T0372800

Innovation in Music

Innovation in Music: Technology and Creativity is a groundbreaking collection bringing together contributions from instructors, researchers, and professionals. Split into two sections, covering composition and performance, and technology and innovation, this volume offers truly international perspectives on ever-evolving practices.

Including chapters on audience interaction, dynamic music methods, AI, and live electronic performances, this is recommended reading for professionals, students, and researchers looking for global insights into the fields of music production, music business, and music technology.

Jan-Olof Gullö is Professor in Music Production at the Royal College of Music, Stockholm, Sweden and Visiting Professor at Linnaeus University.

Russ Hepworth-Sawyer is a mastering engineer with MOTTOsound, an Associate Professor at York St John University, and the managing editor of the *Perspectives On Music Production* series for Routledge.

Justin Paterson is Professor of Music Production at London College of Music, University of West London, UK. He has numerous research publications as author and editor. Research interests include haptics, 3-D audio and interactive music, fields that he has investigated over a number of funded projects. He is also an active music producer and composer; his latest album (with Robert Sholl) *Les ombres du Fantôme* was released in 2023 on Metier Records.

Rob Toulson is Director of RT60 Ltd, who develop innovative music applications for mobile platforms. He was formerly Professor of Creative Industries at University of Westminster and Director of the CoDE Research Institute at Anglia Ruskin University. Rob is an author and editor of many books and articles, including *Drum Sound and Drum Tuning*, published by Routledge in 2021.

Mark Marrington is an Associate Professor in Music Production at York St John University, having previously held teaching positions at Leeds College of Music and the University of Leeds. His research interests include metal music, music technology and creativity, the contemporary classical guitar and twentieth-century British classical music, and his recently published book, *Recording the Classical Guitar* (2021), won the 2022 ARSC Award for Excellence in Historical Recorded Sound Research (Classical Music).

Perspectives on Music Production

This series collects detailed and experientially informed considerations of record production from a multitude of perspectives, by authors working in a wide array of academic, creative and professional contexts. We solicit the perspectives of scholars of every disciplinary stripe, alongside recordists and recording musicians themselves, to provide a fully comprehensive analytic point-of-view on each component stage of music production. Each volume in the series thus focuses directly on a distinct stage of music production, from pre-production through recording (audio engineering), mixing, mastering, to marketing and promotions.

Series Editors
Russ Hepworth-Sawyer, York St John University, UK
Jay Hodgson, Western University, Ontario, Canada
Mark Marrington, York St John University, UK

Coproduction
Collaboration in Music Production
Robert Wilsmore and Christopher Johnson

Distortion in Music Production
The Soul of Sonics
Edited by Gary Bromham and Austin Moore

Reimagining Sample-based Hip Hop
Making Records within Records
Michail Exarchos

Remastering Music and Cultural Heritage
Case Studies from Iconic Original Recordings to Modern Remasters
Stephen Bruel

Innovation in Music
Technology and Creativity
Edited by Jan-Olof Gullö, Russ Hepworth-Sawyer, Justin Paterson, Rob Toulson, and Mark Marrington

Innovation in Music
Cultures and Contexts
Edited by Jan-Olof Gullö, Russ Hepworth-Sawyer, Justin Paterson, Rob Toulson, and Mark Marrington

For more information about this series, please visit: www.routledge.com/ Perspectives-on-Music-Production/book-series/POMP

Innovation in Music

Technology and Creativity

Edited by Jan-Olof Gullö, Russ Hepworth-Sawyer, Justin Paterson, Rob Toulson, and Mark Marrington

Routledge
Taylor & Francis Group

LONDON AND NEW YORK

Designed cover image: Jan-Olof Gullö

First published 2024
by Routledge
4 Park Square, Milton Park, Abingdon, Oxon OX14 4RN

and by Routledge
605 Third Avenue, New York, NY 10158

Routledge is an imprint of the Taylor & Francis Group, an informa business

British Library Cataloguing-in-Publication Data
A catalogue record for this book is available from the British Library

ISBN: 978-0-367-63337-0 (hbk)
ISBN: 978-0-367-63336-3 (pbk)
ISBN: 978-1-003-11881-7 (ebk)

DOI: 10.4324/9781003118817

Typeset in Times New Roman
by Apex CoVantage, LLC

Access the Support Material: www.routledge.com/9780367633363

Contents

v

Preface

The Innovation in Music network brings together experts in the rapidly evolving and connected disciplines of music production, audio technologies, composition, music performance, and the music industry. The Innovation in Music conference is a forum for industry experts and professionals to mix with researchers and academics to report on the latest advances and exchange ideas, crossing boundaries between music disciplines and bridging academia with industry. The conference in 2022 (InMusic22) had as its overarching theme International Perspectives. It was held June 17–19 at the Royal College of Music, Stockholm, having been planned for 2020 but twice postponed due to the pandemic. During three days in June 2022, more than 100 music innovation experts from 22 countries gathered and presented their work in paper presentations, keynote interviews, performances, and panel discussions. A few participants were prevented from travelling to Stockholm due to pandemic travel restrictions and were therefore offered the opportunity to present papers digitally. After the conference, contributors were invited to submit articles for this publication. Due to the many high-quality and interesting contributions, we've decided to publish this volume in two books, each containing two parts. Book 1, *Innovation in Music: Technology and Creativity*, contains 20 chapters in two parts: *Composition and Performance* and *Technology and Innovation*. Book 2, *Innovation in Music: Cultures and Contexts,* contains 17 chapters in two parts: *Creative Production Practice* and *National and International Perspectives*.

The first part of the present volume opens with a contribution by Ambrose Field based on a cycle of 20 traditionally notated pieces for solo flute. This is a work that challenges normative views of the connections between space and compositional workflow by using software tools to explore an acoustically informed compositional design and how technologies for acoustically informed composition change the responsibilities of performers in live realisations when the music is performed. Following this, Christos Moralis' chapter discusses live electronic music performance and how the gap between humans and machines can be bridged. The author presents a model that deviates from prior methods of EDM (Electronic Dance Music) that involve the live version of a musical piece while using the mixing and post-production techniques that would usually be used in a studio setting. In the third chapter, Claus Sohn Andersen presents a project on how acoustics and psychoacoustic aspects may affect musical interplay, interaction, and style during a recording or performance. This is done by analysing changes in recording sessions with an ensemble in different spaces. He concludes that such changes can also be traced to a combination of perceptual learning and the situatedness of perception and cognition. A chapter by Dave Fortune follows, in which he explores the creative potential of using the LFO (low-frequency oscillator) for generating melodic content. This project challenges the conventions of using the piano-style keyboard in combination with a DAW (digital audio workstation) to create melodic content. Next, in Chapter 5, a group of authors, Enric Guaus, Àlex Barrachina, Josep Comajuncosas, Gabriel Saber, and Victor Sanahuja present a project in which they have tested a network setup for real-time music experimentation with a P2P (peer-to-peer) connection setup to find ways of working in the network that goes beyond a pure reproduction of a traditional ensemble environment. The project also shows how latency becomes crucial, greatly influencing the musical result. In Chapter 6, Charles Norton, Daniel Pratt, and Justin Paterson present a technical framework for emulating different instinctual, immediate, and haptic relationships between various acoustic instrument performance aspects through physical controls to specific and meaningful parameters within a given sound-generating construction. They show how electronic parameter mapping is an active and logical process that enables physical controls to realise creative intention and musical expression. In Chapter 7, Matthias Jung and Vegard Kummen explore different concepts of audience participation in live performances and how the audience can experience a performance when they are invited to participate musically, including what significance this can have for participating artists and musicians. This is done with a focus on live chiptune music, a musical aesthetic, and culture in which home computers and video game consoles from the 1980s and 1990s are used for music creation. In the eighth chapter, Samuel Lynch, Helen English, Jon Drummond, and Nathan Scott present a dynamic music composing model for which the music is composed as a collection of short cells that can be seamlessly sequenced together in different combinations to form changeable musical progressions that change according to input. The model challenges the traditional notion of music as a temporally linear art form and expands music to become more malleable, broadening what it means to create and experience a musical work. In the final chapter of Part 1, Stefan Östersjö, Jan Berg, and Anders Hultqvist present artistic research where they explore environmental sounds that are not audible to the human ear but otherwise physically perceptible. The Invisible Sounds project aims to enable trans-modal experiences of a place by creating situations that provide sensation connection. By using participatory methods for the multimodal experience of urban and domesticated soundscapes, augmented with technology, projects of this nature can contribute to developing interdisciplinary approaches, combining landscape architecture and soundscape studies with performance and composition.

The second part of the book opens with a contribution (Chapter 10) by Antti Sakari Saario, who examines Martin B. Kantola's innovation in transducer design. Kantola's microphones are highly regarded by artists and engineers across various genres. The study draws on interviews, studio tests, historical contexts, and existing materials to analyse the factors driving innovation in microphone design, focusing on Kantola's design process. In Chapter 11, Florian Hollerweger presents a project where students in a sonic arts class explored the aesthetic idiosyncrasies of the broadcast listening experience. With guidance from faculty, the students creatively reinterpreted the listening experience using Raspberry Pi and open-source software to develop an experimental audio-streaming server. In different case studies, radio programs were broadcasted that use an automatic speech-synthesized moderator that weaves real-time data retrieved from public web APIs into its narration and automated loading and playback of generative pieces of music. Chapter 12 by Hans Lindetorp is focused on developing a standard for interactive music, an increasingly important development area within music production. Although interactive media have attracted much attention from industry and academia, there is still great potential for further development of tools and formats for content creation and implementation. In this exploratory design study, a JavaScript framework called *iMusicXML* is analysed as a possible starting point for further discussion of standards for the field. In Chapter 13, Henrique Portovedo and Ângelo Martingo present a case study for optimising augmented instruments and transforming performance: Hybrid Augmented Saxophone of Gestural Symbioses – HASGS, that electronically controls parameters in music played on the saxophone, eliminating the need for external electronic devices. It combines acoustic and electronic capabilities, providing composers and performers with a creative agency in multidimensional sonic manipulation and representing the evolving role of academic research in artistic practice. In the following chapter, Bjørnar Ersland Sandvik highlights the importance of considering the role of two-dimensional waveform representations on screens when one discusses digital audio and music production. This project focuses on the role of waveforms on screens with the concept of time manipulation – techniques for experimenting with time, structure, and rhythm in connection with music and digital sound reproduction. Operations of temporal rearrangement and manipulation using waveforms are described and highlight how they shape the interaction with recorded sound in digital music production. This is followed in Chapter 15 with Kirsten Hermes' exploration of the potential translation of chiptune nostalgia to modern MIDI polyphonic expression performance instruments, in which she argues that nostalgia can inspire innovation and new creative expressions. Chiptune emerged from the limitations of old hardware, while modern electronic instruments offer extensive control. The study combines a literature review with a case study of the Chiptune Bubblegum preset pack for a MIDI polyphonic expression software synthesizer. In Chapter 16, Mads Walther-Hansen and Anders Eskildsen explore the relationship between bodily gestures and sound in music production and performance and highlight the challenge of designing user interfaces without haptic or visual feedback that still gives users a sense of agency. The terms 'action' and 'interaction' are examined in the context of musical interface design, recognising that they are interconnected but can vary in the perceived level of agency. Two presented design paradigms for non-haptic music interfaces aim to be intuitive for users with different predispositions towards action or interaction in their musical practice. In Chapter 17, Matthew Lovett explores developments in AI and music to consider potential effects on music production and creativity and to think more broadly about the extent to which human creativity may also be artificial. Two narratives, the claim that the paradigm shift initiated by contemporary developments in AI will have significant consequences for human society and the suggestion that developments in AI have already brought us to a new understanding of our relationship to intelligence, are analysed and discussed. Furthermore, the concept of artificial creativity is also discussed to consider AI's use in various music-related contexts and to learn more about the nature of creative processes. In the next chapter, M. Nyssim Lefford, David Moffat, and Gary Bromham investigate the communication requirements for an intelligently assisted co-creative environment for music mixing. The study draws on existing literature on the cognition of creativity relevant to mixing, as well as human-automation interactions research in other fields and cognitive systems engineering in general. The findings highlight design goals, interaction parameters, and constraints for an intelligent digital collaborator in music mixing. In Chapter 19, Martin Pfleiderer, Egor Polyakov, and Christon-Ragavan Nadar discuss the background and results of a one-year educational project that intended to develop, test, and evaluate several flexibly applicable online teaching modules and tutorials for music analysis based entirely on free and open-source software. The project led to the development of a new software tool for sheet music analysis that allows for computer-aided visualisation and statistical analysis of sheet music and searching for rhythmic and melodic patterns. In the 20th and final chapter of this volume, Mattias Petersson presents a study that explores the potential of a new musical morphology for live electronics ensemble playing. The study involved students who were enrolled in a live electronics ensemble course. It takes a perspective on live electronics as scalable, modular systems of interconnected human and non-human agents to gain new insights into its situated instrumentality and to understand the requirements of musicians participating in a live electronic ensemble.

We thank all chapter authors, conference speakers, and delegates for their support, and we intend that the chapters of this book will be a lasting record of contemporary music innovations and a resource of research information for the future.

Jan-Olof Gullö,
Stockholm, Sweden

Part one

Composition and performance

1

Rethinking the relationships between space, performance and composition in notated acoustic music

Ambrose Field

1 INTRODUCTION

This work explores space from the perspective of understanding ways in which it might interact with the process of making compositions by focusing on workflow methods by which compositions can be created in spatially-informed ways rather than prescribing the nature of those compositions themselves. Views of space as an 'effect', or overlay or augmentation to a performance, are rejected in favour of exploring how the effects of particular acoustic environments can be incorporated with increased precision due to analysis technologies into creative processes involving notated scores. In the workflow proposed, space functions as a complete experimental system (a concept taken from the work of experimental biologist Rheinberger (1995) and adopted by Assis (2018) in a discussion of performance practice, which highlights the need for thinking of creativity as an assemblage of multiple concurrent contexts, not as a part of a supply-chain). This enables the process of creating musical material to be bound together with the spatial effects of a performance in such a way that polarities between *musical material* and *space* are minimised, whilst, importantly, keeping the identity of each.

2 RELATIONSHIP TO EXISTING APPROACHES

Performers can intuitively 'close the loop' between articulation information from the score and perceived acoustic information by reacting to the length and amount of reverberation (and other site-specific cues). In the case of *Quantaform Series*, the composer also takes on this function. To do so, in this case, requires acoustic measurements to be made before compositional design can start. An important part of acoustically informed composition (AIC) is that the process breaks a one-way relationship between information from the environment and a notated score, feeding specific data from a performance space directly back into the fabric of the design. *Quantaform Series* creates links from the environment into the compositional process in such a way that these relationships are supported through performance rather than subverted by it. Mimesis of

DOI: 10.4324/9781003118817-2

environmental features is avoided, and there is no attempt to 'play the resonances' for their own sake, curate or catalogue them – these aspects have been explored extensively by other composers throughout history.

Space as a studio production practice is often enacted as an augmentation, or overlay, to an existing sound. Sounds recorded in one environment can straightforwardly be processed through convolution-based techniques to appear as if they are inhabiting another, although they will still carry the traits of the original recorded environment with them to a degree (less so if the original recording was made in strict anechoic conditions). My aim within *Quantaform Series* was to avoid the creation of spatial overlays, achieving this by reducing any perceived hierarchy between an instrument and the spatial treatment of that instrument. Looking at the sonic contribution of the performance environment from the vantage point of the composition, a spectrum of workflow possibilities exists between mimetic spatial design (such as Messiaen's bird song – see Kraft (2000, p. 20) through to placing an instrument within a spatial environment in a manner similar to placing a sculpture in a landscape (where although combined, space and instrument may function independently or trans contextually), to the design of structures and materials which are created specifically to bridge or highlight gaps between sounds and spaces. Many successful environmental sound installations exist within the latter category. In creating a heightened perceptual gap between installation and environment, Maja S. K. Ratkje, in her installation "Desibel" [sic], draws attention to the ways in which rural landscape is used by replaying high-volume sounds into otherwise tranquil fjords. This isn't simply a musical object introduced into a landscape; both these elements are contingent on each other whilst being critically different in how they are presented to the listener. Maja S. K. Ratkje writes:

> *Desibel* was also made as a protest against the plans of a major mining project in Vevring, a quiet village situated in the district of Sunnfjord. . . . The sound of seagulls is also present – an absurd, over-sized response to the mining company's promise that the mining work will only be as loud as the seagulls.
>
> (Ratkje, 2018)

R. M. Schafer, in his pioneering acoustic ecology work, perceived environmental relationships as being created between sounds and humans. Projects such as *The Vancouver Soundscape* mapped out sounds that were in need of preservation, as they indexed past times and cultures – see Truax (2008). This culturally centred approach can also be found in his instrumental music, such as in *Music for Wilderness Lake,* where the natural surroundings function both as an interactive counterpart to the score and as a stage for the performance. Design features such as pauses and the mimesis of natural sounds create a situation where the environmental response to human musical provocation can be assessed in terms of its living components (wildlife) and the reflective qualities of the physical environment (in creating reverberation). Schafer's creative design is frequently first and foremost a "musical" one – rather than it being primarily sonic, documentary, ecological or activist (although it contains elements of these).

For example. Dufton (2018), in her study of Schafer's environmental music, remarks:

> wolves have responded to my opening melody for Schafer's *Aubade* for solo voice during the pause that follows the sung phrase.

Although *Quantaform Series* contains gestures and features placed in the work to deliberately provoke a reverberant response from the environment, that response is not humanised, nor does it conspire with the human musical text to produce a narrative that is 'about' the environment *per se*. Unlike Schafer's environmental music (particularly that written specifically for wilderness locations), the spaces of *Quantaform Series* are those in which humans are normally found. There is no attempt to provoke the living components of these environments: be they shoppers in the shopping mall, drinkers enjoying a quiet pint in the pub, or climbers on a climbing wall. There is also no musical mimesis of their actions. *Quantaform series* also differs in approach to that taken by artists such as Maryanne Amacher or Bill Fontana, who, grossly summarised, strove for space to become material and material to become space. In *Quantaform Series*, space is simply another contributor to a performance (a performer without human expectations of 'performance'), creating a designed, dynamic relationship between the instrumentality of the soloist and the acoustic response of the environment. Space doesn't need to be anything else in this piece. The music is not a rigid or straightforward algorithmic mapping of spatial analysis onto musical structures: instead, analytical techniques are used to feed information into a traditional, messy, complex and intuitive compositional process, shaping musical lines prior to the performance.

3 RESEARCH AIMS

In a previous publication (Field, 2021a), I suggested a new rationale for framing research questions in creative practice, introducing the idea of the *Creative Question*. Creative questions explore critical and creative responses to defined artistic challenges directly within the medium: each movement of *Quantaform Series* investigates different ways of interacting with an existing acoustic environment, from impressive, large, reverberant spaces (such as aircraft hangars and shopping malls), to small intimate spaces and mundane domestic settings (pubs, domestic bathrooms and hotel rooms). Musically, the works are structured in a form that is as compact as possible: there is no re-statement of material and no development of it in a classical sense. Each piece contains a full repertoire of shapes and gestures from the outset, distributed in a compartmentalised, small-scale 'packet' of material: hence the title, *Quantaform* Series. The aims of this creative work can be summarised as follows:

- to understand how space functions as a complete experimental system in conjunction with creative practice. This rejects the view of space as an acoustic overlay, or augmentation, to a performance; and

- to explore what a process of acoustically informed compositional design might be in a variety of different acoustic environments and to create software tools to achieve this process in an informed way within the workflow and practice of notated composition.

4 WORKFLOW: HOW COMPOSERS DEAL WITH SPACE WITHIN THEIR CREATIVE PROCESS

Musicians can approach working with space in a wide variety of ways. These stretch beyond canonical Western paradigms of concert hall performance, which essentially aligned with specific cultural and stylistic norms to alleviate the need for composers to consider the acoustics in fine detail during the creative process, giving predictable and broadly sonically compatible results across a range of venues. This is not to say that differences between halls could not be heard or were not substantive, Bayreuth is very different from the Vienna Konzerthaus, but from a constructional point of view, composers did not need to concern themselves with the reverberant contribution of the acoustic first and foremost. Canonically, the Gabrielli family, working in St. Marks Venice, typically emerges as an early example of spatial design (for example, see the acoustic reconstruction work of Boren et al. (2013), alongside Notre Dame polyphony (Wright, 1989) in historical significance. However, instrument makers, stretching back over history, have understood the relationship between sound and space as bi-directional: for example, the Wuhan Bell set (bianzhong) of Marquis Yi from China's Warring States period (Foon, 2013) was designed for ceremonial outdoor performance and engineered with this in mind.

Such approaches are intuitive or rely on tacit types of knowledge with regard to how the space impacts the design of music. This knowledge is built from the long-term experience of working or performing in particular spaces – often on a daily basis for cultural reasons or perhaps as part of employment duties. These methods rarely rely on any form of technical measurement to understand the space. Intuitive approaches form one end of a continuum of methods for incorporating space into musical design, whilst at the other end lies technology-based room simulation or auralisation – noting that a variety of hybrid approaches to spatial design are possible along this continuum. Technology-based approaches, such as adding convolution-based reverberation in studio production practices, can provide a highly accurate spatial simulation during creative processes. Such approaches, particularly in the case of impulse-response-based methods, rely on acoustic data sampled from one or more locations within a space. Technology, despite the precision and availability of the data that can be gathered, has, for many musicians, ultimately replicated the functionality from the centuries-old 'intuitive' workflow noted previously: it is possible to create music whilst at the same time hearing the spatial effects of a simulated environment, obviating the need to work with measurements directly. *Quantaform Series* adopts a design methodology that places the evaluation of spatial possibilities closer to stages in my compositional workflow where ideas are formed and malleable. The point at which this occurs in practical terms may differ considerably between composers but is nonetheless identifiable across a variety of working practices.

Before proceeding, it is worth examining how compositional materials might be evaluated by the composer during their design, with a view to understanding how the effects of the performance acoustics may or may not fit within their workflow. Typically (but not exclusively), some of the following processes occur. Composers[1] can:

1   assess musical lines, fragments, ideas, textures or completed sections using internalised listening from mentally replaying the notation (or other symbolic representation);
2   perform/experiment with elements of the score on any instrument to hand or sing/vocalise them, even though this might not be the intended timbre;
3   use software simulations of the intended instruments, often within notation packages or audio workstation software;
4   give completed sections to performers (often undertaken once a body of material has been generated due to practical reasons);
5   work with performers early in the design process on fragmentary ideas of various kinds and operate a co-design process (similar to that encountered when working with improvised music). This may or may not involve the re-notation of the work, a process limited in extent by the number of practical iterations possible.

Notably, it is the live performance elements of these processes that include the quickest, most accurate feedback on spatial design considerations. The act of considering design information derived from the acoustic generally happens *after* musical material has been created – apart from situations where the performance and compositional design are essentially one and the same: in improvised music as mentioned previously, or through real-time composition techniques (such as live coding with technology). Without adopting real-time approaches to composing in situ, composers often need to resort to a much more protracted cycle of hearing their music performed in a particular venue and then making modifications to the score if needed. This work seeks to understand the musical relevance of being able to *pre-auralise the space aided by notation*, yet with the workflow flexibility of an improvised, real-time approach.

To date, there is no current technology[2] that permits the effect of reverberation to be visualised on a musical score so that a composer could fully understand the spectral and time domain impacts of a performance environment on their process of writing a particular phrase or gesture. In notated composition, informed discovery of the interaction of space and material will typically come at the end of the creative process upon realisation. Bringing this experience to earlier in the notated composition workflow has several benefits, noted in what follows. The software tools created for this project attempt to address this problem by providing the composer with musically useful data about the reverberant environment in which their work is to be performed. These software tools, however, do not directly suggest how this information is to be used: that is left to the individual approach of the artist.

All of this may sound like a solution in search of a problem: why would it be necessary to *see* the effects of reverb on a phrase in musical notation when most contemporary software for music notation features a playback engine? Notation, in some styles of composition, is not simply a representational tool – it is the medium through which relationships between different components of a work can be designed and connected. Nattiez (1990) proposed a "tripartition" model where the score was separated both from performance and creative intentionality as a *trace* or *neutral level*. Whilst it is certainly true that a score captures the representation of a musical form to be enacted by performers and brought to life, it is easy to overlook that it has a different type of functionality within the creative workflow as a design medium. Notation also provides the composer with a viewpoint on a piece that is not fixed on one timescale (the 'here and now' of real-time performance or playback), allowing structures to be defined between details on a variety of timescales with relative ease. This aspect of working with reverberant space in a notated context is particularly useful: it becomes clear to the composer if pitch material which is core to the experience is becoming smudged or obscured by the environment, and allows the precise modification of phrases in pitch or rhythmic terms to sculpt how they interact with the acoustic of the performance venue. Whilst such practices are possible by ear, they are more straightforwardly applied to acoustics with longer reverberation times than those that are very short. It is hard aurally to detect the compositionally relevant pitch content of a very short reverberation tail of, say, 0.2 of a second. This is due in part to the degree of spectral masking of pitch content in the reverb by the performed sound and the timescale involved with regard to the mechanisms of auditory perception (see Griesinger (1995)). With an AIC approach based on audio analysis, the pitch content of *any length* of reverberant tail can be harnessed to create greater bonds between the notes being written at composition time and their realisation in the performance environment. This can be useful in a number of practical situations, such as film score realisation, allowing the potential for better matching between the score and environmental elements. Through AIC creative approaches, it becomes possible to go beyond working with the most prominent room modes or outdoor environmental resonances and access more subtle qualities of a space, aided by analysis.

In David Byrne's TED talk (see Byrne, 2013), he points out that music is generally written with the performance context in mind and that the acoustic of the venue has a role in shaping the music that is made in the first place. This also aligns with ideas from Acoustic Ecology research (Truax, 2001), which suggest that the sounding environment affords certain types of functional relationships. He also indicates that in the natural world, such acoustic adaptation is not uncommon as biological species have evolved to communicate in ways that offer the best information transmission methods relative to their environment. Style, though, is only part of the question: parameters related to the reception of the music enter into this complex web of interactions. Byrne (2013, 3'00"–3'56") suggests certain music fits a Gothic Cathedral precisely and that music written for these spaces would, therefore, not have the option of changing key in a way that would be practical in other, smaller venues. Whilst the modal harmony of pre-renaissance music would place tonal developments out of scope even for music written with domestic settings in mind, the personal taste and cultural expectations of a particular set of listeners who needed long, drawn-out experiences of concentrated types also notably aligned to the architectural environment of the Gothic Cathedral: ultimately, culture shapes reverb as much as architecture. *Quantaform Series* looks at this problem from a different perspective: what would happen if music could be written for spaces that might previously be considered 'unsuitable' for certain types of music, where that 'unsuitability' is a complex combination of the listeners' expectations, the composers' intentions and the performers' ability to match the acoustic environment to their performance? The techniques presented in this paper can be expanded to include in consideration of *where* in the building performance might be placed to achieve the particular effects notated in the score or to build into the notation new forms of micro-articulations specifically designed to provoke particular acoustic effects (described in what follows).

5 PERFORMER RESPONSIBILITIES IN AIC

Depending on the degree to which precise acoustic effects are required, performers of acoustically informed compositions will need to re-evaluate how their own intuitive processes for matching the timing of musical materials to the feedback from the acoustic which they are receiving are deployed. These will have been learned through experience in performing in a large number of venues, typically resulting in tempo and articulation adjustments for locations with longer reverberation times. How much can these adaptations be made before they become musically significant, and to what extent does it matter if they do? The closer match between the score and the performance environment – in terms of how rhythms and pitches are constructed – the more natural the integration should feel both for the performer and the audience – see Brereton et al. (2011) for an experimental context. Further research will need to be undertaken to establish the extent of this and the time-window concerned when performing music already designed for particular acoustics. Additionally, perceived outcomes will be influenced by personal taste and cultural conditions, in addition to neurology and physics.

For *Quantaform Series* to be fully effective, it is essential the performer keeps to time. The score itself is almost entirely notated in 2/8 at 60 bpm to achieve a visual representation that foregrounds timing accuracy, for much the same reasons that Berio's Flute *Sequenza 1* was re-notated from the 1958 original for the 1992 edition by the composer with a more conventional approach (see Notaristefano (2013) for a discussion of the notational differences). In *Quantaform Series*, each movement functions as a *block of time* – not a divided, metrical space, working within a concept for proportional duration manipulation inspired by Haddad (2008). The musical material itself is not pulse-based and flows around arbitrary divisions of time, calling on the reverberant environment to help mark important structural moments.

6 QUANTAFORM SERIES – AESTHETICS AND ARTISTIC VISION

Quantaform Series was originally composed in 2010 and intended for performance in local, real-world physical spaces. To do so at the time proved costly to arrange, especially given each movement is relatively short. Therefore, a studio recording was made by Jos Zwaanenberg in 2013 by Sargasso Records, London, with simulated reverberation through a carefully programmed studio effects processor.[3] Only in 2019 did it become possible to realise and document the piece as intended through a film project supported by the Arts Council of Great Britain and Heritage Lottery Fund. The film, "Quantaform", can be found here: Wilson and Field (2021). Each movement is performed within a particular real-world location, selected to match the acoustic characteristics specified in the score.

Aesthetically, *Quantaform Series* has some design similarities to the photographic series of Bernd and Hilla Becher (Stimson, 2012). Their *new topographic* style documented routine and mundane constructions, such as water towers or coal mining winding gear in series, allowing the viewer to draw conclusions about the nature of the relationships therein: between object and environment, individuality and commonality and the human and the environmental. There is no humanisation or romantic pictorialism to these images: they are stark collisions of human and environmental context.

In preliminary evaluation sessions held with conservatoire music students, an opinion was expressed that AIC techniques do not make for 'spectacular' effects, offering instead a 'natural' integration of performer and acoustic. Also, the end result of the work is dependent on how the audience perceives the relationship of space to music as much as that encoded within the piece itself. *Quantaform Series* appears to be, at first glance, a straightforward solo performance and doesn't 'show it's workings' to the audience in a manner such as in Alvin Luciers' *I am sitting in a room* (Broening, 2005), where the contribution from the room acoustic defines the piece and becomes the material in such a way that the listener is led through the process. Whilst some movements in *Quantaform Series* expose this relationship to an extent (such as movements VI and IX), the piece is not *about* resonances *per se*.

7 CUSTOM SOFTWARE FOR VISUALISING THE EFFECTS OF AN ACOUSTIC ON A NOTATED SCORE

The software needed to solve a two-stage problem: firstly, the composer should be presented with musically useful information on which to base compositional decisions initially, such as the number of strongest resonances (defined as a percent of those occurring above the mean amplitude of the reverberant tail), their duration and their pitch. Secondly, once a phrase or segment of musical material has been written with this information in mind, a process is needed by which an impulse response can be *symbolically* convolved with score data, and the results output as musically readable information.

A prototype was made in IRCAM's OpenMusic (IRCAM, 2022) lisp-based patching environment to process data gathered from on-site measurements. Spaces were probed with a sine-sweep signal, which is then deconvolved to produce an impulse response. Ambisonics B-format measurements were taken, offering the potential for a choice of spatial positioning in post-production. The impulse response is converted to an SDIF file and loaded into OpenMusic for analysis. From this analysis, a harmonic map is generated as an aid to understanding which pitches are likely to produce resonances of significant durations. At this point, it would be relatively straightforward to use this data algorithmically to produce a variety of interactions with the space. As I wished to write intuitively, the second stage of work described previously is required to model the effects of a particular line or phrase: a process which is straightforward to accomplish for recorded sound, but less so for notation. An additional OpenMusic patch takes a line or phrase as input, applies a convolution to the pitch and rhythm data and then draws a time-aligned view of how multiple resonances within the space interact with the musical material presented to it. The final step in this process of AIC is conceptual: designing the music so that identified resonances are hit or not hit as part of the musical dialogue. Unlike traditional intuitive workflows, this can now be accomplished with an extremely high degree of precision. A detailed discussion of the software techniques developed for this process can be found in Field, A, in Bresson et al. (2016). *Quantaform Series* represented my first work with this set of techniques I'm now calling AIC. Other works, such as the *Architexture project* documented in Field (2021b) and (Architexture, I, II, III for choir, IV and V for virtual acoustics), offer alternative musical outcomes from these techniques.

The score fragment in Figure 1.1 and the OpenMusic outputs in Figure 1.2 are presented in this case across three timescales so that it is easier to judge how individual components of the phrase become altered by the reverberation.

The result in Figure 1.2 shows compositionally useful considerations, namely:

•   after performance in the reverberant environment, the pitches most likely to be strengthened are upper F# and C# in the mid-flute register; and
•   in the lower flute register, considerable acoustic blurring occurs to rapid textural detail.

The musical phrase could then be reshaped at composition time with this knowledge in mind if required. Please note that the OpenMusic display here is not quantised and the system uses a crotchet to simply

Figure 1.1 Quantaform 16, initial fragment.

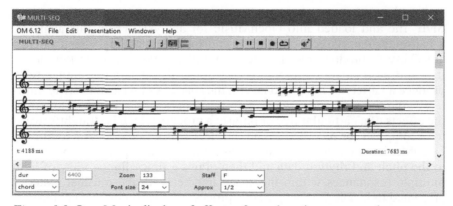

Figure 1.2 OpenMusic display of effects of reverberation on notated passage.

indicate where in time an onset occurs. The horizontal tails indicate the duration of the note. Although this style of output is intended to be a guide rather than a definitive resource, it has proven clear enough to enable the musical design process to accurately strengthen particular resonances and avoid others whilst providing an impression of the relative timing constraints for doing so. Two different examples from the piece illustrate this. Firstly, *Quantaform I* is for an acoustic with a long reverberant tail. In this instance, the reverberation quality and pacing would be relatively easy to judge intuitively through working in the environment, if without some of the detail on texture internals provided by this technique. However, in *Quantaform IV*, the performer is to work within a mid-size room with strong and short early reflections – in this case, a pub. As the composer, the pitch content of the reverberant tail was only recognisable to me through this technique, allowing a relatively precise 'setting' of the musical content into that particular location, even though the end result is not about creating spectacular acoustic provocations. This process led to a workflow for acoustic notated music, which was analogous to working in the recording studio on an electronic music work, where the reverberant effects could be judged before committing to a final version of a line or phrase – something traditionally difficult to accomplish in acoustic music without bringing it into the recorded domain. For example, knowing how to sculpt dense, busy textures so that some will be underpinned by the acoustic and others will work against it is valuable pre-compositional knowledge. In addition to the judgements composers might usually take when composing for 'dry environments' (ones where reverberation does not perceptually dominate the presentation), additional information on frequency-specific timing is valuable in determining the amount of smudging or perceived clarity textures will have. Of course, in reverberant environments with shorter reverb times, the possibilities for making noticeably obvious interplay diminishes. Instead, being able to precisely predict the response of an environment becomes about contributing a subtle sense of fit between the work and the environment. Timing accuracy on the part of the performer becomes even more critical in such situations. The workflow advantage of AIC, in this case, allows the generation and trial of different results, without needing the composer to be present in the venue to 'play the space'. This has the advantage of opening up access to the performance acoustic to a slower, more worked-through compositional process.

8 HOW KNOWLEDGE OF THE ACOUSTIC ENABLES FINE-GRAINED SHAPING OF THE PERFORMANCE: MICRO-ARTICULATIONS

As the relationship between performer, score and acoustic in *Quantaform Series* is a closely coupled system, it becomes possible to create nuanced types of micro-articulation that will have known effects in a particular reverberant environment. Three types of micro-articulation derived from ADSR envelopes found on synthesizers were used in *Quantaform Series* to allow either an onset to be established and then reverberated, to allow previous reverberation to build before an onset, or to sustain a micro-pitch bend on the onset in order to differentiate between the onset of the note and the continuant in how it is presented in the reverberant tail. Symbols for these are positioned over the notation and determine how the note onset is to be shaped. The three types described are shown in Figure 1.3.

Figure 1.3 Quantaform 1.

Source: Field (2019)

9 FURTHER WORK

Further work on this project will involve porting the software from Open-Music to a bespoke application, which is able to accept generic score input from popular notation software as MusicXML files. Such a platform will also enable further performance research on pieces that have been pre-made for particular acoustics.

10 CONCLUSION

The *workflow* presented in this paper has the potential to widen the palette of spatial expression for acoustic music in contexts that are well matched to this methodology: for example, site-based work, installation, or the use of particular spaces in fixed media such as in film applications. These methods are unlikely to create 'portable' works suitable for performance anywhere.

The acoustically informed composition techniques presented in this article have also been useful in extending the range of possibilities for working with spatial environments in subtle and nuanced ways that are not always immediately aurally obvious. In *Quantaform Series,* this has created a sense of dialogue between space, place, instrument and performer, where the design of those interactions has been mediated through the score.

NOTES

1 Those working with notated materials. Composers can, of course, mix any of these methods and involve other methods of non-notated production.
2 That is publicly available at the time of writing and known to the author.
3 In this instance, a Bricasti M7.

REFERENCES

Assis, P. de (2018). *Logic of Experimentation: Rethinking Music Performance Through Artistic Research*. Leuven: Leuven University Press.

Boren, B. B., et al. (2013). 'Acoustic Simulation of Renaissance Venetian Churches', *Acoustics in Practice*, 1(2), pp. 17–28.

Brereton, J., et al. (2011). 'Evaluating the Auralization of Performance Spaces and Its Effect on Singing Performance', in *Audio Engineering Society Convention 130*. New York, USA: Audio Engineering Society.

Bresson, J., et al. (2016). *The OM Composer's Book*. Volume 3. France: IRCAM.

Broening, B. (2005). 'Alvin Lucier\'s I Am Sitting in a Room 1', in *Analytical Methods of Electroacoustic Music*. Routledge, pp. 89–110.

Byrne, D. (2013). *How Architecture Helped Music Evolve*. Available at: www.youtube.com/watch?v=p6uXJWxpKBM [Accessed: 10 July 2022].

Dufton, B. (2018). *A Voice in the Wilderness: A Singer's Guide to the Implications of Performance Context in R. Murray Schafer's Wolf Music*. PhD thesis, University of Toronto Canada.

Field, A. (2019). *Quantaform Series for Solo Flute and Acoustic Resonances (Score)*. Tetractys Publishing. Available at: www.tetractys.co.uk.

Field, A. (2021a). 'Changing the Vocabulary of Creative Research: The Role of Networks, Risk, and Accountability in Transcending Technical Rationality', in Impett, J., ed. *Sound Work: Composition as Critical Technical Practice*. Orpheus Institute Series. Leuven: Leuven University Press, pp. 303–317.

Field, A. (2021b). 'Hearing the Past in the Present: An Augmented Reality Approach to Site Reconstruction Through Architecturally Informed New Music', in *Music and Heritage*. Malaysia: Routledge, pp. 212–221.

Foon, L. S. (2013). 'The Impact of Music Archaeology on Local Community Culture in Wuhan', *Music Dance Environment*, 5, p. 157.

Griesinger, D. (1995). *How Loud Is My Reverberation? Audio Engineering Society*. Available at: www.aes.org/e-lib/online/browse.cfm?elib=7823 [Accessed: 24 June 2022].

Haddad, K. (2008). 'Livre Premier de Motets: The Time-Block Concept in Open-Music', in *The OM Composer's Book 2*. Paris: IRCAM.

IRCAM. (2022). *OpenMusic*. Available at: https://openmusic-project.github.io/openmusic [Accessed: 18 July 2022].

Kraft, D. (2000). *Birdsong in the Music of Olivier Messiaen*. PhD thesis, Middlesex University.

Nattiez, J.-J. (1990). *Music and Discourse: Toward a Semiology of Music*. Princeton: Princeton University Press.

Notaristefano, M. (2013). 'Luciano Berio – Sequenza I', in *De Musica*. Italy: Milano University Press.

Ratkje, M. (2018). *Desibel*. Available at: http://ratkje.no/2009/10/desibel/ [Accessed: 21 July 2018].

Rheinberger, H.-J. (1995). 'From Experimental Systems to Cultures of Experimentation', in *Concepts, Theories, and Rationality in the Biological Sciences*, pp. 1–4. USA: University of Pittsburgh.

Stimson, B. (2012). 'The Photographic Comportment of Bernd and Hilla Becher', *Tate Online Research Journal*, p. 18. Available at: www.tate.org.uk/documents/322/tate_papers_1_blake_stimson_bernd_and_hilla_becher.pdf.

Truax, B. (1984). *Acoustic Communication*. New York: Ablex Publishing Corporation.

Truax, B. (2008). 'Soundscape Composition as Global Music: Electroacoustic Music as Soundscape', *Organised Sound*, 13(2), pp. 103–109.

Wilson, J. and Field, A. (2021). *QUANTAFORM (film)*. Available at: www.youtube.com/watch?v=AueUnE8QqW4 [Accessed: 11 July 2022].

Wright, C. (1989). *Music and Ceremony at Notre Dame of Paris, 500–1550*. USA: CUP Archive.

2

Timing consistency in live EDM

The Performable Recordings model

Christos Moralis

1 INTRODUCTION

Electronic Dance Music (EDM) is a musical genre characterized by its reliance on machine-like aesthetics and its general use of computer technology. The use of computer-aided production techniques based on digital audio workstations (DAW) and other software enables the creation of precise and structured compositions intended to be energetic and danceable (Lyubenov, 2017). To bring the EDM studio recording sound to life on stage, performers attempt to use laptops or other electronic setups to trigger and manipulate pre-recorded material. Others make use of complex electronic controllers and sensors to generate and modify sounds in real time, adding a unique element to their live acts by combining pre-recorded tracks with live performances. These performers might also include live elements such as singing or instrumentation to increase the "live" feel of the show.

If the stage serves as a platform for direct and engaging interaction between musicians and their audience during live performances, then the way musicians perform on stage may influence audience perception and the overall experience of their music. On the one hand, the use of pre-recorded material, long samples, or larger pre-recorded segments or karaoke in live performances may remove the element of human spontaneity and create discrepancies between the visual and auditory elements that challenge the audience and even the performers' perception of reality. On the other hand, using live instruments may introduce an element of unpredictability and human error, as the timing and dynamics of the instruments may not always be perfectly in sync with the pre-produced tracks. The combination of studio recordings with live elements may produce a more organic and dynamic sound but can also result in less accurate and consistent performance. Incorporating live instruments into an EDM performance can add depth and variety to the sound but requires additional skills and resources to maintain the desired level of precision and consistency.

The Performable Recordings model introduces a new way to perform EDM live, deviating from prior methods. This model combines technology with a traditional sense of liveness and authenticity by using a DAW

    DOI: 10.4324/9781003118817-3

in a live performance that follows a structured format and process. The model includes traditional musicians such as a singer, drummer, keyboardist, and DJ/laptop performer and does not include any pre-recorded material. This innovative approach combines the benefits of digital technology with a classic sense of authenticity. The aim of this musical procedure is to gain control over live performances while allowing for flexibility and improvisation. In this way, bands can achieve a cohesive and authentic performance while retaining faithfulness to the selected genre or tradition. The audience can then perceive the music as it is being created in the present moment, with real-time methods, thus reclaiming a traditional sense of liveness and authenticity in the performance. This model provides novel aesthetic potentials within the style of EDM and can also alter how liveliness and authenticity are understood and experienced within this type and setting.

This approach is not intended to compensate for performers who may not have the necessary skill level but rather to address certain elements of musical styles, such as EDM that relies on precise timing, pitch accuracy, and consistent dynamics. The aim is not to find ways to perform "better" but rather to incorporate both "human" and "non-human" elements by requiring performers to interact with technology in new ways. This allows for authentic performances while preserving the integrity of the musical genre, in this case, EDM.

The primary methodology of this study combines ethnographic and autoethnographic techniques, including observations of practice and interviews with the band members (drummer, keyboardist, DJ/laptop performer) and the researcher's participation in the project as the singer and guitarist. This model, called Performable Recordings, was developed by the author of this chapter for the purposes of a doctorate degree at the University of West London. Since most research in this area focuses on recording techniques or electro-acoustic performances, this study contributes to the less explored area of contemporary, excessively mediatized, live EDM performances which are often performed in a more traditional setting. This chapter investigates "timing" and looks at "participatory discrepancies," as discussed by Keil (1995), between quantized and naturally performed elements that serve both the machine feel present in EDM and Carlson's (2004) three concepts for evaluating a performance.

2 BACKGROUND

The incorporation of studio technology into live performances has become a crucial aspect of many artists' exploration of their musical agency, even when these practices contradict traditional beliefs about the appropriate relationship between performers and music (Kjus and Danielsen, 2016). Many music fans may view the phrase "live electronic music" as an oxymoron. Collins and Rincón (2007) argue that it is a common tendency for humans to view the technological and the biological as opposing each other. However, in the context of contemporary bands that use excessive mediation technology during their live performances, what is considered "live"? According to Thorton (1995), the concept of liveness in music emerged only in comparison to recorded music, meaning that the existence of live music is dependent upon the presence of recorded music. However, the electronic music band "The Bays" only perform their songs live and have never created recorded versions of them (Theheritageorchestra. com, 2022). Therefore, the definition of "live" has expanded beyond its original meaning and is not limited to the comparison of recorded and non-recorded versions of a track. This aligns with Cooke's (2011) concept of liveness being a shared understanding between performers and observers that the current moment is unique and distinguished due to the shared context and spatial-temporal relationship. Transmediate (2011) idea of "liveness" occurring between humans and technology, even when they are not spatially or temporally co-present, is also relevant in the context of bands performing live in other settings, for example, over the internet.

When examining the relationship between the physical and the mediated, it is important to consider the specific ways in which they are connected rather than relying on preconceived notions that prioritize the physical over the mediated (Transmediate, 2011). According to Bown, Bell and Parkinson (2014), liveness can be based on the prior perception of the performer's activity or decision-making, and liveness and mediatization can co-occur. The authors argue that in live laptop music, the performance of the mediatized may, in fact, amplify perceptions of liveness and that audiences perceive something as "live" based on this co-occurrence. Auslander also notes that the concept of "liveness" refers to the act of engaging with and bringing an object or experience into full presence rather than the inherent qualities of the object or experience itself (Transmediate, 2011). The manipulation and distortion of live performances have varied over time and across different cultures, styles, and traditions. Therefore, "procedural liveness," defined as the transformation of live sound in real-time, and "aesthetic liveness," defined as the mapping of aesthetically meaningful differences in input sound to output sound, are also relevant in this type of live performance (Croft, 2007, p. 61).

Liveness refers to the sense of presence and immediacy that is created in a live performance (Lalioti, 2012), while authenticity refers to the belief in the inherent value and integrity that is not present in recorded or mediated performances (Moore, 2002). Zagorski-Thomas (2010) argues that in recent years, some performers have attempted to sound more like machines, while computer-based music programs often aim to make machines sound more human-like. Authenticity is shaped by how we interpret and understand things within the context of our culture and history, and it emerges in opposition to forces that seek to destroy, transform, dominate, or disrupt it (Moore, 2002). In EDM, factors such as the performers' stage presence, interactions with the audience, and overall effort can contribute to the authenticity of the performance. More specifically, the activity that performers have on stage is judged by the human perceptual system based on the identification of patterns of connectivity between stimulus and action, but as it is a multi-modal system, any discrepancies between the modes may be perceived as "incorrect" (Zagorski-Thomas, 2014).

The live electronic performance by "Pinn Panelle" (2011), as exemplified in their live cover of "Skrillex – Scary Monsters and Nice Sprites," can be evaluated based on both first- and third-person authenticity criteria. From a first-person perspective, the use of various traditional instruments and EDM production techniques, such as guitars, keyboards, live looping, and sampling, demonstrates the performers' active engagement with the music and their own skills and abilities. However, from a third-person perspective, they may lack timing consistency and pitch accuracy, which lowers the studio sound fidelity and compromises the authenticity of the genre. Submotion Orchestra (2014) uses live instruments and electronic music production techniques to create their music, incorporating a range of instruments such as drums, percussion, trumpet, and keyboards. They showcase their authenticity by actively creating the music using their own skills and abilities. However, from a third-party perspective, the lack of pitch and timing accuracy may impact the authenticity of the studio recording aesthetics. Nevertheless, the group is a good example of the different sub-genres of EDM and the different tolerance of machine-like aesthetics and live elements deviating from the traditional EDM genre. Shawn Wasabi (2015) and Afishal (2014) are both electronic music producers and performers who use MIDI controllers and effects pedals to actively engage with the music and demonstrate their first person authenticity in their live performances. However, their reliance on pre-produced samples and lack of traditional instruments may detract from the authenticity of the performance from a third-person perspective.

Examining live performances through the lens of activity and sound creation, we can see that the concept of "liveness" in live music is largely dependent on the first-person authenticity of the performers, as described by Moore's tripartition of authenticities (2002). In addition, to achieve genuine EDM aesthetics onstage, it is essential to consider both physical and mediated elements rather than favoring one over the other. Authenticity is created from a cultural context, performativity effort, performer stage presence and connection with the audience, as well as technology's ability to achieve the "right" sound for the integrity of the genre. Ultimately, authenticity and liveness rely on a shared understanding between the performer and the audience.

3 METHODOLOGY

An ethnographic approach was employed in this study, which involved observation and study of a specific band. Autoethnographic elements were also used, as the researcher reflected on their own experiences as a musician to better understand the topic being studied. The researcher, a professional producer and performer with over two decades of experience, approached the task of creating a template for live performances using their knowledge and experience to adapt studio production techniques to a live setting in real-time. As a multi-instrumentalist, the researcher also drew on their personal skills and expertise in instrumentation to inform the development of the performance process. The process was adapted and refined through ongoing dialogue and collaboration with other band members based on their feedback. This approach aligns with the principles of autoethnography, as described by Ellis and Bochner (Méndez, 2013), which involves using self-reflection and personal experience to understand and analyze cultural phenomena. By using these tools to inform the creation of their live performance, the researcher was able to adapt the technical aspects to serve both the aesthetics of EDM and the natural feel of the performance.

This musical process relies on the authenticity of live musical performances, with a focus on Moore's (2002) concept of first-person and third-person authenticity. First-person authenticity refers to the emotional connection and genuine expression of the performers, while third-person authenticity refers to the authenticity of the musical genre or tradition being represented, including factors such as the use of appropriate musical instruments and techniques, the coherence between the audio and visual elements, the level of skill displayed, and the adherence to standards of excellence. To achieve this, this project is based on the momentary expressive variations present in a live performance in relation to Moore's (2002) concept of first-person authenticity. This can be assessed using the three concepts proposed by Carlson (2004) for evaluating a performance: appreciation of the performers' use of skill, performativity or entrainment, and an ongoing awareness of a "standard of achievement" against which each performance is judged (Carlson, 2004). According to Davis (2011), the practice of music involves actively considering the formation of music and giving listeners a participatory role in the creation process. This aligns with Small's (1998) concept of "musicking" as a communal activity, even when technology is involved. In this project, the live performance is centered on authenticity, specifically in terms of liveness and creative control, from the perspective of the performer. On a fundamental level, this refers to the relationship between the performer's physical movements and the resulting sound. It also relates to the performer's ability to vary their performance and the audience's sense of agency in the performance. However, it is important to include a component of improvisation in these concerts, as this permits a sense of "composition in real-time" (Bailey, 1993). One way to incorporate improvisation while still utilizing pre-existing mixing techniques is by using the idea of "comprovisation" (Cooke, 2011). This involves combining improvisation and pre-produced, or in this case, pre-structured elements, leading to a show that is both spontaneous and organized.

Based on these fundamental conditions for realism and authenticity in a live performance, the Performable Recordings model combines the DAW "Ableton Live" with laptops, sound cards, digital signal processing (DSP) cards, and digital wireless systems, to deliver the sound characteristics of a studio production and a natural-feeling sonic response to the performers in real-time. This project focused on technologies such as adaptive tonal linearization, pitch-tracking equalization, phase interaction mixing, matching, and adaptive and dynamic equalization for the production and sound design of the sounds used in drum samples, sound fx, and keyboard sounds. In addition, real-time MIDI quantization, real-time envelope shaping, and real-time quantized repetition of small audio segments are used during the live performance.

The creation of the Performable Recordings model focused on each member's individual instrument and their unique production and performance approach. The instruments' sound design, production processes, and performance techniques were based on the researcher's initial design and the aesthetics of EDM, with a focus on both first- and third-person authenticity. However, the process was not linear, as it required feedback from the performers to finalize the audio processes. The final tuning of the model was determined by the group performance and video observations, sonic results, and face-to-face conversations and online discussions. The process was based on the needs, taste, and performance abilities of the performers, the aesthetics of EDM, and the technical aspects and limitations of the system. Considerations included stereo-to-mono compatibility, phasing issues, loudness levels, timbre, pitch accuracy, dynamic response, and timing consistency. The need for a large amount of CPU power and latency limitations led to the adoption of a more musical approach for audio signal fixing such as quantizers, arpeggiators, volume envelope shaping, and a sidechaining process.

4 PRODUCTION

In this section, the techniques used to create timing consistency will be explored, followed by examples in context. Although the research showed that achieving the "live" feel while maintaining the EDM aesthetic requires not only timing consistency but various combinations of fixed and varied musical descriptors, including time, pitch, timbre, and dynamics, this chapter focuses on the timing aspect of this process.

4.1 MIDI-based instruments

4.1.1 Real-time MIDI quantization

MIDI quantization is the process of aligning MIDI events, including notes and control messages, with a specific timing interval or grid, for example, at a 1/4 note, 1/8 note, etc. The strength or "tightness" of the quantization, as well as the threshold for its application, depends on the speed of the song and the size of the deviation of the notes. The main difference between live loopers and DAW-based looping in terms of quantized performances in this model is that correction happens before it can be "heard" within a small window frame of a few milliseconds. To accurately distribute quantized notes over the timing grid, they must be played on or before the defined interval (see Figure 2.1).

4.1.2 Real-time MIDI arpeggiation

To achieve quantized performances, arpeggios have been used as sequences of notes played one after the other in a broken fashion, usually spanning multiple octaves or, in the case of the drums, repeating the same notes to achieve the desired effect. In addition, it is necessary to ensure that the triggered arpeggio pattern is closely aligned with the grid, either by using

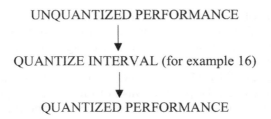

UNQUANTIZED PERFORMANCE

QUANTIZE INTERVAL (for example 16)

QUANTIZED PERFORMANCE

Figure 2.1 MIDI quantization process.

a synthesizer or sampler with this feature or by also using MIDI quantization. This technique can be useful for creating simple or intricate melodic
and rhythmic patterns, even if the performer is not perfectly in time, and
allows the performer to focus on other aspects of the performance, such as
improvisation or the variation of timbre, pitch, and dynamics to achieve a
sense of first- and third-person authenticity (see Figure 2.2).

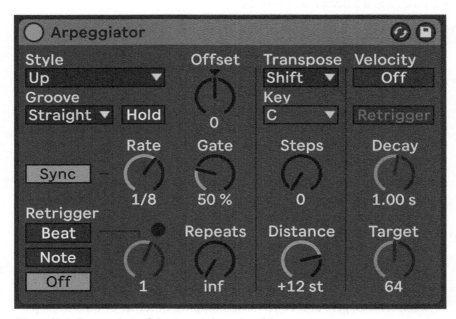

Figure 2.2 Screenshot of the Arpeggiator in Ableton.

4.1.3 Implementation

These techniques have been implemented to maintain timing consistency
on MIDI-based instruments such as drums, keyboards, and certain percussive sounds. The drummer stated that it was not feasible to consistently
play slightly before the click, such as within a previous 64th note, due to the
small division of the note. However, the keyboard player was accustomed
to this procedure, like playing pads or other sounds with slow attack (Moralis, 2019). Therefore, to achieve a first- and third-person authenticity in

this case, the combination of partial real-time quantization and arpeggiation was necessary. For example, in a scenario of four on the floor beat, while the kick and snare were arpeggiated, it was still necessary to perform other elements naturally such as hi-hats, cymbals, and toms. In other cases, where more complicated rhythmical patterns were involved, the use of arpeggiation was used partially with the use of automation to preserve timing consistency on emphasized notes, while others were left naturally performed. The use of MIDI quantization at the beginning of certain bars ensures the quantization and trigger of the arpeggiator in sync with the grid. However, performers must put effort into non-quantized elements to achieve a balance between fixed and varied elements (see Figures 2.3–2.11).

Figure 2.3 Screenshot of the automated parameters in Ableton – Drum Pattern A.

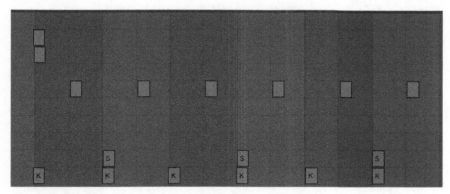

Figure 2.4 Screenshot of the unprocessed performance in Ableton – Drum Pattern A.

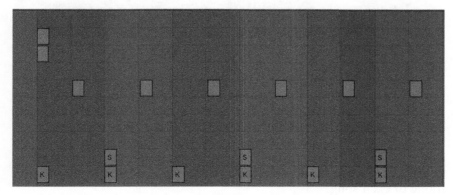

Figure 2.5 Screenshot of the processed performance in Ableton – Drum Pattern A.

Figure 2.6 Screenshot of the automated parameters in Ableton – Drum Pattern B.

Figure 2.7 Screenshot of the unprocessed performance in Ableton – Drum Pattern B.

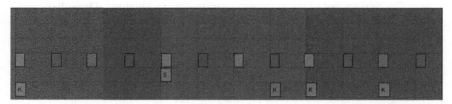

Figure 2.8 Screenshot of the processed performance in Ableton – Drum Pattern B.

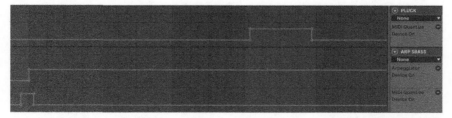

Figure 2.9 Screenshot of the automated parameters in Ableton – Keyboard Pattern.

In other cases, synthesizers with arpeggiators that are synced to the grid allow the performer to activate the process at any point in the song, with the notes automatically adhering to the song's structure. Combining quantized sounds with effects such as delays or reverbs produced by a doubled, non-quantized track creates the desired balance between studio recording and live feel. However, the performer must still try to achieve the desired sonic results within the accepted time variation frame of each song.

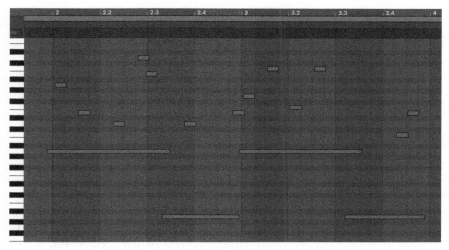

Figure 2.10 Screenshot of the unprocessed performance in Ableton – Keyboard Pattern.

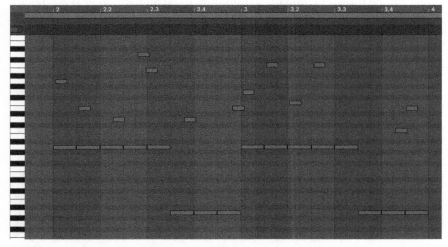

Figure 2.11 Screenshot of the processed performance in Ableton – Keyboard Pattern.

4.2 Audio-based instruments

4.2.1 Real-time volume and tonal shaping

In addition to MIDI quantization and arpeggiation, which allow the performer to play in time, volume envelope controls have been utilized to maintain the perception that the instrument is being played in time. Rather than quantizing the performance, simply processing the volume envelope to align with the grid can give the impression of a polished studio performance. To enhance this common characteristic of EDM in a live setting, volume and filter envelope effects, as well as muting specific parts of the performance that may indicate a lack of entrainment, have been applied in real-time to vocals, guitars, MIDI-based instruments such as drums and keyboards, and other elements performed by the laptop performer. Additionally, real-time volume envelope followers can be utilized between instruments to establish a sense of synchronization and groove, such as adjusting the envelope of the guitar based on the bassline.

4.2.2 Partial live looping

Like MIDI quantization and arpeggiation, repeating small audio segments that are aligned with a grid can produce a combination of fixed and varied performances. This technique allows performers to achieve authentic performances from both a first- and third-person perspective. It can be achieved using the "Beat Repeat" plugin from Ableton Live, which is commonly used to create stuttered and looped phrases. However, it can also be utilized to repeat specific smaller segments, for example, an 8th or 16th note long on a fixed time grid, resulting in a more consistent performance. Like the previously mentioned technique of arpeggiation, the effect can be turned on and off to combine fixed and varied grid aesthetics in a balanced manner. A further synced volume envelope process can create a more polished result.

4.2.3 Implementation

In the example provided, the guitar plays a pattern of 8th notes using open power chords and 16th notes using palm-muted chords. The beat repeater plugin is used to repeat the 16th notes of the palm-muted chords (see Figures 2.12 and 2.13).

Figure 2.12 Screenshot of the live looping effects chain in Ableton.

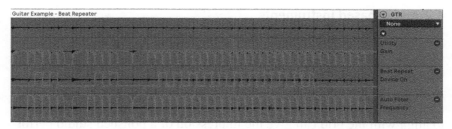

Figure 2.13 Screenshot of the automated parameters in Ableton – Guitar Pattern.

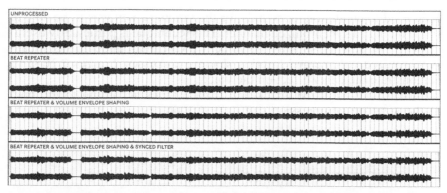

Figure 2.14 Screenshot of the unprocessed and processed performances in Ableton – 6 Bars Guitar Pattern example.

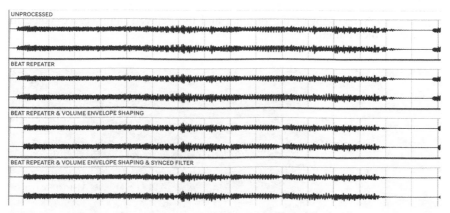

Figure 2.15 Screenshot of the unprocessed and processed performances in Ableton – 1 Bar Guitar Pattern example.

The audio waveforms of the unprocessed, naturally performed versions, as well as the two stages of processing, are displayed in Figures 2.14 and 2.15. It is evident that the audio is quantized while the volume envelopes further shape the sound within the specific timing deviations of the bars.

4.2.3 Synchronized effects

The technique of synchronized effects involves combining live natural performance with fixed to the grid sound effects. In terms of modulation, rather than setting the speed of modulation to a note basis (synced to the bpm of the song), low-frequency oscillators (LFOs) or envelopes can be applied in a similar manner as previously explained with volume envelopes and filters. In addition, it is not possible to create quantized spatial effects, such as delay or reverberation, from non-quantized performances by only setting the parameters to note synchronization unless the performances are indeed quantized. Therefore, unsynchronized decay times have been used to create longer sounds for the volume envelopes to be able to shape them in a synchronized manner. This technique is particularly useful for lead instruments, such as the voice, which cannot undergo significant synchronized volume and filtering shaping processes. Figures 2.16–2.19 demonstrate the delay effect on the voice.

Furthermore, adjusted attack and release times according to the bpm of the song on compression can help this process. As Pretolesi (2015)

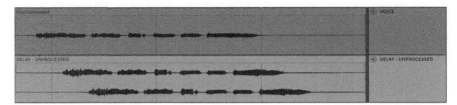

Figure 2.16 Screenshot of the original and the delayed unprocessed voice in Ableton – Voice Pattern.

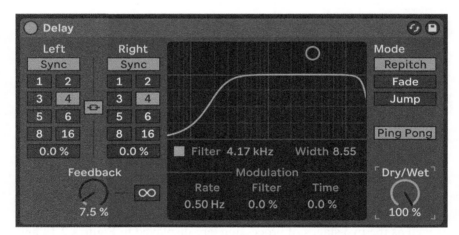

Figure 2.17 Screenshot of the delay effect settings in Ableton (A).

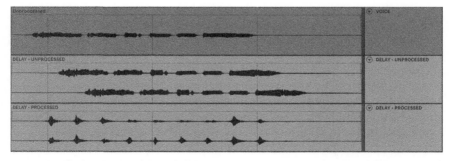

Figure 2.18 Screenshot of the original and the delayed unprocessed and processed voices in Ableton.

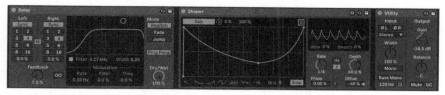

Figure 2.19 Screenshot of the delay effect settings in Ableton (B).

Uncompressed

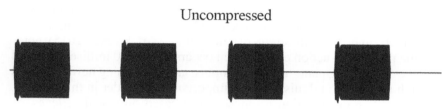

Figure 2.20 Uncompressed sine wave.

Compressed

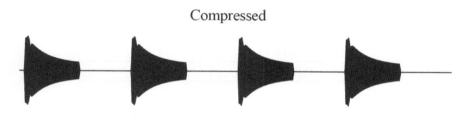

Figure 2.21 Compressed sine wave.

explains, this technique can be used creatively in electronic music to add movement and depth to synthesized or sampled sounds, as well as create space in the mix when prominent sounds like the kick drum hits. An example of synchronized compression can be seen in Figure 2.21, where a quarter note sine waveform is played on every first and third beat at a tempo of 128 bpm, with the compressor's attack time set to 468ms (equivalent to a quarter note at 128 bpm). The release and knee settings are 1.83ms and 0, respectively, and the ratio is set to 2:1. However, it is important to note that this can only significantly help processed performances and quantized elements (see Figures 2.20 and 2.21).

5 PERFORMANCE

The previous section outlined the conditions for implementing a production approach that aligns with the concept of the Performable Recordings model, which involves combining fixed-to-the-grid elements with varied, naturally performed elements in real-time. This section discusses the performance aspect of this hybrid timing technique for musicians.

5.1 Entrainment

The previous section established the conditions for creating a production approach that aligns with the concept of the Performable Recordings model by combining fixed-to-the-grid and varied, naturally performed elements in real-time. This section discusses the performance aspect of this hybrid timing technique for musicians. To effectively integrate technology and processing while avoiding any phasing or entrainment issues, it is necessary for human performances to be "synchronized" with the mechanical processes. According to Human Benchmark (2007), the average human reaction time is between 200ms and 250ms, but individual performers may have different reaction times. Art Works (2015) notes that the perception-action cycle, which occurs every 300 milliseconds and involves evaluating plans, receiving inputs, and developing new behaviors through resonance and mismatch, is important to consider in this context. Figure 2.22 shows reaction response times based on visual reflexes, as measured by the humanbenchmark.com test.

VOCALIST/ GUITARIST:	249ms
DRUMMER:	204ms
KEYBOARDIST:	303ms
DJ:	238ms

Figure 2.22 Response Times.

This table should be viewed as a general guide rather than a scientifically rigorous document. It is important to note that the information presented should be taken as indicative rather than definitive. Factors such as visual perception speed, color usage, mouse-clicking, mood, relaxation, computer performance, and internet connection can all impact the results. However, it seems that musicians who are familiar with percussive elements tend to have better results, with the drummer having the quickest response time. According to Pubnub.com (2017), response times are influenced by various parameters. These parameters include sensory perception, the integration of input into our consciousness, the application of context to the input, and the decision-making process based on the output generated.

Musical-rhythmic performance relies on the entrainment process, which can also help minimize response time by predicting the pulse and tempo. Jones's research (Jones and Boltz, 1989) highlights the distinction between "future-oriented attending" and "analytic attending" in the context of musical aesthetics. "Future-oriented attending" focuses on highly coherent events, which can be divided into two levels of entrainment. The first level, also referred to as "future-oriented attending," involves non-human-performed elements like the click track and allows for a shift in attention to longer time spans, such as the overall tempo. The second level pertains to elements fixed-to-the-grid or synchronized sound effects like arpeggiated kick and snare drums, arpeggiated synthesizers, and audio processing that is synchronized to the grid. This helps participants identify performance entrainment errors and determine whether they were intentional. "Analytic attending," the second mode, is based on human-performed elements and tends to occur when the event stimuli are less coherent and more complex, making it difficult to formulate expectations. An example of this might be a complex rhythmical pattern on the hi-hats with which the musicians may try to synchronize their own groove. Figure 2.23 illustrates the entrainment process in the Performable Recordings model:

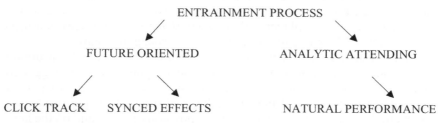

Figure 2.23 Entrainment Process 1.

In this project, the "future-oriented attending" mode precedes the "analytic attending" mode. Participants also use the second level of entrainment to identify "participatory discrepancies" (Clayton, Sager and Will, 2004) and adjust their rhythmic behavior and character during their performance (see Figure 2.24).

Figure 2.24 Entrainment Process 2.

All four participants used a multi-temporal level of attention for entrainment and perceived each sound response and activity differently. The drummer, who is accustomed to playing with a click track, found the entrainment process natural. The keyboardist's entrainment process was based on their own experiences and memories, such as playing pads with longer attack times. The DJ's focus was solely on click track synchronization, and they paid attention to what the other band members were doing to add different musical contexts to their performance. As the creator of this model, the visual cues of audio processing, such as volume envelopes, were helpful in focusing on the entrainment process.

The art of musical expression relies on human variation, personal style, and, as Keil (1995) argues, "imperfections." Additionally, human spontaneity defines live human performance. Integrating all these expressive and entraining elements into a score can be challenging in creating a universal language between band members. However, a model based on music notation has been adopted to serve as a memory aid for performers in terms of emotional expression and timing, including the entrainment process related to MIDI quantization and the performance of musical effects. Different colors have been used in scores to represent both the different notes and their timings, as well as indicate which notes are quantized or arpeggiated. Red notes must be played slightly before the click so that the real-time MIDI quantizer can place them on the grid, while blue notes indicate that there is no such process in place.

The coloring schemes of the drummer and keyboard player are different. The drummer prefers to view only quantized notes and exclude breaks and long bars in naturally performed parts. However, the cymbals, including the hi-hats, are always naturally performed and do not need to be indicated in blue. The keyboard player follows a similar process but leaves arpeggiated notes in black due to the frequency of arpeggiated parts.

For the DJ, most MIDI notes are played but reproduced by a digital workstation, so there was no need to indicate quantized or arpeggiated sounds. However, during the creation of the project and the DJ's part, it was necessary to indicate filters and other real-time effects performances. For example, a specific note indicates the position of the sound on the keyboard, while the arrow indicates the movement of the filter from high to low frequencies. However, the control of this sampler was later transferred to a non-keyboard controller, rendering the pitch of the notes irrelevant and the score used only to indicate the various processes and their position in the song.

The author recalls the musical context of the songs and, therefore, did not feel the need to write scores. However, there were many audio processes, such as volume shaping, that the author could not remember, leading to the creation of a score that displays the final volume process of the guitar. This primarily impacts the overall timing perception, so it is placed as a figure above the score.

6 CONCLUSION

This chapter presented a production and performance model that offers a new approach to performing EDM live that combines technology with a sense of liveness and authenticity. The model employs DAWs and traditional musicians, such as a singer, drummer, keyboardist, and DJ/laptop performer, on stage, without the use of any pre-recorded material. By using this approach, bands can achieve a cohesive and authentic performance while staying faithful to the chosen genre or tradition, and audiences can perceive the music being created in real-time, reclaiming a traditional sense of liveness and authenticity in the performance. This model not only provides novel aesthetic possibilities within the style of EDM but also challenges traditional understandings of liveness and authenticity in live performance. Using a combination of ethnographic and autoethnographic techniques, this study has explored the experiences and perspectives of band members in relation to the Performable Recordings model and its impact on the live EDM aesthetic.

This model focuses on first-person authenticity, defined as the emotional connection and genuine expression of the performers, and third-person authenticity, defined as the authenticity of the musical genre or tradition being represented. The incorporation of improvisation through the concept of "comprovisation" allows for a sense of "composition in real-time" while still using pre-existing elements of the mixing process. In this model, the mechanical processes of studio production are integral tools for making EDM, and the question is not whether it is appropriate or authentic to use them but whether it is possible to create authentic live EDM without them.

The development of the Performable Recordings model was a collaborative process that considered the needs, taste, and performance abilities of the performers, as well as the aesthetics of EDM and the technical aspects and limitations of the system. This project has not been based on questioning multiple audiences but only one specific audience: the band. However, what "live" means to this band and in performance depends solely on the performers' point of view and their cultural background. Although all participants agree that authenticity, creativity, and expressivity in a performance are strong indicators of what "live" means, their cultural differences may result in their perceiving these terms differently.

The ethnographic and auto-ethnographic approach used in this research allows for a deeper understanding of the cultural and personal factors that shape the music production process and the ways in which performers negotiate and adapt to altered performance techniques. It is shown that in this project, as in other musical styles and traditions, performers must alter the form and extent of the expressive practices that they use to fashion their ideas of first-person authenticity to accommodate third-person authenticity. The concept of entrainment plays a crucial role in this hybrid timing technique for musicians, as it allows for the synchronization of human performances with mechanical processes. The distinction between "future-oriented attending" and "analytic attending" helps musicians identify and adjust to any performance entrainment errors, breaking the boundaries of entrainment to a click track only. This project also suggested new methods of notation and score reading for technologies and audio processes. The different coloring schemes and the graphic representation of the audio processes demonstrate ways in which a notation system can be customized to accommodate new technologies.

In conclusion, the Performable Recordings model offers a novel approach for combining technology and live performance in the creation of EDM. This model allows for the creation of authentic and cohesive performances while also challenging traditional notions of liveness and authenticity in live performance. Through the use of mechanical processes of studio production in a live setting, this model offers unique aesthetic possibilities within the genre of EDM. Additionally, the role of authenticity and liveness in the model enhances the immersive experience for both the performers and the audience.

REFERENCES

Afishal. (2014). *David Guetta - Live Remix by AFISHAL*. Available at: https://www.youtube.com/watch?v=NUlZwfh5bpw [Accessed: 23 September 2016].

Art Works. (2015). *How Creativity Works in the Brain*. Available at: www.arts.gov/
    sites/default/files/how-creativity-works-in-the-brain-report.pdf   [Accessed:
    10 May 2017].

Bailey, D. (1993). *Improvisation: Its Nature and Practice in Music*. USA: Da
    Capo Press.

Boltz, M. and Jones, M. R. (1989). 'Dynamic Attending and Responses to Time',
    Psychological Review, 96, pp. 459–491.

Bown, O., Bell, R. and Parkinson, A. (2014). *Examining the Perception of Liv-
    eness and Activity in Laptop Music: Listeners' Inference about What the
    Performer Is Doing from the Audio Alone*. Available at: https://core.ac.uk/
    download/pdf/42385131.pdf [Accessed: 22 April 2015].

Carlson, M. (2004). *Performance: A Critical Introduction*, 2nd ed. New York:
    Routledge.

Clayton, M., Sager, R. and Will, U. (2004). *In Time with Music: The Concept of
    Entrainment and Its Significance for Ethnomusicology*. Available at: http://
    oro.open.ac.uk/2661/1/InTimeWithTheMusic.pdf [Accessed: 26 October
    2017].

Collins, N. and Rincon, J. D'E. (2007). *The Cambridge Companion to Electronic
    Music*. Cambridge: Cambridge University Press.

Cooke, G. (2011). *Liveness and the Machine, Improvisation in Live Audio-Visual
    Performance*. Available at: www.researchgate.net/publication/266316401_
    Liveness_and_the_machine_improvisation_in_live_audio-visual_perfor-
    mance [Accessed: 22 July 2022].

Croft, J. (2007). 'Theses on Liveness', *Organized Sound*, 12(1), pp. 59–66.

Danielsen, A., ed. (2010). *Musical Rhythm in the Age of Digital Reproduction*.
    Surrey: Ashgate Press.

Davis, T. (2011). *Towards a Relational Understanding of the Performance Eco-
    system*. Available at: http://core.ac.uk/download/pdf/4898861.pdf [Accessed:
    10 May 2015].

Human Benchmark. (2007). *Human Benchmark*. Available at: https://human-
    benchmark.com/tests/reactiontime [Accessed: 1 November 2023].

Keil, C. (1995). 'The Theory of Participatory Discrepancies: A Progress Report',
    Ethnomusicology, 39(1), pp. 1–19.

Kjus, Y. and Danielsen, A. (2016). *Live Mediation: Performing Concerts Using
    Studio Technology*. Cambridge: Cambridge University Press. Available at:
    www.duo.uio.no/bitstream/handle/10852/58759/1/Live%2Bmediation.%2B
    Accepted%2Bversion%2B.pdf [Accessed: 2 June 2022].

Lalioti, V. (2012). *Beyond 'Live' and 'Dead' in Popular Electronic Music Perfor-
    mances in Athens*. SIBE. Available at: www.sibetrans.com/trans/public/docs/
    trans_16_08.pdf [Accessed: 22 April 2015].

Lyubenov, B. (2017). *Music Analysis of the Electronic Dance Music*. HPAC. Avail-
    able at: https://hpac.cs.umu.se/teaching/sem-mus-17/Reports/Lyubenov.pdf
    [Accessed: 4 December 2022].

Méndez, M. (2013). *Autoethnography as a Research Method: Advantages, Limi-
    tations and Criticisms, Colombian Applied Linguistics Journal*. Facultad
    de Ciencias y Educación de la Universidad Distrital, Bogotá Colombia.
    Available at: www.scielo.org.co/scielo.php?script=sci_arttext&pid=S0123-
    46412013000200010 [Accessed: 27 December 2022].

Moore, A. (2002). 'Authenticity as Authentication', *Cambridge Journals Online*. Available at: http://journals.cambridge.org/action/displayFulltext?type=1& fid=107752&jid=PMU&volumeId=21&issueId=02&aid=107751 [Accessed: 2 May 2015].

Moralis, C. (2019). *Live Popular Electronic Music 'Performable Recordings', Live Popular Electronic Music 'Performable Recordings' – UWL Repository*. University of West London. Available at: https://repository.uwl.ac.uk/ id/eprint/6560/ [Accessed: 2 January 2023].

Pinn Panelle. (2011). *Skrillex – Scary Monsters and Nice Sprites*. Available at: https://www.youtube.com/watch?v=ZuunY8BTqNs&frags=pl%2Cwn [Accessed: 12 May 2018].

Pretolesi, L. (2015). *Psychology of a Mix Engineer: An Interview with Luca Pretolesi*. Available at: http://modernmixing.com/blog/2015/04/06/psychology-of-a-mix-engineer-luca-pretolesi/ [Accessed: 10 December 2015].

Pubnub. (2017). *How Fast Is Realtime? Human Perception and Technology*. Available at: www.pubnub.com/blog/2015-02-09-how-fast-is-realtime-human-perception-and-technology/ [Accessed: 18 November 2017].

Sanden, P. (2013). *Liveness in Modern Music: Musicians, Technology, and the Perception of Performance*. New York: Routledge.

Shawn Wasabi. (2015). *Shawn Wasabi – Marble Song (Original Song)*. Available at: https://www.youtube.com/watch?v=qAeybdD5UoQ [Accessed: 26 March 2017].

Small, C. (1998). *Musicking: The Meanings of Performing and Listening*, Part 1. Hanover: University Press of New England.

Submotion Orchestra. (2014). *Submotion Orchestra Performance – Bass Music Awards*. Available at: https://www.youtube.com/watch?v=rcZhxtFoXAo [Accessed: 26 April 2017].

Theheritageorchestra.com. (2022). *The Bays – Heritage Orchestra*. Available at: https://theheritageorchestra.com/projects/the-bays/#:~:text=Their%20trade% 2Dmark%20was%20only [Accessed: 1 November 2023].

Thorton, S. (1995). *Club Cultures: Music, Media and Subcultural Capital*. London and New York: Routledge.

Transmediate. (2011). *Digital Liveness: Philip Auslander (us) About Digital Liveness in Historical, Philosophical Perspective*. Available at: https://vimeo. com/20473967 [Accessed: 28 April 2015].

Zagorski-Thomas, S. (2014). *The Musicology of Record Production*. Cambridge: Cambridge University Press.

3

The space is the place

Interplay and interaction in an extreme location

Claus Sohn Andersen

1 INTRODUCTION

In July 2017, my band booked a recording session at Emanuel Vigelands Mausoleum in Oslo, following a weekend of working on improvisation and composition in a relatively traditional way in a conventional recording studio. The mausoleum is, in short, a dimly lit stone vault with omnipresent and evocative artwork, no natural light, and hard, reflective surfaces all around, resulting in a room more reverberant than any cathedral. Interaction, interplay, and even style of music in the recorded improvisations differed considerably from our work in other spaces. This chapter proposes a way to understand and account for the changes to our musicking in the mausoleum. This is done through the lens of an ecological approach to perception, based on Eric Clarke's seminal work *Ways of Listening* (2005). Furthermore, by taking into account Lakoff and Johnson's (2003) claim that metaphorical concepts are crucial to cognition and viewing the space as embodying various such metaphorical concepts, the site-specific impact can be traced in our musicking.

I will look primarily at collective elements, i.e., our interplay and interaction, and compare the choices made in *Tomba* with those the band makes when improvising in regular environments (i.e., in a rehearsal space or recording studio).

Audio and video examples are given throughout, these can be accessed via the accompanying website. Examples are referenced in the fashion "Audio# – Name".

2 BACKGROUND

2.1 The players

The band SVK was formed in 2010 by Håkon Nybø (bass guitar, synths), Kristian Stubbrud Mäkinen (drums, synths) and Claus Sohn Andersen (guitars). In instrumentation, SVK is a classic 'power trio'. However, the music is a mix of post-rock, jazz, ambient and electroacoustic improvisations, heavy on long, repetitive and hypnotic structures. The music is almost entirely instrumental. The band has released three albums and one

 DOI: 10.4324/9781003118817-4

EP (*SVK* (2011), *Rogue Waves* (2013), *Avernus* (2014), *Shitome Us With Roar* (2016)), two of which feature all-improvised material.

As a trio with traditional instrumentation (in terms of Western rock tradition), basic musical roles within the ensemble are typical – at least when playing composed or written material. The drummer keeps time and tempo and creates rhythmic variation and counterpoint. The bassist provides a harmonic/tonal center, aids timekeeping, and adds melodic content and rhythmic variations. The guitarist provides the main harmonic and melodic content and usually serves as the focal point or 'lead voice' of the ensemble. However, given the extensive use of various tools to shape, and at times completely warp, the sound and timbre of our instruments, roles are often in flux – particularly when improvising. Furthermore, SVK employs a decidedly holistic aesthetic approach or 'ethos', where the aim is for the elements to blend rather than stand out in a soloistic fashion. This approach affects all aspects, from composing and arranging to post-production.

Compositions will invariably evolve from an improvisational starting point, whether starting from a free improvisation or based on an idea brought forth by one of the members. All rehearsals are recorded and serve as guidance for further improvisations and, eventually, for working out structures and arrangements.

2.2 The place

The building was erected in 1926 as an atelier by Emanuel Vigeland (1875–1948), the younger brother of sculptor Gustav Vigeland. See Albrektsen (2014) for details on his life and career. It was later repurposed to function as the artist's final resting place, a mausoleum named *Tomba Emmanuelle*. Today, the building is accessible to the public as the Emanuel Vigeland Museum. The entire 800m^2 surface of the walls and ceiling are covered by Vigeland's opus magnum *Vita* – a fresco depicting life and love from conception to death. The urn containing his ashes resides on a shelf above the small entrance (approximately 1.5m in height) to the mausoleum, forcing most visitors to bow to the artist when entering or leaving the mausoleum. In the conversion to a tomb, all windows were bricked up, meaning no natural light enters the room. The limited lighting illuminates parts of the fresco while leaving the rest of the room in a state of perpetual dusk.

The extreme acoustics of *Tomba Emmanuelle* result from geometrical and material properties. The main room is approximately 22m by 10m and has a barrel-vaulted ceiling with a peak height of approximately 12.5m. The importance of room geometry and proportions is well documented (see Everest and Pohlmann (2015) Chapters 13 and 26 or Rossing, Moore and Wheeler (2002), Chapter 25.2), and while *Tomba* does not exhibit ideal proportions, it does facilitate an even reverberation across a wide frequency range. The barrel-vaulted ceiling also contributes to this end. The walls and ceiling have been waxed to protect the fresco, a treatment that also closes all pores in the bricks and plaster, resulting in increased acoustic reflectivity, particularly in the higher frequencies. The floor is

Figure 3.1 Tomba Emmanuelle, looking towards the entrance.

Source: Photo by Kjartan Hauglid

set with equally reflective slabs of waxed granite. This results in a reverberation time of nearly 20 seconds in the low-mid frequency range, coming down to below ten seconds in the higher frequencies (Cox, 2014). In
comparison, a concert hall for classical music with the same room volume
would have a recommended reverberation time of 1.4–1.7 seconds (Standard Norge, 2014) while a medium-sized church would typically be in the
vicinity of three to four seconds.

2.3 The session

The recording session in *Tomba Emmanuelle* came at the tail end of a four-
day session in a traditional recording studio. Here, we had been working
on arrangements and structures in a more traditional sense, taking compositions that had been worked out in the rehearsal space and refining them
in a more controlled environment. On the final day, before our session in
Tomba, we decided to try a simulation of the extremely reverberant environment. We instructed our engineer to add a lengthy reverb similar to
Tomba to the master bus, which was used for monitoring. This approach
was explored for about an hour.

For the session in the mausoleum, we reduced our setups, as we, partly
based on the experience with the simulated conditions, expected that much
of our usual armament would be useless. The drumkit was reduced to bass
drum, snare, hi-hat and a single cymbal. The bass guitar was left behind,

replaced by a monophonic synth with a filterbank included. The guitar setup was reduced from stereo to mono, and the number of pedals and effects was considerably reduced. The recording setup was equally sparse: a single DI for the synth and seven microphones (three room in a Decca tree configuration, one for the guitar amplifier – Vox AC30 and three for the drums). The synth was run through a Genelec 8050 loudspeaker for monitoring and room sound.

The session was freely improvised, except for one section where we stumbled into improvising over a theme we had been working on in the rehearsal room for some months (working title "Balloon Ventures"). In total, the session resulted in nearly two hours of recorded material. The entire session was recorded on video as well as audio.

2.4 Method

Listening back to the recordings from *Tomba Emmanuelle* led to what Brinkmann (2014, 2012) calls a 'breakdown in understanding'. The musical style or expression evident in the *Tomba* recordings differed substantially from our usual sound when improvising, and this inconsistency prompted further investigation. Though this was true for all the material from the session, it was particularly true for the section where we improvised over a pre-existing theme that sparked interest, as this could readily be compared to improvisations on the same theme in different circumstances.

Methodologically, the investigation rests on narrative inquiry (Kim, 2016; Riessman, 2008), which was employed simultaneously in two ways; first – the breakdown led to a recounting of the session in text, eventually resulting in a short autoethnographic account of the session in a narrative form, focused on the subjective experience. This was compared to similar accounts of experiences of being in the rehearsal room and recording studio. The other band members were allowed to read the texts for factual corrections and commentary. Due to limitations of space, only excerpts will be presented in this chapter. Full texts will appear in the author's forthcoming Ph.D. dissertation (Andersen, forthcoming).

Second, recordings of performances from both the rehearsal room and *Tomba* were treated as enacted or performed narratives, emerging through improvisation. This approach is not to be confused with the idea of 'music as narrative' (see Maus (1991) or Almén (2008) for examples), which engages with the composition as a narrative. Rather, the current approach is focused on the *performance*, and in particular, the interactions between performers, as documented in the recordings. This is in part inspired by the emerging field of sound studies, and specifically Gershon (2017). As with other narrative forms, improvised musical performances generally have an opening, a middle and a concluding final section. Each musical statement and interaction can be viewed as part of this narrative – events linked to and partly conditioned by past events while also pointing to future events – i.e., further musical statements and interactions. Furthermore, like other narratives, they are situated in a specific context and enacted by specific individuals with differing backgrounds, abilities, and sensibilities. See also Iyer (2004) for a related approach to narrative in music.

The material from *Tomba*, rehearsal recordings of the theme mentioned in section 2.3 and other recordings of improvisations were all subjected to close listening. The analysis focused on a comparison of the following features across the recordings:

- Instances of interaction and interplay – call/response, mimicry, synchronous or sequential changes, signals/cues, and so on
- Overall dynamic range, both individually and collectively
- Overall tempo and temporal density (amount of sound events within a given time-space)
- Use of timbre and timbral variations, both individually and collectively

Findings from the close listening were then taken together with the text-based narratives and viewed in light of the theoretical perspectives described in section 2.5.

2.5 Theory

To make sense of the findings from the analysis, multiple related theoretical perspectives are employed, outlined in the following section:

- *Tomba Emmanuelle* and the relation to ritual spaces, as outlined by Snekkestad (2017)
- Based on Lakoff and Johnson (2003) and acknowledging the recent move to embodied cognition (see Shapiro and Spaulding (2021) for an introduction), *Tomba* is seen as embodying certain 'metaphorical concepts' that impact the cognition of visitors
- The ecological approach to the perception of music, as described by Clarke (2005) and based on the work of Gibson (1966) and others
- Acoustics, psychoacoustics and 'classic' models of auditory perception

Snekkestad (2017) draws comparisons between *Tomba Emmanuelle*, the Romanesque stone churches of Medieval times, and the painted Paleolithic caves of Central Europe. He points to three 'ritual effects' of such spaces – extended reverberation, demarcation of designated areas for ritual activity and the interplay between limited lighting and works of (religious) art. All three are present in *Tomba*, though demarcation is by far the least pronounced. Furthermore, he argues that throughout human history, we have only encountered such spaces (i.e., those exhibiting ritual effects and in particular, extended reverberation) in connection to religious and/ or ritualistic activity – it has not been a part of our daily lives. Though this changed over the last 100–150 years, with increased access to spaces like concert halls and artificial means of reverberation, the point remains that we as a species are not, in an evolutionary sense, adapted to the sensory input provided by spaces with prolonged reverberation, and that over the course of many millennia, we only encountered such spaces in religious contexts. This leads Snekkestad to conclude that *Tomba Emmanuelle* provides an "acoustic simulation of transcendence" and that, to the secular and disenchanted modern listener, this can "arouse our sedated ears and allow us to re-experience the naïve wonderment that once filled caves and early churches" (Snekkestad, 2017).

The crucial role of metaphorical concepts in cognition has been well-established since Lakoff and Johnson published their seminal work, *Metaphors We Live By*, in 1980. The key points drawn from their work are:

1 Metaphorical concepts and metaphors, to a large extent, arise from bodily experience.
2 Metaphors and metaphorical concepts afford both possibilities and limitations for cognition – i.e., what can and cannot be thought.

Parsons (2007), from the point of view of visual arts, argues further that, in light of the importance of metaphor to cognition, an important role of the arts is to provide new metaphors or novel combinations of existing metaphors and thereby expand our cognitive possibilities. Swanwick (2007), coming from music, arrives at a similar conclusion, albeit in slightly more elevated language: "This is the mission of the arts, to extend metaphorical playfulness and in so doing keep the human spirit open and alive" (p. 501). A central prerequisite to this view of metaphor both in language, the arts and in cognition is that cognition is, at least to a degree, embodied. Such a view has indeed become increasingly common over the last decades; see Shapiro and Spaulding (2021) for an overview. Wilson (2002) outlines six views of cognition that are central to embodiment. In summary, these state that cognition is (often) situated, it is guided by and guides perception and interaction with our environment, it is action-centered and finally, it is body-based – even when working 'offline'.

Going back to Snekkestad (2017), the "acoustic simulation of transcendence" represents an example of a metaphorical concept embodied by *Tomba Emmanuelle* and its acoustic properties. What concepts a specific space embodies is, at least in part, a subjective matter relating to the individual's background (culturally, socially, economically and otherwise), the context in which the individual encounters the space and so on. Nevertheless, certain concepts are likely to be common for individuals with similar backgrounds. All three members of SVK are ethnically Scandinavian, brought up and educated in similar contexts – social democracies historically embedded in Protestant Christianity. On that basis, the following metaphorical concepts are identified (not limited to) as embodied by *Tomba Emmanuelle* and relevant to SVK as a group:

'transcendence', 'eternity', 'divinity', 'death', 'afterlife', 'awe', 'reverence' and 'introspection'.

These concepts arise from the physical (layout, dimensions, materials) and acoustic properties of the space, the omnipresent artwork and the cultural significance of both space and the artist.

Taking his cue from one of the fields contributing to an embodied view of cognition, ecological psychology and the influential work of Gibson (1966), Clarke (2005) provides a thorough account of the ecological approach to the perception of music, summarized in the following quote:

> from an ecological perspective, . . . perception always involves the reciprocal relationship between the opportunities of the environment and the capacities of the receiver.
>
> (Clarke, 2005, p. 148)

This stands in rather stark contrast to the prevailing approach in much writing and research on auditory perception, most of which presuppose a classic computational cognitive model in which the sensory apparatus is a passive input device. While Clarke certainly does not dispute the knowledge this approach has produced concerning the biomechanical functioning of the auditory apparatus, he highlights that such an approach is incapable of explaining the intricacies of how auditory stimuli impact our day-to-day engagement with our environment or how we construct meaning from sensory input. It is worth noting that the 'opportunities of the environment' in the ecological view of perception include the listener's background, experience, emotional state and so on – the ecologic approach, as Clarke describes and employs it, is decidedly holistic and in line with cognition as embodied. The following few key features from ecological perception are particularly relevant to this chapter:

- The *perception-action cycle* – perception guides action, in turn guiding further perception
- *Perceptual adaptation* – the evolutionary adjustment of our perceptual capabilities to our environment and, to an extent, the shaping of our environment to our perceptual capabilities (consider, for example, the evolution of musical instruments)
- A fundamentally different view of *perceptual learning* from the cognitive model – a process of "progressive differentiation, [by which perceivers become] . . . increasingly sensitive to distinctions within the stimulus information" (Clarke, 2005, p. 22) as opposed to the passive gathering and accumulation of information

Finally, Clarke (2005) notes that listening while performing, and particularly when improvising, "highlights the relationship between perception and action, and autonomous and heteronomous perspectives" (p. 152). In short, the autonomous/heteronomous dichotomy here implies listening to music 'only as music', as an aesthetic object with a self-explanatory and self-sufficient (i.e., autonomous) inner logic versus listening contextually – treating the music as any other auditory stimuli. The previous quote points to the fact the improvising musician is simultaneously judging the music (the aesthetic object in creation) and its inner logic while remaining aware of context in various ways and is also engaged in the perception-action cycle in a more technical way (by the physical act of performing).

Furthermore, the perception part of the cycle must also consider both autonomous and heteronomous perspectives and inform further action accordingly. This process becomes increasingly complex if multiple performers improvise together, each with their own aesthetic sensibilities and experience of context to inform their perception-action cycle.

Highly reverberant environments pose some challenges to our auditory system. It is well known that prolonged reverberation has a degrading effect on speech clarity (Rasch and Plomp, 1982) and that different musics or modes of performance have very differing optimum reverberation times. However, even the most 'reverberation-hungry' musical styles rarely demand more than 2–2.5 seconds (see, for instance, Rasch and Plomp (1982, p. 141), Everest and Pohlmann (2015, pp. 171–172)). Research on how acoustic conditions impact musical performance in terms of in-the-moment choices made by musicians is scarce. However, extrapolating from research in psychoacoustics (for example, Bregman (1990), Moore (2013)) and research in stage and performance hall acoustics (Dammerud, 2009), an environment as reverberant as *Tomba Emmanuelle* can incur the following effects (not limited to):

- Sound events with significantly less inter-onset time (i.e., time between attacks) than the room's reverberation time will lead to a blurring of onsets and durations
- Subsequent notes reverberate together if played rapidly relative to the reverberation time
- Masking effects due to spectral content, level and timing become more pronounced

Furthermore, the extreme reverberation of *Tomba*, in a sense, amplifies every sound – even the ruffling of clothes or moving a chair becomes a monumental sound, as evidenced by Audio #3.1 – Chairs – an unaltered recording of chairs dragged across the floor, picked up by three room microphones. Whether this 'audiosensory amplification' leads the visitor to make more or less sound is likely an individual matter, but in any case, it leads to an increased awareness of and attention to sound, especially in combination with the limited lighting. There is, of course, a difference in how we mentally approach a space as performers as opposed to as visitors – the former is supposed to actively use or explore the space in some way, while the latter is expected to take on a passive, observing role. However, it seems that *Tomba Emmanuelle*, through the 'audiosensory amplification', to a certain extent, makes it impossible to be a completely passive and observing visitor. The amplification and prolongation of every sound made within the space makes it nearly impossible to *not* interact with it, intentionally or not.

3 FINDINGS AND DISCUSSION

In the following subsections, I will point to what I see as the most prominent differences to our musicking in *Tomba Emmanuelle*, exemplified by the improvisation over a theme mentioned in section 2.3, compared to

rehearsal recordings of improvisations over the same theme. These findings are then viewed in light of the text-based experiential narratives and
the theoretical perspectives described in section 2.5.

While it surely would be interesting to compare the freely improvised
sections recorded in *Tomba* to free improvisations from other spaces, a
problem of selection criteria arises – free improvisations in other settings
arise from a multitude of starting points (a drum groove, a chord progression, a bass ostinato and so on), which invariably impact on how these
improvisations progress. Selecting the right material to provide a just
and transparent comparison that does not anticipate its own conclusion
becomes a challenge, given a body of work consisting of tens of hours of
material. In other words, such an endeavor would be far beyond the scope
of this chapter. Improvisations over the same theme from different settings
are more readily comparable. For the interested reader, an excerpt of free
improvisation from *Tomba Emmanuelle* is provided (Video #3.2 – Free
improvisation in Tomba), and this can be compared to our releases of fully
improvised studio recordings: *Rogue Waves* (SVK, 2013) and *Shitome Us
With Roar* (SVK, 2016).

3.1 Improvisation on a theme – "Balloon Ventures" in two spaces

"Balloon Ventures" is based on a melodic guitar motif composed on acoustic guitar and presented to the band in November 2016. It served as a starting point for several improvisations in the following months. The analysis
compares the version from *Tomba Emmanuelle* (Video #3.1 – Balloon Ventures in Tomba) to two rehearsal room recordings (Audio #3.2 – Rehearsal
Nov-16 and Audio #3.3 – Rehearsal April-17), representing the first and
last improvisations on that theme prior to the session in *Tomba*.

Recounting the experience of playing "Balloon Ventures" in the mausoleum and listening back to the recording for the first time:

> the way we had played it before never felt right. . . . the minute we
> started playing it in *Tomba*, it just felt right, like this was how it was
> meant to be all along. Listening back, I can hear how I could allow the
> melodic phrases to breathe; slow down, speed up, pause, all without
> the restraints of a rigid meter and tempo.
>
> (Andersen, forthcoming)

This quote points to considerable differences in the subjective experience
of improvising over the theme in *Tomba* as compared to the rehearsal
room. The close listening analysis confirmed the observations made in the
quote, as well as revealed a host of other significant changes. While there
are obvious differences between the two rehearsal-versions, they share a
common aesthetic typical of the post-rock genre: slow build-up to a massive crescendo, start/stop-dynamics, and prominent use of time-based
effects such as reverb and delay.

The initial version, from November 2016, takes some time to 'get going' – the bass steadies the tempo by pumping 8th notes from around 5:50, and the drums enter shy of the seven-minute mark. Prior to this, the phrasing of the guitar motif is best described as 'loose', 'exploratory' and 'unsure'. The solidifying of meter and tempo leads to more rigid and even phrasing. From there, the intensity builds with simultaneous increases in sound level, tempo and temporal and spectral density, while the addition of delays, reverbs and various kinds of distortion further add to these parameters. At around 9:45, the guitar changes to a different theme, building tension. The crescendo culminates at around 14:00, followed by about a minute of quiet, ambient-like synth playing. A count-in on the hi-hat signals a new start – jumping directly to the theme and intensity from the previous crescendo. About midway into this segment, the tonality, which has been largely based on the G-major scale, changes significantly for the first time as the guitar stays on an F for a few bars (implying a shift to the minor key), then starts alternating between E and F, creating a tonal instability (E being part of the G major scale, while F is in the minor scale). The drums signal the ending by 'falling apart'. The crescendos generally take on a 'wall of sound' quality, resulting from high intensity both in terms of spectral width and density, temporal density, sound level, use of distortion and the extensive use of reverb and delay.

The April 2017 version follows much of the same trajectory but shortens the timeframe. First, it dispels the exploratory intro. The bass starts pumping 8th notes straight away, which seems to limit the phrasing freedom of the guitar. Furthermore, a structure with synchronous changes seems to have solidified, for instance, the variation occurring at 2:52 and again at 4:23. Both these variations cue other changes – after the first one, the guitar adds a delay, and the snare drum is played more densely, while the second cues a larger change, including a different guitar theme, eventually leading to a crescendo. This culminates in a lengthy, sparse, ambient sequence lasting roughly four minutes. Around 11 minutes in, the original theme returns, washed in reverberation and at a considerably lower tempo. The phrasing initially remains fairly regular, both in terms of tempo within each phrase and space between phrases. After roughly two minutes, the guitar starts exploring the tonality and elements of the theme in different ways, and as the guitar focuses on the lower register, the synth goes higher. From about 15 minutes, the guitar stops playing, followed by the drums at 15:30, after which the synth abandons the theme and 'dissolves'.

The version from *Tomba Emmanuelle* follows a completely different trajectory from the other two in terms of intensity while retaining some of the thematic structure from the April 2017 version. It is worth noting that we did not *intend* to play "Balloon Ventures" – in retrospect, it seems the sparse groove on the drums, reminiscent of the ending section from April-17, inspired Håkon to play the theme in a somewhat different version, starting at around 1:50. At this point, the guitar is engaged with making noise swells. Eventually, the drums stop, and the guitar joins the synth in playing the theme, but this is done asynchronously – partly as call/response and partly playing different phrases from the same theme simultaneously. In this sub-section, the synth and guitar seem to share the role of focal point or lead voice. From around 4:20, the synth moves into a lower register, playing fewer, longer notes and pushing the guitar to the front. As the drums pick up the initial groove, a section follows, bearing clear resemblance to the ending section from April-17. However, despite the immense natural reverberation, this version is far less dense, and the phrasing on the guitar seems looser. At 9:25, the drums again come to a halt, the synth responding with an ascending B-D-E, cueing a new section of call-response interaction with the guitar. This evolves into a sparse, ambient section containing a sequence of chords on the guitar, supported by single notes from the synth and the occasional rustling of a cymbal or bass drum hit. In the subjective account, I wrote of this section that it "felt like it grew organically out of the main theme, or as if we were exploring the same image through a kaleidoscope" (Andersen, forthcoming). The temporal density of this section is extremely low, with roughly ten seconds between each event. From 15:30, the guitar adds a delay, filling in some of the space between attacks, cueing synth and drums to do the same. The synth takes on an increasingly leading role, especially as the drums enter a steadier groove. This also brings the tonal center back, albeit with an emphasis on the corresponding E minor scale. A chord struck on the guitar at around 18:20 slightly shifts the tonality briefly and signals the ending of this section. The guitar then picks up the original theme again, with the synth partly responding and partly supporting. As the initial groove returns, one repetition of the theme is completed, before the variation from the first section of April-17 (mentioned previously) signals the ending.

As noted, there are strong similarities between the two rehearsal versions – one could say that the exploratory introduction of the first version was moved to function as an outro for the second. The structure is otherwise very similar, but while the first version seems to grow very gradually in intensity, the second version seems to grow a bit more stepwise, with limited change within each step (for instance, the segment 1:45–3:00 represents one step, 3:00–4:35 another). Common to both versions is also the fact that, largely, the guitar remains the focal point or leading voice throughout, and while interactional cues are given from all instruments, the guitar also largely dictates the rate of development and intensity. The version from *Tomba Emmanuelle* differs in both these regards; the leading role is clearly shared with, and at times overtaken by, the synth in several sections; and both pace and direction of development and intensity level are as much dictated by synth and drums as by the guitar. In other words, where the rehearsal versions are guitar-driven, the *Tomba*-version is interplay-driven. Other major differences include:

1   Rehearsal versions vary greatly in level throughout both versions, whereas the *Tomba* version stays at a lower level for its entirety.
2   Similar differences apply to other aspects of intensity; the rehearsal versions generally have a far higher temporal and spectral density,

higher tempo, greater timbral variation and more prominent use of abrasive or 'unpleasant' timbres.

3   While the rehearsal versions *overall* showcase a larger array of timbres, there is still a tendency towards timbral coherence or similarity (for instance – both Håkon and I turn on distortion or add lengthy artificial reverberation), whereas in *Tomba,* the tendency is towards timbral contrast or complementarity – i.e., making our timbres 'fit together' like a jigsaw puzzle rather than like an overlay.

4   Sequential aspects of interplay (call/response, initiating changes, etc.) were far more prominent in *Tomba Emmanuelle*, whereas the rehearsal versions, to a greater extent, relied on synchronous changes based on a common understanding of the direction of the music.

5   In general, the recorded improvisations from *Tomba* display a lower evolutionary rate than improvisations from other spaces – each musical idea was explored to a greater extent before moving on. This is particularly evident in "Balloon Ventures" – the entire 20+ minutes of the *Tomba* version explores the main theme, whereas the rehearsal versions add other, distinctly different, musical ideas.

One could say that the interplay in *Tomba* was more guided by listening and outward attention, whereas the rehearsal versions, even the initial first attempt from Nov-16, were more guided by pre-agreed notions of a common aesthetic (roles, genre and so on), whether these notions were made explicit or not. Furthermore, the restraint (in terms of intensity) we exercised when playing in *Tomba Emmanuelle* led to a decidedly different stylistic outcome – a different 'sound'.

3.2 Piecing it together – discussion and conclusions

Several of the changes noted in the previous section could be ascribed to the acoustic properties of the space in tandem with 'traditional' psychoacoustic models of auditory perception. For instance, the lowering of tempo (understood both as pulse/meter and as temporal density) could be explained by the fact that (prolonged) reverberation will blur transients, particularly when the inter-onset time of events is significantly lower than the reverberation time. This side-effect of reverberation is well known in practice, as evidenced by this statement from producer and engineer Audun Strype:

> if you want to steer the production in some particular direction, if you want them to play a bit slower for instance, . . . a trick could be to put a bit of reverb in the headsets.
>
> (Strype, 2018)

Similarly, the subdued dynamics and the shift towards complementing timbres rather than similar ones can also be viewed as a move made to uphold stream segregation more easily. However, our inclination towards loud, abrasive, 'brick wall' crescendos or soundscapes (exemplified in the Nov-16 version or the four final minutes of the track 'Wormwood' from *Shitome Us With Roar* (SVK, 2016)) would suggest that upholding stream segregation is either not a problem or not a relevant concern for us – 'loud and noisy' is a natural part of our usual style. In other words, while a traditional understanding of acoustics and auditory perception can go a long way in explaining the differences in interplay, interaction and musical choices between different spaces, there are some crucial questions related to the marked shift in aesthetic output that cannot, in my view, be adequately answered from that perspective:

1   Why did we exercise such dynamic restraint on several levels?
2   Why did we 'stay in the moment' more – exploring ideas exhaustively and focusing more intently on each other?

Taking the embodied metaphors of *Tomba Emmanuelle* (outlined in section 2.5) into consideration, within the framework of embodied cognition and ecological perception, the unresolved questions might find an answer. Several changes to our interplay and aesthetics can be seen as responses to the metaphors embodied by *Tomba* – for instance, *'eternity'* and *'transcendence'* are mirrored in the lowered tempo and temporal density, the dynamic restraint and use of largely pleasant timbres are mirrored in the concepts of *'awe'* and *'divinity'* while *'introspection'* and *'reverence'* give rise to modes of interplay more concerned with the here-and-now, and less with preconceived notions of some untold aesthetic goalpost. It could be argued that this is a somewhat speculative inference of causality. I do not mean to imply that these metaphorical concepts will facilitate the same changes in every ensemble or visitor to *Tomba* or even claim that our experience from July 2017 is the only possible outcome for SVK. Rather, I mean to show that *Tomba Emmanuelle*, or any other unique or extreme space, will have an impact on the visitor's perception and cognition. An analysis of what happened in *Tomba* based on ecological perception would naturally include such perspectives as those underlining the metaphorical concepts identified (cultural, social and historical context) in addition to acoustical conditions, the functioning of our sensory apparatus and so on. The ecological approach (and particularly Clarke) emphasizes the situatedness of perception. Clarke, writing on the cultural specificity of perception, notes that such factors, "although arbitrary in principle, . . . take on a fixed character in practice" (2005, p. 40). Lakoff and Johnson (2003) argue that metaphor is not just a matter of language but "a matter of conceptual structure" (p. 235) and that art provides "new ways of structuring our experience" (p. 235). Furthermore, they also argue that one "cannot function within the environment without changing it or being changed by it" (p. 230). Hence – embodied metaphorical concepts have the capacity to 'change us' and provide us with novel ways of structuring our experience.

As implied by Snekkestad (2017), we are not *perceptually adapted* to extreme reverberation, neither do we encounter it sufficiently in our lives (at least not as a physical space and phenomenon) for most to have experienced significant *perceptual learning*; we have not achieved a "differential perception . . . by virtue of environmental exposure/exploration" (Clarke, 2005, p. 24). In other words, we are rather ill-equipped to deal with the audiosensory environment of *Tomba Emmanuelle*. It is my conclusion that the answer to the two unresolved questions is two-fold:

- First, the entire session was a process of perceptual learning through the perception/action cycle – we were familiarizing ourselves with the environment. Before we could push the boundaries of the room and its acoustics, we had to familiarize ourselves with the conditions and explore its nuances. This includes, to an extent, re-learning to play together in a new environment.
- Second, the unique context provided by *Tomba Emmanuelle*, conceptualized by the idea of embodied metaphorical concepts, had a site-specific impact on our cognition, which in turn changed our musicking. This points to both perception and cognition as situated – how and what we perceive and how we think about what we perceive and do is not independent of the situations in which we perceive and do. Put in a popularized term, the 'atmosphere' or 'mood' of the space changed the way we play together.

4 SUMMARY

In this chapter, I have drawn on such fields as acoustics, psychoacoustics, ecological perception and cognitive science to provide a novel way of accounting for site-specific changes to the musicking of an improvising ensemble.

A recording session in *Tomba Emmanuelle* resulted in significant changes to modes of interplay, interaction and musical style, compared to improvisations by the same ensemble in a rehearsal room and recording studio. In an extension of Lakoff and Johnson's (2003) demonstration of the crucial role of metaphors and metaphorical concepts in cognition, the idea of 'embodied metaphorical concepts' was employed and taken together with an ecological approach to perception to account for the changes that could not be fully explained by the acoustic properties of the space. The most significant such changes were:

- A general lowering of intensity in terms of both dynamics, tempo, spectral and temporal density and rate of compositional development
- Heightened sensitivity to the interactional aspect, less regard to the established aesthetics of the ensemble and a willingness to dwell on musical ideas

I conclude that these changes can be traced to a combination of a process of perceptual learning and the situatedness of perception and cognition. This situatedness is expressed by the embodied metaphorical concepts of *Tomba Emmanuelle*.

Looking ahead, I hope that researchers and practitioners across the fields of music production and performance can develop more awareness of how the recording or performance space itself can impact a performance.

REFERENCES

Albrektsen, L. (2014). 'Emanuel Vigeland', in *Norsk kunstnerleksikon*. Available at: https://nkl.snl.no/Emanuel_Vigeland [Accessed: 8 July 2021].

Almén, B. (2008). *A Theory of Musical Narrative*. Bloomington: Indiana University Press.

Andersen, C. S. (forthcoming). *Humanities and the Arts Dissertation*, Ph.D., Norwegian University of Science and Technology, Trondheim.

Bregman, A. S. (1990). *Auditory Scene Analysis – The Perceptual Organization of Sound*. Cambridge, MA: The MIT Press.

Brinkmann, S. (2012). *Qualitative Inquiry in Everyday Life – Working with Everyday Life Materials*. London: Sage Publications Ltd.

Brinkmann, S. (2014). 'Doing Without Data', *Qualitative Inquiry*, 20(6), pp. 720–725.

Clarke, E. F. (2005). *Ways of Listening – An Ecological Approach to the Perception of Musical Meaning*. New York: Oxford University Press Inc.

Cox, T. (2014). 'Extreme Acoustics in the Emanuel Vigeland Mausoleum', in *The Sound Blog*. Available at: http://trevorcox.me/extreme-acoustics-in-the-emanuel-vigeland-mausoleum-2021 [Accessed: 8 June 2021].

Dammerud, J. J. (2009). *Stage Acoustics for Symphony Orchestras in Concert Halls*. PhD. Bath: University of Bath.

Everest, F. A. and Pohlmann, K. C. (2015). *Master Handbook of Acoustics*, 6th ed. New York, NY: McGraw Hill.

Gershon, W. S. (2017). *Sound Curriculum: Sonic Studies in Educational Theory, Method, & Practice*. New York, NY: Routledge.

Gibson, J. J. (1966). *The Senses Considered as Perceptual Systems*. London: George Allen & Unwin Ltd.

Iyer, V. (2004). 'Exploding the Narrative in Jazz Improvisation', in O'Meally, R. G., Edwards, B. H. and Griffin, F. J., eds. *Uptown Conversation: The New Jazz Studies*. New York: Columbia University Press, pp. 393–403.

Kim, J.-H. (2016). *Understanding Narrative Inquiry: The Crafting and Analysis of Stories as Research*. Thousand Oaks, CA: SAGE Publications, Inc.

Lakoff, G. and Johnson, M. (2003). *Metaphors We Live By*. Chicago, IL: University of Chicago Press.

Maus, F. E. (1991). 'Music as Narrative', *Indiana Theory Review*, 12, pp. 1–34.

Moore, B. C. J. (2013). *An Introduction to the Psychology of Hearing*, 6th ed. Leiden: Brill.

Parsons, M. (2007). 'Art and Metaphor, Body and Mind', in Bresler, L., ed. *International Handbook of Research in the Arts Education*. New York: Springer-Verlag, pp. 533–542.

Rasch, R. A. and Plomp, R. (1982). 'The Listener and the Acoustic Environment', in Deutsch, D., ed. *The Psychology of Music*. Orlando, FL: Academic Press.

Riessman, C. K. (2008). *Narrative Methods for the Human Sciences*. Thousand Oaks, CA: Sage Publications.

Rossing, T. D., Moore, F. R. and Wheeler, P. A. (2002). *The Science of Sound*, 3rd ed. San Francisco, CA: Addison Wesley.

Shapiro, L. and Spaulding, S. (2021). *Embodied Cognition. The Stanford Encyclopedia of Philosophy* (Winter 2021 Edition). Available at: https://plato.stanford.edu/archives/win2021/entries/embodied-cognition/.

Snekkestad, P. (2017). 'The Cave and Church in Tomba Emmanuelle. Some Notes on the Ritual Use of Room Acoustics', *Journal of Sonic Studies*, 15. Available at: www.researchcatalogue.net/view/411373/411374.

Standard Norge. (2014). *NS 8178:2014 Acoustic Criteria for Rooms and Spaces for Music Rehearsal and Performance*. Oslo: Standard Norge.

Strype, A. (2018). Research Interview. In: Andersen, C. S., ed. Unpublished.

Swanwick, K. (2007). 'Metaphor and the Mission of the Arts', in Bresler, L., ed. *International Handbook of Research in the Arts Education*. New York: Springer-Verlag, pp. 497–502.

Wilson, M. (2002). 'Six Views of Embodied Cognition', *Psychonomic Bulletin & Review*, 4(9), pp. 625–636.

DISCOGRAPHY

SVK. (2011). *SVK*. Pug-Nose Records. Available at: Spotify [Accessed: 20 August 2022].

SVK. (2013). *Rogue Waves*. Pug-Nose Records. Available at: Spotify [Accessed: 20 August 2022].

SVK. (2014). *Avernus*. Pug-Nose Records/Doognad Records. Available at: Spotify [Accessed: 20 August 2022].

SVK. (2016). *Shitome Us With Roar*. Fnatt Records. Available at: Spotify [Accessed: 20 August 2022].

4

Composing without keys

The LFO as a composition tool

Dave Fortune

1 INTRODUCTION

For several decades, the primary tool for generating melodic motifs within the field of contemporary electronic music has been the Western, piano-style keyboard, frequently used in conjunction with a Digital Audio Workstation (DAW). There are growing trends within communities of practitioners in this field to move away from the established keyboard/DAW configuration and explore alternative tools and interfaces to use for the generation of musical motifs (Rossmy and Wiethoff, 2019). This chapter examines perspectives and justifications behind these trends and explores opportunities created by exploiting one of the most primitive and familiar components of a synthesizer, the Low-Frequency Oscillator (LFO), for melody construction.

The use of the LFO as a compositional tool has been explored by a number of other practitioners (Klobucar, 2017; Boon, 2019; In Vacuo, 2021a), however, this is primarily within the modular Eurorack environment. While this format undoubtedly offers almost limitless options in some respects, it also carries inherent limitations. By employing the Max for Live platform to implement similar functionalities, many of these can be overcome, and additional features can be employed, which increase the scope for this methodology to be both useful and accessible for a wide range of practitioners, including those exploring themes of generativity within their composition practice.

This study will also include the creation of several recorded and performance works, which will be discussed in this chapter. These components, along with other associated audio and video artefacts can be found in the "*LFOizer*" YouTube playlist, which can be accessed at https://tinyurl.com/LFOizer or via the QR code in Figure 4.1.

2 BACKGROUND AND RELATED WORK

Prior to exploring alternative interfaces and composition techniques, it is necessary to appreciate the context behind the current culture of rejecting the DAW and MIDI keyboard-based setup, which has become

        DOI: 10.4324/9781003118817-5

Figure 4.1 QR code to access audio and video artifacts.

commonplace within the sphere of electronic music production. One simply needs to search the word "DAWless" on an online audio forum such as Gearspace or Modwiggler to appreciate the number of practitioners who are interested in moving away from these technologies; however, a more nuanced understanding of the reasons behind this is crucial here. The concept of eschewing seemingly versatile methodologies is not a new one; Stravinsky (1947, p. 65) famously opined that "the more constraints one imposes, the more one frees one's self of the chains that shackle the spirit" and, perhaps in response to this statement, countless musicians since have purposefully limited specific musical parameters in a variety of ways in the hopes of unshackling their creative spirits (Herbert, 2005; Thompson, 2012; Hughes, 2021).

Rossmy and Wiethoff (2019, p. 4) suggest that in modern times this imposing of limitations can be a response to a society so overtly focused on highly efficient software actions: "productivity, workflow and speed experienced in every day work and social interaction have an effect on musician's subconscious expectations when performing music with such machines . . . a growing number of musicians want to slow down when making electronic music and explore creatively instead of pursuing concrete goals". They suggest that in response to this, "musicians are actively choosing regression. They prefer limited devices . . . over the more flexible machines they use every day" (ibid., p. 1). Kris Kaiser of Noise Engineering corroborates this based on his discussions with his customers who reject the use of DAWs in favour of modular synthesis, stating that "they spend so much time at the computer that they really enjoy the tactile experience of modular, of getting out of the box" (Kailus, 2022). The focus here is the "tactile experience"; therefore, any software-based system should also be capable of physical control, a theme which will be explored later.

The use of a traditional, Western piano-style keyboard to control synthesizers and other electronic instruments, while being considered the accepted norm in many musical circles, is deemed undesirable in others. Pinch and Trocco (2002) note that while Moog was the first synthesizer manufacturer to reach a large community of consumer musicians by having their instruments widely available in music stores, their founder, Bob Moog, had reservations about attaching a keyboard to his company's synthesizers but was pressured to do so by his sales representative Walter Sear. This decision may have enhanced Moog's commercial appeal; however, it lost them influential customers such as Vladimir Ussachevsky to Moog's rival Buchla, whom Moog later expressed admiration towards for not "limit[ing] the complexity of his instruments to meet the demands of the so-called marketplace" (Pinch and Trocco, 2002, p. 52). Furthermore, the use of the keyboard left some feeling that making instruments appealing to "both working and amateur musicians ultimately meant reducing their flexibility and thus restricting the use of the instrument to more familiar sonic cultural tropes" (Lanier and Rader, 2021, p. 604). Don Buchla himself has strong opinions on the subject:

> A keyboard is dictatorial. When you've got a black and white keyboard there it's hard to play anything but keyboard music. And when there's not a black and white keyboard you get into the knobs and the wires and the interconnections and the timbres, and you get involved in many other aspects of the music, and it's a far more experimental way. It's appealing to fewer people but it's more exciting.
>
> (Pinch and Trocco, 2002 p. 44)

Carla Scaletti of Symbolic Sound Corporation also suggests that a keyboard is not the most suitable interface for producing electronic music:

> If a musical interface is presented to you in the form of 'notes' that are to be played on 'instruments', it suggests a particular model of the physical world and a way of making music . . . When you encounter a musical interface that does not present you with notes, it encourages you to shift your focus to the sound itself and to create complex structures of sound in time.
>
> (Bjørn, 2018, p. 295)

Levitin, McAdams and Adams (2002, p. 172) discuss significant flaws with using a keyboard to control a synthesizer, concluding that synthesizers with built-in keyboard controllers were "simply a matter of convenience and a marketing decision", while Lanier and Rader (2021, p. 607) note that "the Eurorack community largely eschews . . . the keyboard controller". Given that Eurorack users represent an increasingly large proportion of the electronic music community (Rohs, 2018; Bjørn, 2018; Rossmy and Wiethoff, 2019; Bates, 2021), it is likely that a keyboard-less interface will appeal to a significant number of users, perhaps not just to modular enthusiasts but also those who are interested in alternative methodologies but without the considerable financial resources that are required to build a versatile Eurorack setup.

Ryan (1991), Levitin, McAdams and Adams (2002) and Manning (2004) question the suitability of the keyboard to control a synthesizer's expressive and articulative qualities and, in some cases, explore alternative devices that seek to provide simultaneous control of pitch and articulation within a single device. However, one could argue that the primary methods that many synthesists, particularly in the hardware domain, use to provide these qualities are not intrinsically linked to the 'playing of notes' as they are with most acoustic instruments, such as a woodwind player adjusting the force of the airflow through their instrument, or a string player adjusting the nuances of their plucking or bowing. Rather, they involve changing physical parameter controls relating to oscillators, filters, envelopes or other components, frequently on a device that is separate from the one that is used to 'play', or generate note data. It is, therefore, logical to suggest that an ideal device for a keyboard-eschewing synthesist to generate melodic content needs only to output data for pitch, with the understanding that other parameters necessary for articulation can be controlled by other means.

There is also the consideration of the capabilities of an individual musician's physical control. Ryan (1991, p. 4) examines the attraction of "realtime" [sic] control but warns that "the choice of realtime can have its cost in the narrowing of possibilities"; if an electronic musician's "realtime" control constitutes playing a keyboard or interface in the conventional sense, they pay the "cost" of having limited ability to articulate by manipulating sonic parameters, due to constantly using one or both hands to play notes on the interface. Potential solutions to this problem might require "evolution of higher level representations which leave more of the details to the computer" (ibid.), where in this context the notion of a computer could equally refer to a DAW, or another automated device such a primitive hardware sequencer. This concept is likely to be a factor in Pinch and Trocco's (2002, pp. 143–144) assessment of the keyboard-less Buchla 100 as "an instrument that the performer could really interact with" and use to "make music in real time", compared to the keyboard-controlled Moog that required "endless tape dubs" to produce a full composition.

This perspective could explain the popularity of devices that generate automated note patterns in the modular domain; at the time of writing, the website Modular Grid currently lists 812 modules in the Eurorack format alone, whose primary function is listed as 'sequencer' (Modular Grid, n.d.). Of these devices, many adhere to the step sequencer format, widely established with the release of Moog's Modular Synthesizer 1p in 1969, giving the user precise pitch control of discrete time-based 'steps', usually used to create short, repeating melody patterns. A significant number, such as the Music Thing Modular Turing Machine and the QU-Bit Chance, generate random signals more suited to generative applications, where the user has minimal control over parameters that influence the outputted signal but typically elicit more complex, less repetitive patterns. This paper seeks to augment these methodologies by exploring the area between these two aesthetics, where the user theoretically has precise control over every musical event, but in practice, the line between control and unpredictability is blurred, and constantly evolving patterns that can surprise both the creator and listener are produced.

3 WHY THE LFO?

For several decades, technology has allowed musicians the capability to use a wide range of both software and hardware interfaces to control physical or virtual instruments capable of producing an almost limitless spectrum of sounds. This "separation of the sound controller from the sound-producing device . . . affords an opportunity to think about how controllers can be designed, no longer subject to the constraints imposed by centuries of integrated design" (Levitin, McAdams and Adams, 2002, p. 186). This study chooses to respond to this 'opportunity' through the creative application of the LFO, a component that has been ubiquitous in synthesizer designs for more than 50 years and is most commonly employed to create subtle cyclical variations in pitch, volume or timbre, such as tremolo and vibrato. Most LFO waveforms will produce a constantly moving stream of continuous data, which in the analogue domain would consist of a constantly changing control voltage (CV). If this is used to modulate the pitch of a sound at sufficient amplitude, it will create a sound similar to a siren, rather than a conventional melody. However, if this continuous data is converted into discrete data using a pitch quantizer, so that only notes in a chromatic scale can be played, an atonal melody will be produced. If this is quantized further so that certain notes are eliminated, the melody can be made to adhere to a particular scale or pattern of notes, which may be more appropriate for some musical applications. A basic iteration of this concept is demonstrated in the video "*Generating a melody with a single LFO in VCV rack*" in the "*LFOizer*" playlist, where a sine wave is quantized to just four notes to create a rising and falling melodic pattern. Note that these four notes can be played in multiple octaves if the LFO's amplitude is sufficiently high.

Although quite primitive and limited in some respects, the LFO has a huge benefit in its familiarity to electronic musicians. Bjørn (2018, p. 25) refers to a preferential state where a musical interface "should play its part by being self-explanatory" and offer "no interruptions to the process", resulting in an interface that is both "usable" and "enjoyable". Most practitioners will be so accustomed to devices using an LFO that they should instinctively recognize its controls and functionality almost instantly, thus fulfilling Moog design engineer Eric Church's requirements that an instrument "should act as a frictionless conduit for the user's creative energies" (Bjørn, 2018, p. 84).

The previous comments not only affirm that the LFO can provide an appropriate interface for an electronic musician but also have implications on the specific type of LFO used, of which there is a huge range to choose from. The LFOs of early analogue subtractive synthesizers such as the Arp Odyssey and Moog Prodigy were limited to rudimentary waveforms such as square and triangle waves. Later, more complex synthesizers, such as Oberheim's Matrix series, added additional options, such as random and sample-and-hold LFOs. More recently, software synthesizer manufacturers have implemented a plethora of LFO options: Camel Audio's Alchemy offers no fewer than 82 LFO types while Native Instruments'

Massive features a 'performer' modulation source, essentially a 16-cycle LFO where each cycle can have its own unique waveshape and amplitude setting.

Other practitioners have employed innovative use of Eurorack modules to create varied LFO shapes for the purpose of generating melodic content. Boon (2019) used square wave LFOs and applied additional pulse width modulation and slew limiting to create varying waveshapes. Crucially, his methods involved combining different LFOs set at different rates and amplitudes to generate a greater level of complexity. Klobucar (2017) employed the Intellijel Shapeshifter module due to its large range of waveforms and wave shaping capabilities, meaning very complex patterns can be created with a single oscillator. Clearly, there is an abundance of options when it comes to LFO types; however, to reiterate two points discussed previously, it is the intention that the interface created herein should:

• Impose deliberate limitations to encourage further creativity
• Have an interface that is instantly recognizable and understandable by any proficient electronic musician

With these considerations in mind, it was decided that only the most commonly used and recognizable LFO waveforms, namely sine, triangle, square and sawtooth (in both ramp-up and ramp-down iterations), were to be used with no additional waveshape editing.

4 PRELIMINARY RESEARCH IN THE MODULAR DOMAIN

The initial attempts to apply this methodology took place in the modular domain, specifically in the VCV Rack platform, a virtual modular environment. Figure 4.2 shows one of these initial attempts, audio/video footage of which can be found in the video entitled *"Generating a melody with multiple LFOs in VCV rack"* in the *"LFOizer"* playlist. In this example, three LFOs of varying waveshapes and frequencies are combined at different amplitudes using the "8VERT" attenuverter and combined in the "multiples" module. The output signal is routed via the "QNT" quantizer module to the V/OCT pitch input of the voltage-controlled oscillator, which generates a melody. The purpose of the "Delta" module is to generate a gate trigger every time a change in control voltage is detected from the output of the quantizer; this causes the amplifier and filter ADSR envelopes to be triggered every time there is a change in pitch, applying envelope shaping in a similar way to a synthesizer being played in a more conventional fashion.

The results at this early stage of research were quite satisfactory; as expected, due to the familiarity of the LFO's parameters, it was quite easy to establish interesting melodic patterns and make subtle adjustments, which largely behaved as expected, allowing the user to fine-tune

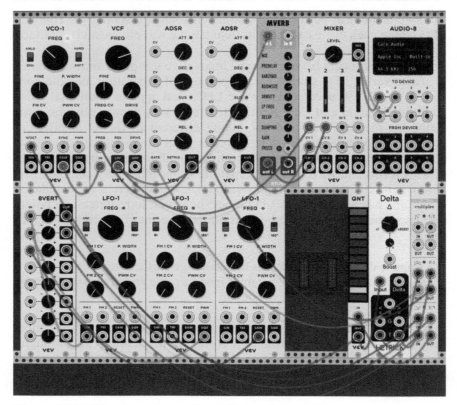

Figure 4.2 VCV rack patch used for preliminary research.

characteristics such as pitch register and speed or direction of note movement. When using larger LFO amplitudes, melodies would occur which
were characterized by notes jumping between large intervals, and various
settings could engender odd, stuttering rhythmic patterns, both of which
sound quite unlike the way most traditional keyboard players would typically approach melodic construction. While some settings elicited quite
calculated results, it quickly became apparent that other settings would
create patterns that could be, at times, far more unpredictable. It was at this
stage that it became apparent that this system was capable of being used
for generative composition applications, at times producing constantly
evolving, unpredictable patterns that could run for a minute or more without noticeable repetition. It should be noted that this system is not technically capable of applying the stochastic processes which generate random,
probability-based parameter changes (Xenakis, 1971; Jones, 1981; Serra,
1993) and, therefore, might be considered by some as not truly generative;
however, the emphasis here is on the creation of patterns that appear random by virtue of the fact that they are unpredictable for both the listener
and the creator.

4.1 Limitations of the modular domain

At this stage, further experiments took place, which implemented various amendments to the patch in Figure 4.2; however, it became apparent that while providing an effective proof of concept, there were considerable limitations to applying this methodology within a modular format, whether using hardware, or a virtual platform such as VCV Rack. The first of these concerns the generative, unpredictable aspect; if the modular patch is played 'live', adjusting parameters relating to both melody generation and articulative sound shaping simultaneously, there are frequent moments where a distinctive melody is generated that could be highly effective in the context of a larger composition, but where the sound is not appropriate or desirable. Then, after adjusting the sound parameters, it is almost impossible to replicate a similar melody. Similarly, there can be moments when very little melodic content worthy of merit happens at all. Eno (1996) encountered similar issues with unpredictability when exploring generative techniques: "[a generative composition is] very difficult just to play to people because you can switch it on and say listen to this, and nothing happens". This phenomenon is acceptable in some contexts; however, not in many contemporary electronic genres where there is a need for immediacy and some element of repetition.

Perhaps in response to this issue, Fortey (2019, p. 9) discussed the creation of randomized, generative works, which were then curated and edited in an attempt to "offer a selection of audio pieces that are both rewarding to listen to devoid of context, and interesting from a theoretical perspective". Morton Subotnick discussed a similar approach when working on his seminal album "Silver Apples of The Moon" in 1967, in that he generated material using the Buchla 100 modular system, purposely not having a specific end result in mind, but later curating and "being critical of the results" (Pinch and Trocco, 2002, pp. 48–49). It is intended that the research herein adopts a similar ethos, but where the preliminary curating and editing is strictly confined to melodic content, ideally as MIDI data – an attribute that is difficult to achieve in the modular format.

Another similar limitation is presented if one wishes to transfer the melodic content generated by devices in a modular format to another sound-generating device, be it hardware or software-based. Both these issues could be overcome to some degree using a CV to MIDI converter in conjunction with a DAW that constantly records MIDI data for later playback and editing; however, there is the potential for this concept to be even better executed with a system where the recording of MIDI data is more seamlessly integrated with the generation of melodic data in a way that allows straightforward implementation of synchronization and parameter recall.

The final, and perhaps the most crucial, limitation is that it is difficult to perform quick harmonic changes, something that is evident in a considerable number of Eurorack-based performances where the user sends control voltages through a pitch quantizer. These performances can lack harmonic movement as a result of the pitch quantizer being fixed to certain notes. In Vacuo (2021a) makes some attempts to add harmonic shifts to his performances, but this is quite limited as he is only able to change one note at a time on his quantizer module. A more versatile system would be one where multiple harmonic shifts can occur in real-time, preferably with hardware control.

5 THE MAX FOR LIVE PLATFORM

In response to this preliminary research, Max for Live was chosen as an alternative platform. The capabilities offered by Max alone can overcome many of these limitations; however, it is Max for Live's ability to integrate seamlessly with Ableton Live and exploit many of its capabilities that made it particularly suitable for these purposes. While this is slightly at odds with the preliminary aims of this paper, specifically rejecting the versatile capabilities of the DAW, there are some overwhelming advantages of this platform in the context of this project. These advantages included:

- The ability to integrate with VST/AU software instruments "in the box", and external hardware instruments either via MIDI or CV
- Seamless recording of MIDI data for further exporting or editing
- Synchronization of time-based parameters to Ableton Live's transport control
- Saving and recalling parameters within a project file
- Straightforward integration with MIDI controllers to permit hardware control
- Precise automation of parameters within DAW project
- Capacity for "exploratory kind of programming" (Bjørn, 2018, p. 292)

It became apparent that these advantages were too much to overlook, provided that the DAW's capabilities were sufficiently limited to adhere to the aforementioned ethos of "actively choosing regression". To elucidate the final bullet point as highlighted in Bjørn's (2018) discussion with Darwin Grosse, Max shares an overwhelmingly advantageous characteristic with the modular environment in that a given 'patch' is constantly running while the user is editing it. This means that any patch changes provide instant feedback, which not only leads to "unexpected and even charming solutions to artistic problems" (Ibid., p. 292) but, for an artistic practitioner, sparks ideas for refinements and improvements as the device is applied to creative applications. While this is true for Max alone, it is even more so for Max for Live, as the patch is being constantly trialled within a DAW studio environment and interacting with additional technologies that further enhance this process of feedback and creative design augmentation.

By applying this process, the existing capabilities previously explored within the modular environment were all implemented, with additional features that considerably enhanced its usability and versatility. The result of this is the creation of the "LFOizer" Max for Live device (Figure 4.3)

Figure 4.3 the LFOizer (full view).

6 THE LFOIZER

The LFOizer features six 'syncable' LFOs, each with identical controls; this number was found to be appropriate to provide sufficiently complex and versatile composite waveshapes while ensuring the control panel was not overly cluttered and would fit the width of a single screen at most resolutions. Additional features include both time quantize and pitch quantize (with remote control), adjustable note length and phase reset controls. Specific features and parameters are explained in greater detail in the tables that follow, accompanied by enlarged images of the control panel:

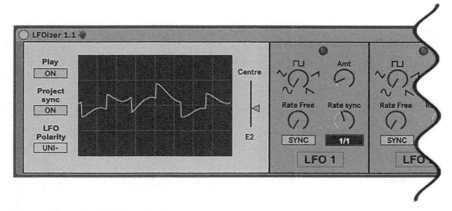

Figure 4.4 The LFOizer left section.

Table 4.1 Left panel controls

Parameter	Function
Play	Starts/stops play.
Project sync	Synchronizes play to start/stop of Live's transport.
LFO Polarity	Toggles polarity of all LFOs between bipolar and unipolar.
Oscilloscope display	Displays resultant waveshape when active LFOs are combined.
Centre	Controls centre pitch from which LFOs modulate pitch.
LED	Illuminates in varying degrees to indicate cycle for each LFO.

(Continued)

Table 4.1 (Continued)

Parameter	Function
Waveform	Selects LFO waveform from sine, triangle, square, saw (ramp up) and saw (ramp down).
Amt	Controls amplitude of LFO.
Rate free	Controls LFO rate in 'Free' mode (displayed in Hz). Values range from 0.01Hz–1.5Hz.
Rate sync	Controls LFO rate in 'Sync' mode (displayed in note value and synchronized to bpm of Live's clock). Values range from 4/1 to 1/4T.
Sync/Free	Toggles between Synchronized and Free modes.
Rate display	Displays LFO rate in note value or Hz depending on mode.
Active/Bypass	Toggles LFO between active and bypass, displays "LFO 1, 2, 3 . . ." when active or "BYPASS" when bypassed.

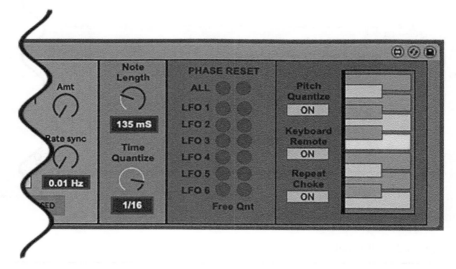

Figure 4.5 The LFOizer right section.

Table 4.2 Right panel controls

Parameter	Function
Note Length	Adjusts note length (displayed in mS); at the leftmost position, 'Legato' mode is activated, where each note is sustained until the next note begins. Values range from 1mS to 999mS.
Time Quantize	Adjusts time quantize value, synchronized to Live's transport; at the leftmost position, quantize is disabled. Values range from 1/4 to 1/16T.

Parameter	Function
Phase Reset	Resets the phase of each LFO individually or simultaneously if ALL is pressed. 'Free' resets the phase instantaneously, 'Qnt' quantizes phase reset to the start of the next bar.
Pitch Quantize	Toggles pitch quantizer On/Off. When 'On', only highlighted notes can be played and notes in-between are quantized to the nearest active note value. When 'Off', any pitch from the chromatic scale can be played.
Keyboard Remote	Toggles keyboard remote control for pitch quantizer On/Off; further details are explained under "The Quantizer Remote" subheading that follows.
Repeat Choke	Toggles repeat choke On/Off. When 'On', repeated notes of the same pitch are removed.
Quantizer Keyboard	Controls pitch quantizer, notes are toggled On/Off by clicking them or by using Keyboard Remote. Active notes are displayed in yellow, inactive notes are grey and active notes turn blue to indicate they are currently being played. *Note: pitch quantizer is adapted from a Max for Live patch by Secret_ Admiral* (Secret_Admiral, n.d.).

7 COMPOSITION WORKS

Following the completion of the LFOizer, the next step of this research project is its application in a series of composition works. To test the LFOizer's effectiveness as a composition device, the limitation was imposed that all parts, with the exception of drums and percussion, are to be generated using the LFOizer. Preserving the ethos of generating material that can be curated and refined, minimal editing is allowed; this can include cutting and pasting of MIDI parts or removing individual notes; however, no editing of other parameters, such as pitch or rhythm, is permitted. Following the recording of audio parts, creative signal processing can be applied; in the example that follows, this includes granular processing to generate sustained pad parts. The composition component of this project is ongoing, and additional works will be added to the *"LFOizer"* playlist upon their completion; the section that follows explores the first such composition, entitled *"Tendrils"*.

The main melody and bassline, which enter at (0:05) and (0:37), respectively, use various LFO waveforms, both in 'Sync' and 'Free' modes. This was found to be highly effective in generating interesting and diverse material due to the interacting LFOs completing their cycles at different points so that any given bar would very rarely elicit a similar melody. There are similarities between this and the principle illustrated by Boon (2020), where he applies differing rhythmic gate patterns to the same voltage-controlled note pattern to elicit varying melodies. With the LFOizer, the rhythmic pattern is fairly consistent and defined by the quantizer. However, it is the LFO-generated melodic pattern that is constantly changing in relation to the quantizer's rhythm; this creates a similar phenomenon, except that it is likely to create even more varied and unpredictable patterns.

Due to this unpredictable nature of the output, long sections were recorded as MIDI clips, which were curated and edited later. While recording MIDI, various parameters of the LFOizer were manipulated, mainly by simply bypassing or activating certain LFOs, but also by subtly adjusting LFO rates, LFO amplitudes and quantizer settings.

The second melody that enters at (1:50) uses very high LFO rates, whereby a full LFO cycle is completed in less time than the 1/16 note quantizer value. In the previous examples, it is possible to hear the movement of the particular LFO shape; however, in this example, far more chaotic, seemingly random patterns are created, even further removed from conventional melodies typically produced using a traditional keyboard interface. In this example, no adjustment of the LFOizer's parameters took place during play, and two resultant melodies with no MIDI editing were played simultaneously, albeit with slightly different sound settings and panned a little to the left and right of the stereo field. In all the examples for this piece, articulation was provided by subtle live parameter automation on the hardware synthesizers.

8 THE QUANTIZER REMOTE

It is notable that "*Tendrils*" was produced using an earlier iteration of the LFOizer that did not feature the quantizer remote. As such, all the melodies and bass lines revolve around the same few notes and are, therefore, lacking in harmonic movement. Despite this, "*Tendrils*" worked quite successfully; however, this might not be the case for other compositions, and many users will require more flexibility to make the LFOizer useful in a variety of musical contexts. Furthermore, the method employed by In Vacuo (2021a) of changing one quantizer note at a time would be insufficient for performing drastic harmonic changes.

In response to this, a system was implemented whereby a MIDI keyboard (or any other device that outputs MIDI note data) can be used to remotely control the quantizer. MIDI notes from C3 upwards toggle quantizer notes on and off, while notes below C3 change the 'Pitch Centre' control. To facilitate quick changes between different chords or note combinations, a MIDI sustain pedal can be used; releasing the pedal after being pressed down deactivates all active notes on the quantizer, allowing the user to quickly select a different note combination using the keys. While using the 'pedal up' rather than the 'pedal down' motion might seem a little odd, in practice, it approximates the same motion typically used by a keyboard player when changing between chord shapes, so it is actually far more intuitive for any user who is a moderately proficient keyboard player.

While the use of a MIDI keyboard is at odds with the earlier discussion of rejecting the use of a traditional keyboard, it should be emphasized that the keyboard is strictly acting as a remote control for the quantizer, not as a device to be used for the 'playing' of notes. Should the user be vehemently against the use of a piano-style keyboard, then any other device that outputs MIDI note data using a non-keyboard interface could be used, for which there are many popular options such as the Ableton Push or Akai MPD series.

The omission of preset scales, which are often found on similar devices, was a purposeful design decision intended to encourage the more exploratory approach to scale and harmony facilitated by the explained system. If a user prefers to use preset scales, this can be done easily by turning off the LFOizer's quantizer and using other tools available within Ableton Live, such as the 'Scale' MIDI effect, or if microtonal tuning is desired, the 'Microtuner' Max for Live device.

9 PERFORMANCE EXAMPLES

While the previously mentioned feature was initially intended to be used for composition applications, in practice, it also transpired to be an effective performance tool, as demonstrated in the videos "*LFOizer performance 1*" and "*LFOizer performance 2*" in the "*LFOizer*" playlist. Both videos show improvised performances that use a standard MIDI keyboard for the LFOizer quantizer remote, an Akai LPD8 to control the LFO bypass and LFO amplitude amounts of the six LFOs, with the LFOizer controlling a Behringer Deepmind 12D synthesizer in monophonic mode; various parameters of the Deepmind are also manipulated throughout the performances to add variation and articulation. In the first of these videos, the user performs frequent changes to the quantizer's note settings to generate most of the melodic variation, with only minimal adjustment to the LFO parameters via the LPD8. In the second video, there is a greater focus on manipulating LFO parameters to generate movement, with only minimal quantizer changes later in the piece. The latter performance also uses the lower octaves of the MIDI keyboard to control the Pitch Centre; this is most noticeable toward the start of the piece where, at times, only a single square wave LFO is used in unipolar mode. This causes longer-held notes in the lower register, which imply bass root notes and provide further harmonic context to the melodic parts in higher registers.

While it was intended that this performance setup would usually be augmented with other pieces of equipment to provide additional musical layers, this minimal setup was purposefully chosen for these demonstrations to illustrate the performance capabilities of the LFOizer when combined with a single monophonic sound source and some very rudimentary MIDI controllers for physical interfaces. These performances illustrate the favourable attributes of the LFOizer in that after a little time is spent configuring satisfactory settings of the six LFOs, only minimal adjustments to the LFO and quantizer parameters are required to elicit interesting and varied melodic patterns. This leaves the user ample time to interact with other devices, which might be used to change the sonic characteristics of the main instrument or, alternatively, to add and manipulate additional parts and layers that might contribute to a larger musical arrangement.

10 CONCLUSIONS AND FURTHER RESEARCH

Following initial experiments, it can be concluded that the LFOizer is largely successful in achieving the aims of this research. While the device does not entirely conform to the 'DAW-less' paradigm, it limits certain functions of the DAW to a sufficient extent that it forces the user to focus not on the inputting of particular patterns of notes but rather on manipulating a broader set of parameters and the refining of the outputted material. If used with external MIDI controllers, the LFOizer can be configured to be used without directly interacting with the DAW at all so that it feels more like a singular instrument rather than an efficient computerized device. The majority of its uses so far have provoked melodic results which are characterized by the subtle eccentricities described previously, which lend an aesthetic unlike what Buchla (Pinch and Trocco, 2002, p. 44) might describe as "keyboard music". The automated nature of its note generation allowed extensive live parameter adjustments to be made on synthesizers, representing the successful implementation of the concepts discussed earlier in reference to Ryan (1991) and Levitin, McAdams and Adams (2002), where separating a sound-producing device from its note-generating interface affords additional expressive opportunities for the composer and performer.

The next stages of this research project are to use the LFOizer for the generation of further musical works and add to the catalogue of compositions in the "*LFOizer*" playlist, as well as inviting other practitioners to use the device and reflect on their experiences. Potentially, further use might reveal alternative applications and working methods, as well as limitations or shortcomings, which could prompt additional features and amendments to be made within the Max environment.

One such shortcoming was observed when using certain settings, typically either high LFO rates, large LFO amplitudes or when several LFOs were combined at varying rates. In these instances, notes are triggered quite quickly so that, even at high quantize values such as 1/16, notes are triggered at every quantize interval. This can result in constant, slightly monotonous patterns that are lacking in rhythmic variation, a characteristic that this device was intended to avoid. In Vacuo (2021b) resolves a similar issue by using an Euclidean Circles Eurorack module to generate rhythmic gates to trigger notes from an LFO-generated control voltage. A similar method could be applied to the LFOizer, perhaps using a step sequencer-controlled trigger; in order to prevent rhythms from becoming too repetitive, further probability-based controls could be added to randomize individual steps or loop points of the step sequencer. Such a device is one potential modification that could be implemented in future iterations of the LFOizer.

REFERENCES

Bates, E. (2021). 'The Interface and Instrumentality of Eurorack Modular Synthesis', in *Rethinking Music through Science and Technology Studies*. London, England: Routledge, pp. 170–188.

Bjørn, K. (2018). *Push Turn Move*, 3rd ed. Denmark: Bjooks Media.

Boon, H. (2019). *Observations on the Utility of Square Waves and Their Applicability in Generative Melodic Applications* (Lecture). SEMPRE Autumn Conference, Bath Spa. 8 November.

Boon, H. (2020). *Modular Synth as Lab – Complexity and the Single Oscillator*. (video) The 21st Century Music Practice Research Network. Available at: www.c21mp.org/session-2-restriction-and-affordance/ [Accessed: 14 June 2022].

Eno, B. (1996). 'Generative Music: "Evolving Metaphors, in My Opinion, Is What Artists Do"', *In Motion Magazine* (website). Available at: https://inmotionmagazine.com/eno1.html [Accessed: 14 June 2022].

Fortey, R. (2019). *Generative Techniques in Composition*. Thesis. University of York. Available at: https://etheses.whiterose.ac.uk/27621/.

Herbert, M. (2005). 'P.C.C.O.M. and P.C.C.O.M. Turbo Extreme Personal Contract for the Composition of Music [Incorporating the Manifesto of Mistakes]', *Matthew Herbert* (website). Available at: http://web.archive.org/web/20071007094518/www.magicandaccident.com/_MH/pccom.php [Accessed: 14 June 2022].

Hughes, T. (2021). 'The Individualist: Todd Rundgren's Approach to Innovation and His 1993 Interactive Album No World Order', in Hepworth-Sawyer, R., Paterson, J. and Toulson, R., eds. *Innovation in Music Future Opportunities*. Oxon: Routledge, pp. 70–88.

In Vacuo. (2021a). *4 LFO Melody Jam* (video). Available at: www.youtube.com/watch?v=_ytk9cGUaz0&ab_channel=InVacuo [Accessed: 14 June 2022].

In Vacuo. (2021b). *Creating Interesting Melody Patterns Using Euclidean Circles and an LFO* (video). Available at: www.youtube.com/watch?v=3Drn3-8xfJE&ab_channel=InVacuo [Accessed: 14 June 2022].

Jones, K. (1981). 'Compositional Applications of Stochastic Processes', *Computer Music Journal*, 5(2), pp. 45–61.

Kailus, K. (2022). 'The Synth-Splosion', *Music Inc.* (website). Available at: www.musicincmag.com/features/detail/the-synth-splosion [Accessed: 14 June 2022].

Klobucar, D. (2017). *Composing with LFO's* (video). Available at: www.youtube.com/watch?v=ddsL6xC8Eyw&ab_channel=DinkoKlobucar [Accessed: 14 June 2022].

Lanier, C. and Rader, S. (2021). 'Synthesizers: An Exploration into the Iconicity of Marketplace Icons', *Consumption Markets & Culture*, 24(6), pp. 598–610.

Levitin, D., McAdams, S. and Adams, R. (2002). 'Control Parameters for Musical Instruments: A Foundation for New Mappings of Gesture to Sound', *Organised Sound*, 7, pp. 171–189.

Manning, P. (2004). *Electronic and Computer Music*. New York: Oxford University Press.

Modular Grid. (n.d.). 'Module Finder', *Modulargrid.net* (website). Available at: www.modulargrid.net/e/modules/browser?SearchName=&SearchVendor=& SearchFunction=11&SearchSecondaryfunction=&SearchHeight=&SearchT e=&SearchTemethod=max&SearchBuildtype=&SearchLifecycle=&Search Set=all&SearchMarketplace=&SearchIsmodeled=0&SearchShowothers=0 &order=tag&direction=asc [Accessed: 23 August 2022]

Pinch, T. and Trocco, F. (2002). *Analog Days the Invention and Impact of the Moog Synthesizer*. Harvard: First Harvard University Press.

Rohs, J. (2018). *A Matlab Implementation of the Buchla Lopass Gate*. Thesis. McGill University. Available at: http://www.music.mcgill.ca/~gary/courses/ projects/618_2018/rohs/MUMT618_Buchla_LPG_Report.pdf.

Rossmy, B. and Wiethoff, A. (2019). 'The Modular Backward Evolution – Why to Use Outdated Technologies', *NIME*, 19, pp. 343–348.

Ryan, J. (1991). 'Some Remarks on Musical Instrument Design at STEIM', *Contemporary Music Review*, 6(1), pp. 3–17.

Secret_Admiral. (n.d.). *Midi Pitch Quantizer* (website). Available at: https:// secretadmiral.com/product/midi-pitch-quantizer/ [Accessed: 14 June 2022].

Serra, M. (1993). 'Stochastic Composition and Stochastic Timbre: GENDY3 by Iannis Xenakis', *Perspectives of New Music*, 31(1), pp. 236–257.

Stravinsky, I. (1947). *Poetics of Music in the Form of Six Lessons*. Cambridge, MA: Harvard University Press.

Thompson, D. (2012). 'Music Technology and Musical Creativity: Making Connections', *General Music Today*, 25(3), pp. 54–57.

Xenakis, I. (1971). *Formalized Music Thought and Mathematics in Composition*, Revised ed. New York: Pendragon Press.

5

Exploring a network setup for music experimentation

Enric Guaus, Àlex Barrachina, Josep Comajuncosas, Gabriel Saber, and Víctor Sanahuja

1 INTRODUCTION

In the last few years, there has been an increasing interest in performing music over the Internet. The Covid-19 pandemic has drastically changed many common activities due to the imposition of social restrictions. Then, music schools and universities moved online in a very short period of time, including activities such as master classes, individual instrument lessons and ensemble rehearsals. In this context, the use of the network was exclusively focused on solving social distancing and the ultimate technological goal was reducing latency down to the imperceptible, that is, in a range of values comparable to the acoustic delays between members in a choir. Since the beginning of 2020, hundreds of forums and webinars proliferated on the Internet proposing solutions for remote music creation over domestic network connections. Based on the original idea behind Jack-Trip (n.d.), a multi-machine audio system used for network music performance over the Internet originally developed by Chris Chafe at Stanford (Cáceres and Chafe, 2010), musicians started using different solutions (for example, Ninjam, Jamtaba, Quaktrip, Jamulus, Sonobus, among others; some of them are described in the following sections). Other creative solutions were also widely used, such as the creation of virtual choirs, or ensembles built up of individual recordings (Zakaria and Astuti, 2020) or those based on general videoconference tools (Rossetti, 2021). Beyond domestic connections, institutions were using very low latency systems based on research networks and advanced network setups such as LoLa for some years (Drioli, 2013), but these systems were not available during the pandemic.

The use of the network for creating music is not new. Conceptually speaking, the piece that can be considered to be the first distance performance is *Imaginary Landscape #4* by John Cage in 1951. It is a composition for 24 performers, 12 radios and a conductor. Performers follow a graphic score with the movements of the radio controls (volume and station) according to the conductor's guidance. In this piece, the sound source is not in the scenario, but in the radio studio, that is, in a different place.

DOI: 10.4324/9781003118817-6

In the late 70s, the League of Automatic Music Composers was considered to be the first computer network band. In 1986, they included a hub in their performances, and in 1987, they created a new collective, The Hub (Gresham-Lancaster, 1998), presenting performances with musicians in remote locations. After that, the introduction of the MIDI protocol and the explosion of the Internet allowed network music to be explored in both artistic and technological ways.

It is worth mentioning an interesting reflection related to latency shared by Tanaka (1999) as a result of his participation in a network performance:

> So, then an essential quality of the network becomes a problem. I would prefer to respect this character of the net, and conceive of a type of music that uses the delay to advantage. After all, no one ever complained about the long reverberation time of a cathedral. It is not a problem, it is acoustic. So, I propose: can we think of IP packet delays as a network acoustic that defines this new space in which we play?
>
> (Tanaka, 1999)

In 2002, Jordà (2002) presented the F@ust Music On-Line (FMOL), an instrument that was used on the Internet by hundreds of musicians for about four years. Although this instrument differs from the typology of works described previously, it is a key work that emphasizes the increasing possibilities the use of the network can provide to the music. These were the embryonic ideas that gave rise, a few years later, to the development of the Reactable, another successful instrument with network capabilities (Kaltenbrunner, 2006).

Some years later, Oliveros (2009) led a telematic concert carried out at different locations in the USA (New York, Stanford and San Diego) using JackTrip developed by Chris Chafe at Stanford (Cáceres and Chafe, 2010). This is an important hit because it can be considered the starting point in which many applications for network music using domestic Internet connections have been developed.

At this point, telematic music and network music are not considered to be the same. According to Lemmon (2019), the first term is more related to the musical practice and its political and social goals while the latter is more related to the technology for creating music. This is an important difference because, as debated later in this chapter, talking about ensemble topologies or musician's roles is a completely different perspective from talking about latency and buffers.

Nowadays, a large list of artists working on telematic or network music using different technological solutions exists (Xambó, 2020), as well as some good reviews on technology resources (Rottondi, 2016), online libraries of scientific work (Pilchen, 2021; Zotero, 2022), digital repositories (Hamido et al., 2020), on-line tutorials (Fasciani, 2020) and conferences (Network Music Festival, Web Audio Conference, Audio Mostly Conference, Computer Music Multidisciplinary Research, Innovation in Music Conference, etc.).

2 OBJECTIVES

The main goal of this research is to explore new musical paradigms provided by different typologies of connections between computers through domestic networks. Specifically, it proposes the use of the network for creating music that can only be conceived in the network instead of using it as a tool for a distant recreation of traditional musical ensembles. For that, it goes deeper with Tanaka's idea exposed previously (Tanaka, 1999), proposing setups that accomplish the following requirements:

- The musical result must exist "*in* and *because of* the network".
- Performers must collectively contribute in real-time to the piece.
- Performers must have the autonomy to decide the nature of their instruments.

The first requirement consists of finding a new way to create music with the network instead of a) using the network for recreating the usual setup in a traditional ensemble and b) organizing hybrid sessions with some musicians on site and other(s) in remote locations. This requirement seeks musical results that can be only obtained through the network, that is, assuming the network is the new medium.

The second requirement implies that, even though performers can be based at different physical locations, the interaction between them must be at a certain musical time scale including all technical inaccuracies (i.e., latency), and this is the only way in which performers may react to the music they are collectively creating through the network. Otherwise, the musical result is assumed to be a simple addition of independent outputs.

The third statement implies that solutions requiring the use of specific software, patches or plugins (beyond the connection layer) are not taken into account. This allows performers to benefit from their best musical skills by using the technical and musical procedures with which they feel more comfortable. In accordance with the research carried out by the League of Automatic Music Composers (Gresham-Lancaster, 1998), every new piece should be shaped by the design of the instruments being used, and, in consequence, each new piece conforms to a uniquely designed configuration. Although the setup process under these conditions is more complicated than using closed software or a fixed setup (providing patches, presets and projects to all the participants), the musical result is supposed to be better.

3 EXPERIMENTS

As detailed previously, when using domestic Internet connections, the latency added by the network, the need for a computer and the presence of audio equipment make it impossible to play as in a traditional ensemble. Then, the relationship between performers, sound and music must be reconsidered (Gresham-Lancaster, 1998). In the following sections, the ideas behind the three proposed configurations are presented. All the explorations presented here are tested using domestic Internet connections without any control of the latency introduced by the network.

3.1 Centralized audio management setup

This experiment is based on Jamtaba (n.d.), a cross-platform open-source program to connect to Ninjam (n.d.) servers and remotely play in an ensemble. Ninjam is an open-source software for connecting musicians via the Internet, native for Reaper (n.d.), a cross-platform DAW, by defining a central server. It's a client-server setup: the audio stream generated by each performer is sent to a central server, and the mix (or individual channels, depending on the software used) is sent back to the performers. These applications are the musical version of traditional video conference software tools (i.e., Zoom, Meet, etc.). In order to minimize the delay introduced by the latency between local performance and the audio from remote participants, Jamtaba artificially increases it and synchronizes each local audio stream at the beat level in a bar so all performers are playing the same beat in a bar, but at different bars.

As Jamtaba allows a high flexibility in the definition of a loop (length, tempo, number of steps, etc.), the schema proposed in Figure 5.1 allows playing music at a given tempo with a certain degree of harmonic structure. In the context of this research, some improvisations based on the notes in a tetrachord arpeggiated in a whole bar in the Jamtaba loop are presented. Results are illustrated in Figure 5.2 and available on YouTube (Barrachina, 2021a).

Figure 5.1 Centralized audio management setup.

Figure 5.2 Members of the Barcelona Network Orchestra playing in a centralized audio management setup.

This setup (and the corresponding piece) allows performers to properly deal with inherent latency and play music in an expressive way. But it is a closed setup. It only allows the performers to play how the Jamtaba developers thought musicians would want to play, that is, in a similar way a traditional ensemble does. It is a very good tool for the adaptation of a traditional ensemble to the new medium, but it does not fulfill our initial objectives.

3.2 Centralized audio with remote control setup

This second experiment is inspired by FMOL (Jordà, 2002) and GroupLoop (Ramsay and Paradiso, 2015) works. They propose a centralized audio generation process with remote control. The performers send control data (i.e., MIDI or OSC) instead of audio streams.

In the context of this research, assuming the difference between remote performing a piece or playing a remote collective instrument is sometimes diffuse (Comajuncosas, 2016), this setup may represent a collective instrument played by performers at different locations. Musicians just handle controls, but they do not generate audio in local nodes. The resulting audio output from the central server is distributed through the network to every performer. The latency experienced by the performers may be a problem in terms of the delay time between the moment musicians perform a physical action and the music reacts as a consequence of that action in their loudspeakers, that is, a delay in the audio feedback.

The schema shown in Figure 5.3 allows remote control of the synthesis process and music generation in a given instrument with clear inputs and outputs. Performers must adapt their own control devices to the central instrument specifications. For this work, the "Network MIDI hub" has been developed. It is a client/server interface to connect multiple clients to a centralized MIDI server in which all the MIDI messages received on the

Figure 5.3 Centralized audio generation with remote control setup.

Figure 5.4 Members of the Barcelona Network Orchestra playing in a centralized audio with remote control setup.

server are forwarded to the server and retransmitted to all the connected clients minus the sender (Sanahuja [Piscue], 2021).

To minimize the effects of latency mentioned previously, the proposed piece is based on an improvisation focused on timbre exploration. Starting from a small snippet of a Nat King Cole piece, the instrument reproduces an extremely slow, time-stretched looped version of the snippet, deleting any temporal or rhythmic references while performers modify some predefined parameters (feedback, loop position, rate, etc.). Subtle changes in control data produce progressive timbre changes in the resulting audio. Performers need to actively listen to the changes and act in consequence.

As temporal references have been deleted from the original audio source, the piece proposed for this collective instrument does not require synchronization at the level of a beat, which makes it more independent of latency values. Results are illustrated in Figure 5.4 and available on YouTube (Barrachina, 2021b).

This setup reveals another interesting approach for creating music with performers at different physical locations. A high degree of independence in relation to the latency can be achieved, but performers just handle controls, so this setup limits the autonomy of remote performers to decide the nature of their instruments. Then, it does not fulfill all of our initial objectives.

3.3 Peer-to-Peer connections for audio streams

Finally, a third experiment based on Peer-to-Peer connections (P2P) is proposed. These connections allow sending data from one user to the other without the need for a central server. This presents a series of advantages from the point of view of musical experimentation:

- Flexibility: each node can be connected to/can receive data from one or multiple nodes without any predefined topology. This configuration can be modified during the performance.
- Decentralized audio setup: the audio processing occurs distributed among the nodes of the network. The use of VST plugins in P2P connections allows performers to use all kinds of tools (any DAW, Max/Msp, Puredata, etc.). Performers can create their own instruments with their own character.
- Latency: Because the processing happens on the node itself, performers can locally feel their performance in real-time, with no latency.

There exist two state-of-the-art solutions for P2P audio connections: Quacktrip (n.d.), available as a Pure Data patch and VST Plugin, and Sonobus (n.d.), available as a VST Plugin.

Inspired by the piece "La Roda" proposed by Comajuncosas (2016), Figure 5.5 shows the connection schema for an interesting example of this kind of setup. Based on the popular Chinese Whisper's game, the instruments (the remote nodes) are linked in a feedback loop configuration with a single shared sound stream flowing from one player to the next. Indeed, the accumulative behavior and heterogeneity of processors involved in the system lead irreversibly to unexpected timbral evolution. The result is non-linear, collaborative and unpredictable at the same time.

This setup, in opposition to the previous ones, uses the network as part of the musical process. As the audio signal is connected in a closed loop, latency plays a central role in the system. It can be established that the sum of all the individual latencies defines the tempo of the piece. Even more, latency is a key player in having a certain control of the rotating speed, allowing the audio result to be stable. It is not possible to play without it.

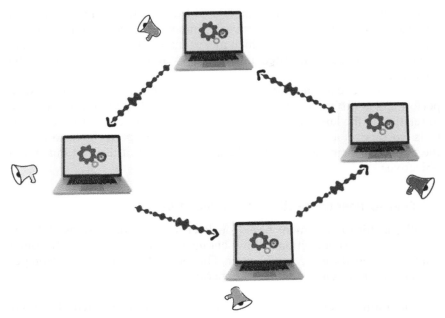

Figure 5.5 P2P decentralized audio setup in a closed circle topology.

Figure 5.6 Members of the Barcelona Network Orchestra playing a P2P decentralized audio setup.

The proposed piece is based on a sequential and accumulative processing of an initially injected audio object, resulting in a progressively distorted version of the original as the sound evolves in the loop. When the sound reaches a certain degree of distortion, it becomes unrecognizable, and performers begin with rhythmic and timbral exploration. Results are illustrated in Figure 5.6 and available on YouTube (Barrachina, 2021c).

This setup is created in the network and for the network. It offers the performers the possibility to shape their own instrument and the feedback is immediate allowing a real-time performance of the piece. So, this setup fulfills all of our initial objectives.

4 DISCUSSION

The previous section has evaluated different scenarios for performing music using the network. All of them allow creative use of the network for digging in the context of experimental music. The third proposed case is the only one that accomplishes all the proposed requirements and brings new musical paradigms to the fore.

What was learned from the first two approaches is that performers need to feel comfortable with their gear and musical background. The two proposed architectures allow a certain degree of flexibility at each physical location except for the communication layer. Internal control signals can be routed through MIDI or OSC, and audio streams can be routed using virtual cables such as Loopback (n.d.) or Blackhole (Existential Audio, 2022), among others. This confidence is reflected in the overall musicality of the pieces and the performers' engagement . For instance, after some rehearsals, including young students, it was observed that fixed environments bother them and cause them to abandon the sessions. In summary, these preliminary experiments open room for exploration in ensemble music composition and performance beyond the limitations of using the network in a particular way.

In relation to the third experiment, new musical paradigms for ensemble playing appeared. First, in opposition to traditional setups, the resulting sound is not the addition of individual sounds (for example, trumpets and trombones in a classic orchestra) but its multiplication. As mentioned previously, each performer works directly on the result of the previous one in the loop. Then, the original sound is sequentially processed by different players until it becomes completely unrecognizable. If the looping speed is not too low, the audience cannot perceive the effect of individual actions. This makes the musical result a completely collective action without room for individual virtuosity.

As a consequence of this multiplicative process, musicians must agree they are not the owners of their sound. No matter how precise, deep or subtle the performer's action is, every player can distort, filter or even mute all the work from the previous players in the loop. In this setup, the only interesting result is the collective output forcing a democratic use of the sound in which experienced and novel musicians can join the jam.

The second paradigm to explore is related to the output. Because each performer is in a different location (and has a specific position in the loop), the sound received by each of the performers is never the same as that received by the others unless a bypass process is applied. The same occurs at the output of each performer: all the outputs will be sonically different. So, which one is the real output of the piece? As there is not a main auditorium, in fact, the piece is a set of multiple outputs, but a specific node can be arbitrarily selected as the main output (see Figure 5.5)

In consequence, as most of the applied processes are not linear, the order of the nodes affects the musical result. In an additive (traditional) setup, the position of the performers is not relevant beyond the acoustic properties of the space. Here, in this non-linear multiplicative setup, it is. The flexibility of P2P communications allows exploration of different positions of musicians in the loop, providing completely different musical results.

Beyond that, and from a musical point of view, different latencies allow playing between rhythmic exploration (low looping speeds produced by relatively high latency values) and timbre exploration (high looping speeds produced by small latency values). Performances with musicians on different continents will inherently sound different than performances with musicians in the same city.

In summary, the last architecture proposed here fulfills the initial objectives, provides new and interesting paradigms for ensemble playing and creates space for artistic research.

5 CONCLUSIONS

The results of the presented research showed different cases of telematic music exploration. The main goal was to find a specific setup that can only be conceived in the network and for the network beyond a mere reproduction of a traditional ensemble environment. After an initial test with a centralized server for managing audio signal created at remote computers and another with a centralized server for managing control data from remote computers with a centralized audio generator, the use of P2P connections discovered a setup that is unique for the network in which latency is part of the ecosystem, and the performance cannot be conceived without it.

The proposed multiplicative workflow between the music elements opens a room for exploration beyond traditional setups. In this sense, this chapter presents new paradigms that emerged for creative processes in music ensembles, such as the difficulty of showing individual virtuosity, the assumption that the player is not the owner of his sound and the need for an agreement in relation to the position of each player in the loop and the node that will be selected as the output of the piece.

All the exploration has been done using free and state-of-the-art software. Each player can use their preferred tools (VST plugins, Max, singing, playing an instrument, etc.) with the only requirement of adapting the resulting audio to the pre-agreed network protocol, resulting in a good musicality of the played piece.

Finally, it is worth mentioning that, in our rehearsals, we used a double network communication channel between performers. First, the main network for audio or control streams depends on the specific setup. In some cases (demo recording, performance, etc.), the screen is also shared using any of the existing platforms. For these connections, we always recommend the use of an ethernet cable instead of Wi-Fi connections unless extra latency is explicitly desired for artistic purposes. On the other hand, a parallel network connection was used for conversations between performers. This communication channel can be established using any of the existing platforms through ethernet or Wi-Fi connections from any device. Specifically, if old computers are used for the performance, the use of a separate smartphone or tablet for verbal communication is recommended. If the local Internet connection is not good enough, video streaming can be disabled.

6 FUTURE WORK

From the artistic point of view, the creation of a specific repertoire for the third network setup exposed here is needed, as well as its performance in front of different audiences. It could also be interesting to perform one of these pieces in a loop around the world.

On the other side, in a higher level of abstraction, given the flexibility and ease of establishing P2P connections, it can be interesting to explore modifying P2P connections in real-time during the performance. That is not an improvisation *in* a given topology but *with* the topology itself. Finally, it would also be interesting to interconnect remote instruments in a complex P2P network for data (or control) streams instead of audio streams. This would allow the performer's actions to affect remote instruments, producing unpredictable results, which is an interesting scenario for improvisation ensembles. This brings the research very close to an updated version of the original configurations from The Hub.

7 ACKNOWLEDGEMENTS

This work has been partly supported by the Escola Superior de Música de Catalunya (ESMUC).

REFERENCES

Barrachina, A. (2021a). *Network Music: Demo Jamtaba* [Video]. YouTube. Available at: https://youtu.be/a0Na_rZPf1s.

Barrachina, A. (2021b). *Network Music: Demo Stretching Nat King Cole* [Video]. YouTube. Available at: https://youtu.be/O9fUnGIMeSw.

Barrachina, A. (2021c). *Network Music: Demo La Roda* [Video]. YouTube. Available at: https://youtu.be/IseiStWTrCw.

Cáceres, J. P. and Chafe, C. (2010). 'JackTrip: Under the Hood of an Engine for Network Audio', *Journal of New Music Research*, 39(3), pp 183–187.

Comajuncosas, J. M. (2016). *Assessing Creativity in Computer Music Ensembles: A Computational Approach*. PhD Thesis. Universitat Pompeu Fabra. Available at: www.tdx.cat/handle/10803/359392.

Drioli, C., Allocchio, C. and Buso, N. (2013, January). 'Networked Performances and Natural Interaction via LOLA: Low Latency High Quality A/V Streaming System', *Lecture Notes in Computer Science*, 7990, LNCS, pp. 240–250.

Existential Audio. (2022). *BlackHole: Audio Loopback Driver*. Github. https://github.com/ExistentialAudio/BlackHole.

Fasciani, S. (2020). *Network-Based Collaborative Music Making*. Available at: https://stefanofasciani.com/2020/03/25/network-based-collaborative-music-making/ [Accessed: 21 July 2022].

Gresham-Lancaster, S. (1998). 'The Aesthetics and History of the Hub', *Leonardo Music Journal*, 8(1), pp. 39–44.

Hamido, O. C., Dessen, M., Pellerin, G. and Penuchot, J. (2020). *Awesome Networked Media*. Available at: https://github.com/omarcostahamido/awesome-networked-media [Accessed: 20 July 2022].

Jacktrip. (n.d.). *JackTrip*. Available at: https://jacktrip.github.io/jacktrip/.

Jamtaba. (n.d.). *Jamtaba: A Free Software to Play Live Music in Online Jam Sessions*. Available at: https://jamtaba-music-web-site.appspot.com/.

Jordà, S. (2002). 'FMOL: Toward User-Friendly, Sophisticated New Musical Instruments', *Computer Music Journal*, 26(3), pp. 23–39.

Kaltenbrunner, M., Jorda, S., Geiger, G. and Alonso, M. (2006). 'The reacTable*: A Collaborative Musical Instrument', in *Proceedings of the 15th IEEE International Workshops on Enabling Technologies: Infrastructure for Collaborative Enterprises*. Manchester, UK: IEEE, pp. 406–411.

Lemmon, E. (2019). 'Telematic Music vs. Networked Music: Distinguishing Between Cybernetic Aspirations and Technological Music-Making', *Journal of Network Music and Arts*, 1(1), pp. 1–29.

Loopback. (n.d.). *Loopback: Cable-Free Audio Routing for MAC*. Rogue Amoeba. Available at: https://rogueamoeba.com/loopback/.

Ninjam. (n.d.). *Cockos Incorporated*. Available at: www.cockos.com/ninjam/.

Oliveros, P., Weaver, S., Dresser, M., Pitcher, J., Braasch, J. and Chafe, C. (2009). 'Telematic Music: Six Perspectives', *Leonardo Music Journal*, 19(1), pp. 95–96.

Pilchen, D. and Wilson, R. (2021). 'Introducing the Networked Music Performance Library', *Organised Sound*, 26(3), pp. 340–353.

Quacktrip. (n.d.). *Quacktrip and Netty NcNetface: Network Audio for Musicians*. UC San Diego. Available at: http://msp.ucsd.edu/tools/quacktrip/.

Ramsay, D. B. and Paradiso, J. A. (2015). 'GroupLoop: A Collaborative, Network-Enabled Audio Feedback Instrument', in *Proceedings of the International Conference on New Interfaces for Musical Expression*, pp. 251–254. https://zenodo.org/records/1179158.

Reaper. (n.d.). *Reaper, Digital Audio Workstation*. Available at: www.reaper.fm/.

Rossetti, D. (2021). 'Live Electronics, Audiovisual Compositions, and Telematic Performance: Collaborations During the Pandemic', *Journal of Network Music and Arts*, 3(1), pp. 1–28.

Rottondi, C., Chafe, C., Allocchio, C. and Sarti, A. (2016). 'An Overview on Networked Music Performance Technologies', *IEEE Access*, 4, pp. 8823–8843.

Sanahuja, V. [Piscue] (2021). *Network MIDI Hub*. Github. Available at: https://github.com/piscue/network-midi-hub.

Sonobus. (n.d.). *Sonobus: High Quality Network Audio Streaming*. Available at: www.sonobus.net/.

Tanaka, A. (1999, March). 'Netmusic – A Perspective', *Catalogue Festival du Web*. Available at: www.academia.edu/44087519/Netmusic_a_Perspective [Accessed: 20 July 2022].

VDO.Ninja (n.d.). *VDO.Ninja*. Available at: https://vdo.ninja/.

Xambó, A. and Roma, G. (2020). 'Performing Audiences: Composition Strategies for Network Music Using Mobile Phones', in *Proceedings of the International Conference on New Interfaces for Musical Expression*, pp. 55–60. https://zenodo.org/records/4813192.

Zakaria, M. and Astuti, K. (2020). 'Hyperreality of Virtual Music Ensemble', in *Proceedings of the 4th International Conference on Arts and Arts Education, Advances in Social Science, Education and Humanities Research*, 552, pp. 192–196. https://doi.org/10.2991/assehr.k.210602.038.

Zotero. (2022). *Networked Music Performance*. Available at: www.zotero.org/groups/2520287/networkedmusicperformance/library [Accessed: 20 July 2022].

6

Performance mapping and control

Enhanced musical connections and a strategy to optimise flow-state

Charles Norton, Daniel Pratt, and Justin Paterson

1 INTRODUCTION

This chapter presents work that seeks to emulate the instinctual, immediate, and haptic relationship of acoustic instrument performance (Saitis, Järveläinen and Fritz, 2018). Further, it explores opportunities to enhance the creative mapping relationship between a performer and their instrument; it investigates the reflexivity between what they can physically touch and manipulate and the electronic (or mechanical) process that creates the sound. In electronic music, the most ubiquitous mapping is the musical instrument digital interface (MIDI) keyboard – a skeuomorph of the acoustic piano, itself an interface that many have tried to augment and manipulate. Historical examples include the 'Matrix' (Smith, 1911) and the circular piano keyboard (Parsons et al., 2013).

Such interfaces tend to map the desired notes to the sound source in the equally tempered chromatic manner to which Western musicians are accustomed (Gann, 2019). Anyone who has witnessed a piano performance understands the relationship between the keys' distribution and the notes' pitch. If this pitch mapping is reversed, the muscle memory that enables the fingers to apply pressure to the desired keys will be literally turned upside down. This polarity change disrupts the musical mapping to a point where the interface must be relearned (Seed, 1998) – this conceptual example underlines the significance of creative mapping. Mapping is neither the musical intention, nor the resultant sound – it is an influential abstract layer situated between the two.

This chapter examines the subset of electronic *parameter* mapping. In the context of both sound and instrument design, such mapping is an active and logical process that enables physical controls to realise creative intention and musical expression. The technical act of routing and combining control signals from physical interfaces and mapping their parameters to a sound-generating device requires focus and attention to detail. This is at odds with the performative intention of achieving the state of flow described by Nakamura and Csikszentmihalyi (2014), which in improvisational performance and gaming vernacular is known as 'being in the zone' (Vyas, 2021).

DOI: 10.4324/9781003118817-7

The process of mapping involves the connection of tactile physical controls to specific and meaningful parameters within a given sound-generating construct. Parameter mapping typically occurs when a musician performs with a traditional MIDI keyboard, knobs, or faders. Alternatively, a performance artist could use movement sensors, or a sound designer might utilise a variety of controllers or develop customised physical interfaces for performance control. The mappings define the possibilities, dimensions, and limitations of creative interaction. Parameter mapping both defines the interaction between humans and machines and enables fluid and intentional performances. The relationship between mapping and sound source mediates the performer's intention as manifested by the resulting timbre and the performance itself.

The chapter presents a technological framework to solve this problem. It examines how sufficient control can be exerted without distracting the performer from their musical intention. To optimise user experience, this research first sought the views of typical 'mapping users'. It employed a mixed-methods research design that combined a quantitative/qualitative survey followed by semi-structured interviews with a focus group. The quantitative data was subjected to statistical analysis, and the qualitative elements were codified using thematic analysis. This information was then used to develop the design of a new system.

2 BACKGROUND TECHNOLOGIES

The configuration of parameter mapping profoundly impacts the timbral range, spectromorphology, and performability of an electronic sound. The concept of mapping is inherently abstract; to conceptualise it requires knowledge of both the source that creates pitch or modulation information and an understanding of how it might be mapped. In addition, we must conceptualise the intended effect upon the target parameter on a sound-generating device such as the Kyma system or a digital audio workstation (DAW) such as Pro Tools. All DAWs provide a protocol to connect to a physical interface with which the user might interact – often inherited from the traditional recording studio. These traditional connective approaches are often utilitarian and based upon legacy protocols with limited published specifications; for instance, Avid removed the MIDI layer from Pro Tools at version 6, leaving only the Mackie HUI protocol for all third parties wishing to map. However, some DAWs, such as Bitwig (bitwig. com, 2022) or Reaper (*reaper.fm*, 2022), take a more contemporaneous open-source approach. McGuire (2019) details the specific requirements of different manufacturers; each appears to take a different approach.

Some creative practitioners map with combinations of technologies that generate musical information. To control this musical information, they construct bespoke interfaces that evolve to individual needs. This process of developing unique assemblages can be so profound that mapping becomes a self-contained activity around which communities such as New Interfaces for Musical Expression (NIME.org, 2022) have grown. For groups such as NIME, mapping sits at the core of its scope, in line with the challenges faced by the research herein. There are numerous references to these mapping challenges in the literature; for example, Hunt, Wanderley and Paradis (2003, p. i) assert that careful mapping "can define the very essence of an instrument", and they discuss the positive impact of exploring the mapping layer, but also acknowledge the non-trivial task of designing new mapping for digital musical instruments. Further, "there is not necessarily an obvious model of the mapping strategies that relate the input device being manipulated by the user/performer to the system being controlled" (Hunt, Wanderley and Kirk, 2000, p. 1). Additionally, NIME designers often lament the limitations they experience with the shortcomings of MIDI protocol – sometimes derogatorily referred to as "Miracle, Industry Designed, (In)adequate" (Cook, 2017, p. 1).

One conclusion that can be drawn is that often, if a newly created interface is to have a lifespan beyond a single original purpose, mapping the creative musical information onto interchangeable sound-generating surfaces must be constructive rather than obstructive, making the mapping process as intuitive as the performance itself. The associated foundations and concerns can be better contextualised by first considering background technologies.

2.1 MIDI 1.0

First introduced in 1982, MIDI provided a protocol and physical connectivity that dramatically impacted music production. Loy (1985) quickly recognised the shift from a 'vertical to horizontal' market situation, which enabled musicians to combine instruments from various manufacturers, as opposed to being locked to a single manufacturer's approach to mapping. Yet Moore (1988) resented several static barriers to the protocol's evolution: directionality, bandwidth, latency, and jitter. It became widely recognised in the 1990s that the protocol required development. As such, the "MIDI 1.0 Detailed Specification captured the state of MIDI as of 1996" (MMA, 2022), offering a timestamp of the evolution of the technology. Igoudin (1997) presented the benefits of this protocol – financial and democratic, plus abundance and portability – to both consumers and manufacturers. Following MIDI 1.0 and in anticipation of an integer upgrade of the protocol, various 'coping strategies' developed over time, e.g., data smoothing and chaining two continuous controllers (CC) for double resolution.

2.2 MIDI 2.0

The subsequent MIDI 2.0 protocol (The MIDI Association, 2020) presented a specification that addressed many challenges and shortcomings. Lehrman (2020) discussed the future possibilities, including bidirectionality, device negotiation, network integration, huge numbers, and universality, all of which are compelling. Unfortunately, despite the formalisation of the protocol, physical integration into commercial devices is still embryonic at the time of writing, and the full benefits of MIDI 2.0 have yet to coalesce.

2.3 Open sound control

In 2002, open sound control (OSC) (2020) came to provide an open-source protocol to transmit musical information via an IP network rather than the dedicated hardware connector of MIDI, providing a way to explore numerous emergent possibilities. Instrument designers could harness OSC to allow adaptable communication between previously un-connectable disparate systems for musical and multimedia purposes. It has long been referenced as an essential tool for enhanced musical communication (Wright, Freed and Momeni, 2003). Since OSC relies on standard networking technology, it is still considered the protocol of choice for prototyping and flexible commercial systems such as Kyma (Scaletti, 2002) and Bitwig (Moßgraber, 2020).

2.4 Multimodality

Many other technologies are suitable for integration into music-oriented communication, and these also need mapping consideration. The research herein also draws from the holistic concept of feedback, and this includes modalities such as *haptic* (Bongers, 1994; Cooper et al., 2011; Carter et al., 2013), *bio* (Coggins, 2014), and *traditional* visual and audible feedback (Bongers, 2000). In these different contexts, each of the authors seeks to address the fundamental problems of control vs. sound-source disassociation by harnessing MIDI alongside these modes, and they accepted that this hybridisation was an initial phase of a much broader exploratory movement. Multimodality offers numerous opportunities to design novel mapping technologies that operate fluidly and seamlessly in the future.

3 A QUALITATIVE FOUNDATION

3.1 Introduction

In order to provide an objective foundation for the subsequent practical development of a novel parameter-mapping system, the views and experiences of a number of electronic musicians and sound designers were canvassed. This data collection also clarified which subsection of this demographic could most benefit from the research. Accordingly, a thematic analysis was designed, and the themes generated from the interview data employed an inductive and cyclic coding process, as described by Braun and Clarke (2006). An interpretive and reflexive approach was applied, starting without a predefined code framework (Braun and Clarke, 2021). From this coding, the emergent thematic framework provided semantic and latent themes that informed the practical prototyping trajectory. Analysis of the data also provided clarity and perspective to the initial investigative research. It was hoped that the themes would provide fresh inspiration for some form of physical control that might unlock previously unexplored techniques.

3.2 Defining a relevant focus group

A survey was used to gather metrics regarding the control of musical systems and provide the respondents with the opportunity to provide written comments on each question. The survey design was developed around preliminary tactile and practical prototyping perspectives, gathering opinions, and inviting discussion of physical control, parameter visualisation, protocols, form factor, and other topics of research interest, such as microtonal experience and click tracks. The initial survey analysis provided the first qualitative dataset to be thematically analysed and acted as a screen to identify a focus group for further dialogue. There were 29 fully completed surveys, and the analysis revealed three broad categories of mapping users:

A] **'Caps-lock Fundamentalists'** – one person used a laptop QWERTY keyboard for all musical duties

This affectionate name reflects their reliance on the 'QWERTY' keyboard and the 'caps-lock' key used by some DAWs to enable the note-input mode. This is often the only input method available by choice, economics, or immediate availability, although because this approach is not velocity sensitive, real-time dynamic control is difficult to perform. Whilst there was only one survey respondent in this category, many students and professionals who input notes in this manner have been encountered.

B] **'DAW Foot Soldiers'** – ten respondents used linear and unambiguous mapping for control in the studio environment

This group of participants relies on a 'one-to-one' mapping topology. Each control is directly mapped in a way that allows one physical element: fader, knob, or button, to be linearly routed to a single control destination: volume, pan, or mute. The mappings' meaning, outcome, and system state are presented in an ergonomic and useable interface. However, the opportunity for customisation, aggregation, and permutation are minimal and usually bound by the implemented protocol: a frustration identified by the following participant category.

C] **'Mapping Warriors'** – 18 participants embraced custom mapping – these people regularly built and used sound-controlling structures

This final and most relevant category map includes the *one-to-many* – where one performance parameter may influence several (say) synthesis parameters at the same time – and the more complex *many-to-many* paradigms described by Hunt and Wanderley (2002, p. 99). This group works with mapping as a crucial part of their workflow in a variety of creative activities, including:

•   'Sound designers', who often use controls beyond faders and pots to increase the number of sources that can be moved with one hand, thus increasing the total number of destinations that can be simultaneously controlled.

- The 'movement and tracking' community generates modulation data from sensors fed to sound-generating systems; they share the same mapping concerns as the sound designers but face the additional barrier of not being the mapping engineer and sharing technical knowledge of the system design.
- 'Sonification artists' often integrate complex modulation topologies in their work, creating relationships between data and sound for scientific or ideological purposes. In this context, mapping is the art.

This taxonomy was instrumental in providing balance to the later software design and helped contextualise the various operational modes the participants discussed. The broad categories of mapping users align with and have evolved from Hunt, Wanderley and Paradis's (2003) definitions.

3.3 Focus group

The tripartite categorisation of participants was also key to subsequently defining and forming the most relevant (online) focus group. The 'mapping warriors' were deemed most suitable as it was clear these participants had the most to both contribute to and gain from this research. An initial online discussion was captured and transcribed. This wide-ranging session provided a foundational data set that solidified the thematic generation. Still, it was evident that one-to-one interviews would also be required to allow participants to explore ideas unhindered by group discourse/discursion, and these then provided the second qualitative dataset for thematic analysis. Before evolving to individuals' interests and specialisms, these semi-structured sessions all began with the same fundamental questions:

- *'Which controllers do you use, and which systems do you control?'* This question had a focus on current activity. Despite being a duplicate of data gathered in the survey, it became immediately apparent how the qualitative data was far more appropriate than the quantitative survey metrics.
- *'What is the most intriguing musical control system you have ever explored?'* Intended to encourage the participant to consider the systems from their previous experience or perhaps operate within different contexts, this question directed the discussion towards broader and legacy perspectives.
- *'Is there a physical controller (musical or otherwise) that you would like to use but can't connect or map?'* This was designed to reveal opportunities to harness physical input devices that participants already possessed but struggled to integrate.

Following this structure, interviews were transcribed and included in the initial coding cycle. Given the richness of the qualitative data, it was decided to adjust the research design to drop the quantitative aspects. The focus-group sessions were instrumental in debating the research direction and purpose.

4 THEMES AND CATEGORIES

Three distinct themes were generated from the surveys, interviews, and focus groups.

4.1 Theme 1 – ubiquity and convenience

This theme represented participants' desire to exert control over whichever system they required with the controller they possess and are familiar with; 189 coded references across three categories contribute to its generation.

Physical Interface: Unsurprisingly, all participants had plenty to communicate regarding their ideal manifestation of tactile controls. For some, the specific number of individual controls was crucial: "*When you have so many, there's a finite number of what's usable and where it becomes better until you have too many and then it becomes just a mess.*" Other perspectives included alternative controls that extend beyond the traditional MIDI keyboard; most participants had something unique that they enjoyed mapping to access musical motion beyond a piano keyboard and faders.

Immediacy: The data revealed a split between participants who need a system to instantly react with no configuration overhead: "*The sound designers I meet, it's not like they're thick. It's not like they can't program. They just don't have time to engage with that sort of stuff. So, they would love to do many-to-many because it would give them subtle, nuanced, or even extreme, and rapid control over getting different new sound rather than having to go program it. But if the mapping process takes any time at all, they're not going do it.*" However, other participants were happy to engage programmatically to achieve their creative goals.

Permanence: This notion was approached differently depending on the context of the creative work. In professional and traditional approaches, the 'one-to-one' topology, where every control has a specific purpose, is the most prized: "*It is important to always have the same function attached to the same knob such as threshold, band frequency . . . regardless of which plug-in is used. Too often, I have to search for the right knob.*" Other participants working in more abstract artistic contexts voiced concerns that also emerge in the next theme.

4.2 Theme 2 – precision and flexibility

This theme evolved from the participants' concerns regarding the nature and specific needs of their mapping activity. One hundred eight coded references across seven categories contributed to the generated theme.

Complexity: A paradox was revealed: participants simultaneously require systems with comprehensible interfaces yet demand increasing configuration complexity. The participants recognised this situation: *"Intuitive interfacing between hardware and software is critical, with software being generally weighty and feature-rich, it is important to have a hardware controller to distil the most important features of the hardware/software into an easily usable and expressive device."* Examples regarding the reduction of complexity by mapping decisions being dynamically assigned: *"I think the focus needs to be on how to make the control surface dynamically assign itself to Kyma/ DAW."* This can be contrary to views such as: *"Especially for people with more than one controller at their disposal is this idea that basically, is – turn this modulation system into a matrix."* The "matrix" in this context refers to the 'EaganMatrix' developed by Edmund Eagan (2022) or the FUN system in VAST Kurzweil Synthesis (Kurzweil, 1999) which both provide the ability to process modulation signals with mathematical functions.

Precision: Reducing latency, jitter, and increasing precision was a regularly coded concern: *"Too many movement-based touch interfaces have poor and latent sensitivity, and worse, many do not have pressure at all."*

Feeling: Coding for this category identified discussion of how a mapping feels rather than functions. There are many factors to nuanced mapping (intentional or a manifestation of a combination of factors): *"As soon as I got it, just a few basic parameters mapped, I wasn't playing the instrument. I was . . . I was becoming the instrument."*

4.3 Theme 3 – feedback

This theme comprises two coding categories that present a desire to see more visualisation in various contexts and to feel the results of the mapping through haptic feedback. Thirty-eight coded references generated this theme.

Visualisation: *"How do I map them consistently and have hands-on control and see what my values are? The engineers answer to that: eight faders and a marker and a scribble strip at the top."* This remark sits firmly in the traditional and practical solution to the mapping visualisation problem but does not offer a solution for constantly changing parameter sets. A technological solution is to provide visual mapping communication closer to the performing interface and away from the sound-generating system.

Haptic: Haptic feedback is something that participants are enthused about but are waiting for creative applications to become readily available: *"I would love to feel the pulsing of the LFO through the control surface."* There is discussion in the literature regarding haptic implementation, e.g., Melchior et al. (2013), who present findings implying the benefits of haptic feedback (in controlling spatial audio).

4.4 Summary of the three generated themes

1] Ubiquity and convenience

Owners of physical control surfaces want to map their existing hardware rather than feeling the need to purchase different interfaces for individual systems. As such, a system should *enable* rather than hinder the mapping process.

2] Precision and flexibility

The legacy of 7-bit MIDI 1.0 is still a default in modern systems. The component codes – complexity, precision, and feeling – dictate that the participants require precise control, wish to lever this precision without too much configuration, and that any technological intervention should enhance rather than degrade or interfere with the feeling of the mapping.

3] Feedback

Within the data – both explicitly and latently, there is a broad desire for more real-time system information to be presented to the performer. Regardless of the context, goals shared by many users include auto-labelling, parameter state, and performative direction provided by the system.

4.5 Theme conclusions

The thematic analysis presented a combination of both conceptual and practical concerns for idealised parameter mapping. This led to pertinent design objectives for the participant-driven hardware-control implementation. These objectives were explored and corroborated by creating practical prototypes that investigated each of the specific areas. Central to this, experiments with various motion-input methods were developed, but the mapping process often hindered their effectiveness. The experiments delivered the conclusion: no matter how many innovative performative evolutions were created, the 'elephant in the room' will always be how to define new mappings without ruining any sense of flow and performative inspiration. The creative context may vary from designing a new instrument to integrating a new physical controller or abstracting a data sonification – but the mapping layer is always *encountered*. The proof-of-concept prototypes will now be discussed.

5 PRACTICAL PROTOTYPICAL SOLUTIONS

5.1 Destination platforms

Until MIDI 2.0 is adopted and coherently implemented by a critical mass of manufacturers, OSC represents a pragmatic protocol for experimentation with mapping concepts, although it is acknowledged that subsequent migration to MIDI 2.0 might prove necessary and perhaps even beneficial.

Focus group participant Alan M. Jackson offered some observations regarding sound designers and their reasons for investing time and money into Kyma – these observations presented Kyma as a viable development platform to consider a variety of artistic, professional, and pedagogical implementations. They also align with the holistic research goals of this study and can be placed into four categories: sound quality, aesthetic originality, practical workflow, and teamwork stability. Kyma users typically map a variety of MIDI controllers or touchscreen applications. Both interfaces have compromises: touch screens are not proprioceptive or velocity-sensitive and can induce latency, whereas physical controllers often rely on MIDI, and each control needs individual mapping and ranging. Kyma does not provide a general-purpose input/output (GPIO) terminal providing direct connections to physical interfaces and data-feedback for circuit-element control (Balachandran, 2009). A particularly relevant feature of Kyma is that it presents all real-time parameters with an open-source specification using bidirectional OSC across a local network. The user must follow multiple steps when connecting an external controller to Kyma. Each parameter must be selected, a menu accessed and then mapped, as shown in Figure 6.1. Whilst each connection can be stored, it must be redefined for each new sound and every parameter – a time-consuming and disruptive process. A typical array of Kyma parameters is shown Figure 6.2.

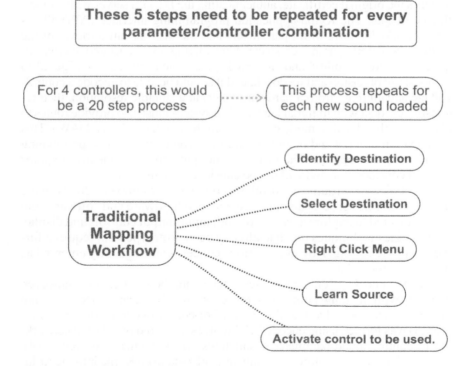

Figure 6.1 A typical mapping workflow.

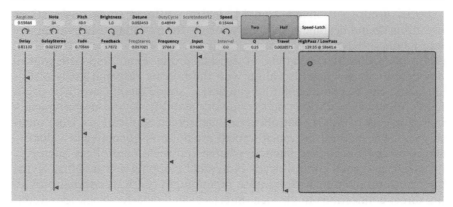

Figure 6.2 The Kyma Virtual Control Surface (VCS).

5.2 Proto host: proof of concept

To experiment with using the 'act of mapping' to identify ways in which topological modifications can improve the connective experience, one approach is to inject oneself like a 'man-in-the-middle attack' in between the source of the modulation and the parameter destination (Callegati, Cerroni and Ramilli, 2009, p. 78). This metaphor is when accessing a website, an HTTPS server sends a public-key certificate to the Web browser, where such an attack replaces the original certificate, authenticating the HTTPS server with a modified certificate. The Kyma application programming interface (API) allows the networked control of all parameters and the near-instant retrieval of the entire modulatory parameter space. Considering the generated themes of 'precision and flexibility' and 'feedback', the system must be configured to demonstrate precision and feedback, and it should be able to encode a control-voltage stream (e.g., from a hardware fader) at a suitable resolution, then retransmit the data with minimal latency. The system must also provide routes to display graphical and numeric content from the target (such as a DAW). This combination of input and output possibilities would enable rapid prototyping of the parameter options. The theme of 'ubiquity and convenience' requires detailed consideration and will not be considered in this text.

The choice of Arduino Uno microprocessor (Arduino.cc, 2022) made initial economic sense as an interface between hardware and software, and it was selected to explore a variety of both input/output controls and display technologies/techniques that had already been prototyped but required further mapping testing. However, various concerns subsequently emerged as the system took shape.

The Arduino Uno only processes integer numbers efficiently; however, working with floating point numbers subsequently became necessary but proved cumbersome. Despite this, a proof-of-concept system (shown in Figure 6.3) was formed using encoded CV sources delivered by UDP IP networking to control sound-parameter destinations on the Kyma (see Figure 6.4). One problem was to capture returning network data from Kyma into the Arduino system – this proved a far more complicated procedure than anticipated. Bidirectionality is an essential topological requirement for delivering visual and haptic feedback (see Figure 6.5). However, this simple initial incarnation

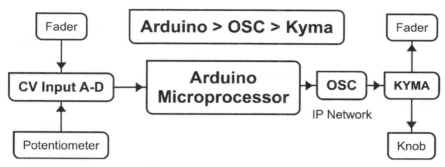

Figure 6.3 Version-one Topology.

Figure 6.4 Basic Input and Visual Feedback using Arduino.

Figure 6.5 XY Control with OLED Display.

provided a fresh perspective on the mapping process. While it was more complex to configure than just clicking 'learn' on the Kyma control surface, correct system implementation in the Kyma API functioned appropriately. This element of the prototyping process implied that the project needed an alternative and more accessible strategy to host the associated experiments.

5.3 A whole new interface

Accordingly, Max (Cycling 74, 2020) and Node.js (Node.js, 2022) presented an alternative route to rapidly prototype without incurring the time overhead of bespoke coding. The Node.js programming framework was an optimal choice for developing the second iteration since the Kyma API presents data in the JSON format (Hebel, 2015). These two applications enabled the easy reception, storage, manipulation, and recall of interface-object details via a native specification. A second software iteration was developed using these new tools to interpret and manage the mapping process.

This system was entitled 'MaxVCS', aspects of which are shown in Figures 6.6, 6.7, and 6.8. Node.js requested a real-time list of sources and destinations from Kyma, enabling a streamlined dataset to be sent to Max. This local dataset provided all the parameter details needed to facilitate mapping experimentation. Max then translated and transmitted any available control input to Kyma with minimal latency via OSC. This system allowed a software front-end to be developed that enabled the user to take advantage of all class-compliant MIDI interfaces, the Max 'hi' object ecosystem (this object allows data input to Max via hardware peripherals), web-APIs, and crucially, Arduino integration. MaxVCS provided a route to quickly explore combinations of all these real-time data sources not natively accessed in Kyma. The critical factor in understanding MaxVCS was that it relied on a Node.js server running in the background that handled the retrieval and storage of all Kyma parameter data. Max could then request all the parameter details without needing further communication from Kyma or, vitally, interrupting the real-time sound playback.

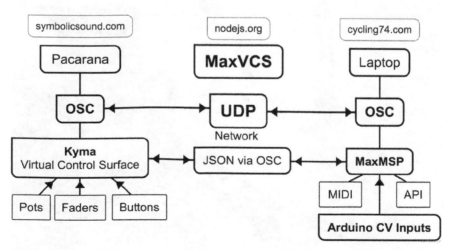

Figure 6.6 MaxVCS.

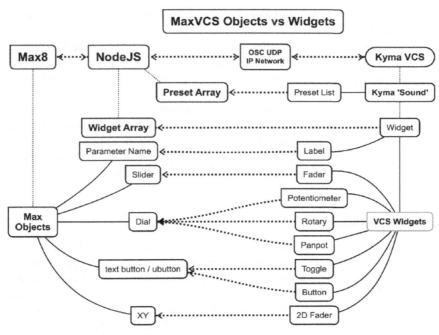

Figure 6.7 MaxVCS Topology.

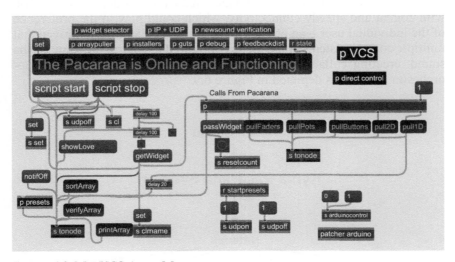

Figure 6.8 MaxVCS Array Manager.

A second iteration was then developed; however, this presented new topological design concerns that centred around either replicating all the controls for the target structure or just being able to use a few pertinent performance controls. If the new system replicated all the targets with an identical style of control, the inherent problems were not solved – merely transported. Whilst this was of some creative benefit, conversely, there

was a need for a refined and reduced set of relevant parameters for immediate mapping.

Kyma provided data regarding the original control type embedded in the
transmitted OSC information, using its graphical object types to organise
parameters in performative priority. This approach facilitated the ability to
add detailed metadata (beyond the parameter name) to each source. A collection of sounds were used to test this functionality (all used this method
to prioritise four relevant controls); it was trivial to instantly match desired
controllers to the most pertinent destinations despite having no stored connection data. This simple exercise functioned as a proof of concept, dem-
onstrating that metadata regarding individual parameter destinations can
be a powerful tool.

6 CONCLUSIONS

The implications of the shift from trying to design a bespoke system to
embracing a broader development topology revealed a range of possibilities not previously considered. The combination of the programmatic
utility of Node.js with Max's immediate and flexible graphical interface
offered a potent framework. This architecture not only met the research
objective of creating a method of rapidly testing prototypical interfaces
but also yielded something far more fundamental and flexible; it created
a dynamic communication method between two unique systems. Connecting the two programming languages enabled a modulation unification
with cogent and speedy connectivity, which could play to the preference
of the individual user – an obvious benefit. MaxVCS has also proven that
multiple control systems could all be configured to control the same Kyma
sound, creating collaborative performance opportunities; a four-laptop-
orchestra scenario is depicted in Figure 6.9.

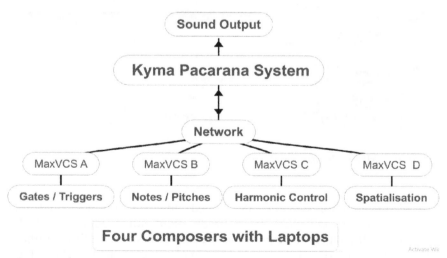

Figure 6.9 Collaborative Mapping.

In a pedagogical context, it was possible to program straightforward Kyma sounds with minimal modulation and provide them to Max students (with the MaxVCS interface), enabling them to explore the sonic potential of Kyma whilst only engaging with the more familiar Max modulation and interface. It was now possible to construct a control interface that could be reapplied to multiple Kyma sounds without needing to constantly re-map configurations. MaxVCS allowed the users to implement a range of GPIO, API, and other Max-specific technologies to control Kyma in ways that extended users' performative ability in a lucid manner, again as before, levering existing skills and knowledge – but in a new performative paradigm – increasing the range of available control, whilst simultaneously decreasing the time and complexity of configuration.

Mapping is a substantial topic with many needs, methods, and outcomes. This research was not initially designed to address mapping as a holistic concern. It was considered too challenging an arena within which to make significant progress. Throughout the research and practical prototyping challenges, mapping became a tiresome foe that would dampen inspiration and disrupt any flow state that was building, yet this proof of concept has overcome its adversary.

7 FURTHER DEVELOPMENT

Now that the concepts have been demonstrated, a set of MaxVCS application states can be considered to function in concert with the requirements of the three mapping-user categories:

- Fully automated mapping – zero configuration for the non-technical mapper.
- One-to-one re-mapping – an intuitive flexible interface for most mapping needs.
- A modulation matrix equipped with the ability to inject formulae into the modulation stream – a powerful re-mapping, manipulation, and re-distribution system.

MaxVCS now requires further user-experience testing with potentially reflexive design. Projecting forward, if the MaxVCS and Kyma OSC implementation (or indeed MIDI 2.0 in the broader context) could provide a method of attaching unique metadata to each control source and destination, significant steps could be taken toward designing a taxonomy of modulation. The creators of sounds could prebuild rapid-mapping possibilities into the interface itself, allowing the designers of control systems and the users of a wide range of physical interfaces to benefit from the reduced configuration overhead. This approach will enable the act of mapping to become real-time and performative. Interesting questions could be posed, such as: could a dancer with sensors control their mapping through bespoke real-time abstraction? Could a toolkit be created for a mapping engineer to further refine and control mappings, combining and shaping multiple sets of movement and performance modulation data?

Despite Max presenting an invaluable set of prototyping and proof-of-concept opportunities, it requires a 'whole computer' to explore this mapping interface. This is not an economical system design considering either cost or energy consumption. The medium-term goal is to transfer Node. js onto a cost-effective microprocessor and implement the GUI as an efficient and flexible hardware interface, using existing class-compliant controllers and easily purchased components.

The related technology is still evolving. The longer-term vision is that a combination of precision latency-free, audio-rate control voltages, combined with the data of digital communication protocols, will coalesce more widely, and it is hoped that this research might even contribute towards that.

REFERENCES

Arduino.cc. (2022). *Arduino UNO R3, Arduino.cc*. Available at: https://docs.arduino.cc/hardware/uno-rev3.

Balachandran, S. (2009). *General Purpose Input/Output (GPIO)*. Available at: www.egr.msu.edu/classes/ece480/capstone/fall09/group03/AN_balachandran.pdf.

bitwig.com. (2022). *www.bitwig.com*. Available at: www.bitwig.com/.

Bongers, B. (1994). *The Use of Active Tactile and Force Feedback in Timbre Controlling Electronic Instruments*. Ann Arbor, MI: Michigan Publishing, University of Michigan Library.

Bongers, B. (2000). 'Physical Interfaces in the Electronic Arts', in *Trends in Gestural Control of Music*. University of Cambridge.

Braun, V. and Clarke, V. (2006). 'Using Thematic Analysis in Psychology', *Qualitative Research in Psychology*, 3, pp. 77–101. https://doi.org/10.1191/1478 088706qp063oa.

Braun, V. and Clarke, V. (2021). 'One Size Fits All? What Counts as Quality Practice in (Reflexive) Thematic Analysis?', *Qualitative Research in Psychology*, 18(3), pp. 328–352. https://doi.org/10.1080/14780887.2020.1769238.

Callegati, F., Cerroni, W. and Ramilli, M. (2009). 'Man-in-the-Middle Attack to the HTTPS Protocol', *IEEE Security & Privacy*, 7(1), pp. 78–81. https://doi.org/10.1109/MSP.2009.12.

Carter, T., et al. (2013). 'UltraHaptics: Multi-point mid-air Haptic Feedback for Touch Surfaces', in *UIST 2013 – Proceedings of the 26th Annual ACM Symposium on User Interface Software and Technology*, pp. 505–514. https://doi.org/10.1145/2501988.2502018.

Coggins, G. (2014). *Augmented Reality Biofeedback Display*. Available at: https://patents.google.com/patent/WO2014056000A1/en.

Cook, P. (2017). '2001: Principles for Designing Computer Music Controllers', in Jensenius, A. R. and Lyons, M. J., eds. *A NIME Reader*. Cham: Springer International Publishing (Current Research in Systematic Musicology), pp. 1–13. https://doi.org/10.1007/978-3-319-47214-0_1.

Cooper, E. W., et al., eds. (2011). *Haptic and Audio Interaction Design*. Berlin, Heidelberg: Springer Berlin Heidelberg (Lecture Notes in Computer Science). https://doi.org/10.1007/978-3-642-22950-3.

Cycling 74. (2020). *What Is Max? | Cycling '74*. Available at: https://cycling74.com/products/max.

Edmund, E. (2022). *EaganMatrix Module*. Available at: https://www.hakenaudio.com/eaganmatrix-module.

Gann, K. (2019). *The Arithmetic of Listening: Tuning Theory and History for the Impractical Musician*. Urbana, USA: University of Illinois Press.

Hebel, K. (2015). *Kyma: OSC Implementation*. Available at: www.symbolicsound.com/cgi-bin/bin/view/Learn/OpenSoundControlImplementation.

Hunt, A. and Wanderley, M. M. (2002). 'Mapping Performer Parameters to Synthesis Engines', *Organised Sound*, 7(2), pp. 97–108. https://doi.org/10.1017/S1355771802002030.

Hunt, A., Wanderley, M. M. and Kirk, R. (2000). 'Towards a Model for Instrumental Mapping in Expert Musical Interaction', in *Proceedings of the 2000 International Computer Music Conference. International Computer Music Conference*. Berlin, Germany: Michigan Publishing. Available at: https://dblp.org/db/conf/icmc/icmc2000.html.

Hunt, A., Wanderley, M. M. and Paradis, M. (2003). 'The Importance of Parameter Mapping in Electronic Instrument Design', *Journal of New Music Research*, 32(4), pp. 429–440.

Igoudin, A. (1997). *Impact of MIDI on Electroacoustic Art Music*. Stanford, CA: CCRMA, Department of Music, Stanford University.

Kurzweil. (1999). *K2000 User Manual*. Available at: www.synthmanuals.com/manuals/kurzweil/k2000/owners_manual/k2000ownersmanual.pdf.

Lehrman, P. D. (2020). 'MIDI 2.0: Promises and Challenges', in *Music Encoding Conference Proceedings. Music Encoding Conference*. Medford, MA: Tufts University, p. 55.

Loy, G. (1985). 'Musicians Make a Standard: The MIDI Phenomenon', *Computer Music Journal*, 9(4), p. 20. https://doi.org/10.2307/3679619.

McGuire, S. (2019). *Modern MIDI: Sequencing and Performing Using Traditional and Mobile Tools*, 2nd ed. Focal Press. https://doi.org/10.4324/9781351263849.

Melchior, F., et al. (2013). 'On the Use of a Haptic Feedback Device for Sound Source Control in Spatial Audio Systems', in *AES 134th Convention*. Rome, Italy: Audio Engineering Society Convention.

The MIDI Association. (2020). *Details about MIDI 2.0™, MIDI-CI, Profiles and Property Exchange, The MIDI Association*. Available at: www.midi.org/midi-articles/details-about-midi-2-0-midi-ci-profiles-and-property-exchange.

MMA. (2022). *midi.org*. Available at: https://midi.org/.

Moßgraber, J. (2020). *Bitwig | OSC, www.bitwig.com*. Available at: www.bitwig.com/en/community/control_scripts/osc/osc/osc_1.html.

Moore, F. R. (1988). 'The Dysfunctions of MIDI', *Computer Music Journal*, 12(1), p. 19. https://doi.org/10.2307/3679834.

Nakamura, J. and Csikszentmihalyi, M. (2014). 'The Concept of Flow', in Csikszentmihalyi, M., ed. *Flow and the Foundations of Positive Psychology*. Dordrecht: Springer Netherlands, pp. 239–263. https://doi.org/10.1007/978-94-017-9088-8_16.

NIME.org. (2022). *The International Conference on New Interfaces for Musical Expression, NIME*. Available at: https://nime.org/.

Node.js. (2022). *Node.js, Node.js*. Available at: https://nodejs.org/en/.

opensoundcontrol.org. (2020). *OSC | opensoundcontrol.org*. Available at: http://opensoundcontrol.org/osc.

Parsons, B., et al. (2013). *Circular Piano Keyboard*. Available at: https://patents.google.com/patent/US20130192444A1/en [Accessed: 25 November 2022].

reaper.fm. (2022). Available at: www.reaper.fm/ [Accessed: 9 December 2022].

Saitis, C., Järveläinen, H. and Fritz, C. (2018). 'The Role of Haptic Cues in Musical Instrument Quality Perception', in Papetti, S. and Saitis, C., eds. *Musical Haptics*. Cham: Springer International Publishing (Springer Series on Touch and Haptic Systems), pp. 73–93. https://doi.org/10.1007/978-3-319-58316-7_5.

Scaletti, C. (2002). 'Computer Music Languages, Kyma, and the Future', *Computer Music Journal*, 26(4), pp. 69–82. https://doi.org/10.1162/014892602320991392.

Seed, C. (1998). *The First Left-Handed Piano*. Available at: www.lefthandedpiano.co.uk/about.html [Accessed: 15 December 2022].

Smith, O. A. M. (1911). *Keyboard for Musical Instruments*. Available at: https://patents.google.com/patent/US1009194A/en?q=invented+the+MIDI+keyboard&oq=who+invented+the+MIDI+keyboard&sort=old.

Vyas, M. (2021). 'Experience of Flow in Games and Using It to Improve Well-Being: A Critical Review', *Indian Journal of Health & Wellbeing*, 12(1).

Wright, M., Freed, A. and Momeni, A. (2003). 'OpenSound Control: State of the Art 2003', in *Proceedings of the 2003 Conference on New Interfaces for Musical Expression (NIME-03)* [Preprint]. (2022). *Haken Audio*. Available at: www.hakenaudio.com [Accessed: 15 December 2022].

7

Hacking the concert experience

Exploring co-creative audience interaction at a chiptune live performance

Matthias Jung and Vegard Kummen

1 INTRODUCTION

The observation that audiences play a central part in musical performances has long been recognized and has been subject to many studies within the field of Popular Music Studies. Auslander explores the idea that musical meaning is produced through the interaction of performers and audiences in his recent book *In Concert: Performing Musical Persona* (Auslander, 2021). The role of audience members in musical performances has also been explored with the idea of active musical contribution. For example, Freeman proposed different roles that audience members can take when contributing to a concert, among them the role of audience members as "influencers" (Freeman, 2005b as read in York, 2019). More recently, communication technology has led to possibilities of networked scenarios by which larger audiences can be included in musical performances in real-time.

The main aim of this study is to explore different concepts of audience participation and learn about the experience they create for both audience members and stage performers. The following questions will be in the center of the study:

- How do audience members experience the performance when being invited to participate musically in the show?
- How do participatory paradigms change the performance from the perspective of the performers on stage?
- Which interaction paradigms are best suited in the context of chiptune live music?

2 BACKGROUND AND RELATED WORK

This section will first briefly review existing participatory work together with the investigated categories and then elaborate on chiptune culture as the musical context for the study.

DOI: 10.4324/9781003118817-8

2.1 Related work

One of the first cases of audience participation connected to Western performance culture can be found in Mozart's *Würfelspiel,* where audience
members could roll dice that determined the arrangement of a cembalo
composition being played by a live instrumentalist (Mozart and Mozart,
1793). Recent participatory works have been proposed to be separated
into pre-smartphone and smartphone-centered works (Hoedl et al., 2020,
pp. 193–194). Examples of pre-smartphone works are *Reflective Paddles*
(Carpenter and Carpenter, 1991), *Dialtones* (Levin, 2001), and *Glimmer* (Freeman, 2005a). *Reflective Paddles* and *Glimmer* both use visual
techniques available for the audience to get involved, whereas *Dialtones*
uses the mobile phones of audience members as playback devices without
their active contribution. Examples of smartphone-centered works include
Echobo (Lee and Freeman, 2013), *Open Symphony* (Wu et al., 2017), and
The Singularity (York, 2019). For an in-depth analysis of participatory
concert strategies, including technological concern of networked topologies, the reader is referred to Weinberg (2005), Renwick (2017), and Serafin et al. (2019). For a deeper analysis of the audience's perspective on
participatory concerts and the preliminaries that influence their experience, a review of the study conducted by Hoedl et al. (2017) is recommended, which includes a questionnaire-based analysis of reception-based
design categories for participatory concerts. More work on design and
implementation can also be found in Lee and Freeman (2013), as well as
in Xambó and Roma (2020), who proposed 13 composition dimensions
that deal with "the role of the performer, the role of the audience, the location of sound and the type of feedback" (ibid.).

Reviewing these previously cited sources, the following investigation
categories are proposed. They are separated into three dimensions – the
individual, technological, and social experience:

- Enjoyment (individual)
- Arousal (individual)
- HCI design (technological)
- Effectiveness and Motivation (social)
- Surprise and Connectedness (social)

The first two categories refer to the individual audience member's experiences, which are inspired by the circumplex model as described by
Juslin (2019). However, the first category of the model, which measures
how positive music is experienced (Valence), is replaced by the category
Enjoyment, which describes how enjoyable audience members rated their
experience. The second category refers to how much excitement the experience creates in the listener (Arousal).

The next category for investigation is the experience of the interface
by which audience members access the participatory parts, referred to as
Human-Computer-Interaction (HCI). This category includes questions

about the user experience of the technology as well as issues and limitations of the smartphone-centered approach that was taken for the study. Turchet (2020) systemizes the HCI design for audience participation as a theoretical fundament.

The last two categories of investigation relate to the social dimension of the participatory concert experience. The one on Effectiveness and Motivation will investigate how impactful audience members and performers perceive their actions and, consequently, how motivated that leaves them for their future contributions to the concert. The second social category is referred to as Surprise and Connectedness, which investigates how the participatory experience reflects the perceived sense of connection and how both groups feel for each other within that experience. Concerning the aspect of surprise, the findings of Erdem and Jensenius (2020), who determined surprise as a central element for the collaborative experience within shared control music making, are followed. As a theoretical backdrop for the part of connectedness, Maibom (2020) is used, who explores artistic empathy in depth.

2.2 Chiptune and hacking culture

There appears to be a lack of research on the effect of audience participation within specific music cultures. This section briefly describes the musical setting the project operates within. The musical context is that of a chiptune show performed by the group *Kubbi*. Chiptune is a technology, musical aesthetic, and culture utilizing the sounds of home computers and video game consoles of the 80s and 90s for music making. On the one hand, it is a sonic aesthetic of low-tech hardware (sometimes reproduced with contemporary software and hardware) characterized by basic audio waveforms, low-resolution samplers, and noise generators. On the other, it is an affinity space (Gee, 2005) with its own norms, practices, creative ideologies, and history that has evolved alongside online communication platforms as well as manifested itself in physical spaces through events, meetups, and workshops. Historically, chiptune culture is considered a product of the 90s programming enthusiast culture known as the 'demoscene' (Collins, 2013, p. 113), but has since evolved to be a sonic expression and aesthetic of its own frequently used in popular music (Márquez, 2014).

The limiting nature of chiptune media also informs a structural dimension of chiptune, for instance, in its limitation as to how many sounds (channels) can be played at once (Collins, 2008). Compositional and sound design-oriented limitations have paved the way for both aesthetics and practice to be oriented around maximizing musical expression within restrictive environments (Carlsson, 2009). To do so, a composer may treat the technology in a way that involves "the manipulation of technological constraints, the process of software and hardware hacking" (Polymeropoulou, 2019, p. 92) to bypass limitations and expand its potential for musical expression. Hacking in this context concerns unconventional usage and creative re-appropriation of technology as opposed to solely illicit and destructive uses, as the term often refers to. In the context of chiptune, it might relate to modifying a Game Boy with a backlit screen and an audio output with a subtler noise floor or increasing the clock speed of its CPU to produce new timbers and effects. In efforts in and appraisal of maximized musical expression on limited media, there seems to be aesthetic value in novel uses of technology for creative interaction (Reid, 2018).

3 RESEARCH DESIGN AND METHODOLOGICAL IMPLEMENTATION

An interactive show has been constructed around the music of *Kubbi*, a musical group and moniker of Vegard Kummen. *Kubbi* has performed music in connection with the chip scene since 2010, mainly at chiptune events, operating within a deeply connected aesthetic and expression to that of the chip scene. However, the music also features characteristics of other musical styles, such as progressive rock, ambient music, classical, and various subgenres of electronic music. Characteristics such as tempo, key, energy level, and sound design vary greatly from song to song. Some parts of the show will contain longer sections of ambient sound design meant to be meditative, while other sections are fast-paced, punk-rock-like parts of high intensity. The performers play traditional instruments: Vegard Kummen on the electric bass and Tobias Øymo Solbakk on the drumkit. Additionally, Vegard controls a selection of Eurorack synthesizers, a 1989 Nintendo Game Boy DMG-01 as well as a MacBook Pro running Ableton Live. Tobias uses an SPDX drum pad, an electric snare, and a kickdrum pedal for triggering sounds via MIDI.

Due to the artistic involvement in the group, Vegard Kummen's role in this project is both as a performer and research contributor. This differentiates this research in terms of analytical perspectives from other works in the field by providing an auto-ethnographic perspective connected to the involvement in an existing musical act. This will introduce bias connected to musical taste and pressure towards producing a 'good show'. While this is important to be clear about, it is also considered a strength of this research and an opportunity to explore audience participation from an insider angle. Yet, this poses restrictions to the findings of the study, which should be seen in the light of the musical context of this show and the researcher's subjectivity.

It is important to emphasize that the sole aim and idea behind the resulting project was to create knowledge around the implementation of audience participation. Vegard, nor the group, made economic profits from the fieldwork, and the concert had no entry fee. The event was staged on April 10, 2022, at *Vaktbua*, a former military checkpoint to a peninsula in Kristiansand, Norway. It was partly funded by the University of Agder's programme *Sundays at Vaktbua* (see Figures 7.1 and 7.2).

Figure 7.1 Audience members at *Vaktbua*.

Figure 7.2 Performing musicians on stage.

3.1 The process of creating the music and participatory parts

The development of the interactive show went through several stages. The first was a phase of exploring existing technologies and navigating the market for suited tools. As ideas for interactive parts materialized, three paradigms were implemented into a live set through *Max for Live, MiraWeb,* and a Wi-Fi-router. These allowed access through a browser-based application via a QR code that was displayed during the concert for the audience to scan with their smartphones. The interaction patches that were then accessed included increment and decrement buttons for musical parameters, which were sent via MIDI CC messages to the onstage Ableton Live setup. This participatory framework aims to create a collective process rather than a system that allows listeners to adjust and play back music individually. It is also connected to the aim of the study, which tries to stay within an ecological concert setting.

The authors are aware that some of the interactive patches use music production terms, such as *cutoff, decay,* or *pulse width,* that audience members may not be familiar with. However, in favor of the ecological nature of the study, it was concluded not to explain musical terminology beforehand but rather include this exploration as part of the experiment. As an additional argument, a varying degree of required expertise might affect the participants' experience and, as such, produce beneficial results for the study.

The following figures show the interface for audience members by which the three interaction paradigms were realized:

- **Interaction 1** (Controlling the musical background): At the beginning of the concert, when the performers weren't on stage yet, audience members had access to the volume control of eight different sounds that were played in the musical background (see Figure 7.3).
- **Interaction 2** (Controlling the musical foreground): In the second part of the experiment, which was placed in the middle of the concert, audience members were invited to control the parameters of the main melody in the musical foreground. Specifically, they were controlling the *volume, cutoff, and decay* parameters of each of the notes generated by an 8-step-sequencer (see Figure 7.4).
- **Interaction 3** (Controlling the instruments): Towards the end of the concert, audience members were given access to parameters of the

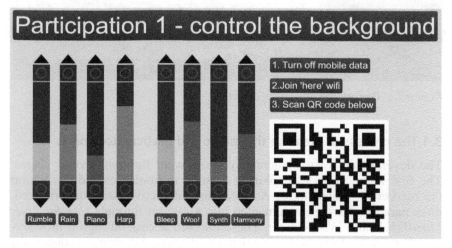

Figure 7.3 Audience interface for Interaction 1.

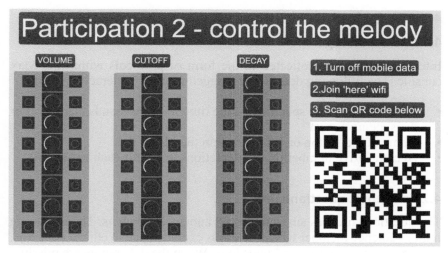

Figure 7.4 Audience interface for Interaction 2.

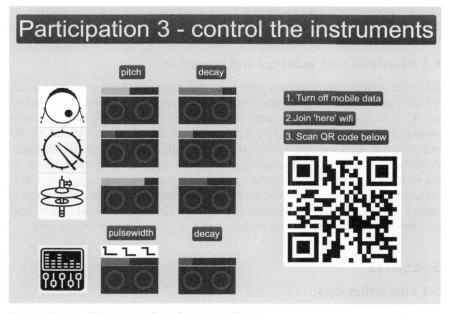

Figure 7.5 Audience interface for Interaction 3.

e-drum instruments (kickdrum, hi-hat, and snare drum) as well as to the Game Boy synths. At this part of the show, the drummer only played these three instruments (the e-drum pads) and didn't use his acoustic drum set. The drum instrument parameters that were offered for change were *pitch* and *decay*. Concerning the melody, audience members could change the parameters *pulse width* and *decay* (see Figure 7.5).

4 DATA COLLECTION

4.1 Interaction logs

Interaction data was collected in the form of protocols within the Max console. The following details were logged for every interaction event:

- Time stamp (more specifically, the time in milliseconds elapsed after the syncing event)
- Name of the button or control within the Max patch
- Accumulative number of all interactions (reset for each paradigm)

4.2 Self-report questionnaire

The questionnaire was answered by 18 audience members. There was one minor audience member whose data was excluded due to ethical concerns. One member left out several questions. When the data points are missing, the number of valid answers is reduced to 17. The self-report includes questions about the backgrounds of the audience members as well as their participatory experience, which will be explained in the result section in detail. Most of the questions were collected on a 7-point Likert scale.

4.3 Interviews with audience and musicians

After the concert, an interview with nine audience members was conducted, which translates to roughly one-third of the audience. The interview lasted ca. 45 minutes, and it was semi-structured along the same investigation points as the questionnaire. The interview with the musicians lasted ca. 90 minutes and used the same structure as the audience interview. Both interviews were transcribed and analysed along the main investigation points, at the same time looking into repeating topics, generating language codes, and collecting additional issues and points for the future development of participatory systems. Miles, Huberman and Saldaña (2018, pp. 70–94) were used as a theoretical framework for coding and analysis of the interview data.

5 RESULTS

5.1 Interaction logs

Figure 7.6 shows a cumulative plot of the interactions that happened among the audience for the first 100 seconds of each participation part. As a measurement entity, the **Quantity of Participation** (QoP) is proposed, which indicates the level of participation over time (named 'Button click count', see Figure 7.6). For the first and the third interactions, a steady curve can be observed, whereas the curve for the second interaction only starts after 20 seconds into the interaction. The volumes of the interactions also differ, with the second interaction showing the highest number of total interactions, followed by the third interaction, and, finally, the first interaction with the lowest interaction QoP values.

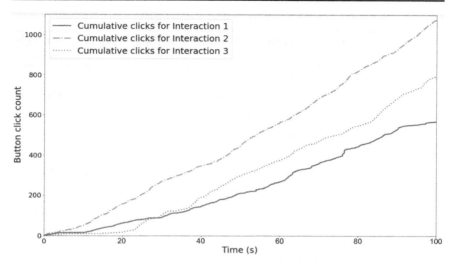

Figure 7.6 Cumulative clicks of the first 100 seconds of the three interactions compared.

5.2 Self-report questionnaires

Background of the audience members. 44.4% of the 18 participants taking part in the survey reported to be female, 56.6% male. Ages ranged from 23 to 73 years, with a mean of 37.7 years. 11 were Norwegian, and the rest came from other European countries. 50% reported they had obtained a Master's degree or higher. 50% reported they had more than five years of musical training; however, the biggest group reported themselves as "music-loving non-musicians". 61.1% reported they practiced music alone, and 50% practiced music in groups. Only 22.2% were versed in digital music production. Based on our observation, the audience wasn't necessarily fans of the band, even if they reported a level of familiarity with the music played at the concert.

Enjoyment. As the survey data shows, audience participants generally enjoyed both the event and the musicians' performance. While the audience participation was rated as still enjoyable, more than the majority (55.6%) of the audience reported that the participation did not enhance their musical experience (see Table 7.1).

Arousal. Almost half the audience reported to be slightly aroused during the participatory parts (44.4%), whereas only 11.1% of the audience felt strongly excited during participation (see Table 7.2).

Human-Computer-Interaction. A majority of the audience members responded they slightly agreed, agreed, or strongly agreed that the interface was easy to use (55.6% combined); however, one-third of the audience only slightly agreed about the software working well for them (33.3%). Enjoyment of the use of the software was rated neutral by one-third of the audience (33.3%), and the software did not hold most people back from dancing during the concert when they felt like it (see Table 7.3).

Table 7.1 Survey results for Enjoyment

Strongly Disagree	Disagree	Slightly Disagree	Neutral	Slightly Agree	Agree	Strongly Agree
I generally enjoyed the event.						
0.0%	0.0%	0.0%	0.0%	11.1%	22.2%	66.7%
I enjoyed the musicians' performance overall.						
0.0%	0.0%	0.0%	0.0%	11.1%	11.1%	77.8%
I enjoyed the audience participation parts.						
0.0%	0.0%	16.7%	11.1%	33.3%	33.3%	5.6%
The participation parts enhanced my musical experience.						
5.6%	27.8%	27.8%	16.7%	0.0%	11.1%	11.1%

Table 7.2 Survey results for Arousal

Strongly Disagree	Disagree	Slightly Disagree	Neutral	Slightly Agree	Agree	Strongly Agree
I felt excited during the audience participation parts.						
5.6%	11.1%	16.7%	11.1%	44.4%	0.0%	11.1%

Table 7.3 Survey results for Human-Computer-Interaction

Strongly Disagree	Disagree	Slightly Disagree	Neutral	Slightly Agree	Agree	Strongly Agree
The interaction software was easy to use.						
0.0%	5.6%	16.7%	22.2%	5.6%	22.2%	27.8%
The interaction software worked well for me.						
5.6%	11.1%	33.3%	22.2%	11.1%	11.1%	5.6%
I enjoyed using the interaction software.						
0.0%	0.0%	16.7%	33.3%	5.6%	27.8%	16.7%
Interacting with my smartphone held me back from dancing when I wanted to.						
16.7%	16.7%	22.2%	11.1%	22.2%	11.1%	0.0%

Effectiveness and Motivation. One-third of the audience members felt neutrally engaged to participate (33.3%), with a positive tendency towards feeling motivated. However, only 11.1% of the audience felt their actions influenced the performance, and they disagreed or strongly disagreed (each 27.8%) about having ownership of the creative work. Lastly, when asked about the performers' reactions to the participatory actions of the audience, the picture is split: 27.8% disagreed or slightly disagreed (5.6%), whereas 22.2% slightly agreed or agreed (16.7%, see Table 7.4).

Table 7.4 Survey results for Effectiveness and Motivation

Strongly Disagree	Disagree	Slightly Disagree	Neutral	Slightly Agree	Agree	Strongly Agree
I felt engaged to participate when it was possible.						
0.0%	0.0%	22.2%	33.3%	16.7%	16.7%	11.1%
I felt that my interactions with the software had an effect on the performance.						
27.8%	11.1%	11.1%	33.3%	5.6%	11.1%	0.0%
I feel the audience has some level of ownership of the creative work.						
5.6%	27.8%	27.8%	16.7%	22.2%	0.0%	0.0%
I felt the performers reacted to what we did as an audience.						
11.1%	27.8%	5.6%	11.1%	22.2%	16.7%	5.6%

Table 7.5 Survey results for Surprise and Connectedness values

Strongly Disagree	Disagree	Slightly Disagree	Neutral	Slightly Agree	Agree	Strongly Agree
I felt that the performance was surprising.						
0.0%	11.1%	11.1%	38.9%	22.2%	5.6%	11.1%
I enjoyed the surprising elements of the performance.						
0.0%	0.0%	11.1%	22.2%	16.7%	22.2%	27.8%
I felt connected to the musicians.						
0.0%	0.0%	11.1%	5.6%	16.7%	33.3%	33.3%
I felt connected to other audience members.						
0.0%	11.1%	22.2%	5.6%	38.9%	11.1%	11.1%
The performance felt like a collaborative act of all people present.						
11.1%	16.7%	5.6%	16.7%	22.2%	16.7%	11.1%

Surprise and Connectedness. Audience members didn't specifically experience the performance as very surprising (38.9% neural, 22.2% slightly agreed). However, 22.2% agreed, and 27.8% strongly agreed to enjoying the surprising elements of the performance. Audience members agreed (33.3%) or strongly agreed (33.3%) to feeling connected to the musicians, and 38.9% agreed to feeling connected to the other audience members. 22.2% slightly agreed to perceiving the performance as a collaborative act of all people present, which is the highest value besides more distributed feedback (see Table 7.5).

Comparing the three paradigms. Interaction 3 was found to be rated the most enjoyable one (66.7%), whereas the result wasn't as clear about the excitement the interactions created. Interaction 3 was also reported as the most exciting (33.3%), followed by Interaction 1 (27.8%), and lastly Interaction 2 (22.2%). It was Interaction 1 that most enhanced the musical

Table 7.6 Survey results for comparison of the three paradigms

Interaction 1	Interaction 2	Interaction 3	None of them	I choose not to say
Which audience participation part did you enjoy the most?				
5.6%	11.1%	66.7%	11.1%	5.6%
Which participation part made you feel most excited?				
27.8%	22.2%	33.3%	11.1%	5.6%
Which participation part enhanced your musical experience the most?				
44.4%	11.1%	22.2%	22.2%	0.0%
Which participation part encouraged you to participate the most?				
11.1%	22.2%	44.4%	16.7%	5.6%
During which participation part did you feel that the musicians reacted most to what the audience was doing?				
16.7%	27.8%	27.8%	27.8%	0.0%

experience of audience members (44.4%), whereas Interaction 3 was rated most encouraging for participation (44.4%). Performer reaction was rated low generally since 27.8% reported that none of the interactions made performers react (see Table 7.6).

5.3 Interviews

Audience interview

Enjoyment. Audience members generally embraced the idea of being able to influence the performed music (*"The concept was really engaging, that you could actually interact and that it worked."*). Some audience members, however, reported they preferred a lean-back experience over the participatory paradigms (*"But . . . when you think about concert experience . . . you just want to listen and enjoy."*).

The clear separation between the participatory parts and the parts where participation wasn't possible pointed to a similar direction and was repeatedly mentioned as a positive characteristic of the concert (*"When the interaction part stopped, it was like a* Kubbi *show, which was really nice. I didn't feel like the interaction overshadowed the fact that we were here to hear your music."*).

Arousal. Being "excited" turned out not to be a very good expression to talk about the experience. It seemed that the interviewed group of audience members felt that it was a bit too personal to share in the recorded interview. However, some audience members reported being excited about the new sections during Interaction 3 (*"Especially when the drum section came, I was really excited."*). In addition, some audience members confirmed a sense of excitement when they experienced common actions (*"And at the parts that everyone was putting it to the top . . . ah we're* *engaging, we agree."*). In that way, excitement could be understood to have a social component that could be related to the later Connectedness values.

HCI. Given the prototypical nature of the created interaction software, many of the comments referring to Human-Computer-Interaction turned out to be critical or suggestive in nature. Connectivity issues were reported multiple times (*"When we scanned the QR code, it took a long time before the page loaded."*). Another issue, it turned out, was the inconvenience of switching between the local server and mobile data (*"If you switch to Snapchat you have to turn on your mobile data and send a snap and turn off and reconnect and that takes two minutes."*). However, some audience members figured out a way to deal with some of the lagging and adapt their behaviour (*"I figured out that I could look at that screen and then it was alright."*).

Several audience members were trying to "hack buttons" in the sense that they tried to acquire full control with many clicks over a specific parameter (*"I didn't have enough time to hear the major difference . . ., so I had to spam the button to keep it low for long enough to notice it."*).

In addition, it was proposed several times that the interactions should be less complex (*"Dumb it down, make it easy."*, *"It was almost as if there were too many options."*). To simplify the participation software, audience members suggested integrating parameters in meta-parameters (*"So the point is that you have one knob that changes a lot of parameters."*).

Effectiveness and Motivation. Some audience members reported issues to determine if it was them who were changing a value (*"It was a little non-transparent."*, *"It's too many chefs on the same menu."*). Several audience members reported losing motivation when this turned out unsuccessful (*"If your experience is that it has no effect you just get disengaged."*).

Suggestions to resolve these issues included a clearer focus on single sections, as well as dividing the controlled parameters into separate groups of audience members (*"So focussing it on sections, like you did, was really cool. And maybe just sharpening that concept a bit more."*, *"I would divide it up to groups, so one group would control this parameter, and one group would control that parameter".*).

Surprise and Connectedness. A specific moment of connectedness was reported during Interaction 2 by one audience member (*"During the second part . . . I felt the most connected with the other people in the audience."*).

Multiple suggestions were made during the interview that could be related to improving the feeling of connectedness (*"More concentrated interaction for a short period of time."*, *"It would be cool to have a longer section of interaction in a way that allowed you guys to respond to the inputs of the audience."*). One audience member suggested preparing the collaboration between the audience and performers before the concert day (*"But if you would do it beforehand, when people buy a ticket, then they get like four bars of a melody to submit."*).

Interestingly, one audience member mentioned that the effect of the participatory setting is that audience members perform closer listening to the single elements of the music to determine subtle changes (*"One very good effect of this is that the audience gets a strengthened listening experience and listening awareness, because you are searching for elements in that sound and you really have to sharpen your listening."*). Seen that way, the focus of the participatory setting would lie rather in the listening itself than the actual musical result of the concert.

Performer interview

Enjoyment. Both performers reported experiencing the participatory parts as enriching. Interestingly, reflections around pleasure-related keywords such as *fun* and *enjoyment* were often connected to themes of novelty *("I have never done something like it before.")*. This might illustrate a fleeting value of audience participation, as the novelty would naturally fade with the repetition of the experience. However, the potential of further developing the experience towards even more enjoyment is highly stressed by the performers, as well as an implication of opening new doors and challenging musicianship in new, creative ways.

Arousal. Further, challenges and memorable experiences of performing alongside the audience were explored with a focus on moments that were experienced as exciting from the perspective of the performers. In improvisatory parts, a sense of habit-breaking was reported *("I feel I kind of disconnected – us drummers love rudiments and all of these muscle memory stuff and usually you can kind of rely on it if you are kind of out of it creatively.")*. However, it is noted that it was challenging to respond musically to the output of the audience participation, indicating a challenge in interpreting the participation to musical material in the moment of performance. This was notably easier with the second paradigm as the participation part was a distinguished musical element, not interacting with the performers' instruments at all. *("Then I get to react to the audience, but the audience is changing like a separate element and then I can answer to that element. So then it becomes that solo interaction, and that's one of my favourite things ever, to listen to phrases and things and repeating if the notes in the arp become long, I switch to more washy stuff, and if it becomes short I dry it up. So, I love that, I could almost go for less control with stuff like that.")*.

HCI. Similar to comments made during the audience interview, direct access to the patches for the audience was appreciated, and the importance of understandable parameters was stressed *("Scan this QR code and you are in and this is amazing. It is about easy access and parameters you can understand.")*. For future iteration of the patches, the idea of developing the interface in a more graphically appealing fashion was suggested *("Make some graphical design that is fun. But there's a point where it still needs to be clear. Because at one point you cannot separate it in the auditive landscape that you are controlling.")*.

Effectiveness and Motivation. There were some doubts mentioned about the audience size and single musical decisions *("Because if 20, 200, 2000 persons are going to vote on what position a filter will be at, then this* *will not always agree with the music, in my head at least. "*). The performers also reported how much attention can be left for listening to the audience's actions while performing the concert (*"The question of headroom always comes down to how well prepared and how good you're feeling on stage. Given that, I would just have that last for 10 minutes and see what happens. "*).

Surprise and Connectedness. Elements of surprise were experienced by the performers (*"So we were playing and I suddenly hear things change, and I thought like "that was cool, did I put that? Wait no, that's the interaction!" . . . I really felt that I wanted to engage with that and respond to it in a musical way. "*). The discussion would often be about what purpose there was in having an interactive part. Regarding connectedness, the question of why audience members participate would be a central theme in the response, and it was stressed that the participation should not feel like a gimmick but rather contribute to the musical composition and the aesthetic experience. (*"You can do this but why should I bother, when there's a show here, I'd rather watch that instead. "*).

6 DISCUSSION

From audience participation to audience interaction. Many participatory concerts are based on the idea of a one-way process, allowing audience members to contribute to a musical performance without allowing performer reaction to feed into the audience interface. However, this reaction of musical performers to the audience's contributions is regarded as critical for a meaningful and sustainable implementation of participatory paradigms. Our data shows that it is essential for audience members to experience a sense of connection to both performers and other audience members, and this could be acknowledged more profoundly. However, most of the participants in our experiment weren't aware of performer reactions that relate to their immediate actions. This should possibly be taken into consideration for future implementations. Consequently, audience participation should be understood rather as an interactive process, allowing two-way interactions between audience members and musical performers.

Individual and collective co-creation roles. The experience that the individual action has a notable influence on the musical performance proved to be a key criterion for audience members to appreciate the participation and stay motivated for future contributions. This is at the same time one of the biggest challenges for participatory settings from a creator's viewpoint. Looking at our audience members' comments and suggestions, there seems to be a great need for an immediate response in the early phases of a participation part. This introductory idea was implemented in the first participation, which turned out to be a successful scenario for audience members to explore before moving into more refined musical contributions such as parameter changes. As suggested by our interview participants, a more elaborate solution allowing to switch between individual and collective modes of listening could be a valid attempt to solve this issue.

Structural composition of the participation parts. Both audience and performer interviews showed that it must be clear at what point it is possible to participate and at what point participation isn't possible. It was also found that shorter, more experimental parts could be better suited for instrumental interactions ('audience-performer solo parts') than longer participations, which should be a more openly constructed interaction space without too much musical structure.

Shared listening. It was found that the possibility of participation itself can lead to a more refined listening experience, given that both the audience and performers want to hear what parameters are being changed. Even if hearing these changes might not always be possible, it can still be seen as a benefit for the co-creative environment. For future implementations, it might be a good idea to take this aspect into consideration and work around sharpened and more focused listening experiences in more depth.

Comparison of the three paradigms. The first paradigm (controlling the background) turned out well-suited for audience members to explore the general concept without interfering with the musical content too much. It seems to fit well with the audience's conventional role, which usually isn't in the center of the musical staging. This is also reflected in the lower QoP values, showing that audience members interacted less. The second paradigm, in contrast, showed the highest QoP values. Audience members seem to interact more when being involved in more central parts (in this case, the central melody). However, this part was experienced as too complex and not understandable enough among most audience members, and only versed musicians engaged and stayed motivated. A better integration in meta-controllers with more understandable names for general audiences without musical backgrounds should be explored. Finally, the third paradigm was experienced as the most experimental and interactive. Here, the QoP values were at a mid-level compared to first and second participations, which seems a desirable level of interaction and hints at a back-and-forth scenario of playing and listening between audience members and performers. Following the performer interview, such parts could be further explored as improvisational settings, and the agency of the audience could be further extended.

Derived from this discussion, it is suggested that future work should include the following aspects:

- **Studies with bigger audiences**: succeeding experiments should include larger audiences for validation of the study results.
- **Movement analysis of audience members**: instead of active participation via a smartphone app, movement data generated by audience members could be used as a contributing input for the performance.
- **Machine-learning as a mediator**: with more audience participation data, it might be interesting to create a machine-learning model that could be used as a more adequate interface between audience and performance.
- **Further exploration of hacking**: hacking culture with its political, ideological, and ethical aspects could be integrated more profoundly

into the concept of audience participation, possibly moving beyond the real-time contribution setting.

- **Audiovisual implementation**: interactive visual elements for future shows should be further explored. This would also relate well to the demoscene and its audiovisual groundings.
- **Learning**: The potential of audience participation for learning purposes became clear during the experiment and could be further explored.

7 CONCLUSION

Three participation paradigms were explored during a chiptune live concert, and results in the categories *Enjoyment, Arousal, Human-Computer-Interaction, Effectiveness and Motivation*, and *Surprise and Connectedness* were presented, finally comparing the three suggested paradigms. The audience and performer interviews gave valuable insights into how the experiences of both groups relate to each other and how the interaction software can be further developed. Finally, it was found that shared, selective listening can be a major benefit of participatory concepts that, in our study, succeeded in the expected musical results during the concert event. Ultimately, chiptune music culture proved well suited as an exploration ground for further participatory studies of how to creatively work together with live audiences.

REFERENCES

Auslander, P. (2021). *In Concert: Performing Musical Persona*. Ann Arbor: University of Michigan Press.

Carlsson, A. (2019). 'The Forgotten Pioneers of Creative Hacking and Social Networking – Introducing the Demoscene', in *Re:live Media Art Histories 2009 Conference Proceedings*, Melbourne: The University of Melbourne & Victorian College of the Arts and Music, pp. 16–20.

Carpenter, L. and Carpenter, R. (1991). 'Reflective Paddles', in *SIGGRAPH*. New York: Association for Computing Machinery.

Collins, K. (2008). *In the Loop: Creativity and Constraint in 8-bit Video Game Audio*. Cambridge: Cambridge University Press.

Collins, K. (2013). *Playing with Sound: A Theory of Interacting with Sound and Music in Video Games*. Cambridge, MA: The MIT Press.

Erdem, C. and Jensenius, A. R. (2020). 'RAW: Exploring Control Structures for Muscle-Based Interaction in Collective Improvisation', in *Proceedings of the International Conference on New Interfaces for Musical Expression*. Birmingham: Birmingham City University, pp. 477–482.

Freeman, J. (2005a). *Glimmer: For Chamber Orchestra and Audience*. PhD thesis. New York: Columbia University.

Freeman, J. (2005b). 'Large Audience Participation, Technology, and Orchestral Performance. *Free Sound*', in *Proceedings of the International Computer Music Association*. Ann Arbor: Michigan Publishing, pp. 757–760.

Gee, J. P. (2005). 'Semiotic Social Spaces and Affinity Spaces: From the Age of Mythology to Today's Schools', in Dave, B. and Tusting, K., eds. *Beyond*

Communities of Practice: Language, Power and Social Context. Cambridge: Cambridge University Press.

Hoedl, O., et al. (2017). 'Design Implications for Technology-Mediated Audience Participation in Live Music', in *Proceeding of the 14th Sound and Music Computing Conference SMC 2017*. Espoo: Aalto University, pp. 28–34.

Hoedl, O., et al. (2020). 'Large-Scale Audience Participation in Live Music Using Smartphones', *Journal of New Music Research*, 49(2). Taylor and Francis, pp. 192–207.

Juslin, P. N. (2019). *Musical Emotions Explained: Unlocking the Secrets of Musical Affect*. Oxford: Oxford University Press.

Lee, S. W. and Freeman, J. (2013). 'Echobo: Audience Participation Using The Mobile Music Instrument', in *Proceedings of the International Conference on New Interfaces for Musical Expression*. Daejeon: Korea Advanced Institute of Science and Technology, pp. 450–455.

Levin, G. (2001). *Dialtones (A Telesymphony) – Mobile Phone Concert*. Linz, Austria: Ars Electronica.

Maibom, H. L. (2020). *Empathy*. New York: Routledge.

Márquez, I. (2014). 'Playing New Music with Old Games: The Chiptune Subculture', *G| A| M| E Games as Art, Media, Entertainment*, 1(3).

Miles, M. B., Huberman, A. M. and Saldaña, J. (2018). *Qualitative Data Analysis: A Methods Sourcebook*. London: Sage.

Mozart, J. C. and Mozart, W. G. (1793). *Anleitung so viel Walzer oder Schleifer, mit zwei Würfeln zu componieren so viel Man Will, ohne musikalisch zu seijn, noch etwas von der Composition zu verstehen*. No place: No publisher.

Polymeropoulou, M. (2019). 'Knowledge of Limitations: Hacking Practices and Creativity Ideologies in Chipmusic', *Volume!*, 16(1), pp. 81–99.

Reid, G. (2018, Springer). 'The Ludomusical Shaping of Identity', *The Computer Games Journal*, 7, pp. 279–290.

Renwick, R. C. (2017). *Topologies for Network Music*. PhD thesis. Belfast: Queen's University Belfast.

Serafin, S., et al. (2019). 'Interaction Topologies in Mobile-Based Situated Networked Music Systems', *Wireless Communications and Mobile Computing*. Volume 2019. Hindawi, pp. 1–9.

Turchet, L., West, T. and Wanderley, M. M. (2020, Springer). 'Touching the Audience: Musical Haptic Wearables for Augmented and Participatory Live Music Performances', *Personal and Ubiquitous Computing*, 25, pp. 749–769.

Weinberg, G. (2005). 'Interconnected Musical Networks: Toward a Theoretical Framework', *Computer Music Journal*, 29(2), pp. 23–39. MIT Press.

Wu, Y., Zhang, L., Bryan-Kinns, N. and Barthet, M. (2017). 'Open Symphony: Creative Participation for Audiences of Live Music Performances'. *IEEE MultiMedia*, 24(1), pp. 48–62.

Xambó, A. and Roma, G. (2020). *Performing Audiences: Composition Strategies for Network Music Using Mobile Phones*. Birmingham: Birmingham City University.

York, A. (2019). 'Transforming Musical Performance: The Audience as Performer', in Hepworth-Sawyer, R., et al., eds. *Innovation in Music: Performance, Production, Technology, and Business*. New York: Routledge.

8

Exploring cell-based dynamic music composition to create non-linear musical works

Samuel Lynch, Helen English, Jon Drummond, and Nathan Scott

1 INTRODUCTION

Dynamic music is a concept that challenges the traditional understanding of music as a linear art form. The term dynamic music, which has varied uses, is used here in a general sense to describe music created with the capability of changing/altering itself based on input variables. While this concept is not a new one, respecting the highly adaptive soundtracks of videogames, the interactivity of musical apps, and the ever-persisting development of computer-automated music generation, dynamic music is still an area that offers much potential for innovation in the overall field of music creation. Moreover, it is seldom discussed purely in the context of composition, leaving room for exploration into how dynamic music practices influence and enhance music creation. This chapter explores dynamic compositional opportunities through a novel approach drawing on the seamless sequencing of short musical segments in variable order. Current experimentation is still in its early stages, but this prototypical work remains to showcase new creative opportunities for composers regarding non-linear musical structures, interactivity, and alterability in music creation. Given the emphasis on composition, this chapter more accurately explores 'Dynamic Composition', a subset of Dynamic Music relating specifically to compositional works designed to vary according to input. The impact of development into dynamic compositional practices could lead to new types of non-linear musical forms, new ways of providing musical works to audiences, and even lead to a democratisation of music composition in which anyone can be afforded agency to dictate how a musical work is arranged.

Dynamic musical forms have existed prior to the advent of digital music composition. However, the emergence of technological advances in digital music production has engendered significant development towards more fluid musical forms of composition. Algorithmic programs replicating compositional processes make dynamic changes to music via the manipulation and/or generation of musical data (Williams et al., 2015a; Williams et al., 2015b; Herremans, Chuan and Chew, 2017; Scirea et al., 2017). Interactive music apps can take similar algorithmic approaches in adjusting

DOI: 10.4324/9781003118817-9

music according to user interaction (Plans, 2017; Stavitskii et al., 2021), or they may instead alter how pre-composed musical sections are layered or sequenced together (Hazzard et al., 2015; Paterson, Toulson and Hepworth-Sawyer, 2019; Sandler et al., 2019). Videogames frequently integrate audio-based methods of sequencing and layering pre-rendered musical material due to a pressing need for higher audio fidelity and musical quality (Plut and Pasquier, 2020, p. 17), and several videogame composers have discussed how they have integrated these principles into their compositional process (Phillips, 2014; Sweet, 2015; Weir, 2017; Whitmore, 2017).

These discussions around dynamic music, however, are often restricted to the context in which the music emerges: videogames integrate dynamic techniques so that the music can adapt to unpredictable narrative progression and avoid excessive repetition (Collins, 2008); algorithmic music research is primarily concerned with the automation of various types of compositional processes; and interactive music research focuses on the design of music systems and how users interact with those systems. There remains an opportunity to explore dynamic music purely in terms of composition such that it may be further distinguished as its own topic within the overall field of music creation. Developments going forward from this exploration will also lead to a broader portfolio of creative opportunities.

This chapter presents a novel approach to composing music that integrates dynamic music methods as a means of arriving at new exploratory compositional outcomes. This approach is defined by its method of composing music as a collection of short 'cells' of audio that can be sequenced together in varying order, allowing for the composition to be dynamically rearranged in real-time. This approach is distinguished by its emphasis on seamless sequencing between audio events, re-constructability, category-based musical structure, and lack of any one pre-defined linear form. Additionally, this approach is not limited to any particular musical style or to any level of audio fidelity.

This research first requires an examination of existing definitions and approaches to dynamic music creation. This forms a foundation from which the research can be contextualised. Secondly, a novel approach towards dynamic music composition is detailed, followed by an analysis of our own creative work and how these techniques have been put into practice. Then follows a discussion about the factors that had a positive and negative impact on musical flow, the influence of this approach on the creative process, and future opportunities within this area. The research shows that dynamic music has much room to evolve, with the potential for music creators to arrive at new types of musical outcomes that expand our understanding (and appreciation) of what a music composition can be.

2 BACKGROUND AND RELATED WORK

2.1 Terminology

It is important to clarify the lexicon around dynamic music. While the term 'dynamic music' is used here to mean music that changes/alters itself according to input, the exact definition and indeed, terminology, used to describe this type of music can be frustratingly elusive and inconsistent when observing this subject from a wider perspective. The most prevalent sources of this disparity derive from classifications of how the music is sourced and how it is directed to change.

How the music is sourced, in this case, refers to what process was used to produce the resulting music. In utilising the term 'procedural music' Karen Collins (2009) draws upon Wooller et al. (2005) and their distinction between *transformational* algorithms and *generative* algorithms in algorithmic music systems to define procedural music as a "composition that evolves in real time according to a specific set of rules or control logics. . . . [T]his can take the form of generative composition or transformational composition, the line between which can be somewhat indistinct" (Collins, 2009, p. 13). To paraphrase Wooller et al. (2005), a generative composition, in this case, is one that is generated from nothing via a certain process, while a transformational composition involves the manipulation of extant musical material at a fundamental level (i.e., transposition, retrograde, etc.) (pp. 116–117). Collins notes that 'transformational' can also apply to musical structure and the addition or subtraction of extant layers. Plut and Pasquier (2020) make a similar distinction in their taxonomy of generative music systems within videogames, in which they clarify that generative music – as opposed to adaptive music – addresses the creation of the musical content itself. However, since they use generative music as a general term, this distinction between 'generative' and 'transformational' is instead made by clarifying 'composition' and 'arrangement' as different types of generative tasks.

Another disparity between terms and definitions of dynamic music lies in what type of input results in changes to the music. The terms commonly utilised in this case include *interactive, adaptive,* and *dynamic,* which are used variably among composers and scholars. The clearest distinction between these terms is again made by Collins (2008), who designates these terms according to either *direct* user input, or *indirect* user input. "*Interactive audio* . . . refers to those sound events that react to the player's direct input. . . . *Adaptive audio,* on the other hand, is sound that reacts to the game states" (p. 4). *Dynamic audio,* then, is used by Collins to encompass both of these terms, thus describing it as "audio that reacts to changes in the gameplay environment or in response to a user" (p. 4). This distinction is commonly referred to by other ludomusicologists and videogame music practitioners (Young, 2012; Summers, 2016; Zdanowicz and Bambrick, 2019; Fritsch and Summers, 2021). However, there are exceptions, as is the case with Phillips (2014) and Sweet (2015), who simply express a preference for the term *interactive* music, along with Paul (2013) and Aska (2017), who indicate that music is part of an interactive system rather than a discrete reactionary component of the game system. With these discrepancies between terminology, definitions of 'dynamic music' are often more general, simply describing music that changes "according to data" (Redhead, 2020) or according to "some kind of input" (Zdanowicz and Bambrick, 2019, pp. 142–143).

2.2 Dynamic music pre-digitisation

Some of the earliest examples of music that could be considered dynamic are the eighteenth-century musical dice games in which individual measures of sheet music were cut out and reordered based on the rolling of dice and the consultation of a provided table (Hedges, 1978). In the twentieth century, many composers began experimenting with indeterminacy in their musical works by providing ambiguous performance directions. Some composers even incorporated indeterminacy into their musical structures, such as Pierre Boulez' *Third Piano Sonata* (1955–1957), Henry Cowell's *Mosaic Quartet* (1962), Stockhausen's' *Klavierstucke XI* (1956), or John Cage's *Winter Music* (1957). In these cases, music was separated into various sections that the performer could move between at their own discretion, thus creating a fluid and non-linear type of work. Included in this period are some interesting examples of film composers who integrated a modular approach to their music writing to overcome issues in synchronising music with film. Music could be composed as a collection of modules that would repeat until a certain cue within the film was reached, enabling an easier means of matching music to visuals before the popularisation of digital tools (Walus, 2011; Schneller, 2012; Müller and Plebuch, 2015). It is important to consider these approaches as they form a fundamental underpinning to more recent developments in dynamic music composition.

2.3 Generative and algorithmic music

With the emergence of digital technology, there are many examples of the use of computers and algorithms to automate various musical tasks, including the generation of fluid and dynamic musical forms. These types of generative systems do not inherently fall under dynamic music since, in many cases, their function is only to produce new musical outcomes, as opposed to real-time musical changes. However, there do remain cases in which algorithmic music systems are designed to exhibit some kind of dynamic behaviour as surveyed by Plut and Pasquier (2020) in the context of videogame music and Williams et al. (2015b) in the context of affective music. Various algorithmic methods have been outlined by Herremans, Chuan, and Chew (2017), who provide a functional taxonomy of algorithmic music systems regarding their processing techniques and their musical functions (e.g., melody, harmony, or rhythm generation). This may include things such as Markov chains, factor oracles, or neural network processing to reconfigure or generate musical data (commonly MIDI). These systems will generally induce alterations to music by changing certain fundamental features of the music, such as pitch height, volume, mode/scale, harmony, rhythm, and so on.

These types of generative/algorithmic approaches towards dynamic music have been used to suit various purposes. For instance, some systems have been designed to exhibit affective intentions by altering various fundamental aspects of generated music, such as pitch, harmony, loudness, timbre, or rhythmic frequency (Scirea et al., 2017; Williams, 2018; Hutchings and McCormack, 2020). Prechtl (2016) designed a system that generates chords that seamlessly vary in dissonance and consonance based on proximity to 'enemies' within a videogame environment while maintaining smooth voice leading. Some interactive music apps also integrate generative methods, such as Brian Eno's Bloom app, which will generate a constant corpus of ambient tones while allowing users to add to these tones by simply touching anywhere on the screen (Milani, 2009). Another app named Endel generates music based on various factors such as user heart rate, weather, light, and motion (Gaskin, 2019). It has been theorised that this type of data-driven music generation could lead to the automatic generation of musical soundtracks (Müller and Driedger, 2012).

As some have noted, however, such algorithmic or computational-based approaches are seldom incorporated in contexts that reach wider audiences due to difficulties in achieving the high audio fidelity that is often more achievable with audio-based approaches (Plut and Pasquier, 2020). There is also the issue of the ambitious interdisciplinary skillsets in both music making and computer programming that are required to achieve dynamic music in this way, something not explored in common music education, which more often favours linear music production (Collins, 2009).

2.4 Dynamic music via audio representations

An alternative approach to engendering changeability to music is to dictate how individual sections of audio that make up a musical work are layered and/or sequenced together to realise dynamic musical structures. Videogame composer Winifred Phillips (2014) describes this type of approach as rendered music, considering that the comprising audio events are complete rendered audio files, while Medina-Gray (2014, 2016, 2019) refers to it as modular in that it is made up of separate components that can be reconfigured. Paterson and Toulson (2018) use the term Interactive Recorded Music to describe the manipulation of recorded or 'printed' music, similar to how DJs shape and remix musical recordings. Techniques that fall under this more audio-based approach have been discussed within the context of music playback apps (Paterson, Toulson and Hepworth-Sawyer, 2019) and interactive art (Redhead, 2018), though there is notably more discussion about these types of audio-based techniques within the context of videogame music. Various videogame composers have talked extensively about the methods and techniques that incorporate recorded music and how they can be used to suit the specific requirements of videogames (Paul, 2013; Phillips, 2014; Sweet, 2015; Whitmore, 2017). Within the context of videogames, these techniques are generally described as being either vertical or horizontal in nature, meaning changes will be made to the layers of music that are sounding simultaneously (vertical) or to how music progresses over time (horizontal) (Kaae, 2008; Phillips, 2014; Medina-Gray, 2014, 2019; Sweet, 2015; Aska, 2017; Zdanowicz and Bambrick, 2019; Plut and Pasquier, 2020).

In the case of vertical methods, musical layers may be added, subtracted, or altered to rapidly change the overall sound and even the perceived level of energy or tension in a game like 'Red Dead Redemption 2' (2018) in which musical layers are added when the player is engaged in combat. This may be referred to as 'vertical layering' (Phillips, 2014) or 'vertical remixing' (Sweet, 2015) when adding or subtracting musical layers, or it may be referred to as 'vertical reorchestration' (Sporka and Valta, 2017), more often when referring to substituting existing layers for alternate ones. This approach has also been used in music apps such as Oiid (oiidAS, 2021) and Bernhoft's Islander app (Bernhoft, 2014), which enables users to adjust the volume and panning of individual musical stems of various songs (Paterson, Toulson and Hepworth-Sawyer, 2019). This idea was taken a step further by the variPlay app format, which allowed musicians to provide multiple versions of their music. Listeners could move between the versions in real-time as the app would adjust the combination of stems that made up the music depending on how users interacted with a 2D touch interface (Paterson, Toulson and Hepworth-Sawyer, 2019).

Horizontal methods, on the other hand, sequence separate musical sections together at designated points to allow music to progress towards new musical ideas altogether. This approach is often regarded as 'horizontal re-sequencing' (Phillips, 2014; Sweet, 2015; Sporka and Valta, 2017) or simply as 'dynamic sequencing' (Berndt, 2019) and is commonly used as a means of transitioning between different linear music loops with varying degrees of seamlessness depending on the required immediacy of the change.

Both vertical and horizontal approaches have their own shortcomings. Vertical approaches are unable to fully display narrative progression on their own, given that they cannot move to new sections of music; they can only change the combination of musical layers within the currently playing section. Horizontal approaches can counter this issue; however, they present difficulties in musicality when attempting to move toward a new musical section in a seamless and timely way. Additionally, the majority of horizontal approaches in videogame music exist just to move towards what is essentially another linear piece of music, though there are notable exceptions, such as Guy Whitmore's music for 'No One Lives Forever' (2000); the iMUSE system in the game 'Monkey Island 2' (1991) (Land and McConnell, 1994); Houge's (2012) cell-based musical approach for game 'Tom Clancy's Endwar'; and the NLN-Player (tot Pannerden et al., 2011). All these examples work at a much more granular level by segmenting music into smaller sections that can be quickly sequenced one after the other rather than moving between looping sections of music. Regardless, videogames will commonly implement both vertical and horizontal methods in their music to overcome their individual shortcomings.

Collins (2008) notes that dynamic music within videogames is used to deal with aspects such as length of gameplay, listener fatigue, and player interactivity, and as such, these aspects unique to videogames influence compositional decisions. Given this influence, the compositional approaches and methods that have been so often discussed by videogame composers and scholars are limited because the techniques emerge as solutions to these inherent issues. While the techniques are innovative, there is a lack of discussion about what this concept of dynamic music means from a purely compositional perspective. Interactive music playback apps arguably suffer a similar issue in that the musical techniques they employ are influenced by their specific purposes. However, their prominent issue lies in the relatively restrictive dynamic techniques they employ, which rarely explore beyond remixing layers of recorded audio.

There remains room for exploration into this area of dynamic music as a compositional opportunity rather than a solution to inherent problems. Investigation into what these audio-based dynamic techniques afford composers in terms of how they may make new types of music could lead to new understandings of musical structure and creation.

3 CELL-BASED DYNAMIC MUSIC COMPOSITION

This section outlines a novel approach to creating a type of dynamic musical work simply referred to here as a dynamic composition, a non-linear musical work comprised of a collection of individual segments of musical audio. This approach is distinguished by several aspects: the seamless sequencing between brief audio events via a method of dovetailing, the construction of a non-linear structure based on the categorical identification of musical cells, and the composition of musical parts with no definitive linear progression.

3.1 Cell-based composition

In exploring how dynamic music methods can lead to new types of non-linear musical works, an approach was developed in which a composition is created as a collection of short 'cells', defined as recorded/rendered segments of musical audio ranging from approximately one to eight measures in length (Figure 8.1). These cells can then be re-sequenced together horizontally in variable order. Since the comprising music, in this case, exists as a collection of separate events, the overall musical work becomes more of a map of potential progressions rather than a singular musical sequence.

A key aspect of these cells is that they represent a complete musical phrase; the term 'phrase' in this case is used to mean 'a substantial musical idea that makes sense on its own and ends with a sense of resolution'. This can take the form of a melodic phrase, a harmonic progression, a

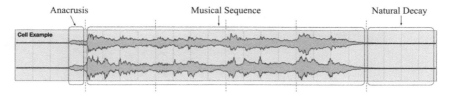

Figure 8.1 Cell Diagram.

percussive groove, or all the above. By composing cells in this way, it is possible to ensure a coherent musical flow between interconnecting musical ideas as an entire idea is heard fully before moving towards another. This approach expands on the 'cut and paste' concept of eighteenth-century dice games in which individual measures were sequenced together (Hedges, 1978); rather than single measures, longer sections of music can be strung together to form musical structures in real-time.

It is important to consider how these individual musical cells interconnect with each other to form a coherent flow of music over time. To do this, we adopt an approach that we refer to as 'dovetailing', a method of overlapping the natural decay of one cell with the beginning of a following cell (Figure 8.2). As noted in section 2.4, this technique has been incorporated in various ways before (tot Pannerden et al., 2011; Houge, 2012; Hulme, 2017). This method of overlapping the ends of cells replaces the need for crossfading since each audio event can be played to completion. For example, if cell '1' contains four measures of music, cell '2' will start playing at the exact moment measure five would begin while cell '1' continues to play out the extra few seconds of natural audio decay. Cell '2' may also contain an anacrusis, in which case the cell will begin a necessary amount of time prior to the beginning of measure five (Figure 8.2).

The main compositional challenge lies in composing cells so that they flow between each other musically and do not clash with each other during their overlap. The rubric developed by Medina-Gray (2014, 2019) provides a method of analysing smoothness between musical modules in videogames by identifying similarities in aspects of meter, timbre, pitch, and volume between them. When composing cells to be similar in these aspects, one could expect there to be minimal clashing when dovetailing. In our own experience, the main cause of clashing came from inconsistent volume and intensity during the overlap points of cells, causing an abruptness to the musical flow. Additionally, main melodic instruments can often clash with themselves when the melodic content of both cells' overlap points is sounded at the same time and by the same instrument, causing an uncanny effect during the transition. Extra care is needed for

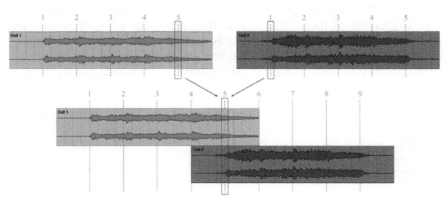

Figure 8.2 Dovetailing.

musical styles employing Western harmonic traditions to ensure that harmonic progression between cells isn't too abrupt. For example, one might maintain relatively sound cadential movement by beginning each cell on a mediant chord (I, iii, or vi) and ending each cell on a dominant or predominant chord (ii, IV, or V). This gets increasingly complicated when dealing with alternate modes and more complicated harmonic movements, such as key changes or secondary dominants.

Further difficulties simply lie in the fact that each cell needs to dovetail effectively with a plethora of other cells, posing limitations on exactly how music is composed in order to avoid all potential clashes. However, by implementing the dovetailing method, clashes are not as noticeable or abrupt as the alternative method of crossfading. There is much more exploration that needs to occur before formulating solid guidelines for avoiding musical clashes while maintaining solid musical coherency. Further, there is plenty of room for exploration into how this approach can be used in more experimental ways, for example, what might occur by randomly sequencing cells of varying keys, tempos, meters, and so on. There are many ways in which this approach could be taken advantage of to lead to new types of musical outcomes.

3.2 Category-based structure – pools of musical identities

The structure and form of dynamic music is a challenging concept, considering traditional linear music derives its form from its pre-defined progression over time. Videogame music generally takes a branching route in which it follows the many possible paths and endings of a game's narrative (Collins, 2008). However, this type of branching structure is defined by the game, not the music itself. In contrast, we propose a framework for determining the non-linear structure of a dynamic composition that can change freely by organising cells into pools representing common musical identities in lieu of definitive sections and narrative points.

- A '**Pool**' refers to a collection of musical cells that may be defined by a common musical identity (Figure 8.3).
- '**Musical identity**' in this case refers to an identifiable musical quality that can be used to wholly describe/categorise that piece of music; this could be an emotional quality such as 'joy' or 'sadness', a musical quality such as 'major' or 'minor', or a general quality such as being a part of section 'A' or 'B'.

This framework of cells organised into pools of various musical identities offers a means of arranging musical ideas non-linearly yet still allows for the creation of a distinctive musical structure based on how constituting cells are organised and categorised. So, rather than a musical structure based on a linear progression of musical sections such as A, B, or Verse, Chorus, etc., music is structured around distinctive pools from which the progression of musical cells can be built. When it comes to playback, cells from these pools are sequenced together in real time to form unique

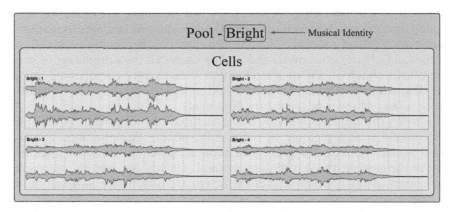

Figure 8.3 Example model of a Pool.

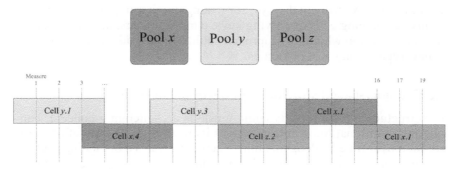

Figure 8.4 Playback of cells from different pools.

progressions of musical ideas. In this sense, the music is dynamically arranged in how it progresses over time (Figure 8.4).

How these pools are categorised and structured is entirely up to the composer. They can be designated varying musical identities such as major, minor, energetic, sombre, and so on. There are many possibilities in how pools are categorised, as well as in how they function. For example, one pool could contain material that only connects material from two other pools together, or several pools could exist within a larger pool. The challenge then becomes, what categories are the cells composed to suit? What is the macro non-linear structure of the composition? And what rules are set in place regarding which cells are allowed to connect together? This framework of dynamic structure is admittedly rather indefinite; however, so long as music composed to be non-linear can be organised and categorised in a categorical manner, it is possible for a composer to formulate a more definitive musical structure despite its non-linearity.

4 PRACTICAL IMPLEMENTATION

This section overviews our own exploration of these approaches to dynamic composition and details how they have been put into practice.

4.1 Creative work

A cell-based dynamic composition can arguably be in any style, but for the purposes of this research, our exploration into the topic draws on Western styles and harmonic traditions. This is so we can utilise the established framework of Western music theory to analyse and communicate our ideas at this developmental stage.

The musical work we created using this cell-based approach is simple in its structure, consisting of only three different pools, each containing four cells of music (Figure 8.5). Each pool is intended to reflect a different level of 'brightness'. This is achieved by composing cells using different scales: those being D major for 'most bright', B minor for 'medium brightness' and D minor for 'dark' or 'least bright'. By structuring the music this way, it can seamlessly alternate between these levels of musical brightness, thus allowing for a changeable progression of musical emotion.

The music within every cell was composed at 120 bpm and contain four measures of music with an additional measure of audio at the beginning and end to leave room for any natural decay and anacruses to allow for effective dovetailing. The melody of each cell was composed to make up a complete melodic phrase that ended somewhat resolutely to ensure musical changes only happened at resolute points and avoid disjunct transitions. Additionally, each cell contained an average of two chords, commonly beginning on tonic or mediant chords and ending on either dominant or pre-dominant chords, with occasional exceptions. Organising harmony in this manner creates conditions for various types of cadential movement to occur, allowing smooth transitions between cells. For example, if each cell ends on a dominant chord and is followed by a cell beginning on a tonic chord, then a perfect cadence will occur as they connect. Or alternatively, the following chord may begin on a VI chord in which a deceptive cadence will occur.

The cells within the 'bright' pool and the 'dark' pool are variations of the same melodies composed in different scales. This has the benefit of maintaining a common musical relationship between cells, sounding like a type of melodic exposition if heard sequentially. An audio-visual demonstration of the work is available online (Lynch, 2023).

4.2 Technology utilised

To demonstrate the dynamic behaviour of the music, we used the program Wwise developed by Audiokinetic, which is an audio middleware

Figure 8.5 Structure of the creative work.

program designed to implement audio and music into videogames. On its own, Wwise can replicate how music may act within a videogame by implementing rendered audio elements and establishing a set of control logics that dictate how these pieces of audio are played back.

There are several other audio middleware programs such as FMOD Studio, CRIWARE ADX, and Elias; however, we chose Wwise due to its extended capability regarding horizontal dynamic techniques. It is capable of dovetailing cells of audio together in a more intuitive manner than alternate programs, which often focus on the vertical. Wwise also provides a more granular level of control over how audio behaves and is organised than other programs, though it does have limitations, as a program designed specifically for use in videogames.

5 DISCUSSION

5.1 Effective musical flow

Factors that have a noticeable impact on the musical flow and seamlessness of musical ideas include effective anacruses, variable instrumentation, and harmonic consideration. When an anacrusis is included in a following cell, it generally sounds more musical and seamless than when there isn't one. But despite this, there is always the possibility that an anacrusis could clash with a previous cell. One method of overcoming this is by altering the instrumentation slightly between every cell. However, this doesn't overcome potential tonal clashes if a following cell is in a different key. But by varying the main instrument that performs the melody, not only is there more interesting variation in how music progresses over time, but it avoids the possibility of the most prominent instrument overlapping with itself and sounding unnatural. This somewhat counters the idea noted by Medina-Gray (2019) that the smoothest connection between cells/modules occurs when all of the same instruments occur before and after the seam/transition. Additionally, in the cases where interconnecting cells result in a coherent cadence, they seem to flow in a more musical way.

Other factors that seem to hinder the flow between cells include the overlapping of material that is too similar and sudden changes in timbral intensity and volume. Since cells from the 'bright' and 'dark' pools are variations of each other, there are occasional issues when similar variations are sequenced together, causing either harmonic or timbral clashes, given that the music is similar but not identical. There are also cases when a cell ending in a higher level of timbral intensity is suddenly followed by a cell that begins at a lower intensity. This occasionally leads to abrupt changes in the overall emotion of the music that makes the transitions obvious. This could potentially be overcome by more careful composition of cells such that they begin and end at a similar dynamic level or by including a short transitory phrase between cells that are too dissimilar.

5.2 Creative process

Applying this approach to our own music-making had interesting effects on the overall compositional process. Rather than thinking of music in terms of linear progression, we were instead able to explore a wider variety of musical ideas that were not explicitly influenced by what came before or after. It forced us to think in terms of semi-complete cellular ideas that needed to act like interconnecting building blocks from which a whole piece of music could be constructed. Even composing musical cells of a similar disposition was interesting when considering how the music might seem totally different if cells were randomly rearranged. It was a liberating experience to think of music as a set of separate locations that one could freely move through. Thinking of ways to make that experience as musical and interesting as possible was a unique challenge.

5.3 Further opportunities

There is much scope for further research into dynamic composition and, indeed, dynamic music as a whole. This research highlights a limited approach to the affordances that exist. The methods outlined thus far emphasise the potential of horizontal methods in dynamic music creation. However, there remains room to explore how these methods could be combined with vertical techniques to create exponentially more dynamic musical behaviour. For instance, cells could contain multiple variations of musical layers, or layers within cells could be added or subtracted to evolve their overall sound. The pools that make up a composition's structure could be greatly expanded; they could contain a larger collection of cells, pools could be nested within each other, pools could have specific functions like containing transition material or material that only plays at the end of the composition, and so on. Our own future work in this area is aimed at assessing the compositional affordances of multiple independently controlled dynamic musical layers and composing these layers such that spontaneous and interesting musical interactions occur.

There is potential for more appropriate technology to be created to enable even more creative ideas to spawn. The most appropriate program for this type of music creation we have been able to discern thus far is Wwise. However, since Wwise is designed specifically for videogames and interactive media, it can be difficult to learn and impractical to use as a purely musical device. There is yet to be a system specifically designed for implementing and playing back audio-based dynamic music.

While this research is still in its very early stages, the seamlessness and approachability of this cell-based compositional approach towards dynamic music is anticipated to lead to the development of further creative approaches. This approach could promote new means of exploring personalised and affective music which is often explored using algorithmic methods (Williams, 2018). Furthermore, music could be designed to be customisable with the potential for use in rehabilitation contexts to help regulate emotion (Agres et al., 2021, p. 6). It also leads to a consideration of how music consumers are able to rearrange the music to suit their own purposes, for instance, adapting music to match the cues of a film or video. This leads towards a concept of democratising the music composition process and providing music to others that they may arrange, construct, or simply explore as they wish, something that becomes increasingly possible with the development of dynamic music creation.

6 CONCLUSION

This chapter has outlined an approach to composing music that can dynamically change by sequencing individual musical ideas, referred to as cells, in varying order. Cells are fully rendered audio files containing a resolute musical phrase ranging from one to eight measures. To seamlessly sequence cells together, the beginning of a following cell will start playing while the initial cell continues to sound out its natural audio decay once its musical phrase is complete. A method of formulating non-linear musical structures is also proposed in which cells are organised into pools representing predetermined musical categories.

In our own exploration of this compositional approach, we found that it was possible to create music that could move to any other section of composed material while maintaining a seamless musical flow. Music, in this sense, was created like a set of building blocks from which many different musical structures could be formed. The work was presented as a distinctive approach to existing methods of cell-based music composition. There remain challenges regarding musical coherency between cells, as inconsistent compositional decisions can cause abrupt and noticeable transitions. But, the ability for the music to be quickly rearranged in real time demonstrates a fascinating opportunity for music to be extremely malleable and for audiences to interact with it. This stage of our research suggests that the development of dynamic music has room to expand compositional outcomes and broaden what it means to both create and experience a musical work.

The outworking of our research presents a new model for dynamic composition and is anticipated to influence future music-making. Further research and exploration into the compositional implications of dynamic music may hold many prospects not only for music creators but for anyone engaging with music, owing to the inherent democratisation of music composition.

REFERENCES

Agres, K. R., Schaefer, R. S., Volk, A., van Hooren, S., Holzapfel, A., Dalla Bella, S., Müller, M., de Witte, M., Herremans, D., Ramirez Melendez, R., Neerincx, M., Ruiz, S., Meredith, D., Dimitriadis, T. and Magee, W. L. (2021). 'Music, Computing, and Health: A Roadmap for the Current and Future Roles of Music Technology for Health Care and Well-Being', *Music & Science*, 4.

Aska, A. (2017). *Introduction to the Study of Video Game Music*. Milwuakee: Lulu Press.

Berndt, A. (2019). 'Adaptive Game Scoring with Ambient Music', in *Music Beyond Airports – Appraising Ambient Music*. Huddersfield: University of Huddersfield Press, pp. 197–226.

Bernhoft. (2014). *Islander. Apple App Store*. Available at: www.hdthreesixty.com/bernhoft-islander.html.

Boulez, P. (1963). *Troisième Sonate, Formant 3 – Constelation-miroir*. Edited and Arranged by Robert Piencikowski (music score). Vienna: Universal Edition.

Cage, J. (1957). *Winter Music* (music score). New York: Edition Peters. EP 6775.

Collins, K. (2008). *Game Sound: An Introduction to the History, Theory, and Practice of Video Game Music and Sound Design*. Cambridge, MA: MIT Press.

Collins, K. (2009). 'An Introduction to Procedural Music in Video Games', *Contemporary Music Review*, 28(1), pp. 5–15.

Cowell, H. (1962). *String Quartet No. 3, Mosaic Quartet* (music score). New York: Associated Music Publishers.

Fritsch, M. and Summers, T. (2021). 'Creating and Programming Game Music: Introduction', in *The Cambridge Companion to Video Game Music Cambridge Companions to Music*. Cambridge: Cambridge University Press, pp. 59–130.

Gaskin, C. (2019). *How Endel and Toro y Moi Are Shaping the Future of Music and Digital Wellness*. digitaltrends. Available at: www.digitaltrends.com/cool-tech/toro-y-moi-and-endel-talk-the-future-of-music-and-digital-wellness/ [Accessed: March 2022].

Hazzard, A., Benford, S., Chamberlain, A. and Greenhalgh, C. (2015). 'Considering Musical Structure in Location-Based Experiences', in *Proceedings of the International Conference on New Interfaces for Musical Expression*. Baton Rogue: Louisiana State University, pp. 378–381.

Hedges, S. A. (1978). 'Dice Music in the Eighteenth Century', *Music & Letters*, 59(2), pp. 180–187.

Herremans, D., Chuan, C.-H. and Chew, E. (2017). 'A Functional Taxonomy of Music Generation Systems', *ACM Computing Surveys (CSUR)*, 50(5), pp. 1–30.

Houge, B. (2012). 'Cell-Based Music Organization in Tom Clancy's End War', in *Demo at the AIIDE 2012 Workshop on Musical Metacreation*. Palo Alto: AAAI Press.

Hulme, Z. (2017). 'Killing-off the Crossfade: Achieving Seamless Transitions with Imbricate Audio', *G| A| M| E Games as Art, Media, Entertainment*, 2(6).

Hutchings, P. E. and McCormack, J. (2020). 'Adaptive Music Composition for Games', *IEEE Transactions on Games*, 12(3), pp. 270–280.

Kaae, J. (2008). 'Theoretical Approaches to Composing Dynamic Music for Video Games', in Collins, K., ed. *From Pac-Man to Pop Music*. London: Routledge, pp. 75–91.

Land, M. Z. and McConnell, P. N. (1994). *Method and Apparatus for Dynamically Composing Music and Sound Effect Using a Computer Entertainment System*. USA Patent no. 5315057 [Online]. Available at: https://patents.google.com/patent/US5315057A/en

Lynch, S. (2023). *Cell-Based Dynamic Music Composition – Cell Playback Demo*. Available at: https://youtu.be/-VZp2WSWihI.

Medina-Gray, E. (2014). *Modular Structure and Function in Early 21 st-Century Video Game Music*. New Haven, CT: Yale University Press.

Medina-Gray, E. (2016). 'Modularity in Video Game Music', in *Ludomusicology: Approaches to Video Game Music*. Shefield: Equinox, pp. 53–72.

Medina-Gray, E. (2019). 'Analyzing Modular Smoothness in Video Game Music', *Music Theory Online*, 25(3).

Milani, M. (2009). *Peter Chilvers: Visual and Tactical Music*. Digimag: Digicult. Available at: https://digicult.it/digimag/issue-048/peter-chilvers-visual-and-tactical-music/ [Accessed: April 2022].

Müller, J. and Plebuch, T. (2015). 'Toward a Prehistory of Film Music: Hans Erdmann's Score for Nosferatu and the Idea of Modular Form', *The Journal of Film Music*, 6(1), p. 31.

Müller, M. and Driedger, J. (2012). 'Data-Driven Sound Track Generation', in *Multimodal Music Processing*. Wadern: Schloss Dagstuhl, pp. 175–193.

oiidAS. (2021). *oiid. Apple App Store*. Available at: https://apps.apple.com/no/app/oiid/id977918521.

Paterson, J. and Toulson, R. (2018). 'Interactive Recorded Music: Past, Present, and Future', in *Audio Engineering Society Convention 145*. New York: Audio Engineering Society.

Paterson, J., Toulson, R. and Hepworth-Sawyer, R. (2019). 'User-Influenced/Machine-Controlled Playback: The variPlay Music App Format for Interactive Recorded Music', *Arts*, 8(3).

Paul, L. J. (2013). 'Droppin' Science: Video Game Audio Breakdown', in Moormann, P., ed. *Music and Game: Perspectives on a Popular Alliance*. Wiesbaden: Springer Fachmedien Wiesbaden, pp. 63–80.

Phillips, W. (2014). *A Composer's Guide to Game Music*. Cambridge, MA: The MIT Press.

Plans, E. (2017). 'Composer in Your Pocket: Procedural Music in Mobile Devices', in *Music on Screen: From Cinema Screens to Touchscreens. Musicology Research* [Online], p. 51.

Plut, C. and Pasquier, P. (2020). 'Generative Music in Video Games: State of the Art, Challenges, and Prospects', *Entertainment Computing*, 33.

Prechtl, A. (2016). *Adaptive Music Generation for Computer Games*. The Open University [Online]. Available at: http://oro.open.ac.uk/45340/ [Accessed: April 2022].

Redhead, T. (2018). 'The Emerging Role of the Dynamic Music Producer', in *Australasian Computer Music Conference 2018: Reflecting Worlds: The Promise and Limitations of Mimesis in Electronic Music*. Perth: Edith Cowan University.

Redhead, T. (2020). *Dynamic Music the Implications of Interactive Technologies on Popular Music Making*. Newcastle, Australia: The University of Newcastle.

Sandler, M., Roure, D. D., Benford, S. and Page, K. (2019). 'Semantic Web Technology for New Experiences Throughout the Music Production-Consumption Chain', in *2019 International Workshop on Multilayer Music Representation and Processing (MMRP)*. New York: IEEE, pp. 49–55.

Schneller, T. (2012). 'Easy to Cut: Modular form in the Film Scores of Bernard Herrmann', *The Journal of Film Music*, 5(1–2), pp. 127–151.

Scirea, M., Togelius, J., Eklund, P. and Risi, S. (2017). 'Affective Evolutionary Music Composition with MetaCompose', *Genetic Programming and Evolvable Machines*, 18(4), pp. 433–465.

Sporka, A. J. and Valta, J. (2017). 'Design and Implementation of a Non-Linear Symphonic Soundtrack of a Video Game', *New Review of Hypermedia and Multimedia*, 23(4), pp. 229–246.

Stavitskii, O., Bulatsev, K., Petrenko, P., Bezugly, D., Gurzhiy, E. and Evgrafov, D. (2021). *System and Method for Creating a Personalized User Environment* [Online]. Available at: https://patft1.uspto.gov/netacgi/nph-Parser?Sect1=PTO1& Sect2=HITOFF&d=PALL&p=1&u=%2Fnetahtml%2FPTO%2Fsrchnum. htm&r=1&f=G&l=50&s1=10948890.PN.&OS=PN/10948890&RS= PN/10948890.

Stockhausen, K. (1956). *Klavierstücke XI* (music score). Vienna: Universal Edition.

Summers, T. (2016). *Understanding Video Game Music*. Cambridge: Cambridge University Press.

Sweet, M. (2015). *Writing Interactive Music for Video Games: A Composer's Guide*. London: Pearson Education.

tot Pannerden, T. V. N., Huiberts, S., Donders, S. and Koch, S. (2011). 'The NLN-Player: A System for Nonlinear Music in Games', in *International Computer Music Conference Proceedings, Huddersfield, UK*. Ann Arbor: Michigan Publishing.

Walus, B. P. (2011). 'Modular Structures in Film Music: The Answer to Synchronization Problems?', *The Journal of Film Music*, 4(2), pp. 125–154.

Weir, P. (2017). 'Sounds of No Man's Sky', in *Game Developer's Conference*. Available at: https://www.gdcvault.com/browse/gdc-17/play/1024067.

Whitmore, G. (2017). 'Game Composer Guy Whitmore Interviewed', Interviewed by Valerio Velardo, *Game Music Town*. Available at: https://www. gamemusictown.com/interview-game-composer-guy-whitmore/

Williams, D. (2018). 'Affectively-Driven Algorithmic Composition (AAC)', in Williams, D. and Lee, N., eds. *Emotion in Video Game Soundtracking*. Cham: Springer International Publishing, pp. 27–38.

Williams, D., Kirke, A., Eaton, J., Miranda, E., Daly, I., Hallowell, J., Roesch, E., Hwang, F. and Nasuto, S. J. (2015a). 'Dynamic Game Soundtrack Generation in Response to a Continuously Varying Emotional Trajectory', in *Audio Engineering Society Conference: 56th International Conference: Audio for Games*. New York: Audio Engineering Society.

Williams, D., Kirke, A., Miranda, E. R., Roesch, E., Daly, I. and Nasuto, S. (2015b). 'Investigating Affect in Algorithmic Composition Systems', *Psychology of Music*, 43(6), pp. 831–854.

Wooller, R., Brown, A., Miranda, E. and Diederich, J. (2005). 'A Framework for Comparison of Process in Algorithmic Music Systems', *Generative Arts Practice*, pp. 109–124.

Young, D. M. (2012). *Adaptive Game Music: The Evolution and Future of Dynamic Music Systems in Video Games*. Ohio University Honors Tutorial College [Online]. Available at: http://rave.ohiolink.edu/etdc/view?acc_ num=ouhonors1340112710 [Accessed: March 2022].

Zdanowicz, G. and Bambrick, S. (2019). *The Game Audio Strategy Guide: A Practical Course*. New York: Routledge.

9

A deepened 'sense of place'

Ecologies of sound and vibration in urban settings and domesticated landscapes

Stefan Östersjö, Jan Berg, and Anders Hultqvist

1 INTRODUCTION

This chapter discusses participative approaches to sound art and how such artistic and scholarly practices may be enhanced through audio technologies. It builds on preliminary results from *Invisible Sounds*, a compositional and ecological sound art project that explores place through the minute detail of sound and vibration, extending beyond the limits of human listening. With participation and artistic action as a method, the project wishes to create a heightened awareness of our environment, seeking to highlight nested ecological spaces through a widened sense of sound and place. By studying structurally meaningful musical and sonic interaction through combining instrumental and sound composition with sensor technologies, the project also aims to expand some of our human understanding of and engagement with the "more-than-human" world.

Paraphrasing Heraclitus, Norbert Wiener (1988), the father of Cybernetics, described Homo sapiens as "nothing but whirlpools in a river of everlasting water. We are not subjects that remain, but patterns that perpetuate themselves" (p. 96). A human being is not a biological entity but is continuous with the world rather than existing independently from it. Bateson (1979, p. 18) goes as far as claiming "that our loss of the sense of aesthetic unity was, quite simply, an epistemological mistake". Martha Senger (2005, p. 5), in turn, points to how

> Bateson demonstrated that the formative imagination is not limited to the subjective sphere but is in fact the transformative matrix of an interdimensional reality; a recursive 'loop' structuring that flows continuously between subject and object, self and world, order and chaos, in rhythmically cohering and complexifying patterns.

In this chapter, we discuss how methods for approaching such "complexifying patterns" can be developed through a participatory engagement with sound. An important origin for this work is found in the ecological sound art practices developed in the Landscape Quartet, a group of four

 DOI: 10.4324/9781003118817-10

sound artists of which the first author has been a member since its found-ing in 2012. As the central point of departure for the group, Bennett Hogg (2015) articulated the shared observation of how

> representations of landscape, and in many respects the aestheticisa-tion of landscape in general, conspire to maintain the separation of culture and nature, of humans from the rest of the planet. Though rep-resentation has played a powerful role in many projects whose ethical grounds are admirable, representation can also stand as an obstacle to other approaches where participation, for instance, might open alter-native models of understanding that are less oppositionally structured. . . . In challenging the separation of culture and nature, the project sought to model possibilities for a more ecosystemic approach to 'acoustic ecology'.
>
> (Hogg, 2015, p. 283)

The four members of the group – Bennett Hogg, Matthew Sansom, Sabine Vogel and Stefan Östersjö – developed artistic methods for direct inter-action with the affordances of a site, often through the use of acoustic instruments. The discovery of aeolian guitar performance – which allows for direct interaction with the phenomenon of wind-induced sound, as known since antiquity in the form of the aeolian harp – is one example of these practices: an acoustic instrument stringed around one or more trees with fishing-line which stretches out several meters from the bridge. The extended strings allow the wind to excite harmonics in the instrument, and Stefan Östersjö has developed techniques for how to interact with the wind and shape these aeolian sounds (Östersjö, 2020). This entails the control of pitch by shifting the tension of the strings and choosing the number of strings actually sounding. Hereby, melodic lines and chordal structures, drawn from the overtone series of each string, can be created (for video examples and further discussion, see Östersjö, 2020; Stefans-dottir and Östersjö, 2022).

In Invisible Sounds, a project created by the composer Anders Hultqvist and Stefan Östersjö, the aeolian guitar became a layer in an exploration of the elements at play in the urban soundscape of the Gothenburg industrial harbour, created for the Gothenburg Art Sounds Festival in 2016. A second instalment was created in Piteå Harbour in September 2018, with Jan Berg in charge of the audio engineering. In addition to the interaction with the wind, we captured ground vibration with an accelerometer and underwater sounds with a hydrophone. In the Gothenburg performance, carried out in collaboration with the engineer Per Sjösten, we also used solar data to create electronic sounds. In Gothenburg, all these layers were mixed live and diffused to a multi-speaker setup on site (Hultqvist and Östersjö, 2019). In the first round of work in Piteå, we instead collected the data for a soundscape composition that premiered at the *Intonal Festival* in Malmö in March 2019. The present chapter draws its central examples from the third iteration of the project, which started out in September 2021 with recordings made at Västra Kajen in Piteå, a marina near the city centre.

These recordings were made using a series of different approaches, going beyond standard formats for surround recording and reproduction, for instance, through the combination of close-up recording of water waves with underwater recordings using hydrophones.

2 BACKGROUND

Much "acoustic ecology" approaches the environment and its sounds in objectifying terms, making recordings of "environmental" sounds as raw material for artworks. Numerous cultural critics have noted that our cultural tendency to objectification is rooted in the empirical sciences, in taxonomic systematisation and measurement, and in the generalised and ubiquitous dominance of sight over sound (Attali, 1985; Ingold, 2011; Voegelin, 2010). The fact that "soundscape" – derived from "landscape" – is often deployed as a synonym for acoustic ecology practice betrays such indebtedness to the visual at the expense of the sonic. Contemporary understandings of the relations of humans to the world's ecosystems have begun to move away from a "preservation" model to one of "sustainability", insisting upon the inescapable interdependence of humans and their environments, a model that sees humans as participant members of a world rather than its users.

Since the 1960s, artists have explored the environment as not only a place for art but as artistic material. Richard Long and Andy Goldsworthy, among many others, make interventional actions in the landscape, while "soundscape" composers, such as Murray Schafer, Hildegard Westerkamp and Barry Truax, have used environmental recordings as raw material for electroacoustic composition. Acoustic ecology has grown from Schafer's "World Soundscape Project", producing remarkable creative, philosophical and political fruit. Current developments in landscape architecture build on acoustic ecology, pointing to its remaining relevance. A recent example is the Soundscape Actions approach developed by Cerwén, Kreutzfeldt and Wingren (2017) built on a design tool in three main categories: Localisation of Functions, reduction of Unwanted Sounds and Introduction of Wanted Sounds.

However, we argue that much acoustic ecology relies on the model of preservation (recording), an ecological strategy that has less and less credence in contemporary environmental debate. Against this is proposed a participative approach to the sonic environment, where performers and audience produce sounds in dialogue with the specific sites explored, in keeping with the more participative and engaged turn in contemporary environmentalist thinking. Such an approach seeks to model a participative approach to environmental sound art that moves beyond preservation, as a model of ecology, towards interaction and cooperation with the environment, participation rather than representation (Hogg, 2015; Östersjö, 2020).

2.1 Ecological perception, engagement, and interaction

The structure and meaning of musical and sonic interaction may be investigated another way as well, from the perspective of ecological psychoacoustics. Ecological approaches to perception presume that the perceiver, in this case, the audience, is an active participant in shaping their sensory experience. Varela, Thompson and Rosch (1991) suggest that a perceiver's physical form and ability to navigate the environment, its embodiment, is that perceiver's primary connection to the environment. Embodied cognition is a powerful theory for understanding musical creativity and has allowed researchers to acquire new knowledge in this field through detailed study of movement as well as the interaction between user and instrument, widely speaking. But, as Lakoff and Johnson noted, the embodied mind is manifest as "either universal or widespread across languages and cultures" (Lakoff and Johnson, 1999, p. 6). Hence, as argued by Tim Rohrer (2007):

> the body of embodied cognitive science is not limited to physiological and neurophysiological influences on mind, nor to that plus the physical body's interactions with the physical world, but also incorporates the experiences of the social and cultural body as well. In other words, it has to take account of the socio-cultural context within which a particular body is situated.
>
> (p. 348)

Embodied music cognition must similarly build on the grounds of how cultural and social conventions are embodied by the individual and form a habitus that shapes the nature of the interaction between user and instrument.

Hence, not only the audience's perceptions shape their experiences but also their knowledge, past experience, values and emotions, which is constitutive of their listening habitus (Becker, 2010). These influences direct attention and determine what is meaningful and significant or not, and as a result, shape the audience's response. Outside the artistic context, we find examples of attention being directed toward invisible sounds, and values, knowledge and vantage skewing perceptions and subsequent active participation with these invisible sounds. One such case is wind turbines, which produce infrasound pulses at frequencies of 1–10Hz (van Kamp and van den Berg, 2018). Despite the overt benefits of sustainable energy, concerns over wind power's noise pollution negatively impact its broader adoption. In conjunction with the musical elements, the Invisible Sounds project aims to recontextualise those frequencies and vibrations by placing them in creative contexts that afford perceivers different, new vantages. Positive experiences in creative contexts influence similar encounters with similar invisible sounds elsewhere.

A musician's interaction with an instrument, in which the kinaesthetic and the proprioceptive perspectives are interwoven, is a manifestation of the transmodal nature of human experience, an all-enveloping experience of the kind that Ingold (2011) refers to as atmospheric. But, at the same time, such interactions between human and instrument can also be isolated and compared. For instance, the nature of a specific instrument can be understood through the specific qualities it brings about in the relation between action and sound. Thelle (2010) suggests that the interaction between human and instrument in contemporary practice can be analysed into the five levels of action-sound-separation, from incorporated to direct, mechanical, analogue electronic and digital electronic. The first three levels, Jensenius (2013) describes as action-sound couplings and the two latter as action-sound relationships: "a tone played on an acoustic piano is based on an action-sound coupling, while a tone played on a digital piano is based on an action-sound relationship" (p. 181).

2.2 Spatial sound recording and reproduction

One of the many challenges in audio recording is to represent spatial features. From the use of the depth dimension in early monophonic recordings to the lateral positioning of sound in 1950s stereophonic recordings, a breakthrough in audio recording has been the possibility of recording more than two channels simultaneously. The term "surround sound" refers to systems, e.g., the 5.1 (ITU, 2022), that are able to create the sensation of being surrounded by sound(s). Both stereophonic and surround sound recording techniques, as well as methods to assess their performance in terms of their spatial quality, are reviewed by Berg (2002). Research in surround sound shows that attributes like naturalness, envelopment and feeling of presence correlate. Hence, audio systems that can capture and reproduce environmental cues will support the perceived presence in that environment (Berg and Rumsey, 2002).

A feature of complex soundscapes containing numerous individual sound sources is that they tend to be perceived as a whole rather than individual sound events (Guastavino et al., 2005). However, standard surround sound systems suffer from the inability to reproduce the sensation of height (if some minor elevation effects are neglected). Also, certain sound source positions are harder to reproduce accurately. The contemporary development in spatial audio is often found in parallel with applications for visual virtual reality, where one of the aims is to attain a perceived congruence between sound and vision. When no visual cues are present, all information about the environment has to be carried by sound only. Rudi (2021) found that for visitor experience in a hybrid virtual environment of a museum exhibition setting, sound is an essential component that contributes to a high degree of perceived realism in the sense of being "there".

Even if immersion is a concept that is subject to discussion due to its dependency on multiple factors, recent work shows that immersion can be assessed as a unidimensional quality (Agrawal et al., 2021). This is a valuable observation when the impact of soundscapes is to be assessed. The physical quality of audio systems today for certain parameters exceeds the limit of human hearing, e.g., the noise floor and the upper frequency limit. Hence, the resolution of the audio system is not the limiting factor, but rather issues that live on the border between art and technology like microphone positioning, signal processing and reproduction system configuration. Over the years, proprietary software solutions for 3D sound have continued to develop where different input formats are used for rendering output signals to headphones and/or loudspeakers. The recording of 3D audio, i.e., the acquisition of acoustical signals, is still under development and mainly builds on elements from surround sound recording (Lee, 2019). Consequently, there is no "off-the-shelf" solution that solves all aspects of 3D recording; research together with artistic needs and/or considerations are still essential.

3 INVISIBLE SOUNDS AT VÄSTRA KAJEN IN PITEÅ

In September 2021, the third instalment of Invisible Sounds started out with Hultqvist, Berg and Östersjö making recordings by Västra Kajen in Piteå, a marina near the city centre. Recordings were made using a series of different approaches, going beyond standardised formats for surround reproduction, for instance, through the use of additional close-up recording of water sounds while simultaneously recording underwater using hydrophones.

One important factor of a recording is the perception of space. In the case of audio recording and playback, we must primarily consider two types of spaces: the space in which a recording is carried out and (potentially) the space where a recording is reproduced. Regarding the latter, e.g., in the case of an art gallery installation, the acoustical properties of the space can be retrieved, understood and to some extent controlled, whereas a CD recording may be reproduced in any space outside the artists' control. The space of the recording context, however, can often be controlled and is normally given significant attention in almost any audio production as it provides several essential cues for the listener, e.g., the proportions of the recorded space and the sensation of being present in this place (Berg and Rumsey, 2000). In the current project, several recording techniques were used to capture the soundscape in its full complexity. These techniques differ in microphone spacing and directional characteristics, resulting in combinations of interaural differences in time (ITD) and level (ILD), giving rise to differently perceived spatial qualities (Berg and Rumsey, 2002).

Another aspect of spatial sound cues concerns the spatial distribution of sound sources in the mix. Techniques for creating spatial distribution have been used in stereophonic recordings since its introduction and have subsequently been developed into different spatial reproduction formats that add further possibilities. As discussed by Mitchell (1998), building on observations made at the time when 5.1 surround sound was becoming more widespread, when setting up recordings and mixes, it is necessary to consider, e.g., whether the listeners should be situated as an audience in a traditional concert or as someone within the performance, being surrounded by its sound sources. In the current project, both approaches have been used, depending on the venue of the performance.

As the project aimed to "visualise" sounds that are either not acoustically present or not normally the focus of attention, it follows that there was no obvious reality to be used as a reference for the recordings; rather, the end result combined many different materials, recorded using various types of transducers, picking up sound travelling through air, water and solid matter. Recall Anderson's (2007) observation of how reality is not a recording, and a recording is not a reality. The current project utilised complete sessions where all sounds were recorded simultaneously, as well as performers overdubbing their contributions to previously recorded material. But the third instalment also expanded the interaction between human and environment in the recording situation by inviting members of the Norrbotten NEO chamber ensemble to explore the sound captured through these different recording techniques and to engage in site-specific performance. In audio example 1, we hear how their violinist, Lovisa Ehrenkrona, weaves the sound of a powerboat into a solo improvisation on the site.[1]

As previously mentioned, microphone arrays for spatial recording were used to capture the outdoor space air-borne sounds. These mainly picked up both naturally occurring sounds, outside the control of the authors or the invited artists, generated by nature or man-made. These were complemented by sensors in the form of transducers able to acquire vibrations in water, a hydrophone, and, in solid matter, an accelerometer. The hydrophone is able to pick up activity that often is inaudible above the surface of water but clearly detectable in water. The most prominent sounds are from propulsion systems (engines/motors) and pumps, which reflect and emphasise human activity within the environment. The accelerometer is attached to an object and thus susceptible to vibrations of the object, which may be any solid item, including organic material such as trees.

The importance of having relevant auditory cues as a performer was confirmed by Berg, Johannesson and Nykänen (2022) in the context of monitor mixing for stage performances. In the current project, the musicians were provided with headphones connected to an auxiliary send where selected microphone signals were fed back to them. Each musician had an individual master volume control. To record each musician, dedicated microphones were added. There were two spaced microphones per instrument with unidirectional characteristics to capture spatial cues from the single instrument as well as to enable a necessary level difference between the instrument and the environment.

Recordings of this kind have to start with a site-specific approach, i.e., to make suitable reconnaissance prior to the recording to gauge the particulars of the venue and to adjust equipment and planned workflow accordingly. Also, an outdoor recording brings additional challenges for the recording engineer, who must be able to deal with varying and unpredictable weather conditions like wind and rain in combination with transport of equipment to possibly remote places with limited access to mains power supply. In the current project, the venue was at the marina's camping ground close to the city, where mains were easily available and windscreens were used to protect microphones from picking up wind noise.

As one of the key features of the current project was to acquire and emphasise sounds that are not normally perceived by humans, the use of non-airborne vibrations is particularly interesting. With the use of sensors, we were able to capture sound inside trees by the water. In audio example 2, the listener may zoom into these sounds, starting out with the distant representation of the sawmill just across the water; a listener may experience a sound giving the impression of water rising in the tree in the evening.

The hydrophone was submerged in the water approximately two metres from the quay at a depth of one metre. The idea was to pick up as much activity resulting in water-borne vibrations as possible. Earlier tests showed that not only boat sounds but also different sorts of mechanically induced sounds, e.g., from machinery, travelled well through water. The sound of approaching vessels received a more complex character when hydrophone sounds were added to the normal air-borne sounds. As sounds travel faster in water compared with its velocity in air, delay effects were noted. Underwater sound lacks a lot of the normal ambience that could be heard through a standard microphone in air, which, as one result, created a sensation of being confined in an environment where the occurring sounds became more focussed and protruding.

An accelerometer is sensitive to the structural vibrations of the object it is attached to. As with the hydrophone, it emphasises other sounds than a standard microphone in air, which makes the accelerometer and its attached object possible to use as an acoustic probe into the object itself as well as into anything that the object is mechanically connected to. In an earlier recording situated at *Piteå Port*, an accelerometer was attached to a ladder partly encapsulated in the quayside. The accelerometer picked up numerous sounds of the sea but filtered through the concrete structure of the quay. In the current project, the accelerometer was attached to a tree close to the edge of the water, where some tree roots reached into the water. The output of the accelerometer contained waves hitting the tree, branches creaking and cracking and leaves caught by the wind, but also ambient sounds like bird song and the noise from the sawmill across the water. Also, as mentioned previously, fluid-like noise was recorded, which we interpreted as water moving through the tree. From these recordings, one observation is that sensors in the form of transducers like the hydrophone and the accelerometer, in addition to the sound sources they pick up, also affect how the space of the recording is perceived. The use of transducers that allow for a broader input of signals conveying a variety of spatial cues when combined with the recording sessions' different approaches (outdoor, overdubbing, studio) and reproduction systems that excite the spatial dimensions to a fuller degree gives the composition a finer granularity and a higher complexity, which in its turn contribute to the sense of a "whole", as noted by Guastavino et al. (2004).

In the on-site recordings with members of Norrbotten NEO, the aeolian guitar, performed by Östersjö, was also an important vehicle for the interaction. An instance of such performative explorations of place can be heard in audio example 3, which captures an improvisation with two (overdubbed) bass clarinets and the aeolian guitar. This track provides an example of how, in the project, several different recording sessions were executed, adding and combining environmental and ambient sound with musical instruments, finally adding a solo cello improvisation. The first session recorded sounds naturally occurring at the venue, arriving via air, water and solids through microphones and sensors. The next session extended this by adding the aeolian guitar and the violin interacting with the environment while continuing to record the environment through all microphones and sensors. This session was subsequently used in new sessions, still on-site, where flute and bass clarinet (one at a time) were added to the previous through overdubbing. This meant that the musicians had to listen to and interact with the previous takes while still being in the outdoor environment.

The final recording session was carried out with the entire Norrbotten NEO ensemble in a recording studio at LTU Piteå. Prior to this session, Anders Hultqvist created a score with mainly through-composed materials for the entire group related to selected sound files from the sessions at Västra Kajen. The compositional process, enacting a series of loops (with reference to Bateson) between the inner hearing of the writing process and the concrete listening to the pre-recorded sound from the site, also displaying the nested character of such an engagement with composition and soundscape listening. The written and improvised material is created in a sort of double mirroring: the written material takes as its point of departure both the raw sound recordings and the musicians' on-site improvisational reactions to the sounding *milieu*.

The score and the associated sound files defined the situation in which the ensemble performed, but in addition to recordings of the scored materials, improvisations to selected sound files were recorded, both with individual performers and the entire group. The ensemble was recorded through both individual microphones as well as a main microphone setup. The pre-recorded sound files were played back to the ensemble through headphones. The sound files influenced the musician's interpretation of the written score, just as it had been a more direct inspiration for some of the compositional material. Similarities and contrasts between details of the recorded *milieu* and the written material were put into the score in different constellations. These various outcomes are then evaluated from different, also aesthetic perspectives for inclusion in the next step of composition/improvisation. A third musical level then becomes actualised when the ensemble has gotten familiar both with the score, and some of the original soundscape recordings, and are able to improvise with these soundscapes. A sounding geography is created where detailed acoustic events are put into a clear relief but also in relation to, and included in, larger ambient-sounding *milieus*.

An example of such working within, and at the same time creating, these nested loops can be heard in audio example 4. In this preliminary edit, a scored material (section K to L as found in Figure 9.1) was recorded in the studio, with field-recording materials played back as stimuli to the musicians. Starting at section L, another layer is added, in which a new set of interactions was created between an aeolian guitar recording, fed back through a 10-string guitar using a transducer. This created a new nested loop, where Östersjö's 10-string guitar became a resonant object, through which the aeolian guitar from the site was brought back into the studio.

Figure 9.1 Excerpt from Anders Hultqvist's score to *Sounds in Water and Trees*, p. 14.

The first artistic output from the third set of recordings will be an album, mixed in Dolby Atmos, in which music composed for and recorded by Norrbotten NEO will be integrated with the many different representations of place which Invisible Sounds enables, in the manner outlined previously.[2] When the music for the album is completed, the aim is to produce a version that combines a fixed media installation with a live performance by the ensemble. This will give us an opportunity to add at least one more dimension by having the musicians physically move around the room in relation to the speaker installations. By playing with and against the sounding material in new constellations, a fluid conversation arises with the content and position of the different speakers in the spatial design, expanding the experience/understanding of the given soundscape.

4 DISCUSSION AND CONCLUSIONS

An ambition of the Invisible Sounds project is to make visible a widened structural and deepened soundscape of living and "material" things. Not to, in the more traditional way, make artistic artefacts that are based on recorded environmental soundings, but to create sonic landscapes that form these material layers lived by humans, but not that only. An ongoing project combining artistic and technical approaches with very similar aims is Natasha Barrett's research "Reconfiguring The Landscape", which seeks to combine electroacoustic composition with analysis of high-resolution ambisonic recordings of the soundscape (Barrett, 2020). Barrett's project develops a method built on analysis, an approach different from that of Invisible Sounds, and also does not explore participation as does Invisible Sounds. However, we see great potential for cross-fertilisation of findings and method development in the two still ongoing projects.

By including deeper sonic layers and memories in realising, writing and excavating an enlarged and Heightened Sense of Place, a widened sense of nested spaces and places is sought through connecting dots in an enlarged network. As Stengers and Debaise (2017) observe in Parse Journal on Speculation: "Nothing of what is real is self-sufficient. There is no such thing as an isolated fact" – and they continue by citing Whitehead: "Connectedness is of the essence of all things and all types. It is of the essence of types that they be connected. Abstraction from connectedness involves the omission of the essential factor in the fact considered" (2017, p. 15). From this perspective, thinking is always a matter of thinking through the *milieu*, through the many affordances of tools, objects and instruments, and also through the culturally and sociologically grounded nature of our perception (Östersjö, 2020).

Tim Ingold (2011), in his critique of the notion of the soundscape, makes some observations that allow for a deepened understanding of the interaction between humans, nature and culture, such as expressed in the eco-systemic approach of the Invisible Sounds project. He argues that while landscape encompasses all forms of sensorial experience, the technologically manifested concept of the soundscape only becomes possible through the mediation of recording and playback technologies, typically reproduced in a dark or darkened room, in which the listener is deprived of other sensory input. However, according to Ingold's integrated understanding of subject and object, the sensorial experience of sound in a landscape cannot be reduced to the domain of hearing:

> When we look around on a fine day, we see a landscape bathed in sunlight, not a lightscape. Likewise, listening to our surroundings, we do not hear a soundscape. For sound, I would argue, is not the object but the medium of our perception. It is what we hear *in*. Similarly, we do not see light but see *in* it.
>
> (Ingold, 2011, p. 138)

Ingold's argument builds on a more radical understanding of the situated nature of cognition, breaking down the confines between subject and object. Along the same lines, Borgo (2012) argues that human experience is conditioned not only by the "physical and social specifics" of a given environment but also "by their perceived 'place' in a social process" (pp. 206–207).

> The sight, hearing and touch of things are grounded in the experience, respectively, of light, sound and feeling. And if the former force[s] us to attend to the surfaces of things, the latter, by contrast, redirect our attention to the medium in which things take shape and in which they may also be dissolved. Rather than thinking of ourselves only as observers, picking our way around the objects lying about on the ground of a ready-formed world, we must imagine ourselves in the first place as participants, each immersed with the whole of our being in the currents of a world-in-formation: in the sunlight we see in, the rain we hear in and the wind we feel in. Participation is not opposed to observation but is a condition for it, just as light is a condition for seeing things, sound for hearing them, and feeling for touching them.
>
> (Ingold, 2011, p. 129)

Ingold proposes an atmospheric perspective on human existence, in which we participate in what he calls a weather-world "under the great dome of the sky" (2011, p. 132). Through such a widened ecological understanding of human experience, we must account for our interaction with the environment not as mere inscriptions on the body but as evolving relations. Hence, Ingold (2011, p. 87) argues that "nature is not a surface of materiality upon which human history is inscribed; rather history is the process wherein both people and their environments are continually bringing each other into being".

The Invisible Sounds project aims to enable transmodal experiences of a site through the creation of situations that afford sensation-coupling. But how can similar immersive experiences of place be created in a concert hall, theatre, or gallery space? Marc Leman (2008) identifies possibilities for the development of "embodied music mediation technology" (p. 235), arguing that "in many cases music mediation technology is effective when it becomes invisible" (p. 237). However, the Invisible Sounds project seeks rather to achieve the opposite; by engaging in technologies that are *not* transparent – like the use of an accelerometer to capture sonorities inside a tree – we seek to create augmented experience. However, drawing on Leman's assertion that perspectives from embodied music cognition may inform the development of embodied music mediation technology, we propose that immersive technologies may engender similarly transmodal experiences in which both performers and audiences may be swept up into the currents of the elements. But such experience, we believe, is dependent on similarly nested loops as described in the encounters between composer-percept-score in the writing situation and the more complex performative situation with the entire ensemble in the recording studio, in which they may find themselves again listening to a site-specific recording in which they were once themselves performing, and in the now, interacting as an ensemble in response to the composer's score, a pre-recorded sound file, in a listening situation combining the micro-sonic listening (Östersjö, 2020) to the track in the headphones, and the ensemble, sounding the acoustics of the recording studio.

Beyond the outcomes of such artistic experimentation, it is our hope that the developments of participative methods for a multimodal experience of urban and domesticated soundscapes, expanded by technology, may contribute to the development of interdisciplinary approaches, combining landscape architecture and soundscape studies with performance and composition.

NOTES

1 All audio files referenced in this chapter are found on the publisher's web page dedicated to the present publication, see link in the front of the book.
2 The album, including a mix in Dolby Atmos, is found following this link https://footprintrecords.com/product/sounds-by-water-and-trees/

REFERENCES

Agrawal, S., Bech, S., Bærentsen, K., De Moor, K. and Forchhammer, S. (2021). 'Method for Subjective Assessment of Immersion in Audiovisual Experiences', *Journal of the Audio Engineering Society*, 69(9), pp. 656–671.

Anderson, J. (2007). 'Reality Is Not a Recording/a Recording Is Not Reality', *The Journal of the Acoustical Society of America*, 122, pp. 2945–2945.

Attali, J. (1985). *Noise: The Political Economy of Music*. Minneapolis: University of Minnesota Press.

Barrett, N. (2020). 'Deepening Presence: Probing the Hidden Artefacts of Everyday Soundscapes', in *Proceedings of Audio Mostly (AM'20)*. New York: ACM, pp. 77–84. https://doi.org/10.1145/3411109.3411120.

Bateson, G. (1979). *Mind and Nature, A Necessary Unity*. New York: E.P. Dutton.

Becker, J. (2010). 'Exploring the Habitus of Listening', in Juslin, P. and Sloboda, J., eds. *Handbook of Music and Emotion: Theory, Research, Applications*. Oxford: Oxford University Press, pp. 127–157.

Berg, J., Johannesson, T. and Nykänen, A. (2022). 'Mixing for In-Ear Monitors: Understanding the Work of Monitor Mixing Engineers', in *AES 152nd Convention*. Audio Engineering Society. Available at: https://www.aes.org/e-lib/browse.cfm?elib=21718

Berg, J. and Rumsey, F. (2000). 'Correlation Between Emotive, Descriptive and Naturalness Attributes in Subjective Data Relating to Spatial Sound Reproduction', in *Presented at AES 109th Convention*, 25–22 September, Los Angeles. Paper Number 5206. Audio Engineering Society. Available at: https://www.aes.org/e-lib/browse.cfm?elib=9132

Berg, J. and Rumsey, F. (2002). 'Validity of Selected Spatial Attributes in the Evaluation of 5-Channel Microphone Techniques', in *AES 112th Convention*,

10–13 May, Munich, Germany. Paper Number 5593. Audio Engineering Society. Available at: https://www.aes.org/e-lib/browse.cfm?elib=11338

Borgo, D. (2012). "Embodied, Situated and Distributed Musicianship." In Brown, A. R., ed. *Sound Musicianship: Understanding the Crafts of Music*, Newcastle upon Tyne: Cambridge Scholars Publishing, pp. 202–213.

Cerwén, G., Kreutzfeldt, J. and Wingren, C. (2017). 'Soundscape Actions: A Tool for Noise Treatment Based on Three Workshops in Landscape Architecture', *Frontiers of Architectural Research*, 6, pp. 504–518.

Debaise, D. and Stengers, I. (2017). 'The Insistence of Possibles: Towards a Speculative Pragmatism', in *Parse Journal No.7*. Gothenburg: University of Gothenburg.

Guastavino, C., Katz, B., Polack, J.-D., Levitin, D. and Dubois, D. (2005). 'Ecological Validity of Soundscape Reproduction', *Acta Acustica United with Acustica*, 91(2), pp. 333–341.

Hogg, B. (2015). 'Healing the Cut: Music, Landscape, Nature, Culture', *Contemporary Music Review*, 34(4), pp. 281–302.

Hultqvist, A. and Östersjö, S. (2019, December 18). 'Invisible Sounds in a Nested Ecological Space', "Sonic Argumentation I," special issue, *Seismograf Journal*. Available at: https://seismograf.org/fokus/sonicargumentation-i/hultqvist_ostersjo [Accessed: 28 February 2022].

Ingold, T. (2011). *Being Alive: Essays on Movement, Knowledge and Description*. Abingdon: Routledge.

ITU. (2022). *Multichannel stereophonic sound system with and without accompanying picture*. Recommendation ITU-R BS.775-4. International Telecommunication Union.

Jensenius, A. R. (2013). 'An Action – Sound Approach to Teaching Interactive Music', *Organised Sound*, 18(2), pp. 178–189.

Lakoff, G. and Johnson, M. (1999). *Philosophy in the Flesh: The Embodied Mind and Its Challenge to Western Thought*. New York: Basic Books.

Lee, H. (2019). "http://www.aes.org/e-lib/browse.cfm?elib=19883" Capturing 360° Audio Using an Equal Segment Microphone Array (ESMA), *Journal of Audio Engineering Society*, 67(1/2), pp. 13–26.

Leman, M. (2008). *Embodied Music Cognition and Mediation Technology*. Cambridge, MA: MIT Press.

Mitchell, D. (1998). 'Toward an Aesthetic in Mixing for Multichannel Music Presentation', in *AES 105th Convention*, 26–29 September, San Francisco. Paper Number 4818. Audio Engineering Society. Available at: https://www.aes.org/e-lib/browse.cfm?elib=8362

Östersjö, S. (2020). *Listening to the Other*. Leuven: Leuven University Press.

Rohrer, T. (2007). 'The Body in Space: Dimensions of Embodiment', in Ziemke, T., Zlatev, J. and Frank, R. M., eds. *Body, Language and Mind*. Berlin: Mouton de Gruyter, pp. 339–378.

Rudi, J. (2021). 'Designing Soundscapes for Presence in Virtual Reality Exhibitions: A Study of Visitor Experiences', *Visitor Studies*, 24(2), pp. 121–136. https://doi.org/10.1080/10645578.2021.1907151.

Senger, M. (2005). 'G2 Institute for Integral Aesthetics, Aesthetic Phase Shift – Lecture and Event Series', *Academia.edu*. Available at: www.academia.edu/39088613/The_Coming_Re_Formation.

Stefansdottir, H. S. and Östersjö, S. (2022). 'Listening and Mediation: Of Agency and Performative Responsivity in Ecological Sound Art Practices', *Phenomenology & Practice*, 17(1), pp. 116–136. https://doi.org/10.29173/pandpr29464.

Thelle, N. J. W. (2010). *Making Sensors Make Sense: Challenges in the Development of Digital Musical Instruments*. MA dissertation. Oslo: University of Oslo.

van Kamp, I.,and van den Berg, F. (2018).'Health effects related to wind turbine sound, including low-frequency sound and infrasound'. *Acoustics Australia*, 46(1), pp. 31–57.

Varela, F., J., Thompson, E., and Rosch, E. (1991). *The Embodied Mind: Cognitive Science and Human Experience*. Cambridge, MA: MIT Press.

Voegelin, S. (2010). *Listening to Noise and Silence: Towards a Philosophy of Sound Art*. New York: Continuum Books.

Wiener, N. (1988). *The Human Use of Human Beings: Cybernetics and Society*. Boston: Da Capo Press.

Part two

Technology and innovation

10

"Yesterday's charm, today's precision"

Martin B. Kantola and the design of a new 'classic' microphone (Nordic Audio Labs NU-100K)

Antti Sakari Saario

INTRODUCTION

This paper investigates innovation in transducer design by the sound engineer, inventor and designer Martin B. Kantola, who, in the words of the late Bruce Swedien, is "the microphone guru of life" and "knows more about microphones than any guy I have ever met" (Swedien, 2018, 2009). Kantola's boutique microphone business Nordic Audio Labs (NAL), is based in the village of Karperö in the Swedish-speaking part of Finland, where all the microphones are hand-built in-house by Kantola and his team of family members plus one employee.

Drawing primarily from new interviews with Kantola and conversations from a 2012 site visit to NAL, the paper is supported by secondary research into related historical and studio production contexts, available microphone user and designer comments, and other existing materials and exchanges relating to Kantola's work.

Due to the fundamental role of transducers in recorded sound production, the affordances and constraints of specific models shape the recorded sound with an immediate and direct effect, affecting and shaping the whole production process. More so than with loudspeakers, microphone choices tend to be wedded to 'classic' models and their contemporary reinterpretations or 'clones'. Although primarily known for its high-end versions of the venerable Neumann U 47, the company refocused its business model in 2016 around a single new microphone model – the NU-100K (see Figure 10.1) – with the aim to produce "a new classic" (Kantola, 2020), a 'new type' (Nordic Audio Labs, 2019) and a 'new class' of a microphone (Kantola, 2022a).

Kantola's 30+ year pursuit of producing a 'new classic' maps a Deleuzian enterprise of 'de-designing' a classic microphone: the Neumann U 47. This enterprise takes the form of an affective-transductive quest initiated by his encounter with a 1953 vintage Neumann U 47. Crucially, the U 47 is not seen as a definitive point of origin or a destination but as being "in the middle" (Deleuze and Guattari, 1988), one node in an open 'map' or a network of transducer innovation potentiality. Kantola explores and 'charts

DOI: 10.4324/9781003118817-12

Figure 10.1   Nordic Audio Labs NU-100K large diaphragm condenser microphone.

open' contingent, unpredictable and 'productive' design options (Martin and Kamberelis, 2013), challenging the notion of a classic microphone and that of a classic sound, opening them to be accessible and transmutable and arguably mouldable by the end user. The paper presents Kantola's design thinking being one of nomadic affectivity, where the affective dimension of the transduction and the affinity of transduction to the sonic experience are valued over the technical correctness or accuracy of transduction (Braidotti, 2005).

MARTIN KANTOLA AND NORDIC AUDIO LABS

Kantola worked as a full-time professional sound engineer during 1990–2011 with notable work including recording of the 'legendary' acoustic performances by Björk with the Brodsky Quartet at Union Chapel, London, in 1999, released on *Family* Tree (2002). He is particularly known for productions that draw from a meticulous approach to microphone technique, and there is a clear parallel and a genealogy in terms of skill set and

Figure 10.2 Nordic Audio Labs control room.

Figure 10.3 Nordic Audio Labs workshop area.

approach to those of American recording engineers and producers Bruce Swedien (1934–2020) and Al Schmitt (1930–2021), both of whom Kantola has worked with.

The purpose-built NAL studio complex (see Figures 10.2 and 10.3) was established in 1995 (Luukkanen, 2011), with the facility functioning as a hybrid space offering multiple modalities to Kantola's operation as a recording studio, RND lab and fully-fledged manufacturing site. Being situated adjacent to the Kantola family home in a quiet rural location enables him to work with minimal distractions, retain "long thoughts" (Kantola, 2022a) and 'stay' with a single focused idea that he would have upon awaking throughout the day, thus facilitating "deep work" (Newport, 2016).

Favoured by artists and engineers in various production contexts from orchestral recording to contemporary pop production, famous users and owners of NAL microphones include Björk, James Hetfield, Michael Jackson, Jennifer Lopez, Max Martin, Al Schmitt and Bruce Swedien.

SWEDIEN, BJÖRK AND THE NU-47 AFFECT

Since meeting in 1992, Swedien and Kantola forged a lifelong creative partnership governed by their "ears first" and "music first" mottos (Swedien in Gearspace, 2021). Kantola's designs are notably informed by the values he shares with Swedien in terms of listening, engineering and desired sonics (e.g., foregrounding of recording process, microphone choice and technique; simultaneous use of close and distant miking techniques; use of mono-stereo hybrid 'sound objects'; harnessing of available acoustics and 'acoustic support'; quality of stereophonic image and the importance of spectral, dynamic and spatial contrasts and details). During 2007–2010, Kantola taught regularly (three to four visits per year) at the "In The Studio With Bruce Swedien" (Swedien, 2016) residential recording workshops at the West Viking Studios, Florida, USA, where participating 'students' ranged from amateur and semi-professionals to multiple Grammy awarded engineers (Kantola, 2022a) (see Figure 10.4).

Swedien provided input and feedback on the early designs and prototypes of the NU-47. He commented how "on a certain vocal it will make you cry" (Swedien, 2018) and how all of his clients "went bananas" on hearing their "voice through that mic for the first time" (Swedien in Grönholm, 2010).

Figure 10.4 Kantola at West Viking Studios with Bruce Swedien, Al Schmitt and Ed Cherney (L to R).

Björk, who absolutely loves the sound of this incredible new microphone. She told us that, 'It captures both the small and the big sounds that I make!'

(Gearspace, 2021)

Describing the microphone as "really sober" and not having "any additional fluff" (Björk in Nordic Audio Labs, 2017) is crucial for Björk, as "everything else is secondary" to transmitting and not taking away the "vibe and a feeling she wants to keep intact" (Taylor in Colletti, 2011).

AMPHION LOUDSPEAKERS

Kantola worked as a product designer for Finnish loudspeaker manufacturer Amphion from 2011 to 2019 before continuing as a consultant for the company. He was responsible for the creation and sound of the Amphion Create series of professional studio monitors and LF-extension units. The 1998-established Amphion had focused purely on Hi-Fi products until the launch of the Create range, with which the company reimagined its image and product line, disrupting the professional monitor marketplace with their passive designs, new approach to crossover frequency in two-way designs, implementation of waveguides and passive radiators and Kantola's new concept of "base systems" which shifted the subwoofer paradigm in full-range studio monitoring by transforming "a two-way monitor into a seamless three-way monitoring solution" (Amphion, 2022a).

Kantola met Amphion Founder and CEO Anssi Hyvönen in 2010 after Hyvönen saw the documentary *Mikrofon Mannen* (2010) about Kantola's work and "instantly decided that [he] had to contact this gentleman" (Nevalainen, 2022) as he sensed a convergence for their respective "transducer quests" (Saario, 2012). Their listening to old stereo and multi-track recordings made by Swedien through Amphion Ion and Argon speakers and a Harrison 32-series console, a unit favoured by Swedien for both recording and mixing (Kantola, 2008; Saario, 2012; Harrison Consoles, 2022; Nevalainen, 2022, Shanks, n.d.), marked the genesis of the Create range. This led to the design of the first Amphion pro-version of the Ion, the Ion+, which Kantola took to West Viking for feedback from Swedien and other engineers (Amphion, 2012; Nevalainen, 2022). Amphion monitors have since become near ubiquitous in professional studios and are associated with an ever-increasing list of A-list users (Amphion, 2019a, 2019b, 2022a, 2022b). The commercial success of the Amphion speakers inspired Kantola to persist, believing that he is "onto something", supporting his decision to commit full-time to the NU-100K project (Kantola, 2022a).

The pair make explicit references to the 'magic' and lost quality that was present in classic 50s and 60s recordings (Saario, 2012; Hyvönen, 2012a), with Hyvönen placing primary importance on the resolution of the studio monitoring system in this regard, as it enables "exact" placing of microphones and thus the production of tracking material that "competes with the best recordings from 50s and 60s even in its uncompressed and untreated 'rawfeed' form" (Hyvönen, 2012a). The *Amphion Presents* session with Finnish duo Eva and Manu (Amphion, 2015) demonstrates this quality that can be obtained with minimal to no processing through careful microphone positioning and high-resolution foldback mixes. The track was recorded and mixed at NAL solely with NAL microphones, with the mix comprising level balancing and panning, with any dynamics and EQ processing having been applied only during mastering. Kantola found Amphions monitors to be the first speakers that he could rely on when developing microphones in close listening to get the necessary levels of sonic detail and intimacy without having to resort to headphone-based listening (Kantola in Hors Phase, 2016).

AFFECTIVE-CRITICAL LISTENING

Hyvönen's ability to "remember exactly how something sounded at a certain place at a certain moment" and his sensitivity to "sound's energy and emotion" have helped him in his "40 years of listening to music and developing loudspeakers", particularly when working on final voicing of loudspeakers. Hyvönen highlights the importance of *affective listening* (Jing, 2012, Jing, 2016) in product design, stating it has "always been easy to know when the product is ready: we stop tweaking when the hairs on my arms stand up. And it appears that what works for my arms, causes similar reactions in others!" (Nevalainen, 2022).

An *affective-critical* listening practice and relationship to sound connects Hyvönen and Kantola, who recount how they listened to proto-types focusing on their sonic micro-inflictions and spatial-emotive-affective impact – the 'affective hit' (Massumi, 2015) – of the speaker. Whilst a number of Kantola's design ideas were not picked up by Amphion, he and Hyvönen never disagreed on what sounded good and right in terms of design, material or component choice (e.g., cone material), or what was deemed 'right' for what was being worked on. They dismissed drivers even if the units measured correctly but did not 'sound right', and for Kantola, it is essential that experiential evaluation and any measured performance are considered together, in convergence, and not to rely on 'flat' or any other set curve or measurement figure. He stresses the importance of developing sensitivity to differences without losing the big picture and awareness of the musical or sonic context (Kantola, 2022a).

TUNTEMATON SOTILAS (2017)

> Walking in the woods tells me what it should sound like and it's something very hard to put in words, but I try to work with texture and have a reference point in my memory of how it sounds out in the forest and how it sounds here and I can work with the *difference*.
>
> (Kantola, 2022a)

Tuntematon Sotilas (2017) was "the highest-grossing film of 2017 in Finnish cinema" and the most expensive film ever produced in Finland (The Hollywood Reporter, 2018, Wikipedia, 2022). Composer Lasse Enersen and conductor Dima Slobodeniouk explicitly wanted to use a Finnish symphony orchestra, as well as the "best possible technology" for the recording sessions and commissioned Kantola to design new microphones to that end. Kantola built three NU-100K microphones that were utilised as the main orchestral microphones alongside 50 other support microphones at the recording sessions with Sinfonia Lahti (Haavisto, 2017; Kröger, 2017).

The commission acted as an accelerant for the capsule designs that Kantola had commenced in 2015 (Haavisto, 2017), resulting in a "working prototype which sounded decent" in 2016. Soon after this, Kantola paused the production and promotion of all other NAL microphone models and resigned from his full-time role at Amphion to be able to "fully focus on just one model", thus reimagining the NAL business model (Kantola, 2022b). Kantola is particularly interested in the high-frequency spectrum, with the sound of an un-amplified string section, the quality of the treble in a nice concert hall, and the feeling of walking in the forest – the sense of resolution, softness and detail of the treble in nature sounds – acting as his references (Kantola, 2022a). This high-frequency 'quality' can be difficult to capture "as microphones can often produce too glaring or brash and hard sound", and with the NU-100K, Kantola wanted to create a sound "that is both clear and soft" (Translated, Kantola in Haavisto, 2017). Notably, already with the 1999 Union chapel recordings, Kantola utilised two pairs of DPA cardioid microphones, one set of which he had modified as he was not happy with the high-frequency *texture* and feel produced by the stock models (Kantola, 2022a).

TRANSDUCING EXPERIENCE

> He [Kantola] lives in his own world where cold and hot water sound different from each other, and a quiet room like the sounds of a rainforest.
>
> (transl. from Luukkanen, 2011)

Kantola conceives microphones as portals, which, with loudspeakers, form a system of transducer/transductive portals that connect one dimension or medium to another, where "one part of the system allows the listener to sit in 2022 and be transported into another place and time. It is very exciting to be transported into a recording, a musical event" (Kantola, 2022a). He also views microphones 'being' like a submarine window into an underwater world that is 'not compatible' with the one inside the submarine, making direct translation impossible by default (Kantola, 2022a).

> You cannot experience it as being out there. You have to compensate for the lack of a perspective or size or whatever. What you really want to transmit or to bring from the 'other side', is not the most precise exact technical experience but the actual emotional experience, and as such the question really becomes does the transducer enhance the experience or destroy it?
>
> (Kantola, 2022a)

There is an uncanny connection to Helmreich's transductive realisation of 'transductive anthroploogy' inside the *Alvin* research submarine. Similarly to Helmreich's proposition that for him and the accompanying scientists inside *Alvin* to have been able to imagine themselves as being "immersed in a submarine soundscapes, depended on transduction" (Helmreich, 2015), Kantola proposes that for the listener to be able to reach into and be immersed in – and thus affectively connected with the sonic event – is dependent on the 'quality' (feel, texture, space) of transduction and that transduction always 'shapes' the experience (i.e., transduction extends into experience). Furthermore, for Kantola, transduction and the transducer(s) do not 'vanish' "as the mediating operation" in the system (or chain) that enables the listener to hear and experience the 'given' sonic event (Helmreich, 2015, p. 226). The notion of a loudspeaker as a window and an "unreliable mediator" (Prior, 2021) parallels both Kantola's view of microphones and how both music production and microphone design practices purposefully draw from the colour and characteristics of 'tone', spectromorphological behaviour and the inter-and intra-actions that transducers afford as creative tools. There is an active desire for the mediation and the associated value implication of (vintage) transducers and tones (Smalley, 1997; Fink, Latour and Wallmark, 2018), for the 'texture affect' of recorded sound (Hemment, 2004).

Kantola repeatedly refers to sounds as objects with *texture*. This notion of texture is fundamental to his perception of the 'quality' of a microphone, a loudspeaker or a given spectral energy (e.g., self-noise), particularly with high-frequency spectrums and characteristics ('contours'). Thus, the microphone's characteristics and limitations must be considered as affordances and constraints in their function to connect a listener affectively to a (given) recorded sonic event. In microphone design, it is then about making informed decisions in terms of these critical-affective qualities (e.g., about the amount of boost in a given frequency area, or the benefits of more distortion of specific 'quality' over less distortion, when voicing a microphone). Typically, it is about quality over quantity – "simply put, the spectrum of the noise floor is more important than the amount" (Kantola, 2022a) – "the problem is not to render everything coherent, the question is to know where you're going to put the accent" (Deleuze, 1977, p. 216) to ensure the primacy of 'experience' in transduction.

U 47 AND THE DARK FOREST

As the first multipattern condenser, the U 47 ushered in the era of the modern studio mic, and even more than 50 years after its birth, it remains one of the world's most sought-after and desirable studio tools.

(TECnology Hall of Fame, 2004)

My idea was always to go back in time to a point where we had something exciting in microphones and investigate if there would be another way forward than the one we took, to find another path through the forest . . . These wonderful vintage microphones are appreciated for a reason . . . they have qualities and we are missing some of those qualities . . . I'm not trying to reinvent but to move forward, to go deeper into the forest, so to speak. . . . Hence the name, the NU or the new microphones.

(Kantola, 2022a)

Kantola's oft-cited microphone 'quest' (Grönholm, 2010; Luukkanen, 2011; Hors Phase, 2016; Nordic Audio Labs, 2021) was initiated by his sonic-affective 'encounter' with a 1953 'long body' U 47, which he restored (Kantola, 2006; Nordic Audio Labs, 2021). Not driven by nostalgia towards classic designs or comprising components, nor romantic ideals of perfection, but by curiosity and desire to "bring learning together" (Kantola, 2022a), he wants to understand what made the U 47 so good, why 'we' have not been able to improve or move beyond the early designs from 40s and 50s, namely the U 47, and AKG C12 (and the subsequent Telefunken ELA M 250 and 251 and the Siemens rebranded SM204) (Burgess, 2014, p. 57), and most importantly to map what "other options and routes out of the dark forest" were and are available to microphone designers (Kantola, 2022a). Sometimes, these new paths might be produced by small design decisions or advancements in available materials and technology, but crucially, they are about not accepting given 'proven' solutions as the only or the best available ones, and thus not missing effective design and build options due to oversight (Kantola, 2022a).

Given the desirability and high market value of an original U 47, due to the limited number of available microphones and replacement parts and the need for regular servicing to ensure a reliable operation, it is not surprising to find a whole marketplace focusing on recreating this classic microphone and http://ww.u47clones.com/ lists 24 contemporary 'clones' by 22 different manufacturers. Whilst the site 'trumpets' "All bow to the King of microphones . . . The Holy Grail of Vintage Tube Microphones . . . The Neumann U47", demarking it as a superlative point of origin that cannot be surpassed, Kantola stresses the importance to move beyond the familiar: "People do not know what they like. They like what they know. I mean they've heard this certain sound on so many records and they just love it because it sounds familiar" (Kantola, 2022a). Adapting from Chanan's account of the fetishisation of recorded music (Chanan, 1995, p. 18), Kantola's design principles and pursuit of knowledge and new options resist the fetishisation of classic microphones and its tendency to produce the fetishising of the specific and accidental characteristics or features of a microphone. Designs that move away from classic models also resist the dominant tendency of vintage equipment and techniques to function as "metaphors for professional knowledge and embodied heritage" (Meynell, 2020, p. 97).

Warning against the status quo and assuming the necessity of any design feature, Kantola calls for the 'need' to move beyond any 'requirements' (e.g., to have a tube in the microphone just to get the desired response or to rely on vintage/replica capsules and/or transformers in the design). These 'design turns' must be made "without losing what was so beautiful and good about them" (Kantola, 2022b), thus calling for a deep critical-creative evaluation of all design choices and parameters and for understanding of their respective function, effect and affect in the whole. For example, Kantola is "kicking out" the transformer altogether whilst having the design perform the transformer's 'step' function, as well as retaining the desirable sonic characteristics of third harmonic distortion, natural HPF effect and pleasant 'bump' in the low-frequency response (Kantola, 2022a).

When transducer designers are not able or empowered to trust their 'ears' in decision-making, combined with a strong marketing push and market-place demand for classic models or vintage sounds, there is an increased risk of manufacturers seeking to copy, clone or impose characteristics to designs that can compromise their performance. Kantola described the Neumann M147 frequency response as a "caricature of a classic Neumann curve . . . as if they forced this oversized curve" to the design as a result of not having listened themselves and having 'listened' to the market audience in terms of "what they want" (Kantola, 2022a).

Typical design pitfalls and decisions that compromise sound quality encountered by Kantola include poor implementation of phantom power in non-tube condenser microphones (i.e., what was lost as a corollary when moving away from external PSUs), unnecessary miniaturisation or enlarging of studio microphones, reliance on valves or transformers in circuits, in particular, the use of inferior quality valves and valve-designs for the sake of producing a piece of 'tube-gear' (Kantola, 2022a). As "harmonic content and dynamic range are important" (Kantola, 2022d) it is about moving forward from these points with "new choices and other ways to add character" (Kantola, 2022b) (e.g., with non-linear circuits). "It is not about 'bringing back the warmth' but not losing it in the first place" and it is of fundamental importance not to equate design decisions and choice as compromise, including cost factor considerations (Kantola, 2022b).

Whilst the NU-47 (1997), utilising the original VF-14 tube and M7 capsule, was already 'matched' to Kantola's vintage U 47, it was the NU-47V (2013) that completed the quest to recreate the U 47 without reliance on NOS or vintage parts. Being "matched in sound", it produces the same feeling, emotion, and mood as Martin's vintage U 47 (Hors Phase, 2016). The aim to match the experience – to create the *affect* of the U 47 – and not copy the specification and measured performance *per se* is a key differentiating factor in Kantola's designs in relation to the other U 47 'clones' and how he views microphone design in general. The U 47, with its "enormous musical quality" (Nordic Audio Labs, 2013; Hors Phase, 2016), is an inspiration and something that is 'behind' the classic sounds – something to "match the experience" of and "discover what was lost and what could be extended" (Kantola, 2022a).

'U-TURN'

When researching capsule designs from the 1930s, Kantola noticed how the frequency curves which "looked funny and like modern Neumann curves" (Kantola, 2022a) were actually hand-drawn. The designers had "drawn what they heard because they didn't have the equipment to measure response" as 'flat' capsules did not exist yet (Kantola, 2022a). When Georg Neumann worked on the U 47, "he had to rely a lot on his ears and the finetuning and shaping of the sound was done with ears and not with measuring" which "shows in all the details including how the grille affects the response" (Kantola, 2022a).

Kantola recounted an anecdote from Microtech Gefell staff of Neumann's visit to East Germany to give instructions pertaining to the build of his microphone designs. Telling staff to "stick to the recipe and not to improvise or trust their ears", resulted in overt reliance and focus on measurements, machining specifications and other details from Neumann's 'formula', and rather unsurprisingly, Microtech Gefell "ended up doing really good measurement microphones" (Kantola, 2022a).

This semantic turn away from the primacy of the listening experience in the design and tuning of microphones was compounded by advances in measurement technologies, initially making engineering departments play a more prominent role, only to be superseded in turn by the marketing departments, in terms of driving the design agenda and leading to what Kantola refers to as a "full blown disaster . . . happening because what was important was forgotten in a way" (Kantola, 2022a). Reminiscent of classical producer Walter Legge's account of when a more controlled use of ambience in stereo recording, as afforded by advances in microphone and tape recorder designs, enabled the pursuit of making records to sound "exactly like they would be hear[d] in the best seat in an acoustically perfect hall" (Schwarzkopf, p. 73), and how he had to fight with the technical and sales departments over the use of stereo. "They believed that the public wanted the 'gimmick' of stereo . . . It took a long time for me to induce these people that their ideas of stereo were opposite of what musicians and the musical public wanted" (Schwarzkopf, 1982, p. 73).

The decline of listening and experience-informed praxis in microphone design was paralleled in sound engineering practices in general. Chanan notes how tacit knowledge of 1950s sound recording practices – of the time when advances in microphone designs afforded the emergence of microphone choice and placement became an art form (Schmidt Horning, 2013, p. 111) – was very much lost by 1970s (Chanan, 1995). Schidmt Horning's 1999 interview with Walter Sear adds weight to the argument of the importance of experiential intra-action with, and aural evaluation of, audio hardware design choices and adjustments and the desired – or most importantly 'known' – target sound.

> Explaining their lasting appeal, Sear described the care with which Summerlin and Shenk built these early equalizers: "They were two guys who set up a production line, but every unit that came off, they'd sit there and diddle around – you know, change a resistor here", and make various minute adjustments "until they got *sound*. Well they had ears; they knew what it should sound like when it was right." By "sound" Sear simply meant that they heard the Pultec perform as they intended.
> (Schmidt Horning, 2013, p. 114)

Significantly, the 1947-introduced Pultec programme equaliser was "designed to match timbres between recordings when mastering from different studios or recording dates" (Meynell, 2020, p. 91) (i.e., to 'match' sounds by ear by the sound engineer).

PARADIGM SHIFT

> There was a certain sound with condenser microphones that was not present in ribbon microphones and I wanted to move away from that sound.
>
> (Kantola, 2022a)

From comparing the affordances and constraints associated with the U 47 and ELA M 250 microphones, as well as those of different transduction principles and diaphragm sizes, Kantola wanted to produce a microphone that combines affordances from different microphone models and types with as few operational limitations as possible and without design compromises in terms of sonic performance. Additionally, the microphone had to be able to cover the whole spectrum of recording and production scenarios and work with a wide range of sound sources and microphone techniques, in close or distant miking, with solo voices/ instruments or backing elements, in ensemble or ambient recording, for quiet and loud acoustic or amplified sound sources and to function either as the sole microphone in a given production or as part of an arsenal of microphones.

Drawing from the "to keep" and to "get rid of" qualities of U 47 and ELA M 250 (Kantola, 2020), the NU-100K was designed to have an extended frequency response with full support for the body of the voice, clarity and warmth with a "silky top end" and a "nice dynamic range", but without a tube or a transformer in the design. Crucially, it must not possess a "strong pre-EQ sound" to enable desirable amounts of "shaping" to take place during the recording and/or mixing stages. This potential for post-microphone-processing is afforded by the microphone's response not highlighting or bringing out any elements of the source sound too much (Kantola, 2020).

As the pre-equalisation produced by the condenser capsule's resonance cannot be undone with equalisation, the NU-100K has to function as a 'clean slate' that would afford it to be layered and shaped as desired by EQ and/or dynamics processing (Kantola, 2020). This should not be mistaken for neutrality or 'flatness', neither of which are wanted or needed, except with test microphones (Kantola, 2022a, 2022b) (see Figure 10.5). To be able to be processed "heavily", there must be a "lack of issues and plenty of detail/information in the signal. . . . In optics there is image distortion and limited dynamic range, in audio there are capsule resonances which become more and more annoying with each dB of EQ or compression" (Kantola, 2022c). To achieve his goals, Kantola had to design and build a brand-new capsule type for the NU-100K (Kantola, 2019), marking a paradigm shift in his microphone designs.

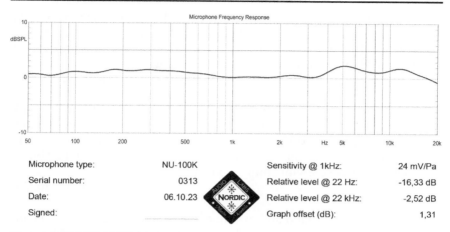

Figure 10.5 NU-100K frequency spectrum.

Table 10.1 NU-100K Specification

Weight	395 g
Color	Black/Black, Grey/Gold, Gold/Gold
Pickup patterns	cardioid, omni, figure-8
Sensitivity	31 mV/Pa (−30.2 dBV)
Max SPL	137 dB(A) @ 1% THD, 6kOhm load
Noise floor	13dB(A)
Phantom power	5.3mA, 48V
Output impedance	22 Ohms
Dimensions	192.5 mm long, 38 mm diameter

'NU-TURN'

> The challenge really has not been coming up with an idea and seeing if it works but being able to go through with it. I mean, I had to.
>
> (Kantola, 2022a)

To answer 'what produces innovation', Kantola identifies three areas that produce conditions for innovation: practical situations, technical or logical steps forward and daydreaming. With the first type, "you have something that you need to make it work, producing a very practical innovation" – a solution to clear practical problem. The second scenarios tend to be "possible technical innovations that are based on a technical principle". It is this (cross)application of principles (e.g., finding new materials to use in loudspeakers and then exploring their potential in microphone designs) and the 'what if' type questions (e.g., what if we utilised AC high frequency instead of a static magnetic field in ribbon microphones) and the potential of technical engineering that Kantola "love investigating and learning about" (Kantola, 2022a). The final category of innovation is about:

> Having a vision of something that you can dream up. You are not even sure that it can exist. . . . It might be just an illusion. It might be impossible. . . . But this is an important driving force in my thinking: what if we could have this, and then I start exploring.
>
> (Kantola, 2022a)

> I was able to go into the workshop with a fresh idea of how to think and make progress, to draw it up in CAD, do the CAM programming, CNC machine the part, build it with the electronics, and have it ready for testing, listening and recording that afternoon, and then be able to go back and do the same thing next day.
>
> (Kantola, 2022a)

To be able to design, build and manufacture all parts of the NU-100K in-house required considerable upskilling and reimagining of the NAL setup. Kantola learnt 3D CAD (computer aided design) from scratch as well as CAM (computer aided manufacturing) tool paths for CNC (computer numerical control) of the machining tools (e.g. drills, lathes, and for milling). The aim was to be self-contained in a 'closed system' that enabled Martin to have an idea, remain with it, and be able to build and test it 'immediately' in the studio, without having to rely on other people for the machining, fine-tuning or feedback (Kantola, 2022a).

Due to no funding for the three-year RND period, speeding-up of the design process became a priority, with both Martin and Suvi Kantola quitting their music industry jobs to focus exclusively on the project. Key in foreshortening the time to produce a completely new design from the groundup was to make use of rapid prototyping and rapid experimentation techniques whilst working with DFM (design for manufacture) principles and purposefully staying within the 'limits' of available setup and abilities (ProductPlan, n.d.). Hence, the initial establishing of the 'ground' was crucial as it becomes the 'ceiling' in a DFM context (Sild, 2021) where "your options dictate the design in a way you are working" (Kantola, 2022a), indicating the importance of being able to work with emergent ideas and 'qualities' both 'ground up' and from an 'abstract idea down' (e.g., Martin built a welding machine to be able to weld the mesh grille around the capsule). Interestingly, Kantola perceives these 'limits' as drivers for creative solutions and potential (Kantola, 2022a), and he purposefully worked in "narrow paths" only on what was essential, focusing on 'real-time' learning to match the needs of the current task or sub-project, instead of "bank learning" that would later be "mined" (Kantola, 2022b).

Kantola's rapid cycle of idea-to-test-to-revision, directly disrupts the typical prototype development and test cycles of large(r) microphone business(es) where engineers typically have to wait for written feedback after test units are sent out for studio testing, thus reducing the number of designs that can be effectively tested, and for listening to re-emerge as an essential part of the design process. Written communication can also be difficult as: "it's so so hard to communicate these things. I mean, I can keep this in my own head and I can do the next version, which is

slightly different" (Kantola, 2022a). NAL was set up with two independent machinery 'stratas', one for build and one for production machinery,
with the latter intended to run 'smoothly' without Martin's input, to allow
him to focus on new 'things' and stay with the 'long thoughts' (Kantola,
2022a).

III (2021)

The 2021 album *III* by Eva and Manu demonstrates the effectiveness
of the NU-100K in relation to its design aims. Producer Manu Laudic
explains how the NU-100K afforded the duo options both at the recording and mixing stages, explicitly noting the ease of mixing, malleability
of the recorded sound that enabled extensive use of layering of sounds
(e.g., composite piano sounds comprising five layers), being able to process sounds extensively and to add character to the recorded signal in the
digital domain. The NU-100K allowed the utilization of both close and
distant miking techniques more readily than before as well as to track
elements 'clean'. Due to the quality of captured tone and performances,
Laudic could rely less on compression and create effective contrasts with
compression for feel, colour, character and/or for adding a desired spectromorphological behaviour (e.g., heavy Beatles-style piano compression). Whilst Shure SM57 was used for some 'narrower' guitar overdubs,
everything else on the album was recorded either with a NU-100K or
a NAL Black Pearl. Being able to work primarily with a single microphone model produced workflow efficiencies as they were able to have
the microphone(s) ready-to-record at all times (Nordic Audio Labs, 2020;
Eva and Manu, 2021).

CONCLUDING NOTES: AN AFFECTIVE DE-DESIGN

Understanding microphones and loudspeakers as affective tools that
enable not only the technical but also the experiential transduction helps
us understand and situate the innovation in Kantola's work. With "music
as an affect, as an intensity that carries an ability to affect and be affected"
(Hemment, 2004, p. 77), microphones and loudspeakers form a system of
affective tools or portals that shape and affect both the sounding and listening bodies. When viewing sound, music and transducers as affect and
affective relationships, we can see how Kantola has effectively negated
Neumann's transductive 'u-turn' that casts out the 'ear' ('body') from
the microphone design and brings listening ('sensing') and designer's
tacit knowledge back into play. Kantola's initial transducer quest can be
read as a "Deleuzian de-designing" (Hemment, 2004, p. 89) of a classic microphone where the U 47 becomes de-territorialized, de-composed
and de-designed in the exploration of the relationship between different
materials, design features and decisions, and their sonics, spectromorphological and affective qualities and potential. Approaching a classic microphone through a de-design process produces a difference-in-repetition that
"displaces an economy of imitation and re-presentation, and the practice

of [microphone design] comes to be seen in terms of turning a prism to reveal different facets or aspects of a field of possibility" (Hemment, 2004, p. 89), which in this instance has evoked the potential for the creation – of a line of flight (Deleuze and Guattari, 1988) – of a new class of a microphone. Kantola's design praxis is really one of exploring the dynamics of difference in and repetition.

By reimagining his working practices out of practical necessity, Kantola disrupted and innovated the typical design-proto-type-test-evaluate-revise process by making it faster and more effective, experiential and affective, through the increased number of product optimisation model test-revise cycles. The ability to produce capsules in-house was pivotal in empowering the circumnavigation of the innovation 'bottleneck' imposed by reliance on vintage capsules, capsule designs, and/or their clones or contemporary recreations in microphone designs and to advance his strategy of competing in the global microphone market solely on the basis of quality (Haavisto, 2017).

To conclude, Kantola's "dedication to excellence" (Swedien in Grönholm, 2010) and transductive quest have produced affective tools that 'resonate' with listeners globally without the 'unwanted resonances' that we might expect from the designs typically associated with them and this is something exemplified in the design and build of NU-100K.

REFERENCES

Amphion. (2012). *Bruce Swedien Listening to Amphion Ion+*. YouTube. Available at: https://youtu.be/2EC8aLIbFRs [Accessed: 29 July 2022].

Amphion. (2015). *Amphion Presents: Eva & Manu//"I've Learned" @ Nordic Audio Labs*. Available at: https://youtu.be/PPoUIs_bKL4 [Accessed: 29 July 2022].

Amphion. (2019a). *Acustica Audio on Using Amphion in Their Plug-in Development*. YouTube. Available at: https://youtu.be/Uh4PvtxCWyk [Accessed: 25 August 2022].

Amphion. (2019b). *Oeksound Relies on Amphion for Their Plug-in Development*. YouTube. Available at: https://youtu.be/QFrVQ1FpFDw [Accessed: 25 August 2022].

Amphion. (2022a). *Amphion*. Available at: https://amphion.fi. [Accessed: 29 July 2022].

Amphion. (2022b). *Amphion BaseTwo25: NAMM TEC Award Nominee*. Available at: https://amphion.fi [Accessed: 29 July 2022].

Braidotti, R. (2005). 'Affirming the Affirmative: On Nomadic Affectivity', in *Rhizomes*, Issue 11/12 Fall 2005/Spring 2006. Available at: www.rhizomes.net/issue11/braidotti.html.

Burgess, R. J. (2014). *The History of Music Production*. New York: Oxford University Press.

Chanan, M. (1995). *Repeated Takes: A Short History of Recording and Its Effects on Music*. London: Verso.

Colletti, J. (2011). *Behind the Release: Björk Biophilia*. Available at: https://sonicscoop.com/behind-the-release-bjork-biophilia/ [Accessed: 29 July 2022].

Deleuze, G. (1977). 'Vincennes Seminar Session May 3, 1977: On Music', in *Discourse*, 20.3, Fall 1998, pp. 205–288. Available at: http://www.jstor.org/stable/41389512 [Accessed: 29 July 2022].

Deleuze, G. and Guattari, F. (1988). *A Thousand Plateaus: Capitalism & Schizophrenia*. London: Athlone.

Fink, R., Latour, M. and Wallmark, Z. (2018). 'Chasing the Dragon: In Search of Tone in Popular Music', in Fink, R., Latour, M. and Wallmark, Z., eds. *The Relentless Pursuit of Tone: Timbre in Popular Music*. New York: Oxford University Press, pp. 1–17.

Gearspace.com Community. (2021). 'Interview with Bruce Swedien', *Gearspace*. Available at: https://gearspace.com/board/interviews/1363147-interview-bruce-swedien.html#post15669795 [Accessed: 29 July 2022].

Grönholm, K. (2010). *Mikrofonmannen*. [Film]. YLE Fakta. FST5. Available at: https://youtu.be/5bCOO1ZCsAk, https://youtu.be/iUGHoTYiA30, https://youtu.be/U2vMgFvzgzM [Accessed: 29 July 2022].

Haavisto, A. (2017). *Maailman luokan mikrofonit valmistuvat käsityönä*. YLE. Available at: https://yle.fi/uutiset/3-9592516 [Accessed: 29 July 2022].

Harrison Consoles. (2022). *Harrison Consoles: History*. Available at: https://harrisonconsoles.com/history/ [Accessed: 29 July 2022].

Helmreich, S. (2015). 'Transduction', in Sakakeeny, M., ed. *Keywords in Sound*. Durham: Duke University Press, pp. 222–231. Available at: ProQuest Ebook Central [Accessed: 13 July 2022].

Hemment, D. (2004). 'Affect and Individuation in Popular Electronic Music', in Buchanan, I. and Swiboda, M., eds. *Deleuze and Music*. Edinburgh: Edinburgh University Press, pp. 76–94.

Hors Phase. (2016). *Audio Days: Meet the Makers – Martin Kantola (Nordic Audio Labs/Amphion)*. YouTube. Available at: https://youtu.be/izvWtAPpUuU [Accessed: 29 July 2022].

Hyvönen, A. (2012a). *Email to Antti Saario*, 30 June.

Jing, A.-W. (2012). 'China's Experimental Music and Sound Art Practice', *Journal of Sonic Studies*, 2, Listening. Available at: https://www.researchcatalogue.net/view/229681/229682 [Accessed: 29 July 2022].

Jing, A.-W. (2016). 'Affective Listening as a Mode of Coexistence: The Case of China's Sound Practice', *Representations*, 136, pp. 112–131. Available at: https://www.jstor.org/stable/26420581 [Accessed: 29 July 2022].

Kantola, M. (2006). 'New U47', in *Gearspace*. Available at: https://gearspace.com/board/product-alerts-older-than-2-months/79992-new-u47-2.html#post848952 [Accessed: 29 July 2022].

Kantola, M. (2008). 'Harrison Desk?', *Gearspace*. Available at: https://gearspace.com/board/so-much-gear-so-little-time/171239-harrison-desk.html [Accessed: 29 July 2022].

Kantola, M. (2020). *NU-100K Design Goals*. Nordic Audio Labs. [Video]. Available at: www.youtube.com/watch?v=7IeG85PKtDc [Accessed: 29 July 2022].

Kantola, M. (2022a). *Nordic Audio Labs: In Conversation w/Martin Kantola – Part 1*. Interview by Antti Saario [MS Teams], 27 May.

Kantola, M. (2022b). *Nordic Audio Labs: In Conversation w/Martin Kantola – Part 2*. Interview by Antti Saario [MS Teams], 7 June.

Kantola, M. (2022c). *Email to Antti Saario*, 12 June.

Kantola, M. (2022d). *Instagram*. Available at: www.instagram.com/p/CggKT-JoKPDYmIpiAYtlCYT59zlA3PDakvh_yag0/ [Accessed: 29 July 2022].

Kröger, T. (2017). *Tuntemattoman sotilaan musiikki tulee Lahdesta – äänityk-set jo käynnissä*. Available at: https://yle.fi/uutiset/3-9578515 [Accessed: 29 July 2022].

Luukkanen, T. (2011). *Kantolan Maailma*. Vaasa: Vaasan Ylioppilas Lehti.

Martin, A. D. and Kamberelis, G. (2013). 'Mapping Not Tracing: Qualitative Educational Research with Political Teeth', *International Journal of Qualitative Studies in Education*, 26(6), pp. 668–679.

Massumi, B. (2015). 'After the Affective Turn: Reassessing Affect', *ISEA 2015: 'Disruption' Conference Keynote*. Vancouver, Canada.

Meynell, A. (2020). 'How Does Vintage Equipment Fit into a Modern Working Process?', in *The Bloomsbury Handbook of Music Production*. Bloomsbury, pp. 89–106.

Nevalainen, J. (2022). *My Story, Our Story*. INNER [Website]. Available at: www.inner-magazines.com/audiophilia/my-story-our-story/ [Accessed: 29 July 2022].

Newport, C. (2016). *Deep Work: Rules for Focused Success in a Distracted World*. New York: Grand Central Publishing.

Nordic Audio Labs. (2013). *NU-47 Microphone Project Announcement*. YouTube. Available at: https://youtu.be/9m0B1pKZRT4 [Accessed: 29 July 2022].Nordic Audio Labs. (2017). *Björk Talks about a Mic She Got 20 Years Ago*. YouTube. Available at: https://youtu.be/iQvhjqbaT9E [Accessed: 29 July 2022].

Nordic Audio Labs. (2019). *NU-100K Microphone*. YouTube. Available at: https://youtu.be/ioJquq5jBio [Accessed: 29 July].

Nordic Audio Labs. (2020). *Coffee with Manu Laudic*. YouTube. Available at: https://youtu.be/-yryM0619go [Accessed: 29 July 2022].

Nordic Audio Labs. (2021). *Nordic Audio Labs – Music, Microphones and More!* [Website]. Available at: https://nordicaudiolabs.com [Accessed: 29 July 2022].

Prior, D. (2021). 'The Unreliable Mediator: Loudspeakers in Sound Art Heard through *Music on a Long Thin Wire*', in Grant, J., Matthias, J. and Prior, D., eds. *The Oxford Handbook of Sound Art*. New York: Oxford University Press, pp. 191–202.

ProductPlan. (n.d.). *Glossary: Rapid Prototyping*. Available at: www.product-plan.com/glossary/rapid-prototyping/ [Accessed: 27 July 2022].

Saario, A. (2012, July). *Conversations with Martin Kantola and Anssi Hyvönen During Nordic Audio Labs Site Visit*. Karperö: Nordic Audio Labs.

Schmidt Horning, S. (2013). *Chasing Sound: Technology, Culture & the Art of Studio Recording from Edison to the LP*. Baltimore: John Hopkins University Press.

Schwarzkopf, E. (1982). *On and Off the Record: A Memoir of Walter Legge*. London: Faber and Faber.

Shanks, W. (n.d.). *Bruce Swedien and the Harrrison 32C Console*. Available at: www.uaudio.com/blog/bruce-swedien-harrison-32c/ [Accessed: 29 July 2022].

Sild, S. (2021). *Design for Manufacturing*. Available at: https://fractory.com/design-for-manufacturing-dfm/ [Accessed: 29 July 2022].

Smalley, D. (1997). 'Spectro-Morphology: Explaining Sound-Shapes', *Organised Sound*, 2(2), pp. 107–126.

Swedien, B. (2009). *In the Studio with Michael Jackson*. New York: Hal Leonard.

Swedien, B. (2016). *In the Studio with Bruce Swedien*. Available at: https://inthestudiowithbruceswedien.com/ [Accessed: 29 July 2022].

Swedien, B. (2018). *Bruce Swedien Talks about the NU-47 Microphone*. Nordic Audio Labs. Available at: https://youtu.be/JO8SUnMtxyo.

TECnology Hall of Fame. (2004). *TECnology Hall of Fame 2004*. Available at: http://legacy.tecawards.org/hof/04techof.html#9 [Accessed: 29 July 2022].

DISCOGRAPHY

Björk (2002). [CD] *Family Tree*. London: One Little Indian Records. Disc 4 and 5.

Enersen, Lasse (2017). *Tuntematon Sotilas*. Available at: TIDAL: [Accessed: 1 July 2022].

Eva + Manu (2021a). [digital release] *III*. Helsinki, Finland: Bandcamp.

Eva + Manu (2021b). *III*. Available at: TIDAL: [Accessed: 1 July 2022].

11

Audio beyond demand

Creative reinventions of the broadcast listening experience

Florian Hollerweger

1 INTRODUCTION

While 'streaming' enjoys ever-increasing popularity, the term's actual meaning has undergone a significant shift in popular discourse over the course of its existence. Whereas in the late 1990s and early 2000s, it referred exclusively to *live*-streamed media, such as web radio (Lind and Medoff, 1999; Priestman, 2001), it is now as frequently used to refer to media experiences that are served *on demand* through a combination of web and file serving (Xiph.org, 2004–2022), such as (in most cases) on Spotify, Netflix, SoundCloud, or YouTube.

This linguistic shift arguably reflects the underlying development of listener and viewer habits and expectations. Live-streamed media are consumed in a fashion similar to the traditional radio and TV broadcasts that they were originally modeled on, with all recipients tuning into the same content at the same time – an experience for which the very term 'stream' provides an adequate metaphor. With the popularization of podcasts and, more recently, services such as Spotify and Netflix, however, users are getting increasingly used to being in full control of their media experience and like to decide for themselves what they listen to or watch, and when they do so. Specifically, it is becoming increasingly normal to be able to start, stop, pause, and resume playback of a 'stream' on an individual basis at any time without affecting other listeners or viewers. Rather than submitting oneself to a flowing river, a more suitable metaphor for this kind of listening experience might be that it seeks to turn the listener into a 'God with a remote control'.

Even though live streams (such as radio) remain a common form of technologically mediated aural experience, they may seem to be, at least from a technological perspective, gradually rendered obsolete by the aforementioned developments and on-demand media consumption habits. In contrast to such a view, this chapter aims to demonstrate the continued relevance of live audio streams for musical innovation. By facilitating an idiosyncratic form of technologically mediated aural experience that we shall define and refer to as *broadcast listening*, live audio streaming addresses the inherent limitations of algorithmic music recommender

DOI: 10.4324/9781003118817-13

systems. This offers creative opportunities for developing alternative ways in which aestheticized listening can be algorithmically mediated, manifested by a variety of sonic arts practices that can be summarized under the term *procedural broadcasting*.

Towards this goal, the *Streaaam* experimental audio streaming server has been created from Free/Libre Open Source Software (FLOSS) in a higher-education context. Whereas a previous publication focuses on *Streaaam*'s technical implementation (Hollerweger, 2021) and a second paper discusses a sonic artwork created for the server as an individual student project (Thompson and Hollerweger, 2022), the present chapter presents some of the artworks created by students for the server in the context of two small classes of six and ten students, respectively. The *Streaaam* project's artistic goal is to offer an opportunity to consider audio *beyond* demand and to creatively explore and reinterpret the broadcast listening experience by means of artistic research (Klein, 2017). This chapter's main contribution is grounded in the numerous artistic strategies that students have, under faculty guidance, devised in this regard.

2 BACKGROUND

2.1 The broadcast listening experience

Listening to a live stream represents an idiosyncratic form of aestheticized aural perception that is qualitatively different not only from on-demand listening but also from other forms of technologically mediated aural experience, such as live music performances. For the purpose of the discussion in this chapter, it shall be referred to as the *broadcast listening experience*, which can be defined according to three key characteristics.

1   Broadcast listening is an *acousmatic experience* in the sense of Pierre Schaeffer and Jérôme Peignot, where sounds, such as those on the radio, are being heard with no visible cause (Chion, 1983, 1991); a definition that explicitly excludes audiovisual broadcasts, such as television. Voegelin (2010, p. 38) argues that "[t]he invisibility of radio-sound enables a multiplicity of perception" in what she explicitly and repeatedly refers to as a form of "innovative listening"; perhaps because it is situated at an individual level through the specifics of the respective listener's circumstances, such as the acoustic properties (frequency response, directivity, etc.) of their playback system.

2   Broadcast listening is a *simultaneously individual and collective* experience in so far as every listener (a) receives the same stream at the same time and (b) knows this to be the case. Voegelin describes radio listeners as "a collective of individuals" (2010, p. 38) who "produce a collective solitariness" (p. 39) by "listening all together alone" (p. 38) in "an invisible social network" (p. 114). This "invisible co-audience" (p. 115) is arguably absent in an on-demand listening experience, which in this sense falls short of radio's "potential to produce site-specificity not tied to a place as architectural fact but as the temporal location of my auditory imagination" (p. 160). This rootedness of broadcast listening in *time*

distinguishes it from the (asynchronous) ways in which listeners of on-demand media compare their respective experiences through online comments or other forms of social media.

3   Crucially, broadcast *listeners have limited control over what they listen to*. Rather, the decision to tune into and out of a broadcast at a given time is often the only form of direct control that its listeners can exercise, short of adjusting the playback volume. This open form is a characteristic that broadcast listening notably shares with generative music (Eno, 1996; Collins, 2008), but clearly distinguishes it from on-demand listening, where listeners can pause, rewind, or fast-forward on an individual basis, and which therefore does not exhibit the same "constant stream of now" with "literally no end in sight" (Voegelin, 2010, p. 38). Brian Eno's dualism of "control and surrender" (Loydell and Marshall, 2016; Loydell, 2014) represents a suitable framework for contrasting these two types of technologically mediated listening: on-demand media emphasizes the listener's ability to control their experience, whereas a live stream requires the listener to surrender such control.

The analysis that follows will focus, in particular, on the last of these three characteristics. Despite its seeming inconvenience of a lack of control, broadcast listening appears to remain attractive to listeners, as is evident from the fact that even on-demand media providers such as Spotify aim to emulate this experience on their platforms (e.g., Spotify Radio). This confirms that Eno's observation that "[w]e've treasured the controlling part of ourselves and neglected the surrendering part" (Tan, 2011) is also valid in a 'streaming' context. We can hypothesize that the continued affinity for broadcast listening is not merely due to listener nostalgia but that rather, in the sense of Eno's dualism, broadcast listeners *voluntarily* surrender control to the stream's curator for the sake of chance discoveries that are not primarily mediated by their own previous choices. The conclusion that can be drawn from this analysis is that broadcast listening remains worthy of continued exploration in the sonic arts, for example, to demonstrate alternative approaches to the algorithmic mediation of listening, which addresses artistic considerations beyond consumer choice.

2.2 The limitations of music recommender systems

A holy grail of on-demand music services is to provide useful recommendations to their users, who "are overwhelmed by the choice of what to . . . listen to" (McInerney et al., 2018, p. 31). Algorithmic music recommender systems, such as the one employed by Spotify, initially focused on making such recommendations based on an "exploitation" (McInerney et al., 2018) of the listener's previous choices. The collection of such information then enables the system to issue personalized recommendations for what Snickars (2017) summarizes as "more of the same". A particular challenge for such systems is posed by newly subscribed listeners and newly added music for which no previous data exists. Interestingly, for our discussion, one strategy that has proven successful in this regard is a deliberate "exploration" of less reliable recommendations, even though it ultimately serves the purpose of "gathering more information" to then be further exploited (McInerney et al., 2018).

In recent years, several observers have noted that Spotify's recommender algorithm tends to converge on a surprisingly small subset of songs from the company's vast archives (access to which is, after all, what users pay for). Some have referred to the algorithm as "a disappointment" in this regard (Snickars, 2017, p. 206), deduced that "Spotify is making you boring" (Timberg, 2016), and hypothesized that "music in the age of the algorithm" generally leads to narrowing musical tastes (Hunter-Tilney, 2016). Others have put the onus of countering such developments on the listeners themselves, who are allegedly "using Spotify wrong" and advised them to "hijack the recommendation algorithm" for the "purpose of tricking Spotify into thinking you have a wide variety of music that you like" (Ranallo, 2021). Yet others have questioned the actual randomness of Spotify's 'shuffle play' mode and claimed that listeners "feel cheated" if it does not provide a reliable element of "unpredictability and surprise" (Bendet, 2020). Crucially for musical innovation, it has also been argued that music recommender systems result in narrower scopes not only of music being consumed but also of music being produced.

> If [as a producer] you start in a place where you are listening to the [music recommender] algorithm, you're probably not gonna come up with something that's gonna change things. We don't need more of what's here."
>
> (Nick Littlemore of Pnau in Stoppa et al., 2022, 29:24)

To summarize, these perceived shortcomings of music recommender systems have been pervading the recent popular discourse to the degree that The Guardian (2022) recommended to "[i]gnore the algorithm [and] listen to music outside your usual taste" as one of "100 ways to slightly improve your life without really trying".

2.3 Audio beyond demand: surrendering control to become a listener

The conclusion that "we don't need more of what's here" reassuringly suggests that music listeners and producers regard music as more than mere consumables that fulfill listeners' aural desires according to predictable patterns such as 'customers who listened to X also listened to Y'. It appears that well beyond "more of the same", music listeners actively seek "something that's gonna change things", whether that change concerns a simple broadening of their personal musical horizon or – more ambitiously – the listener themselves as a political human being (Attali, 1977).

> [N]ew experiences change man. Whenever we hear sounds, we are changed, we are no longer the same, and this is more the case when we hear organized sounds: music.
>
> (Stockhausen, 1972, 2:22)

This active desire for new sensory input appears to point to an essential property of the human mind and, by extension, of creative expression and the reception of art. The human sensory system constantly adjusts itself to a shifting environment, and various manifestations of sensory adaptation illustrate the specific perceptual relevance of changing (rather than static) external stimuli (Wohlwill, 1974; Wark, Lundstrom and Fairhall, 2007; Webster, 2012; Adibi, Zoccolan and Clifford, 2021). This "differential sensitivity" (Fechner, 1860) of our sensory apparatus is perhaps especially inherent to the sense of hearing, which perceives the oscillations of a vibrating medium such as air. Without change (of an oscillation's amplitude over time), there simply is no sound to be perceived. The ear, in other words, literally demands change. Perhaps we can speculate that in this sense, listening represents a frontier of consumerism that, by illustrating the limitations of personal choice (i.e., that which we *want*), instead points us to things *beyond* those that we demand (i.e., what we allow ourselves to be curious about).

Ironically, a key ingredient for such aural discoveries seems to be the limited amount of control on behalf of the listener that was defined earlier as a key characteristic of the broadcast listening experience. For example, anecdotal evidence suggests that the live stream through which the *Streaaam* server presents sonic artworks recently produced by students at our department made it easier for some faculty to get a broad overview of these works than an interactive website. The characteristically fragmented experience of clicking through a potentially overwhelming number of available choices stands in contrast to the only real choice that a broadcast listener has to make: 'I shall now devote a chunk of time to listen to this broadcast'; a choice that, by the way, is entirely compatible with music's inherent temporality.

The limited control that a broadcast listener exercises over their experience is, therefore, not merely an unfortunate side effect of an outdated technology that has since been superseded by the superior convenience of on-demand listening. Rather, we can hypothesize that broadcast listeners *deliberately surrender control*, in Eno's sense of these terms (Loydell and Marshall, 2016; Loydell, 2014), to the broadcast's curator(s) for the sake of encouraging aural surprise and chance discoveries of favorable sonic constellations. The artistic and aesthetic value of the broadcast listening experience appears to lie in the listener's exposure to new sensory input that does not directly rely on previous personal choices (or an illusion thereof), thereby preventing the creation of auditory filter bubbles that would otherwise restrain such novel experiences. In this fashion, the listener's lack of control ironically grants them an autonomy that the 'burden of choice' in on-demand listening does not, and which could be described as the essence of what makes them a 'listener' as opposed to a mere 'user' of the audio they are being served.

Such a characteristic aural experience arguably warrants further artistic development, which is what the *Streaaam* project attempts. As a nod to the historical roots of radio art (Brecht, 1932; Khlebnikov, 1985; Marinetti and Masnata, 1992), the stage for these inquiries will next be set in the

form of a (hopelessly polemic and deliberately unacademic) artistic manifesto (Puchner, 2006). It represents the author's personal reflection on two
semesters of artistic discourse with his students and the sonic artworks that
they have created in response, which will then be discussed in section 3.

2.4 Un-demand audio! A broadcasting manifesto

Ancient life was all sonic surprises. But in the twenty-first century, with
the commercialization of the internet, audio-on-demand was born. Today,
on-demand audio is triumphant and reigns sovereign over the aural sensi-
bility of people (cf., Russolo, 1916).

For too long, algorithms have been reading our every sonic wish from
our ears and fed us an aural diet exclusively based on what we allegedly
'demanded'. But we never asked for these auditory filter bubbles, the endless (re)cycles of sounds that they claim we 'also' want to hear. They know
our ears better than ourselves. They prevent us from finding in ourselves
the listener we do not yet know to be, the ears we do not yet know how to
use.

We must listen to audio beyond demand! We vow to give up control to
again become listeners in search of the auditory unknown!

Enough of algorithms that turn us into products! Enough of the endless
regurgitations of the culture industry's (Horkheimer and Adorno, 1987)
'more of the same'! They will converge into one single last surviving song
in the same way that the loudness race ultimately ends in silence. Enough
of echo chambers! Enough of speeches! Enough of speech!

Our eardrums want to be tickled with unheard sensations, devoid of
purpose and goals – freed of messages and signs (Schaeffer, 1966). Our
souls want to indulge in sounds that are not a means to an end but an end
to all meanings. A human and artistic autonomy of sound creation, utter-
ance, and perception.

We shall un-demand audio!

3 CASE STUDIES IN THE CONTEXT OF THE *STREAAAM* PROJECT

Streaaam (Hollerweger, 2021) is an automated experimental audio streaming server that has been devised as a vehicle for an artistic exploration of
algorithmically mediated broadcast listening experiences. It represents a
collaborative educational project that operates at the intersection of radio
art, generative music (Eno, 1996; Collins, 2008), and procedural audio
(Farnell, 2014), a research context previously explored through projects
such as *Eigenradio* (Recht and Whitman, 2003), *rand()%* (Dodson, 2003),
Generative.fm (Bainter, 2019), *Tweetspaces* (Hermann et al., 2012), or
Alternator (Clester and Freeman, 2022).

Over the 2021/22 academic year, the *Streaaam* server was used in a variety of higher education contexts at Columbia College Chicago's Department
of Audio Arts and Acoustics. They include, for example, Izaak Thompson's
ongoing sonification of COVID-19 case and death figures, whose sonification

strategies, synthesis techniques, and implementation in Pure Data (Puckette, 1996) are discussed elsewhere (Thompson and Hollerweger, 2022). This section aims to complement this discussion with a primarily artistic consideration of sonic artworks created by students in two other classes taught by the author. Its goal is to illustrate multiple ways in which the creation of broadcast listening experiences continues to offer a rich context for innovation in music.

The first of these two classes forms the backbone of a Bachelor of Science in Music Technology program and was devoted to the topic of *Broadcasting as a Sonic Art Form*. It yielded several new programs of sonic artworks created by students for the *Streaaam*, which will be discussed in sections 3.1 through 3.4. The second class, whose outcomes are presented in section 3.5, was concerned with the programming of digital audio effects. It provided an opportunity to artistically interpret generative music in the unusual context of processing existing sounds rather than synthesizing them from scratch.

Because the outcomes of these two classes represent artifacts of individual artistic expression, the author considers it appropriate to include their respective titles as well as the names of their creators in the following discussion. The artworks are presented here in this form with the explicit permission of the participating students.

3.1 Radiophonic poems

For the semester's first assignment in the first class, students were asked to create a 'radiophonic poem', a term that stems from the subtitle of the broadcast *Private Dreams and Public Nightmares*, written by Frederick Bradnum and realized by Daphne Oram and Desmond Briscoe at the BBC Radiophonic Workshop (Niebur, 2010; Netherwood, 2014) in 1957. Two other classic pieces of radio art served as role models for students to base their own sonic artwork on: *The Dreams* (1964) by Delia Derbyshire, as well as Barry Bermange and Glenn Gould's contrapuntal radio documentary *The Idea of North* (1967). Both of these works center on the human voice as their primary sound material, which students were encouraged to also artistically explore, either in recorded or speech-synthesized form, in a fixed-media composition. This focus on the human voice readily connects the assignment to its poetry-related theme, while *Streaaam*'s automated moderator Hal, one of its most recognizable features (Hollerweger, 2021), provided a context for an artistic exploration of speech synthesis.

Ed Hein's piece *Condensation* explores voices synthesized by means of artificial intelligence to convincingly create different characters purely by sound, who complement each other in the reading of a poem whose polyphony resembles Gould's. It also pays homage to Derbyshire's piece by replicating the disconnected sense of time and space that characterizes many dreams, letting the voices draw the listener's aural attention against a background that slowly transitions from one ambient space to another. The surprisingly expressive voices in Hein's piece reveal how synthesized speech is used almost exclusively for utilitarian (but rarely artistic) purposes.

Line Out by Jacob Clark portrays an inner monologue by overlaying recordings of the composer's own voice, a technique that resembles one also employed in the *Pre-Composition* by Mark Applebaum (2004). Reflecting Clark's interest in aphantasia, the work's meandering counterpoint of voices – sometimes focused, sometimes free-floating, sometimes intelligible, sometimes getting into each other's way – sonically represents the fleeting state of ideas and thoughts in our minds in an instantly recognizable fashion.

In *Tales from the Uber Days™* (2021), Autumn Hill uses the composer's own recorded voice to narrate to an imaginary audience one of many anecdotes from her experience of working as a driver for a popular rideshare service to finance her studies, using self-produced music and a fast-paced sound design to enhance the story's comedy in an artistically original fashion.

Kat Kamarulzaman's *The Last Voicemail from Me* wraps the characteristically acousmatic situation of listening to one's voicemail inside a composition that is itself acousmatic. The voicemail messages that form the basis of the work serve, in the composer's words, "as a symbolic pipeline of communication" to condense the spectrum of emotions experienced during the five stages of grief (denial, anger, bargaining, depression, and acceptance) into a deeply personal piece.

Nick Soto's piece *Three Friends* aims to capture the sonic essence of hanging out on a Discord call in good company. The composer achieves this by editing actual recordings of such calls according to the musical idioms of jazz, with 'drum fills' and 'solos'. Like Clark's, this work oscillates between an artistic use of the human voice as an intelligible sign in a language on the one hand and an abstracted sound object appreciated through reduced listening (Chion, 1983) on the other.

3.2 Oppressistance!

For the second assignment in the previously discussed class, students reflected on the history of audio broadcasting as a vehicle for oppression on the one hand and for resistance on the other. Based on a text by Frantz Fanon (1965), as well as various in-class readings and listenings on the propagandistic use of radio in the Third Reich, students created a fixed-media composition that was to artistically foreground the typical sonic artifacts of broadcasting (noise, crackles, etc.) as musical material. The resulting works mirror the definition of manifesto art by Puchner (2006, p. 6) as "aggressive rather than introverted; screaming rather than reticent; collective rather than individual".

For his piece *Resistance*, Nick Soto repurposed a Bluetooth-to-FM transmitter, playing a pre-produced recording of a self-authored text off a phone, whose signal was then, via the transmitter, received by a radio that the composer manipulated while re-recording its output. Soto then re-recorded the resulting signal on a reel-to-reel tape machine and back into a digital audio workstation, adding yet another layer of sonic artifacts whose identifiability in the resulting piece attests to the extreme subtleties that the human auditory system is capable of decoding. The result convincingly conveys the archetypical sonic experience of tuning a receiver to an ephemeral station on the ether, akin to, in the composer's words, "hearing a radio message that is coming from a resistance base".

Jacob Clark's work *The Right to Broadcast* creatively re-assembles quotes from the FCC's website, which rationalize the regulation of the radio spectrum by arguing that no fundamental right to broadcast can be derived from the free speech right enshrined in the First Amendment of the US Constitution. The work's artistic expressiveness stems from the manner in which its editing, without altering the original quotes per se, highlights the negative side effects of a legal framework that effectively silences marginalized communities while giving a voice primarily to the wealthy and big business.

In *Radio Anarchy*, Ed Hein imagines a dystopian society through a fictional news broadcast by a government that has banned other sources of information, which is eventually interrupted by rebels who take over the airwaves to inspire others to support their cause. Hein weaves various forms of noise and distortion that are characteristically encountered on terrestrial radio into a realistic sound design.

Nicholas Vitacco's *Changing Stations* critiques the tendency of mainstream radio to talk "about a sensationalized state of the world all of the time . . . with the intent of scaring people into tuning in". Like Soto, the composer achieves this through a sound design that mimics the experience of tuning a radio's frequency dial, illustrating that noise cannot just be found between the stations but also in the indistinguishable messages of mainstream media. This critique is emphasized by highlighting coincidental appearances of the word "normal" across different stations, a sonic twist that manifests the piece's musicality.

3.3 From Scratch

For their final project in this class, students autonomously decided to create an automated radio talk show entitled *From Scratch*, to be moderated by the stream's speech-synthesized moderator Hal (cf., Hollerweger, 2021). After the fixed-media pieces that students created for the previous assignments, they were encouraged (but not required) to creatively explore procedural audio techniques (Farnell, 2014) in Pure Data for this project.

Both Jacob Clark's *Erratic Hourglass* and Nick Soto's *[po'sole]* contrast generatively synthesized background layers, which change each time they are being played, with a static linear monologue in the foreground, although in artistically very different fashions. Soto refers to his piece as a "sonic cooking show" in which the foreground monologue represents the cook going through the process of preparing posole while explaining the recipe and process along the way, accompanied by an ever-shifting background loop of drums and synthesizer chords. In Clark's piece, the composer further develops the idiosyncratic use of his own voice, already familiar from his radiophonic poem. It provides an anchor of tranquility, "unaware and unaffected by the chaos around", as the composer says. The latter is created by a vivid background of generative granular synthesis, creating radically different sonic textures at different times of the day.

Ed Hein's piece *Poetics*, in contrast, uses procedural techniques at both the micro level of procedural sound synthesis and the macro level of artistic form. The former is used, for example, to convey the stochastic character of the sounds of a glowing fire, whereas the latter determines which of ten poems is read at the end of a scene in which the listener is acoustically guided from a stormy winter night into the coziness of a room with an open fire and a kitchen. Although the poem selection, which leaves the listener in suspense also upon repeated listening, is randomized and automated, the technique resembles interactive theater plays with multiple possible outcomes, such as the musical *The Mystery of Edwin Drood* based on an unfinished Charles Dickens novel.

While Autumn Hill's *An Informational Broadcast* and Kat Kamarul-zaman's *19 Hz* do not incorporate any procedural elements, they further illustrate the variety of artistic strategies that students devised for their creative explorations of audio broadcasting. Against a powerful self-produced foreground, Hill's piece's background weaves a dense net of sonic quotations from various listenings that students encountered during the semester, including the characteristic endless recitations of encrypted messages broadcast on Cold War 'numbers stations' (Moon, 1987; Schimmel, 1994; Pierce, 1994; Smolinski, 1998; Bury, 2007; Beaumont, 2012, 2013; Friesen, 2014). Kamarulzaman's work, in the composer's words, "references the sounds that played a monumental role in the compositions I have written over the past year".

Nicholas Vitacco, rather than contributing his own sonic artwork to the program, was responsible for providing the radio talk show frame in the form of a shell script that loads the other students' pieces and introduces them by letting Hal read the works' titles and descriptions from the metadata of the sound files representing the works. The script also implements various talk segments moderated by Hal, including a standup comedy show with randomized jokes and audience laughter and a conversation with a celebrity guest whose voice is synthesized through the Uberduck web service. Some aspects of this script are implemented in a procedural fashion, such that the jokes told during the standup comedy segment, for example, vary with each occurrence of the program on the stream.

3.4 Procedural theme music

Procedurally synthesized sounds feature on the *Streaaam* not only in the form of self-contained sonic artworks but also in the form of much shorter snippets that are woven into the context of a larger program. An example is the re-implementation of the BBC's iconic Greenwich Time Signal (Wikipedia contributors, 2021) in Pd, which opens our stream's hourly news segment and is generated on-the-fly every time it is played. Another example is the shortened version of Izaak Thompson's *Pure Covidata* (Thompson and Hollerweger, 2022), which sonifies only the current day's COVID-19 case and death figures for Cook County, Illinois, and concludes the same news segment.

A third example is given by the mid-term project of the previously discussed class, for which students were asked to create short 'dynamic theme music' for the *Streaaam* server by means of procedural sound synthesis in Pure Data. They were given the option of either creating a 'sweeper' for the stream as a whole or a 'jingle' for one of its existing programs. A requirement was for this sonic theme to change every time it is being played while at the same time retaining its recognizable 'sonic identity'. In addition, students were asked to artistically reflect on the theme of 'giving a voice to someone' through their work.

The five students who submitted work for this assignment addressed these challenges through a variety of artistic means. Two of them relied exclusively on sound synthesis, while two others mixed synthesized sounds with pre-produced sound files. The fifth student implemented a form of granular synthesis, whereby a program jingle is constructed from recycling whatever sound file was previously heard on the stream. The other works also employed techniques such as additive and subtractive synthesis as well as waveshaping. All works made use of Pd's internal random object to create variations of their jingle. Four of them additionally used the date or current time of day to create further variety in a more deterministic fashion. For example, Ed Hein's *Sleepy Chicago* contrasts nature sounds in the morning with urban sounds in the afternoon and generates different sounds based on whether the piece is being played during the first or the second half of the hour. Using the techniques listed previously, students varied parameters such as oscillator frequencies, melodic pitches, envelope durations, filter cutoff frequencies, playback speed, sound file selection, and wavetable read points. Despite these deliberately introduced variations, all five works succeeded in retaining an immediately recognizable 'sonic signature'.

3.5 SFX Flags

SFX Flags is a 'sonic theme park' that students envisioned as their final project in the second class discussed in this chapter, which was devoted to the creation of digital audio effects. Since audio effects do, by definition, not generate any sound themselves but instead transform a potentially unpredictable input signal, the question presented itself how students could present their final projects on the *Streaaam* server. It was decided to re-route the server's regular (and, for this purpose, randomized) playlist through the effects created by the students in Pure Data (Pd). The result is a non-deterministic, procedural program of generative music, in which every effect creates a differently sounding output each time the program is scheduled, depending on which input signal it happens to be fed at that time.

The granulator that Purusottam Samal created for his effect, *The Shimmer,* generates sonic gestures and musical-formal trajectories that are instantly recognizable, regardless of the source material that they process.

Taryn Stroman's *Shooting Star* mimics the popular 'Superman Tower of Power' theme park ride, whose characteristic vertical upwards and downwards motions it emulates by speeding up and slowing down, respectively, the playback of a short sound snippet recorded from the input signal. In a similar fashion, Jacob Clark's *Boomerang* uses three independent delay lines that record sound from the input signal and play it back at varying speeds.

X2 by Alexander Espinosa replicates a theme park ride of the same name, a rollercoaster that additionally spins on its tracks. Stereo panning mimics the ride's spin, amplitude modulation frequency, its shakiness, and amplitude envelopes the ups and downs of the rollercoaster.

Nick Soto's *Raging Bull* is inspired by the two drops of an equally named rollercoaster and relies on a bit crusher and additional distortion to create a sound that is as wild as the ride that lends it its name.

An Alice-in-Wonderland-like sense of a sonic world spinning around the listener is conveyed by Holland Sersen's *SpinPot* by means of a frequency-dependent panpot that is implemented with FFT-based techniques.

Stanley Rex Godfrey's *The Deep* conveys the acoustic depths of the ocean through classic guitar-pedal effects such as flanging and reverb. Similar effects are also employed in *Canyon* by Noel Gutierrez, which is a reference to both the 'Canyon Blaster' ride as well as a guitar effect pedal of the same name.

Tien Nguyen's *Bone* emulates a theme park ride entitled 'Skull Mountain' through sudden movements, pitch, and playback speed changes, as well as through delay lines to mimic this indoor coaster's cave-like acoustics.

The outcomes of this program challenge the traditional notion of audio effects as *tools* (rather than artifacts) of the sonic arts in so far as they arguably represent artworks in their own right, each with a strong sonic identity. It was unexpectedly easy to reliably identify each student's effect solely by ear while testing the program on the server with a variety of input signals. Each student's effect conveyed the respective artistic theme of their 'ride' quite successfully and in a perceptually relevant fashion.

4 CONCLUSIONS AND FUTURE WORK

The sonic artworks presented in the previous section illustrate the artistic potential of 'audio beyond demand', of broadcast listening as an idiosyncratic form of aestheticized aural experience. Specifically, these works implement numerous artistic strategies for the algorithmic mediation of aural experience that go well beyond choice-driven music recommendations and instead point towards many other opportunities for musical innovation. The following concluding remarks provide some pointers in this regard.

4.1 Towards procedural broadcasting

While generative music and procedural audio (Farnell, 2014) techniques are commonly discussed in the context of non-linear, interactive media such as computer games, the *Streaaam* server ironically employs them for the linear, non-interactive medium of live audio streaming. Their usefulness for the latter stems from the fact that on a fully automated system such as *Streaaam*, the desired sonic variety (cf., section 2.2) needs to be generated algorithmically rather than by more immediate forms of human intervention. The sonic art created for the *Streaaam*, therefore, seeks to forward a procedural understanding not only of sound but also of other media, such as text, from which the server generates sound in a variety of ways, be it through speech synthesis, data sonification (Thompson and Hollerweger, 2022), or other means (cf., Hollerweger, 2021). One could refer to such a genre, which combines an inherently dynamic understanding of data with classic radio automation techniques (Baelde, Beauxis and Mimram, 2011; Mimram and Beauxis, 2021) as *procedural broadcasting*. The further development of this genre represents the central artistic vision for *Streaaam*'s future.

4.2 Beyond sound files

One observation that stems from the artistic explorations in the context of *Streaaam* is how surprisingly poorly equipped existing software frameworks are for the implementation of such procedural broadcasting systems. The resulting technological challenges illustrate the degree to which music technology still defaults to an understanding of sound as a fixed rather than dynamic medium. For example, one mundane reason why the *Streaaam* server can load code written in Pure Data, SuperCollider, Csound, and ChucK (cf., Hollerweger, 2021) is the simple fact that there are no widely agreed-upon data formats for procedural audio comparable to standardized (and easily convertible) fixed audio file formats such as .wav, .aiff, .flac, etc. A similar workaround is employed in the *Alternator* project (Clester and Freeman, 2022).

When will listeners be able, on a large scale, to load procedural sound 'files' on their devices that can adapt to the playback conditions? Since RjDj put forward the notion of 'reactive music' in 2008 (Reality Jockey Ltd., no date), surprisingly little has happened. While the standardization of procedural audio arguably represents a trickier problem than that of fixed-media audio file formats, the WebAudioAPI (World Wide Web Consortium, 2021) represents an important step in this direction.

5 ACKNOWLEDGMENTS

The author would like to thank the students of the two classes at Columbia College Chicago who created the sonic artworks discussed in section 3, where their creators' names are listed as well. Pedro Lopes at the University of Chicago deserves a special mention for inspiring the 'audio-un-demand' pun in that original form.

REFERENCES

Adibi, M., Zoccolan, D. and Clifford, C. W. G. (2021). 'Editorial: Sensory Adaptation', *Frontiers in Systems Neuroscience*. https://doi.org/10.3389/fnsys.2021.809000.

Applebaum, M. (2004). 'Pre-composition', in *Intellectual Property*. Audio CD 602. Innova Recordings.

Attali, J. (1977). *Bruits: Essai sur l'économie politique de la musique*, 1st ed. Presses Universitaires de France, Paris.

Baelde, D., Beauxis, R. and Mimram, S. (2011). 'Liquidsoap: A High-Level Programming Language for Multimedia Streaming', in *Proceedings of the International Conference on Current Trends in Theory and Practice of Computer Science (SOFSEM)*. Heidelberg: Springer, pp. 99–110. https://doi.org/10.1007/978-3-642-18381-28.

Bainter, A. (2019). 'Generative.fm', in *Proceedings of the International Web Audio Conference*. Trondheim, Norway: NTNU, p. 148.

Beaumont, P. (2012). 'Numbers Stations: A Modern Perspective (Part 1)', *RadioUser*, November issue, pp. 50–53.

Beaumont, P. (2013). 'Numbers Stations: A Modern Perspective (Part 2)', *RadioUser*, January issue, pp. 50–55.

Bendet, N. (2020). 'Is Spotify's Random Play Button Really Random?', *UX Collective*. Available at: https://uxdesign.cc/randomly-not-random-2fd53536513c [Accessed: 27 August 2022].

Brecht, B. (1932). 'Der Rundfunk als Kommunikationsapparat', *Blätter des Hessischen Landestheaters*, 16, pp. 181–184.

Bury, J. (2007). 'From the Archives: The U.S. and West German Agent Radio Ciphers', *Cryptologia*, 31(4), pp. 343–357. https://doi.org/10.1080/01611190701578104.

Chion, M. (1983). *Guide des objets sonores: Pierre Schaeffer et la recherche musicale*. Paris: Éditions Buchet/Chastel.

Chion, M. (1991). *L'art des sons fixés ou la musique concrètement*. Fontaine: Metamkine.

Clester, I. and Freeman, J. (2022). 'Alternator: A General-Purpose Generative Music Player', in *Proceedings of the Web Audio Conference*. Cannes, France. https://doi.org/10.5281/zenodo.6767436.

Collins, N. (2008). 'The Analysis of Generative Music Programs', *Organised Sound*, 13(3), pp. 237–248. https://doi.org/10.1017/S1355771808000332.

Dodson, S. (2003). 'Web Watch', *The Guardian*. Available at: www.theguardian.com/technology/2003/dec/04/internet.onlinesupplement [Accessed: 1 July 2022].

Eno, B. (1996). *Generative Music: A Talk Delivered in San Francisco, June 8, 1996*. Available at: https://inmotionmagazine.com/eno1.html [Accessed: 11 July 2022].

Fanon, F. (1965). *A Dying Colonialism*. New York: Grove Press.

Farnell, A. (2014). 'Procedural Audio Theory and Practice', in Collins, K., Kapralos, B. and Tessler, H., eds. *The Oxford Handbook of Interactive Audio*. New York: Oxford University Press, pp. 531–540. https://doi.org/10.1093/oxfordhb/9780199797226.001.0001.

Fechner, G. T. (1860). *Elemente der Psychophysik*. Leipzig: Breitkopf und Härtel.

Friesen, C. (2014). 'Spy "Numbers Stations" Still Enthrall', *Radio World*, 38(2), pp. 12, 14.

The Guardian. (2022). *100 Ways to Slightly Improve Your Life Without Really Trying*. Available at: www.theguardian.com/lifeandstyle/2022/jan/01/marginal-gains-100-ways-to-improve-your-life-without-really-trying [Accessed: 27 August 2022].

Hermann, T., et al. (2012). 'Tweetscapes: Real-time Sonification of Twitter Data Streams for Radio Broadcasting', in *Proceedings of the International Conference on Auditory Display*, pp. 113–120. Available at: http://hdl.handle.net/1853/44424 [Accessed: 1 July 2022].

Hollerweger, F. (2021). 'Streaaam: A Fully Automated Experimental Audio Streaming Server', in *Proceedings of the Audio Mostly Conference*. Virtual/Trento, Italy: Association for Computing Machinery, pp. 161–168. https://doi.org/10.1145/3478384.3478426.

Horkheimer, M. and Adorno, T. W. (1987). 'Kulturindustrie: Aufklärung als Massenbetrug', in *'Dialektik der Aufklärung' und Schriften 1940–1950*. Frankfurt am Main: S. Fischer Verlag GmbH.

Hunter-Tilney, L. (2016). *Music in the Age of the Algorithm*. Available at: www.ft.com/content/fc9db5d6-2cc9-11e6-bf8d-26294ad519fc [Accessed: 27 August 2022].

Khlebnikov, V. (1985). 'The Radio of the Future', in Douglas, C., ed. *The King of Time: Selected Writings of the Russian Futurian*. London and Cambridge, MA: Harvard University Press.

Klein, J. (2017). *What Is Artistic Research?* https://doi.org/10.22501/jarnet.0004.

Lind, R. A. and Medoff, N. J. (1999). 'Radio Stations and the World Wide Web', *Journal of Radio Studies*, 6(2), pp. 203–221. https://doi.org/10.1080/19376529909391723.

Loydell, R. (2014). 'Out of Context: "Control & Surrender" Revisited and Remixed', *Journal of Writing in Creative Practice*, 7(1). https://doi.org/10.1386/jwcp.7.1.111_1.

Loydell, R. and Marshall, K. (2016). 'Control & Surrender: Eno Remixed – Collaboration and Oblique Strategies', in Albiez, S. and Pattie, D., eds. *Brian Eno: Oblique Music*. London: Bloomsbury Academic, pp. 175–192. https://doi.org/10.5040/9781501325007.ch-009.

Marinetti, F. T. and Masnata, P. (1992). 'La Radia', in Kahn, D. and Whitehead, G., eds., Sartarelli, S., trans. *Wireless Imagination: Sound, Radio and the Avant-Garde*. Cambridge, MA: MIT Press, pp. 265–268.

McInerney, J., et al. (2018). 'Explore, Exploit, and Explain', in *Proceedings of the 12th ACM Conference on Recommender Systems*. Vancouver, BC, Canada: Association of Computing Machinery, pp. 31–39.

Mimram, S. and Beauxis, R. (2021). *The Liquidsoap Book*. Available at: www.liquidsoap.info/doc-dev/book.html [Accessed: 8 July 2022].

Moon, H. (1987). *Uno, Dos, Cuatro: A Guide to the Numbers Stations*. Lake Geneva, WI: Tiare Publications.

Netherwood, N. (2014). *An Electric Storm: Daphne, Delia and the BBC Radiophonic Workshop*. Obverse Books, Edinburgh.

Niebur, L. (2010). *Special Sound: The Creation and Legacy of the BBC Radiophonic Workshop*. Oxford: Oxford University Press.

Pierce, L. (1994). *Intercepting Numbers Stations*. Perth: Interproducts.

Priestman, C. (2001). *Web Radio: Radio Production for Internet Streaming*, 1st ed. New York: Routledge. https://doi.org/10.4324/9780080520919.

Puchner, M. (2006). *Poetry of the Revolution: Marx, Manifestos, and the Avant-Gardes*. Princeton, NJ: Princeton University Press.

Puckette, M. (1996). 'Pure Data: Another Integrated Computer Music Environment', in *Proceedings of the Second Intercollege Computer Music Concerts*. Tachikawa, Japan, pp. 37–41.

Ranallo, A. (2021). 'Why You're Using Spotify Wrong', *Becoming Human: Artificial Intelligence Magazine*. Available at: https://becominghuman.ai/why-youre-using-spotify-wrong-b827eb47c249 [Accessed: 27 August 2022].

Reality Jockey Ltd. (n.d.). *RjDj: The Sonic Experiences of the 21st Century*. Available at: www.rjdj.me [Accessed: 20 September 2014].

Recht, B. and Whitman, B. (2003). 'Musically Expressive Sound Textures from Generalized Audio', in *Proceedings of the International Conference on Digital Audio Effects*. London. https://www.dafx.de

Russolo, L. (1916). *L'arte dei rumori: Manifesto Futurista*. Milano: Edizioni Futuriste di 'Poesia'.

Schaeffer, P. (1966). *Traité des objets musicaux: Essai interdisciplines*. Paris: Éditions du Seuil.

Schimmel, D. W. (1994). *Underground Frequency Guide: A Directory of Unusual, Illegal, and Covert Radio Communications*, 3rd ed. Solana Beach, CA: High Text Publications, Inc.

Smolinski, C. (1998). 'Spy Numbers Stations: Have You Heard Them?', *Popular Communications*, pp. 8–10.

Snickars, P. (2017). 'More of the Same: On Spotify Radio', *Culture Unbound: Journal of Current Cultural Research*, 9(2), pp. 184–211.

Stockhausen, K. (1972). *Four Criteria of Electronic Music*. Available at: https://youtu.be/7xyGtI7KKIY [Accessed: 11 September 2020].

Stoppa, N., et al. (2022). *Tracks: Songwriting Special: Pop Music: The Great Recycling Business*. Available at: www.arte.tv/en/videos/106757-005-A/tracks-songwriting-special [Accessed: 27 August 2022].

Tan, I. Z. M. (2011). 'Brian Eno: Drums Between the Bells', *Sputnik Music*. Available at: www.sputnikmusic.com/review/44311/Brian-Eno-Drums-Between-The-Bells/ [Accessed: 9 January 2023].

Thompson, I. and Hollerweger, F. (2022). 'Pure Covidata: An Automated Sonification of the COVID-19 Pandemic's Recent State', in Rönnberg, N., et al., eds. *Psychoacoustics in the Loop: Proceedings of the 7th Interactive Sonification Workshop*. Delmenhorst, Germany: Hanse Wissenschaftskolleg (HWK). https://doi.org/10.5281/zenodo.7552251.

Timberg, S. (2016). *Spotify Is Making You Boring: When Algorithms Shape Music Taste, Human Curiosity Loses*. Salon. Available at: www.salon.com/2016/06/10/spotify_is_making_you_boring_when_algorithms_shape_music_taste_human_curiosity_loses/ [Accessed: 27 August 2022].

Voegelin, S. (2010). *Listening to Noise and Silence: Towards a Philosophy of Sound Art*, 1st ed. Continuum, London.

Wark, B., Lundstrom, B. N. and Fairhall, A. (2007). 'Sensory Adaptation', *Current Opinion in Neurobiology*, 17, pp. 423–429. https://doi.org/10.1016/j.conb.2007.07.001.

Webster, M. A. (2012). 'Evolving Concepts of Sensory Adaptation', *F1000 Biology Report*, 4(21). https://doi.org/10.3410/B4-21.

Wikipedia Contributors. (2021). *Greenwich Time Signal*. Available at: https://en.wikipedia.org/wiki/Greenwich_Time_Signal [Accessed: 10 May 2021].

Wohlwill, J. F. (1974). 'Human Adaptation to Levels of Environmental Stimulation', *Human Ecology*, 2(2), pp. 127–147. https://doi.org/10.1007/BF01558117.

World Wide Web Consortium. (2021). *Web Audio API*. Available at: www.w3.org/TR/webaudio/ [Accessed: 3 June 2022].

Xiph.org. (2004–2022). *Icecast FAQ*. Available at: https://icecast.org/faq [Accessed: 27 August 2022].

12

Towards a standard for interactive music

Hans Lindetorp

1 INTRODUCTION

Interactive media has become one of the most important forms of entertainment and education over the last decades, and sound and music play a big role in those formats, including music for games (Collins, 2008) and interactive movies. Even if the technology has matured over the years from the 8-bit sound in early game consoles and computer sound cards into high-quality, multi-channel, surround audio, there is still room for improvements in strategies, tools, processes, and formats regarding the making and implementation of sound design and music for interactive media (Redhead, 2018). This has been explored and used primarily in computer games and is referred to as "adaptive music", "interactive music" or "dynamic music", and even if the term varies, it often refers to musical building blocks that are arranged and played back in real-time controlled by data from a hosting application. There are different technical approaches to achieve interactive music. It can be very responsive and even generated in real-time using algorithms and virtual instruments, or it can be less responsive, simply cross-fading between different music when an interaction occurs. The focus of this study is Interactive Recorded Music (Paterson and Toulson 2018), which is an approach that can be both responsive and have the sound quality of a traditional recording. This technique uses multiple audio files that are structured, triggered, looped and mixed by the hosting application.

Since the advent of HTML5 (Hickson et al., 2022), web technologies have matured to become a solid and powerful platform for building accessible applications for almost any purpose. Since Web Audio API (Adenot and Choi, 2022) became a "web recommendation", applications for music production will most likely be subject to a lot of changes in the near future. Web technologies are fostered and further developed by a consortium with many stakeholders (Berners-Lee et al., 2022) and are built upon Open Standard Principles (OpenStand Advocate, 2022) that aim at "improving the way people around the world develop new technologies and innovate for humanity" (Berners-Lee, 2022). In regards to sound and music, web technologies have led to many initiatives in research and education, and

DOI: 10.4324/9781003118817-14

commercially, web audio applications are now available, ranging from small demos (Google, 2013) to experimental interactive audio platforms (Robaszkiewicz and Schnell, 2015) and commercial software for music production (Soundtrap, 2023).

In contrast to standard music production and music notation, there is no shared file format or well-defined terminology for interactive music. This makes it hard to share content as well as knowledge between different user groups. The current solutions and terminologies tend to be proprietary and unique to different applications or hidden in unknown minor projects.

This study seeks to contribute to the discussion and the ongoing standardization of such standards with insights from designing and evaluating iMusicXML (Lindetorp, 2016b) – a language and a plugin for implementing music in web-based interactive applications. Contrary to similar products on the market, it uses artistic goals rather than commercial as a driving factor for feature specification. It targets multiple types of applications rather than only commercially viable platforms like computer games. The code is open source, and the documentation of the design process is available to contribute useful research output for the wider community.

2 BACKGROUND

In this section, related technologies and research are presented, and the culture of integrated research and education at the Royal College of Music (KMH), where the study was performed, is described to give an understanding of the environment where the ideas and solutions have emerged.

2.1 Applications for music production

There are many applications available for music production. The ones most used by the students participating in this study are called Digital Audio Workstations (DAWs) and are built on metaphors from the music studio, like a tape recorder with tracks, a mixing console with channels and many different virtual representations of instruments and audio processors.

These DAW applications, like Apple Logic (Apple inc., 2022) and Pro Tools (Avid, 2022) have their own terminologies for different features but often share concepts that have an analog representation (like "track" or "mixer"). There are also music production tools aimed at live performances, like Ableton Live (Ableton, 2022), that share some concepts with music for interactive media. Applications like these are used as a first step for producing audio files for the projects covered by this study, and their terminology is used, when possible, in the design of iMusicXML.

2.2 Applications for game music

In order to make music integrate into a computer game, the music produced in a DAW needs to be implemented into the game environment. To solve this task, a type of program called "middle ware" has emerged; popular examples are Fmod (Fmod, 2022), Wwise (Audio Kinetic, 2022) and Elias Studio (Elias Software, 2022). They offer features to import, structure and connect the musical content to the game interactions. The current study focuses primarily on these tasks and shares terminology with some of the middle ware applications.

2.3 Experimental interactive sound and music

There is a range of platforms available for making interactive music that have become popular tools on the experimental scene. They generally have a focus on connecting interactions with audio processing rather than dealing with musical structures and queueing audio files. Some examples are CSound (Vercoe, 1985), Pure Data (Puckette, 1997), and SuperCollider (McCartney, 2002). They can be used to connect interaction variables to control various aspects of a sound and are often used to build new Digital Musical Instruments. This aspect of declaring variable mapping to sound parameters using XML has been explored and presented in the WebAudioXML project (Lindetorp and Falkenberg, 2021).

2.4 Interactive music-playback apps

There have been various attempts at finding new and interactive ways to deliver music. Releases like Björk's "Biophilia" (Björk, 2011) with limited user interactions and Massive Attack's "Fantom" (Monroe, 2016) that used input from various sensors, including the camera, clock, microphone and the user's heart rate demonstrate how music can be experienced in various engaging ways. The research project "variPlay" (Paterson, Toulson and Hepworth-Sawyer, 2019) explored new formats for letting the user controlling the mix and even the style of a song through a simple and accessible interface. A related type of applications are DJ-apps, where the user can manipulate the playback of different tracks in real-time. The release of the Traktor DJ iPad app from Native Instruments has also led to an extension of MPEG-4, where four different tracks can be shared using an open file format (Stems-Music, 2015). All these initiatives are important steps towards a possible open standard for fully interactive recorded music.

2.5 Education and research

At KMH, music production education is built on a problem-based, learner-centered approach (Walker, 2015). Research and the education are highly integrated, and the students contribute with research data as well as benefit from learning from the last findings. The courses and methods are regularly evaluated and improved (Hansen et al., 2019). Interactive media has always been an important part of education but, like related studies (Xambó et al., 2020; Xambó Sedo et al., 2019), it has been noted that the demanding technical tasks involved in making interactive media create a high barrier for artists to start creating interactive media. Earlier studies have shown that technical challenges sometimes cause students to abandon their artistic ambitions (Lindetorp, 2019) and never try their potential.

These challenges have led to the design of various tools for entering interactive music production from an artistic angle, and this study is a summary of the most important insights from this work.

3 OVERVIEW OF INCLUDED PROJECTS

This study is performed on data collected from more than 100 student projects at KMH during a period of eight years. The students (aged 19–35) were studying music production at bachelor's or master's level. Many of them have a background in pop music production and are in various courses also exposed to composing and producing music for film, games and interactive installations. A typical structure for such a course is a series of lectures, labs, an artistic project and, finally, a reflection and evaluation of the result. All the projects included in this study start from a given template made for the specific course and are led by the students' artistic visions. The projects are very different and span from simple web pages with adaptive music to large-scale interactive music installations at museums, but they are all built with web technologies and iMusicXML. An overview of the projects are described in what follows.

3.1 Interactive stories

All bachelor students create an "Interactive Story" with images, video, text, audio, and music. The story could be either linear or have an open form, but the progression of the story is always determined by the users' actions. The focus of the music production is to match the story and the graphical style with the music and to support smooth transitions between the different pages and meaningful changes in the music according to the interactions. This challenge requires solutions for playing music in a sequential order.

3.2 Online games

Some students create their own computer game. The musical challenge is to make adaptive music that gives the game the right energy and feel. It is also a goal for the music to reflect the current intensity of the game, which requires features for working with stems and layers of music. Another important aspect of the game projects has been to respond musically to the different events and user interactions, which require features for triggering musical phrases in sync with the other tracks.

3.3 Adaptive music in museum exhibitions

The students have several times been invited to produce music for interactive exhibitions at museums in Stockholm (Kulturhuset, 2022; Stockholm City Museum, 2022) and the "Nobel Creation" exhibition (Gullö et al., 2015). The musical challenge for these installations has been to make music that communicates the message of the exhibition in harmony with the objects and the general design of the room and to respond to the visitors' actions without being too repetitive for the staff working at the museum. These challenges require solutions for dealing with variation and randomness.

3.4 Multi-sensory music installation

The Swedish Museum of Performing Arts (Museum of Performing Art, 2022) includes a large-scale, multi-sensory, accessible, digital instrument called the "Sound Forest" (Bresin et al., 2016; Paloranta et al., 2016) that allows visitors to play with light-emitting strings attached between the ceiling and the floor. Two groups of master students from the Music Production education program have composed interactive music for this instrument, and several studies have contributed with important insights on how to compose effectively for a multi-sensory experience like this (Frid and Lindetorp, 2020; Frid et al., 2019). The musical focus in these projects has been to make sounds and vibrations that are fun for the visitors to interact with and a background loop that is also effected by the interactions in the room.

3.5 Smartphone instruments

Finally, there is a group of projects that have aimed at creating interactive musical instruments using ordinary smartphones. The instruments have been tested both in a multi-channel super-surround speaker setup called "Klangkupolen" (Figure 12.1) (Frisk and Brunson, 2014; Lindetorp, 2019) at KMH and with the built-in speakers and headphones (Lindetorp and Falkenberg, 2022). These projects require features for dealing with multiple sensors, audio parameter mappings and multi-channel output routing.

Figure 12.1 Smartphone instrument in multi-channel super-surround speaker setup.

4 METHOD

The current study is an evaluation and report from an ongoing exploratory design study where the research activities are integrated into the bachelor's and master's education mentioned in section 3. The design practice is used as a method to generate research data (Löwgren, 2013) and can be viewed as "research through design for the arts" (Frayling, 1993). The following sections describe the technical platform and the method for collecting data in more detail.

4.1 Technical platform

All projects covered in this study and all design activities are collected in one framework called iMusicXML. It is a JavaScript framework and XML language for implementing interactive music in web pages. The development started as a pure JavaScript plugin that offered high-level methods for structuring and controlling the playback of audio loops but has, in later years, also been expanded with an XML language to abstract the features even more. iMusicXML builds upon Web Audio API (Adenot and Choi, 2022) and relates to a framework called WebAudioXML (WAXML) (Lindetorp, 2022b), presented at the Sound and Music Computing Conference (Lindetorp and Falkenberg, 2020, 2021). WAXML is an XML abstraction for configuring audio objects and mapping audio parameters in an application, and iMusicXML is structuring and synchronizing audio files in a musical context. This study focuses on the latter, even if many of the included projects also use features from WAXML.

4.2 Iterative design process

The design strategy is sequential (Redstrom, 2017, p. 24) and is based on an iterative process where a group of students formulate artistic ideas and needs for a project. These ideas inform the design of new technical solutions that are evaluated and finally turned into new features and ideas. The cyclic process results in new versions of the technology after each student project and makes up the new starting point for the iteration with the next student group (Figure 12.2). The source code (Lindetorp, 2016b) is annotated, the features are documented (Lindetorp, 2016a) and the XML language is finally specified in an XML Schema Definition (XSD) file (Lindetorp, 2022a).

4.3 Data collection

In the study, data from the XSD file are analyzed. This file contains all musical objects and all settings and is the output of the cumulative process of building the framework in close relation to the student projects. The objects, features and terminologies are grouped and presented in categories (structure, variation, transitions, user interaction and accessibility) that are derived from the learning objectives in the different courses.

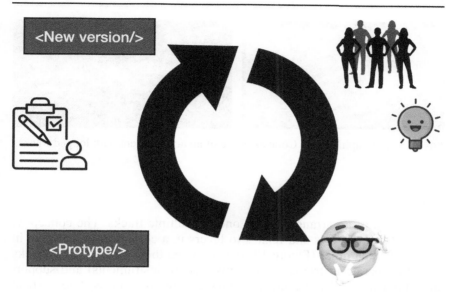

Figure 12.2 The iterative design process from student ideas, new solutions and evaluation.

5 RESULT

The following sections present the concepts and features in the current state of iMusicXML. They are the result of an exploratory design study with multiple iterations with student projects and will serve as a stepping stone for further development and a broader discussion about general concepts and possible standards.

5.1 Structure

In all student projects, the musical content needed to be structured in a way that was neither hard to understand nor too limiting in its possibilities. The structural parts that have emerged as a result are presented in what follows.

Arrangements

An "arrangement" is a section of music targeted for a specific scene or part of an application. Compared to a musical score, it refers to a range of bars in a composition and supports an approach in adaptive music sometimes referred to as "the horizontal method". To use a computer game as an example, arrangements typically play at a certain location or during a specific event in the game.

The length of an arrangement is not set, and the content can either play once or be looped. The arrangement holds musical settings like tempo, time signature, and information for controlling when and where a transition to another arrangement can appear.

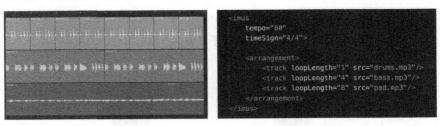

Figure 12.3 Graphical and Code example of an arrangement with looped tracks.

Tracks

The content of an arrangement is one or multiple tracks. The concept is inherited from DAWs and relates to layers in a composition that play in sync with each other (Figure 12.3). Compared to a musical score, tracks refer to separate instruments or stems (sets of instruments) and support an approach in adaptive music sometimes referred to as "the vertical method". In computer games, this is used to change the intensity of the music by adding and removing tracks inside a looped section. Tracks can have individual settings for looping and cross-fades and can be routed to a mixer channel strip in WAXML.

Loops

The way most students have chosen to create an open musical form is to loop tracks until a change is required. Traditional loops are often cycling between one or more bars, but the use of different instruments has challenged how the loop feature has to be implemented. The musical content in the student compositions has led to loops with both a head and a tail that are layered on top of the next iteration of the loop. The head preserves audible pick-up just before the downbeat like a strummed guitar chord, and the tail keeps the sustaining sound in an instrument like a cymbal (Figure 12.4).

Motifs

A "motif" feature has been needed in almost all student projects and is the way to trigger smaller blocks of musical content at any time in sync with other blocks. Compared to a musical score, this is like a note, a sound or a phrase that can be played on cue. In film scoring and computer games, this is sometimes referred to as "motifs" or "stingers". A motif is typically played on top of all other tracks and has settings for controlling how it synchronizes with the rest of the arrangement.

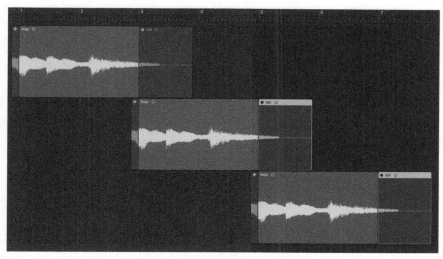

Figure 12.4 Example of a loop with both head and tail.

5.2 Variation

One important learning objective in the courses has been to explore how to give variation to the music and avoid static loops. This has resulted in a set of features that makes it possible to select different variations of the same object depending on the following factors described in what follows.

User control

Music often has its internal timing with a clock measuring bars and beats, and this "musical time" can be used to apply musical variation to user interactions. A typical approach has been to play different options of a motif depending on the time left until the next beat occurs in the currently playing arrangement. In iMusicXML, this is specified with the "upbeat" attribute that can apply both motifs and lead-ins.

Random control

The students focusing on producing music for museums and public spaces have specifically asked for features to randomize the composition to various degrees. The most wanted features have been the ability to have different loop lengths for different tracks and different loop lengths for each loop iteration. Another approach was to use the "active" attribute to control the likeliness of an object to play. This feature led to a minimalist approach where the students composed lots of small, looped blocks that triggered very rarely but together would build up a chance-based musical

```
<motif retrig="other" quantize="1/4">
    <option src="A.mp3"/>
    <option src="B.mp3"/>
    <option src="C.mp3"/>
    <option src="D.mp3"/>
    <option src="E.mp3"/>
</motif>
```

Figure 12.5 Code example of a motif with variations.

pattern. One feature that was often used for motifs is to have different options for a musical phrase that is selected randomly each time the motif is triggered. The students also wanted to control the randomness to various degrees, which led to having settings for controlling how different options were selected (Figure 12.5).

Musical control

The students that explored randomized variation further requested features where they could build up rules for how different parts of the composition could control other parts. One example is a feature where a randomly selected variation on a track controls the selection of a user-triggered motif. This makes it possible for a random chord progression on a track to control the pitches in the phrase in a user-triggered motif. This system is built upon an internal structure for variables in iMusicXML, where the composer does a markup of the hierarchical relations between different musical objects and events.

5.3 Transitions

To make seamless transitions from one state in the music to another, there has been a request for arrangements that work as an interlude between two arrangements and for shorter musical blocks that build up to the change. Such a block is called a "leadin" and typically contains musical content leading up to the next barline. The audio is superimposed on top of the rest of the arrangement. The leadin object also supports multiple alternative versions that are chosen automatically depending on the time from the event that triggered the transition until the next barline.

5.4 User interaction

The two types of interactions the students have worked with are events and continuous changes. It is reflected by connecting events to trigger changes

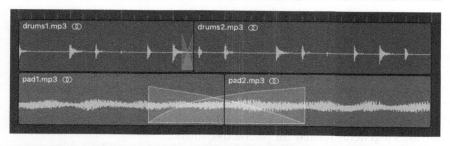

Figure 12.6 Different cross-fades settings for different instruments.

of arrangement or a motif to play and to connect the continuous changes to cross-fade between different tracks. Like the findings in the variPlay project (Paterson, Toulson and Hepworth-Sawyer, 2019), the result from this study confirms that different musical content needs to be treated differently. Some parts of the music, like bass lines and melodies, need to be exchanged quickly with a short cross-fade to avoid unwanted layers. More ambient or slow sounds often need a slow cross-fade to avoid a too abrupt change (Figure 12.6). Some instruments need to cross-fade on specific musical time positions. Typically, percussive sounds need to change just before a transient, and chord instruments need to change where the harmony changes. Other instruments benefit from a continuous change of the timbre, like connecting a continuous user interaction to the cutoff frequency of a low-pass filter controlling the timbre of a synth pad.

5.5 Accessibility

While most of the participating students have little or no prior programming experience, it has been important to make the features accessible without a lot of technical training. iMusicXML started as a pure JavaScript framework but important feedback from the students led to the expansion with an XML language and, most recently, also an XML Schema Definition (XSD) that supports the coding process. In order to avoid JavaScript coding altogether, iMusicXML implements a set of custom HTML attributes to control the playback of the music with interaction events.

In addition to mouse and touch events in web pages, many of the students have asked for input data from a variety of sources like MIDI (Mozilla, 2022), socket.io (Arrachequesne, 2022), OSC (Wright and Freed, 1997) and smartphone sensor data, which has led to support of all these environments.

6 DISCUSSION

The process of developing music technology in a tight relation to education and student projects has arguably led to many features and solutions that might not have evolved through a more commercial design process. In this section, the most important findings are discussed, and the method and precautions are criticized on how they might have affected the result. This leads to a wider discussion on important perspectives when working towards a general format for interactive music.

6.1 Important features

One observation when reviewing the result is that many of the objects and naming conventions used in the code are inherited from tools already familiar to the students. So, even if they could have been completely unique to how music is structured in an interactive environment, they have rather been chosen from a terminology with which most students felt comfortable. This also points towards the strength of using common terminology and finding solutions from the current practice to build tools that become useful for the creators. The differences between the student projects also played an important role in challenging existing solutions toward more flexible and general features. This applies especially to the different ways of responding to user interactions depending on the musical content.

A specific feature that arguably carries one of the most important insights from the study is the loop, which deals with the audio in a more musical way than looping features in most DAWs. The result indicated that audio content that exists before and after the loop cycle is important for some musical content. Finally, the result indicates that the user interface for coding is important. The XML abstraction improved the students' experience a lot, and a further development towards a graphical interface might improve the result even more.

6.2 Impact from tradition

All design work is performed within a paradigm of values and traditions (Redstrom, 2017, p. 99), and the work in this study is not an exception. This means that many solutions and features might inherit limitations from how they are currently defined. In this study, it becomes clear when looking at the result from a genre perspective. The idea that music is structured in arrangements with layers of synchronized musical blocks derives from DAWs that build on the metaphor of a multi-track tape recorder. This means that the current state of iMusicXML is under a lot of influence from Western music and technology and that it can only play a limited part in contributing to the discussion of a possible future standard. Input will be needed from many different traditions, genres and cultures to arrive at an inclusive technology for interactive music.

6.3 A future standard

Even if this study is a small-scale project compared to many commercial products, the result indicates a potential for an open standard where many participants with different aims contribute to the specification. The work has also contributed to easier ways for sharing and spreading content, which in turn has led to a cumulative process of growing knowledge and experience among the students. If taken to a global scale, this approach to development could contribute to shared content and knowledge on a cross-cultural level. There are inspiring examples from web standards that can lead the way for a new level of interactive sound and music with common terminologies, technologies and formats.

7 CONCLUSION

The study presents objects and features that have been designed, implemented, and evaluated through an iterative design process with more than 100 student projects. It also points out limitations in participatory studies like this, where the result depends a lot on the users' earlier experiences, the learning objectives in the courses and the template files provided for the projects.

The terminology used in iMusicXML partly overlaps with existing tools, which points towards a potential for a common standard with terminology, file formats and sharing possibilities. There are also benefits from terminology that encourage the sharing of knowledge and ideas between different user groups. One potential risk for a project that aims at standardizing a format for interactive music is that one genre, one purpose, or one culture could take precedence in the process, and it would therefore be preferable to see a wide range of users, genres and applications participating in a continuing discussion.

REFERENCES

Ableton. (2022). *Ableton Live*. Available at: www.ableton.com/.

Adenot, P. and Choi, H. (2022). *Web Audio API: W3C Recommendation, 17 June 2021*. Available at: www.w3.org/TR/webaudio/.

Apple Inc. (2022). *Apple Logic Pro*. Available at: www.apple.com/logic-pro/ [Accessed: 11 January 2023].

Arrachequesne, D. (2022). *Socket.IO – Bidirectional and Low-Latency Communication for Every Platform*. Available at: https://socket.io/.

Audiokinetic. (2022). *Audio kinetic Wwise*. Available at: www.audiokinetic.com/en/products/wwise/.

Avid. (2022). *Avid ProTools*. Available at: www.avid.com/pro-tools.

Berners-Lee, T. (2022). *W3C Mission*. Available at: www.w3.org/Consortium/mission.

Berners-Lee, T. et al. (2022). *W3C – About*. Available at: www.w3.org/Consortium/facts.html.

Björk. (2011). *Biophilia. App.* Available at: https://apps.apple.com/gb/app/bj%C3%B6rk-biophilia/id434122935 [Accessed: 9 January 2023].

Bresin, R. et al. (2016). 'Sound Forest/Ljudskogen: A Large-Scale String-Based Interactive Musical Instrument', in *Sound and Music Computing 2016*. SMC Sound and Music Computing Network, pp. 79–84. Available at: https://urn.kb.se/resolve?urn=urn:nbn:se:kth:diva-192919.

Collins, K. (2008). *Game Sound: An Introduction to the History, Theory, and Practice of Video Game Music and Sound Design*. Cambridge, MA: MIT Press.

Elias Software. (2022). *Elias Studio*. Available at: https://eliassoftware.com/elias-studio/.

Fmod. (2022). *Fmod*. Available at: www.fmod.com/.

Frayling, C. (1993). 'Research in Art and Design', *Royal College of Art Research Papers*, 1, pp. 1–5.

Frid, E. and Lindetorp, H. (2020). 'Haptic Music – Exploring Whole-Body Vibrations and Tactile Sound for a Multisensory Music Installation', in *Sound and Music Computing Conference Torino, 2020*. SMC Sound and Music Computing Network, pp. 68–75. Available at: https://www.diva-portal.org/smash/record.jsf?dswid=-6735&pid=diva2%3A1474725.

Frid, E. et al. (2019). 'Sound Forest: Evaluation of an Accessible Multisensory Music Installation', in *Proceedings of the 2019 CHI Conference on Human Factors in Computing Systems (CHI '19)*. New York, NY, USA: Association for Computing Machinery, Paper 677, pp. 1–12. Available at: https://doi.org/10.1145/3290605.3300907.

Frisk, H. and Brunson, W. (2014). 'Building for the Future – Research and Innovation in KMH's New Facilities', in *Sound and Music Computing Sweden: Bridging Science, Art, and Industry*. SMC Sound and Music Computing Network. Available at: https://www.diva-portal.org/smash/get/diva2:797019/FULLTEXT01.pdf#page=13.

Google. (2013). *Google Web Audio Samples*. Available at: https://google-chromelabs.github.io/web-audio-samples/.

Gullö, J.-O., Höglund, I., Jonas, J., Lindetorp, H., Näslund, A., Persson, J. and Schyborger, P. (2015). 'Nobel Creations: Producing Infinite Music for an Exhibition', *Dansk Musikforskning Online*, pp. 63–80.

Hansen, K. et al. (2019). 'Student Involvement in Sound and Music Computing Research: Current Practices at KTH and KMH', in *Nordic Sound and Music Computing Conference 2019*, pp. 36–42. Available at: https://zenodo.org/records/3755825.

Hickson, I. et al. (2022). *HTML Specification*. Available at: https://html.spec.whatwg.org/.

Kulturhuset, S. (2022). *Kulturhuset, Stockholm*. Available at: http://kulturhuset-stadsteatern.se.

Lindetorp, H. (2016a). *iMusicXML – Manual*. Available at: https://github.com/hanslindetorp/iMusicXML/wiki.

Lindetorp, H. (2016b). *iMusicXML*. Available at: https://github.com/hanslindetorp/iMusicXML.

Lindetorp, H. (2019). 'Immersive and Interactive Music for Everyone', in *Proceedings of the Nordic Sound and Music Computing Conference*. SMC Sound and Music Computing Network, pp. 16–20. Available at: https://www.diva-portal.org/smash/record.jsf?dswid=-6735&pid=diva2%3A1471294.

Lindetorp, H. (2022a). *iMusicXML, XML Schema Definition Language (XSD)*. Available at: https://hanslindetorp.github.io/iMusicXML/scheme.xsd.

Lindetorp, H. (2022b). *WebAudioXML*. Available at: https://github.com/hanslindetorp/WebAudioXML.

Lindetorp, H. and Falkenberg, K. (2020). 'WebAudioXML: Proposing a New Standard for Structuring Web Audio', in *Proceedings of the Sound and Music Computing Conference. SMC2020.* Zenodo, pp. 25–31. Available at: https://zenodo.org/records/3898655#.X3HgbC0zLa4.

Lindetorp, H. and Falkenberg, K. (2021). 'Audio Parameter Mapping Made Explicit Using WebAudioXML', in *Proceedings of the Sound and Music Computing Conference 2021.* Zenodo. Available at: https://doi.org/10.5281/zenodo.5038686.

Lindetorp, H. and Falkenberg, K. (2022). 'Evaluating Web Audio for Learning, Accessibility, and Distribution', *JAES*, 70(11), pp. 951–961.

Löwgren, J. (2013). 'Annotated Portfolios and Other Forms of Intermediate-Level Knowledge', *Interactions*, 20(1), pp. 30–34.

McCartney, J. (2002). 'Rethinking the Computer Music Language: SuperCollider', *Computer Music Journal*, 26(4), pp. 61–68.

Monroe, J. (2016, January 21). 'Massive Attack Launch App Containing New Musi', *Pitchfork*. Available at: https://pitchfork.com/news/61596-massive-attack-launch-app-containing-new-music/ [Accessed: 9 January 2023].

Mozilla. (2022). *Web MIDI API.* Available at: https://developer.mozilla.org/en-US/docs/Web/API/Web_MIDI_API.

Museum of Performing Art. (2022). *Museum of Performing Arts.* Available at: http://scenkonstmuseet.se.

OpenStand Advocate. (2022). *Open Standards.* Available at: https://open-stand.org/about-us/principles.

Paloranta, J. et al. (2016). 'Interaction with a Large Sized Augmented String Instrument Intended for a Public Setting', in *Proceedings of the 13th Sound and Music Computing Conference (SMC).* Zenodo. Available at: https://www.diva-portal.org/smash/record.jsf?pid=diva2%3A931469&dswid=-7903, https://zenodo.org/records/1400818.

Paterson, J. and Toulson, R. (2018). 'Interactive Recorded Music: Past, Present, and Future', *Engineering Brief 460*, in *Audio Engineering Society Convention 145.* Audio Engineering Society. Available at: https://www.aes.org/e-lib/browse.cfm?elib=19725.

Paterson, J., Toulson, R. and Hepworth-Sawyer, R. (2019). 'User-Influenced/Machine-Controlled Playback: The variPlay Music App Format for Interactive Recorded Music', *Arts*, 8(3), p. 112. https://doi.org/10.3390/arts8030112.

Puckette, M. S. (1997). 'Pure Data', in *Proceedings: International Computer Music Conference 1997*, 25–30 September. Thessaloniki: Hellas.

Redhead, T. (2018). 'The Emerging Role of the Dynamic Music Producer', in *Australasian Computer Music Conference 2018: Reflecting Worlds: The Promise and Limitations of Mimesis in Electronic Music.* Edith Cowan

University.   Available   at: https://computermusic.org.au/proceedings/
ACMC2018-proceedings/09Redhead.pdf.

Redstrom, J. (2017). *Making Design Theory*. Cambridge, MA: MIT Press.

Robaszkiewicz, S. and Schnell, N. (2015). 'Soundworks – A Playground for Art-
ists and Developers to Create Collaborative Mobile Web Performances', in
Proceedings of the International Web Audio Conference (WAC'15). Paris,
France. Available at: https://hal.science/hal-01580797.

Soundtrap by Spotify. (2023). *Soundtrap*. Available at: www.soundtrap.com/
[Accessed: 11 January 2023].

Stems-Music. (2015). Available at: www.stems-music.com/ [Accessed: 12 January
2023].

Stockholm City Museum. (2022). *Stockholm City Museum*. Available at: http://
stadsmuseet.stockholm.se.

Vercoe, B. (1985). *Csound*. Available at: https://csound.com/.

Walker, A. (2015). *Essential Readings in Problem-Based Learning: Exploring
and Extending the Legacy of Howard S. Barrows*. West Mafayette, IN: Pur-
due University Press.

Wright, M. J. and Freed, A. (1997). 'Open Sound Control: A New Protocol for
Communicating with Sound Synthesizers', in *International Computer Music
Conference*. International Computer Music Association (ICMA). Available
at: http://www.adrianfreed.com/content/open-sound-control-new-protocol-
communicating-sound-synthesizers.

Xambó, A., Støckert, R., Jensenius, A. R. and Saue, S. (2020). 'Learning to Code
Through Web Audio: A Team-Based Learning Approach', *Journal of the
Audio Engineering Society*, 68(10), pp. 727–737. https://doi.org/10.17743/
jaes.2020.0019.

Xambó Sedo, A., Støckert, R., Jensenius, A. R. and Saue, S. (2019). 'Facilitating
Team-Based Programming Learning with Web Audio', in *Proceedings of the
International Web Audio Conference (WAC)*. NTNU, pp. 2–7. Available at:
https://www.duo.uio.no/handle/10852/77532.

13

Transforming performance with HASGS

Research-led artistic practice with an augmented instrument

Henrique Portovedo and Ângelo Martingo

1 INTRODUCTION

Drawing on the development and technical possibilities of the Hybrid Augmented Saxophone of Gestural Symbioses (HASGS) as a case study, this chapter aims to discuss the optimization of augmented instruments and the role of research in the transformation of performance. HASGS, as demonstrated in www.henriqueportovedo.com/hasgs/, was developed as an academic project aimed at enhancing performance by electronically controlling parameters in mixed music performed via the mechanical instrument, thus reducing recourse to external control devices for electronic purposes. After three preliminary prototypes, the current system is comprised of an ESP32 card, providing Bluetooth and Wi-Fi connectivity, while based on a digital production solution able to be directly integrated into the instrument's body, thus transforming the saxophone into a hybrid instrument – both an acoustic instrument and an electronic controller. The remaining HASGS components include a ribbon sensor, a four-button keypad, a trigger button, two pressure sensors, up and down selectors and an accelerometer.

In a performance-practice context in which the interpreter is required to be a creative agent within a multidimensional context of sonic manipulation, improvisation and expressive extension and augmentation, HASGS emerges both as a means of contributing to optimizing this new virtuosity and as a result of the changing role of academic and musical research in the transformation of artistic practice, as illustrated in the detailed description of a recent piece 'Study 1b'.

2 UNDOING THE ELECTRONIC/INSTRUMENTAL DIVIDE

Although instrumental music is technologically mediated, digitalization has fundamentally changed music production, transmission and reception (Cook, 2020a, 2020b) in ways perhaps not fully foreseeable at its origins. Writing at the dawn of electronic music, Stockhausen (1961[1959], p. 59)

DOI: 10.4324/9781003118817-15

suggested that "physical nature of traditional instruments", reflecting a musical language from which new composers would distance themselves, were unsuitable for "new musical ideas concerning form". The composer then poses a fundamental question: *"Does the rise of electronic music mean the end of the age of interpretation? Are interpreters condemned to play in future only the old instrumental music for 'collegium-musicum' concerts and for music museums on tape?"* (Stockhausen, 1961[1959], p. 65). Stockhausen proposes that electronic music and performed music pertain to separate worlds, with each exploring its own specific possibilities. Furthermore, the development of expressive resources for a changing musical language was not confined to electronic music – complexity and timbric research found ample terrain in instrumental writing (Andrikopoulos and Martingo, 2019; Martingo, 2019), resulting in the development of new instruments (e.g., Redgate, 2015, 2019) and in a panoply of extended techniques (several authors, in Martingo and Telles, 2019) which, according to Heaton (2012, p. 783ff, 2019, p. 53ff), were developed mainly in the decades between 1950 and 1980 and in the meantime assimilated into standard practice.

The integration of digital technology and mechanical instruments would not only deconstruct this distinction between electronic and instrumental music and enormously amplify the scope of extended techniques but would also question, according to Baalman (2017), the traditional understanding of composer, performer and instrument, and their interrelationships. In recent years, the proliferation of new digital musical instruments has been enormous in conjunction with the recent resurgence of electronic instruments incorporating mixed characteristics. Examples include analog-hybrid and digital-analog synthesizers that can be modular, include a keyboard or be wind-controlled. These wind-controlled synths display performative interfaces similar to those of wind instruments, not only in terms of fingering but also in terms of articulation, their dynamics, amplitude and other physical characteristics. This is especially noteworthy given that many instrumentalists and even composers no longer need to develop a virtuosic or highly developed piano technique, moving them away from electronic exploration via the keyboard-based interface model. In response to the proliferation of electronic technology associated with new musical and hybrid musical instruments, and especially as regards these hybrid instruments, the terms "extended" (Penny, 2009) (Normark, Parnes and Andersson, 2016), "augmented" (Schiesser and Schacher, 2012; Thibodeau and Wanderley, 2013; Kimura et al., 2012) and prefixes such as hyper- (Machover and Chung, 1989; Palacio-Quintin, 2003), meta- (Impett, 1994; Burtner, 2002), infra- (Bowers and Archer, 2005) and even mutant- (Neill and Jones, 2010) were coined to emphasize the different approaches adopted.

Systematizing the interactions between digital media and the performer, Keislar (2009) describes these as occurring either in the form of an input to the performer, an output from the performer or as a networked performance. In the case of performer outputs, Keislar points to a fundamental shift in performance in that, instead of a univocal relationship, there is a 'gap' between instrumental gesture and the sound resulting, within which there are, according to Keislar (2009, p. 30), *"one or more software layers that map the physical gestures to synthesis parameters or to higher-level musical events in a thoroughly flexible fashion*". In this context, Hardjowirogo (2017) states that the definition of instrument – 'instrumentality' – underwent a transformation, suggesting that musical instruments would perhaps be better defined functionally (the purpose for which they are made) rather than ontologically (something an object is or is not) (cf. Cance, 2017). In the same vein, and further considering contextual and cultural differences, Théberge (2017, p. 59) indicates that rather than "physical objects", "*musical instruments are better understood in terms of their place in a network of relationships – an 'assemblage' – with other objects, practices, institutions and social discourses*".

The 'hybrid augmented saxophone of gestural symbioses' (HASGS) instrument will now be discussed. It fits the previously mentioned context particularly well insofar as it is the product of performance practice, academic research, and professional composition. Initially developed as a product of academic research leading to a PhD (Portovedo, 2020), it aimed to offer a potential solution for performance practice that fostered close collaboration between performers and composers. Over time, it has generated a dedicated repertoire.

3 DEVELOPING HASGS

Nilsson (2011) describes the development of digital instruments as a process divided into two stages – Design Time and Play Time. Design Time comprises planning and implementing decisions and Play Time is devoted to evaluating an instrument in terms of both its performance and the expressive possibilities provided. Both playing an instrument and constantly testing its response in light of the perceived experience are important components of the instrument design process. Waisvisz (1999) goes a step further in proposing the essential nature of interrupting instrument development and taking a step back in order to test and evaluate its augmented elements in both performance and composition.

This was the case in the development of HASGS, which employed an artistic action-research methodology in line with research aimed at enhancing performative efficiency and addressing issues related to the performance of mixed electroacoustic works. Hitherto, the different stages in the development of HASGS had resulted in the addition and subtraction of technological resources based on accessing their worth as compositional and performative features. HASGS was initially conceived as an Electronic Wind Instrument (EWI) integrated into an acoustic instrument, but such a design soon proved to be unsuitable. This was due not only to the excessive number of sensors in the physical structure of the instrument but also to the unsuitability of the performance ergonomics. The design required a myriad of adjustments to technique that might have jeopardized the virtuosity developed over more than 20 years of instrumental practice. We, therefore, decided that the augmentation process should not be intrusive in relation to the mechanical material of the acoustic instrument, adding possibilities without compromising its organic qualities, and that the standard technique and the defining sonic characteristic qualities of the saxophone were to be maintained. In that context, the term "Reduced Augmentation" was used to describe the system (Portovedo et al., 2021), denoting the search for a balanced usage of technology. The MIGSI3 Trumpet by Sarah Reid (Reid et al., 2016), the IRCAM Augmented Violin Project (Kimura et al., 2012), the Magnetic Resonator Piano (McPherson, 2010) or the more recent SABRE2 by Matthias Mueller would be cases in which the design strategies are comparable to those put into practice for HASGS.

Prior to its current version, HASGS included the development and testing of three prototypes. The first included a pressure sensor on the mouthpiece in order to detect the pressure exerted by the embouchure during performance. The HASGS digital information was processed by an Arduino Nano plate communicating to the computer through a serial port using a USB connection and by running a Node.js application simulating a MIDI port. The second prototype maintained the characteristics of the earlier version but had the addition of an accelerometer to attribute musical meaning to gestural movements. The third HASGS prototype included swapping the previous computing board for an ESP8266, allowing wireless communication between the augmented instrument and the host computer. The elements of the system were connected via an API and linked by a phone hotspot serving as a router. Throughout the process, decisions regarding updates were based on the suitability for instrumental performance, optimization of technology and, above all, the requirements dictated by the repertoire. For example, sensors that were seldom used by composers were discarded, such as the mouthpiece pressure sensor in the first prototype.

The current version of HASGS (Figure 13.1) reflects the considerable amount of repertoire specifically written for the instrument and tested in performance. This is structured around an ESP32 card, providing Bluetooth and Wi-Fi connectivity. For a better attachment to the instrument's body, we adopted a 3D-printing solution with a better fit to the instrument's body, taking advantage of the saxophone's side protection plate. Several improvements and updates were also made to the sensors, which now include two up and down selectors, two piezo sensors, a ribbon sensor, an accelerometer and gyroscope, four trigger switches and some status LED indicators (for multiple functions). Similar to any augmented instrument or electronic equivalent, HASGS introduces an arbitrary factor into performance as the acoustic properties of the instrument's material and shape do not determine the sounds emitted. Indeed, mapping constitutes an entire invisible dimension of the instrument, mediating physical gestures and the sounds heard (DeLahunta, 2010). For this reason, the performer can experience a feeling of freedom with HASGS in determining how a certain gesture creates or modulates a sound or timbre. In each work, the composer gains the opportunity to change the processing of each sensor's data in a very flexible manner. This break in linearity necessitates that the composer's knowledge of the instrument should not be limited to standard techniques and the capabilities of the acoustic saxophone. Furthermore, the performers must constantly modify their techniques to meet these new demands. In order to create common ground, expand knowledge about HASGS, and encourage new writing for the instrument, a table of instructions was sent to several composers describing the range of possible communications between the sensors and the software and standardizing software usage. The objects and the attributes of each sensor's mapping were also provided in Max (Figure 13.2), the programming language adopted.

Figure 13.1 Current version of HASGS.

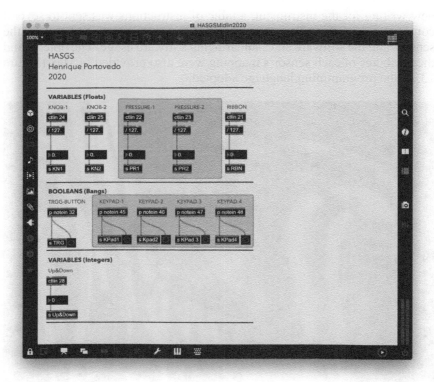

Figure 13.2 Mapping through Max.

4 BUILDING A COMPOSITIONAL COMMUNITY AROUND HASGS

The use of augmented instruments is often limited to their creators, who mostly value improvisation and an aesthetic of free expression (Palacio-Quintin, 2003). Moreover, these factors significantly impede the proliferation and longevity of augmented instruments. To counteract this, those developing augmented instruments should strive to build musical communities that not only contribute to the sustained improvement and full exploration of augmented instruments but also to their widespread usage and longevity. Such was the case with HASGS, which was initially developed within a "do it yourself" logic in order to play a specific contemporary repertoire for saxophone and electronics before evolving in response to the challenges posed by new works written for the system. Most of the pieces that were developed specifically for HASGS were composed after 2015, with some resulting from project presentations at conferences such as EAW, ICLI, SMC, ICMC and NIME. Composers writing for the project include Stewart Engarts, Rodney Duplessis, Nicolas Canot, Tiago Ângelo, Pedro Louzeiro and Henrique Portovedo.

Indeciduous, by Stewart Engarts, is a free blues piece on an electronic drum loop. Durations of different phrases, as well as musical gestures based on improvisational fluency, are provided as suggestions. The notated pitches are performed to be incorporated into the recorded loop and later triggered by the performer. The looper can be controlled using a trigger button, and periods of relative inactivity are recommended, particularly when the looper buffer returns to the previously recorded material.

Disconnect, by Rodney Duplessis, explores HASGS' discrete and continuous control in order to achieve an organic performance of electronic processing elements. The electronic component consists of a set of buffers for recording and reproducing the saxophone material, including the loop of that material and a bank of filters. The latter is defined with formants for three different vowel sounds, namely, (ə) ("uh"), (ɪ) ("ih"), and (ɑ) ("aw"). There are two sections in the work: the first is based on a loop of melodic material, which creates a web of complex harmonic relations, albeit in a language close to tonal development through the accumulation of elements; the second section uses some of the previous material in loops in which timbre and formants are explored. In this second section, the sounds produced display a 'windy' character, amplifying the blown air inside the aerophone and the sounds of the consonants "sh", "t" and "f".

Composed by Nicolas Canot, *Cicadas Memories* is an improvisatory work in which the performer must deal with two temporalities: determining the future score and improving on past gestures. Specifically, the performer's gestures change, with a one-minute delay, the texture of the electronic sounds, providing a sonic background to the saxophone's melodic discourse and rhythmic impulses. Therefore, the performer needs to simultaneously consider two moments: the present (i.e., the standards imposed by the software but created by the past action of the performer) and the future (i.e., the gestural connection with the sensors). *Cicadas Memories* can, therefore, be defined as a multitemporal feedback loop.

Composed by Tiago Ângelo, *Verisimilitude* is written for the tenor saxophone and HASGS system and deploys a single loudspeaker placed in front of the performer at the same height as the saxophone bell. A mixture of acoustic and electronic sound sources (processing and generation) based on computer music techniques are conducted in three sections. Each section applies specific processors and generators by implementing different mappings at the control level, either from the HASGS controller or from real-time sound analysis. Electronic sound events arise from the sound emitted by the instrument itself. The timbre's coloring, combined with slight oscillations from the fundamental note of the entire work, creates a rich sonic environment. The augmented system fully controls the electronic parameters without relying on automatic effect generation from computational algorithms, except for a looping effect that is auto-generated in the closing bars of the piece.

Comprovisador represents a system composed and programmed by Pedro Louzeiro, which allows for interactive mediation between soloists and ensembles through a listening machine, algorithmic composition and dynamic notation via a networked environment. As the soloist improvises, the *Comprovisador*'s algorithms generate real-time notation that is immediately read by a group of instrumentalists, thereby creating a coordinated response to improvisation. The interaction is mediated by a performance director. The implementation of this system requires a series of network-connected computers in order to display the notation in separate parts for each of the ensemble's players.

In the piece *Comprovisação nº9*, HASGS serves as a double action musical interface – it feeds *Comprovisador*'s algorithms with improvised musical material via an acoustic instrument and controls several parameters through its sensors and controllers to claim some of the performance director's mediation tasks to the benefit of the interactive flow. The synergies between HASGS and *Comprovisador* bring about a greater degree of interactivity between the improviser, the ensemble musicians and the sight-readers – in real time between the improvised material and the composition. By enabling the soloist to control selected parameters that are expressive, compositional, and formal in nature, we can expect more consistent interactions. Furthermore, this also enables the performance director to become more aware of the macrostructure.

The community surrounding any augmented instrument may consist of artists or creators with different roles. However, in the case of HASGS, which involves coding, the compositional process becomes more complex when the composer and programmer are not the same person (Portovedo, Lopes and Mendes, 2018). Both the programming language and building an algorithm involve decisions that programmers may consider compositional. Additionally, the programmer may not be limited to engineering – the compositional concept may undergo alterations through the exchange between the composer and the programmer. However, in some other cases, the composer takes on the roles of the programmer and performer, eliminating issues of authorship. In such cases, the complexity arises from the same individual having to excel in multiple tasks and competencies. This is the case with 'Study 1b', which will now be briefly described to provide an example of the process involved in composing for HASGS and the potential of its system.

5 STUDY 1B

'Study 1b' (Figure 13.3), a recorded performance available at www.youtube.com/watch?v=ClbbqofjZGk, belongs to a series of pieces written by Henrique Portovedo for multiple saxophones. These pieces were developed with a specialized algorithmic composition software named Slippery Chicken (Figure 13.4), developed by Michael Edwards, written according to the principles of the common Lisp object system (CLOS). The piece explores the microtonal relations of tone pitches and layers of multiphonic permutations using two different methods and software, SaxMultis and Multi2Sax. 'Study 1b' was premiered in 2022 at the New Interfaces for Musical Expression (NIME) conference. The piece was composed and organized into several layers, including (1) writing code in Slippery Chicken to generate a musical structure and score; (2) converting the musical score into MIDI files for processing by two different analog synthesizers, a bass and a subtractive synth, and further recording them into audio files; (3) live processing of the saxophone sound through FFT analysis to develop the granular synth and ring modulator; and (4) integrating the mapping structure of HASGS into a Max program for live performance, establishing four different presets.

The rhythms and harmonic content of the electronics are triggered by two different playlist objects defining the piece's musical structure over which the saxophonist improvises. The live input of the saxophone is analyzed by ZSA descriptors (centroid and freqpeak) to control the grain rate of a granular synth and the frequency of the modulator in a ring modulator. Several parameters and effects (Table 13.1) are chunked into four presets that can be switched, including

(1) ring modulation changing with variable centroid; (2) ring modulation changing with variable centroid and affecting grain rate and grain size; (3) ring modulation with an 8 Hz modulator and freqpeak affecting grain rate and grain size; and (4) ring modulation changing with variable centroid and freqpeak affecting grain rate and grain size while maintaining a freeze on grain flow.

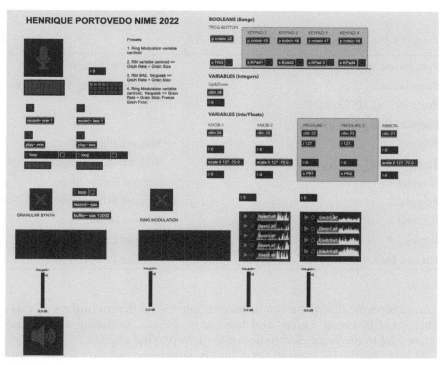

Figure 13.3 Performance Patch of 'Study 1b'.

Figure 13.4 SC Code for Structure and Rhythm Generation in 'Study 1b'.

Table 13.1 Mapping Parameters for 'Study 1b'.

Potentiometer 1	Volume of Granular Synth
Potentiometer 2	Volume of Ring Modulation
Pressure 1 (Left Thumb)	
Pressure 2 (Right Thumb)	
Ribbon	Volume Playlists
Trigger	Trigger and Change Playlists
Keypad 1	Record Buffer One
Keypad 2	Trigger Buffer One
Keypad 3	Record Buffer Two
Keypad 4	Trigger Buffer Two
Up and Down	Change Preset

The saxophone discourse can be looped into two different buffers of variable sizes to create layers and masses of sounds, colliding and mixed according to the fixed electronics of the two playlist objects.

While 'Study 1b' constitutes a highly structured, heavily technology-reliant composition, audiences perceive it as primarily improvisational.

The perceived improvisation contributes to the flow of the performance and smoothly mapping the performative gesture to sound output.

6 CONCLUSION

Developed as an academic project leading to a PhD, HASGS can be seen as an example of how artistic practices can benefit from research, challenging the conventional definitions of "instrument," "performer" and "composer". Indeed, HASGS results as much from a digital system as from the acoustic instrument to which the system has been added.

The resulting augmented instrument, with mapping at its core, challenges the traditional divide between instrumental and electronic music. HASGS retains essential elements of traditional technique while simultaneously challenging the performer to acquire new skills, such as improvisation, structural listening and extended notation. Moreover, creating music with HASGS implies coding and mapping produced signals into perceived output. In cases where the performer is also the composer and programmer, as is often the case, its role is irreducible to reproduction since mastering distinct competencies is necessary. In cases where the composer and programmer are distinct members of the creative process, coding affects compositional options and deconstructs authorship. 'Study 1b' provides a detailed account of a work by the HASGS developer, where the performer was also the composer and programmer. Other works illustrate the community of composers established around HASGS, further stimulating its development and testifying to its relevance for musical creation.

In summary, this performance research has led to the development of a hybrid instrument that has fostered a developing community of composers, challenging established notions of instrument, performer and composition in a productive way.

7 ACKNOWLEDGEMENTS

HASGS research was supported by National Funds through the FCT – Foundation for Science and Technology under the project SFRH/BD/99388/2013, from 2014 to 2019. Fulbright has been associated with this project in supporting the research residency at the University of California Santa Barbara. We acknowledge all the composers with pieces mentioned here, as well as the research center INET-md, University of Aveiro.

Henrique Portovedo is a Member of XPerimus, research funded by the project "Experimentation in music in Portuguese culture: History, contexts and practices in the 20th and 21st centuries", co-funded by the European Union through the Operational Programme Competitiveness and Internationalization, in its ERDF component, and by national funds, through the Portuguese Foundation for Science and Technology.

REFERENCES

Andrikopoulos, D. and Martingo, A. (2019). 'Da expansão sonora à expansão técnica: práticas performativas na recente escrita para instrumentos de corda', in Martingo, A. and Telles, A., eds. *Musica instrumentalis: experimentação e técnicas não convencionais nos séculos XX e XXI.* V. N. Famalicão: Húmus, pp. 13–29.

Baalman, M. A. J. (2017). 'Interplay Between Composition, Instrument Design and Performance', in Bovermann, T., de Campo, A., Egermann, H., Hardjowirogo, S.-I. and Weinzierl, S., eds. *Musical Instruments in the 21st Century: Identities, Configurations, Practices.* Singapore: Springer, pp. 225–241.

Bowers, J. and Archer, P. (2005). 'Not Hyper, Not Meta, Not Cyber But Infra-Instruments', in *Proceedings of the 2005 Conference on New Interfaces for Musical Expression.* Vancouver, Canada: National University of Singapore, pp. 5–10.

Burtner, M. (2002). 'The Metasaxophone: Concept, Implementation, and Mapping Strategies for a New Computer Music Instrument', *Organised Sound,* 7(2), pp. 201–213.

Cance, C. (2017). 'From Musical Instruments as Ontological Entities to Instrumental Quality: A Linguistic Exploration of Musical Instrumentality in the Digital Era', in Bovermann, T., de Campo, A., Egermann, H., Hardjowirogo, S.-I. and Weinzierl, S., eds. *Musical Instruments in the 21st Century: Identities, Configurations, Practices.* Singapore: Springer, pp. 25–43.

Cook, N. (2020a). *Music: A Very Short Introduction.* Oxford: Oxford University Press.

Cook, N. (2020b). 'Música 2.0: como foi a música modificada pela tecnologia?', in Martingo, A., org. *Musica Humana.* V. N. Famalicão: Húmus, pp. 207–230.

DeLahunta, S. (2010). *Shifting Interfaces: Art Research at the Intersections of Live Performance and Technology.* PhD thesis. University of Plymouth. Available at: http://hdl.handle.net/10026.1/2711 [Accessed: 4 January 2023].

Hardjowirogo, S.-I. (2017). 'Instrumentality. On the Construction of Instrumental Identity', in Bovermann, T., de Campo, A., Egermann, H., Hardjowirogo, S.-I. and Weinzierl, S., eds. *Musical Instruments in the 21st Century: Identities, Configurations, Practices.* Singapore: Springer, pp. 9–24.

Heaton, R. (2012). 'Instrumental Performance in the Twentieth Century and Beyond', in Lawson, C. and Stowell, R., eds. *The Cambridge History of Musical Performance.* Cambridge: Cambridge University Press, pp. 778–797.

Heaton, R. (2019). 'Técnicas não convencionais no clarinete', in Martingo, A. and Telles, A., eds. *Musica instrumentalis: experimentação e técnicas não convencionais nos séculos XX e XXI.* V. N. Famalicão: Húmus, pp. 51–62.

Impett, J. (1994). 'A Meta Trumpet(er)', in *International Computer Music Conference Proceedings* (ICMC 1994). Aarhus, Denmark, 12–17 September. Ann Arbor: Michigan Publishing, pp. 147–150. Available at: http://hdl.handle.net/2027/spo.bbp2372.1994.037 [Accessed: 4 January 2023].

Keislar, D. (2009). 'A Historical View of Computer Music Technology', in Dean, R., ed. *The Oxford Handbook of Computer Music.* Oxford: Oxford University Press, pp. 11–43.

Kimura, M., Rasamimanana, N., Bevilacqua, F., Zamborlin, B., Schnell, N. and Fléty, E. (2012). 'Extracting Human Expression for Interactive Composition with the Augmented Violin', in *International Conference on New Interfaces for Musical Expression*. Ann Arbor, Michigan, 21–23 May. NA, France, pp. 1–1. Available at: https://hal.archives-ouvertes.fr/hal-01161009/file/index.pdf [Accessed: 4 January 2023].

Machover, T. and Chung, J. (1989). 'Hyperinstrument: Musically Intelligent and Interactive Performance and Creativity Systems', in *International Computer Music Conference Proceedings* (ICMC 1989). Columbus, Ohio, 2–5 November. Michigan: Michigan Publishing, pp. 186–190.

Martingo, A. (2019). 'Do timbre como desconstrução: Makrokosmos I/II de George Crumb', in Martingo, A. and Telles, A., eds. *Musica instrumentalis: experimentação e técnicas não convencionais nos séculos XX e XXI*. V. N. Famalicão: Húmus, pp. 193–202.

Martingo, A. and Telles, A., eds. (2019). *Musica Instrumentalis: experimentação e técnicas não convencionais nos séculos XX e XXI*. V. N. Famalicão: Húmus.

McPherson, A. (2010). 'The Magnetic Resonator Piano: Electronic Augmentation of an Acoustic Grand Piano', *Journal of New Music Research*, 39(3), pp. 189–202.

Neill, B. and Jones, B. (2010). 'Posthorn', in *Proceedings of ACM CHI 2010 Conference on Human Factors in Computing Systems, CHI 2010, Extended Abstracts*. Atlanta, Georgia, 10–15 April. New York: Association for Computing Machinery, pp. 3107–3112. https://doi.org/10.1145/1753846.1753927.

Nilsson, P. A. (2011). *A Field of Possibilities: Designing and Playing Digital Musical Instruments*. PhD thesis. Goteborgs Universitet. Available at: https://gupea.ub.gu.se/handle/2077/27953 [Accessed: 4 January 2023].

Normark, C., Parnes, P., Ek, R. and Andersson, H. (2016). 'The Extended Clarinet', in *Proceedings of the International Conference on New Interfaces for Musical Expression*. Brisbane, 11–17 July. Brisbane, Australia: Queensland Conservatorium Griffith University, pp. 162–167. http://doi.org/10.5281/zenodo.1176090.

Palacio-Quintin, C. (2003). 'The Hyper-Flute', in *Proceedings of the International Conference on New Interfaces for Musical Expression*. Montreal, Canada, 22–24 May. Montreal, Canada: McGill University, pp. 206–207. http://doi.org/10.5281/zenodo.1176549.

Penny, J. (2009). *The Extended Flautist: Techniques, Technologies and Performer Perceptions*. DMA, University of Melbourne. Available at: www.jeanpenny.com/uploads/5/5/4/3/55434199/penny_the_extended_flautist.pdf [Accessed: 4 January 2023].

Portovedo, H. (2020). *Performance Musical Aumentada: Prática Multidimensional Enquanto Co-Criação e Hybrid Augmented Saxophone of Gestural Symbiosis*. PhD thesis. Portuguese Catholic University. Available at: https://repositorio.ucp.pt/handle/10400.14/32145 [Accessed: 4 January 2023].

Portovedo, H., Lopes, P. F. and Mendes, R. (2018). 'HASGS: The Repertoire as an Approach to Prototype Augmentation', in Gomes, A., Carvalhais, M. and Penha, R., eds. *Proceedings. ICLI 2018, 4th International Conference on Live Interfaces: Inspiration, Performance, Emancipation*. Porto, Portugal, 14–16 June. Oporto: Universidade do Porto, pp. 45–51.

Portovedo, H., Lopes, P. F., Mendes, R. and Gala, T. (2021). 'HASGS: Five Years of Reduced Augmented Evolution', in *Proceedings of the International Conference on New Interfaces for Musical Expression*. Online and Shanghai. New York University Shanghai, 14–18 June. https://doi.org/10.21428/92fb eb44.643abd8c.

Redgate, C. (2015). 'Creating New Music for a Redesigned Instrument', in Doğantan-Dack, M., ed. *Artistic Practice as Research in Music: Theory, Criticism, Practice*. Farnham: Ashgate, pp. 203–217.

Redgate, C. (2019). 'A transformação do oboé: inovação técnica e técnicas não convencionais', in Martingo, A. and Telles, A., eds. *Musica Instrumentalis: experimentação e técnicas não convencionais nos séculos XX e XXI*. V. N. Famalicão: Húmus, pp. 31–42.

Reid, S., Gaston, R., Honigman, C. and Kapur, A. (2016). 'Minimal Invasing Gesture Sensing Interface (MIGSI) for Trumpet', in *Proceedings of the International Conference on New Interfaces for Musical Expression*. Brisbane, 11–17 July. Brisbane, Australia: Queensland Conservatorium Griffith University, pp. 419–424. http://doi.org/10.5281/zenodo.1176106.

Schiesser, S. and Schacher, J. C. (2012). 'SABRe: The Augmented Bass Clarinet', in *Proceedings of the International Conference on New Interfaces for Musical Expression*, 21–23 May. Ann Arbor, MI, University of Michigan. http://doi.org/10.5281/zenodo.1180587.

Stockhausen, K. (1961[1959]) 'Two Lectures', *Die Reihe*, V, pp. 59–82.

Théberge, P. (2017). 'Musical Instruments as Assemblage', in Bovermann, T., de Campo, A., Egermann, H., Hardjowirogo, S.-I. and Weinzierl, S., eds. *Musical Instruments in the 21st Century: Identities, Configurations, Practices*. Singapore: Springer, pp. 59–66.

Thibodeau, J. and Wanderley, M. (2013). 'Trumpet Augmentation and Technological Symbiosis', *Computer Music Journal*, 37(3), pp. 12–25.

Waisvisz, M. (1999). 'Gestural Round Table', in *STEIM Writings*. Available at: http://web.archive.org/web/20050425074722/www.steim.org:80/steim/texts. php?id=4 [Accessed: 4 January 2023].

14

Waveforms as means of time tinkering

Bjørnar Ersland Sandvik

1 INTRODUCTION

This chapter concerns the idea that standardized graphical forms of sound notation and representation become "invisible" and embedded in our lives, thus shaping what we think of as sound and music at different historical moments. Specifically, it will argue for the importance of considering the role of waveform representations on screens when one discusses digital audio and music production. Approaching sound through waveforms has become so habitual that we take little notice of their influence, even though they quietly constitute our sense of the capacities of recorded sound and musical composition today. Waveforms not only present sound but also represent an important means of producing sound.

People have long thought about and understood sound as waves propagating through the air (or other media). Toward the end of the eighteenth century, inventors started trying to capture what sound waves actually look like – or rather, as Sterne reminds us, what the "effects" of sound waves look like (Sterne, 2003, p. 33). Édouard-Léon Scott de Martinville's phonautograph, invented around 1860, is the earliest known device for recording and storing sounds, which it did by drawing two-dimensional visual inscriptions of sound waves. A stylus transcribed the sound waves as a line traced on smoke-blackened paper or glass; only later would Edison's phonograph reverse the process and convert the inscriptions back into sound again. For Scott de Martinville, meanwhile, the possibility of actually hearing inscribed sounds played back again seemed unlikely. Instead, he imagined people would eventually read waveforms like a new language and hear the performances in their "mind's ears" (Feaster, 2014). Today, it seems that Scott de Martinville's proposition that people would one day read visual depictions of waveforms as a language has, in fact, come to be, especially in certain specialized audio production contexts.

With the pervasiveness of multimodal media, this notion of thinking about and looking at sound waves has become almost as natural as hearing the actual sound itself, and the basic two-dimensional waveform graph – representing changes in amplitude levels over time – is by far the most prevalent way of depicting recorded sound in mainstream Western culture.

DOI: 10.4324/9781003118817-16

For example, several companies offer to sell what they call "soundwave art." From people's favorite songs and recordings of loved ones' voices to baby's heartbeats, these companies sell framed pictures of enlarged wave-form representations (see, for example, Sound Wave Picture, n.d.; Artsy Voiceprint, n.d.). Judging from all this, most people accept that this is one way that sound "looks" today – at least in a Western industrialized context. More significantly, perhaps, the two-dimensional waveform representation of sound has become a standardized means of depicting and representing sound and audiovisual content in different music and media production contexts, including amateur media productions and social media platforms such as TikTok and SoundCloud – and it has consequently become integral to the procedures for editing and sequencing audio events in specialized music-making software. In short, working with waveform representations has become synonymous with composing and interacting with musical sound on screens across a range of contexts and genres.

Of course, we are not actually able to hear sounds by looking at their waveform representations, but a trained eye can discern an incredible amount of information from them, and, more importantly, they facilitate a range of different operations and perspectives that are not possible in real-time sonic experience. In particular, two-dimensional waveform rep-resentations enable one to manipulate and control the temporal dimen-sion of sound in ways that would be impossible if one were accessing them directly within their temporal domain. After all, by becoming a mode of image processing, the graphical editing of sound transforms the time domain into the spatial domain. To be clear, whereas the term "spatial" is generally used in audio-technical discourse to refer to the recreation of real-world or virtual sound spaces (for example, in descriptions of stereo, surround, binaural, and "spatial" systems such as Dolby Atmos), we are here concerned with a different kind of spatialization – the spatialization of the time axis. Time becomes operative through what Kittler famously called technical media's capacity for "time storage" and "time axis manip-ulation" (Krämer, 2006; Kittler, 2017). Stated more succinctly, time only becomes a feature of sound manipulation once the sounds are inscribed and interacted with in space. In the present case of two-dimensional waveform representations on screens, this process of spatialization and operability of the time axis is especially salient (even though waveform representations can map a range of different parameters against time, I will restrict my investigations here to amplitude over time, that is, changes in sound pressure levels). Now, of course, tape, too, stores time spatially and thus affords various techniques of time axis manipulation, but once sounds are committed to a linear ribbon of oxide, any edits are performed on a new continuous whole. In contrast, two-dimensional visual inscriptions of sound have always rendered sounds into discrete and interchangeable forms, frozen as individual events in space contrasted by the empty spaces between them. Moreover, through abstraction, waveforms project differ-ent dimensions of sound (time, frequency, amplitude) onto a flat surface, making them more easily managed, either from afar or up close, as well as cut up, reversed, or recombined – in short, controlled (Bruyninckx, 2018, p. 155).

This chapter is specifically interested in the role of waveforms on screens in what I call "time tinkering" – that is, techniques of experimentation with time, structure, and rhythm in the context of music and digital sound reproduction. This role is approached via the different ways in which waveforms have influenced how digital composers conceptualize and interact with recorded sound. First, the chapter describes the introduction of waveform representation into digital audio workstations (DAWs) in the 1980s and 1990s. Then, it presents certain consequential features of waveform representations in terms of music composition/production, and especially time tinkering. In particular, this chapter evaluates how sounds are spatially organized and arranged in a manner reminiscent of pencil-and-paper writing, how they are sequenced on a horizontal timeline and micro-edited to create innovative rhythmic feels, and how they are sliced up and stretched to be recombined in new expressive ways. Whereas sound recordings are elsewhere considered to capture and accurately store real live events, they are, in the context of DAWs, indexical only to the left-to-right timeline grid on our screens. Lastly, the recent arrival of more tactile manners of waveform interaction that reinforce the conceptual linking of sound interaction with waveform displays is discussed.

2 THE EMERGENCE OF DIGITAL WAVEFORM REPRESENTATIONS IN DAWS

Sampling, which refers to the recording of snippets of audio – or "live" sound, as it was often described at the time – became popular in the 1980s. The first graphical pattern-based sequencer that sequenced such sounds on a screen (that is, ordered them in time) was Page R (Real-Time Composer) on the Fairlight CMI Series II released in 1982 (Harkins, 2020, pp. 51–52). It mimicked staff notation and served as a visual-spatial step-sequencer with tracks stacked vertically and time mapped horizontally, and it displayed traditional notes and not waveforms in the sequencer itself (Figure 14.1).

The adoption of the MIDI protocol in 1983 allowed musical devices to be compatible in a standardized format. Rather than transducing and passing sound as electric signals directly through wires, MIDI signals only transmitted digital information about how sounds should be produced and controlled, and thanks to the correspondingly reduced requirements for storage and processing power, this was a game changer, making digital samplers and sequencers more affordable and widely available. At the same time, the personal home computer became increasingly widespread and capable, and audio waveform representations on computer screens appeared with increasing frequency in dedicated sample-editing software such as Digidesign's Sound Designer (1985) and Blank Software's Alchemy (1988), intended to edit samples from hardware samplers (Wiffen, 1985, 1988). The recording and sequencing of samples were

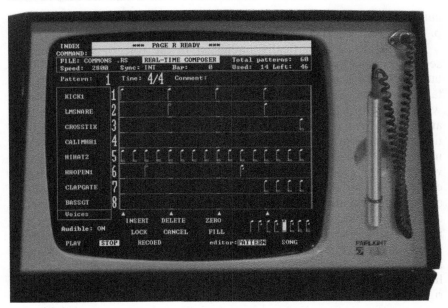

Figure 14.1 The Page R sequencer on Fairlight CMI Series II (released in 1982).

Source: Joho345, 2011. Wikimedia Commons, CC BY-SA 3.0

still not feasible on the computer itself. Instead, they were typically first recorded on a sampler, then transferred and edited on the computer via distinct, time-consuming operations before being transferred back into the sampler again for sample-replay and MIDI sequencing.

In the early 1990s, the coming of age of direct-to-disk recording and new possibilities for non-destructive graphical multitrack sequencing led to the rapid establishment of new conceptual models for digital audio production that have remained remarkably persistent. In 1989, Digidesign's Sound Tools (the ancestor of Pro Tools) introduced two-channel audio recording to disk, thanks to new dedicated hardware. Essentially an extension of Sound Designer, it displayed the two tracks as continuous editable graphical waveforms (Lehrman, 1989). One year later, in 1990, Opcode's Studio Vision and MOTU's Digital Performer relied on Digidesign's new hardware to integrate this new possibility of hard-disk recording into their already popular MIDI sequencers (Vision and Performer). Arranging both discrete audio waveforms and MIDI notation in the same view opened up for manipulating the timeline of multitrack sequencer-based grooves using nothing but one's personal computer (Brøvig-Hanssen and Danielsen, 2016, p. 104). Other software followed soon after, including Pro Tools (1991), Cubase Audio (1992), and Emagic's Notator Logic Audio (1993 – later Apple's Logic Pro) – all of which included their versions of this new integrated arrange view, a design layout that has remained remarkably stable.

The incremental addition of features to match the developing storage and processing power of personal computers meant that the DAWs of the mid-1990s were often large and complicated, and new specialist developers soon appeared with simpler, dedicated sequencers and editors devoted entirely to sample replay and loop-oriented sequencing. In the early 2000s, new DAWs, such as Ableton Live and FL Studio, incorporated features from loop-based sequencers and, among many other things, introduced new ways of interacting with waveform representations. In the 2010s, new tactile touchscreen interfaces further reinforced the link between manipulable audio and waveform representations. In our current screen-saturated culture, operations such as cutting and recombining, slicing and time stretching, as well as the reshaping of audio using signal processors, often rely on interaction with waveforms (more on this in sections 6 and 7).

3 SPATIAL AND SYNOPTICAL ORGANIZATION

Bell, Hein and Ratcliffe (2015) reason that the "writing" that occurs in the informal contexts of laptops and mobile devices in contemporary music production "often takes the form of exploratory and improvisatory recording and sequencing, a process bearing little resemblance to pencil-and-paper composition" (Part Two section, para. 20). In the case of the standardized arrange view (still widely used in most DAWs today), however, I will suggest that it is exactly through its resemblance to pre-technical writing that it differentiates itself from analog tape recording in terms of enabling new kinds of composing with recorded material. Despite its many metaphorical design references to the analog recording studio – including the tape transport functions of starting, stopping, fast-forwarding, and rewinding – in operation, the arrange view effectively combined the concept of sound recording with the techniques of pre-technical forms of spatial writing such as sketching, notation, and perspective drawing.

Once fixed onto a flat surface in a standard layout, sounds from disparate sources can then be made optically consistent. Historically, this has enabled people to represent sounds synoptically by juxtaposing them in the same plane – first with staff notation, later with piano roll (and MIDI) notation, and finally with soundwave inscriptions. In this sense, through the cultural technique of "flattening out," sequencing waveforms have turned into a mode of what Krämer calls "operative writing" (Krämer and McChesney, 2003; Krämer, 2017). Composing in a waveform arrange view attains the "notational iconicity" of writing not only due to its visuality but also through the two-dimensional spatiality and operativity of writing:

> This kind of operational iconicity is inherent to almost all written texts and is based on the fact that written texts materially and perceptively present themselves synoptically and simultaneously. Inscribed surfaces open up a neatly arranged and controllable space of aesthetic presentation and tactile manipulations: Every written configuration

can be reconfigured; thus writing is a paper-tool, a laboratory for cognitive and aesthetic activities.

(Krämer, 2017, p. 303)

Importantly, operative writing can sustain a place-value logic so that it is the spatial location of events that makes them subject to rearrangement. Moreover, in operative writing, both the eye and the tool (the pencil or mouse pointer) can move multi-dimensionally. Working with pencils on paper affords experimental, erasable, and non-durable writing and rearrangement, as does organizing waveforms on a screen. To paraphrase Krämer, we do not merely think with our screens; we think on them.

A range of sample- and mix-based, or "recombinant" (Sterne, 2006), music styles exist today, many of which rely on audio waveforms as their basic building blocks. The synoptical capacities of early arrange views encouraged a new kind of fractal organization and spatial thinking, wherein sounds could be added, removed, and shuffled around with an efficiency and economy that simply did not exist in any audio recording context before. Over time, the centralization of tools and techniques, together with increasing storage space, has led to a de-emphasizing of the "capture" element of classic hardware samplers (Nash, 2021). Instead, the conceptual models of "importing" or drag-and-dropping pre-existing audio files from a vast sound library have become habitual, and sounds recorded from somewhere else are then treated the same way once they are fixed on the unifying graphical timeline. Indeed, software designed to afford creative interaction with already recorded sound (as "content" visually represented on screens as discrete building blocks) has become the dominant mode of music composition and production. This has led to new approaches to composition with discrete bits of sound, as described by Brøvig-Hanssen and Danielsen:

> The visual representation of the music now arguably influences how we compose it in the first place. For instance, using the cursor to drag and drop chunks of "music" across the timeline of the arrange window encourages us to think about music as consisting of bits and fragments that can be easily shuffled around, rather than as a continuous flow that evolves organically through time.
>
> (2016, p. 14)

It is not only tiny bits and fragments that are shuffled around, however – another key feature of early arrange views is that they were scalable. While zooming in is often mentioned in the context of the unprecedented precision of digital editing (more on that in section 5), the ability to zoom out was, of course, just as new at the time. By changing the structural resolution of the view, the user could get an overview of the whole track or its constituent regions and, in principle, arrange a whole composition of recorded sound visually. As DAWs have become more and more sophisticated, the design of arrange views has introduced additional visual cues to help organize and arrange a song, from different-colored tracks and clips to the grouping and collapsing of several tracks into larger building blocks – all to afford attending to different structural levels in the composition.

To the extent that arrange views encourage tinkering with the rearrangement of events fixed in space, they work as spreadsheets or diagrams that organize data on spatial addresses. Scholars have in recent years narrated a shift in DAW design from what is considered the traditional linear horizontal timeline view to a vertical and non-linear, grid-based design (see, for example, Brett, 2019; D'Errico, 2022; Reuter, 2020). Ableton Live's Session View is the typical example, with its grid of clips inviting experimentation with audio and MIDI as interchangeable blocks of sound. But it seems that, in a very basic sense, the now taken-for-granted waveform arrange view has allowed non-linear interaction all along, and in a way that is hard to replace or leave out (most DAWs still have one). If the sequencer allows for the freezing or stabilizing of sounds in the same view and then the ability to move them around freely in relation to a fixed timeline, it likewise allows for the careful and iterative non-linear process of time tinkering.

4 STRUCTURING TIME ON A LINE

To sequence waveforms in an arrange view is, in the simplest of terms, to order time on a line. The consequences of this simple fact are, however, important to consider. As Bruyninckx explains:

> Whereas listening necessarily takes place in time and thus takes time, inscriptions stabilize time – allowing the reader to move back and forth or cut across sections more or less at will. It is this stabilization and reversibility of time that matters, more so than the visual organization of sound per se.
>
> (2018, p. 157)

An important consequence of the mapping of time to space is order: every possible manipulation in an arrange view – from trimming audio clips to arranging and drawing automation curves – is ultimately contingent on the left-to-right metaphorical logic of structuring time on a line. Furthermore, because ordering events in time is conceptual in nature, it necessarily involves abstraction; it means ignoring everything else about the events except their order and unfolding in time. But this abstraction – reducing sound's complexity into two dimensions (amplitude against time) – also allows comparisons and inferences: what events precede another, what are the relevant inter-onset-intervals, and are there any discrepancies in timing?

This capacity for comparisons and inferences presupposes what Krämer calls the "visibility of spacing" between events (Kramer and McChesney, 2003, p. 524). The prerequisites to the procedures of visual tinkering with timing and structure are, of course, blanks: "a chain of signification can only be constructed and reconstructed with varying combinations if there is a distinction between empty and filled spaces" (Krämer, 2006, pp. 98–99). Along the same lines, Siegert reminds us that, indeed, the grid-based notational system "presupposes the ability to write absence, that is, to deal equally efficiently with both occupied and empty spaces" (Siegert, 2015, p. 97). Here, we encounter a defining difference in the quality of recorded sound before and after the era of digital reproduction. While analog recording systems and sequencers obviously afforded the recording and programming of sophisticated rhythms as well, graphical timeline-based interfaces instrumentalize vision and spatialization in a way that affords certain kinds of thinking over others. It is the graphical sequencer's inclusion of the empty spaces between sounds that invites one to reckon with the sequentiality of individual sound events and to experiment and tinker with their precise timing.

Moreover, the way in which waveforms render the temporal envelope of sounds visible in the arrange view itself differentiates them from other forms of digital notation (including MIDI notation). Instead of depicting boxes that show when an event starts and stops, waveforms provide high-resolution information about when the relevant transients – peaks, low points, and other important moments – within the sample occur in time. This visual "data" about the sound makes it possible to edit, cut and paste, reorder, and time warp audio within the arrangement itself, which, together with the visibility of spacing between sounds, has resulted in a range of different expressive techniques for ordering sounds on a timeline.

5 MICRO-TIME MANIPULATION

Waveform editing and sequencing have also facilitated new operations at the micro level of rhythm. Expressive timing and groove are often described in terms of systematic departures from regularity (see, for example, Keil, 1987; Danielsen, 2006). Producing effective grooves necessitates the careful manipulation of what Kvifte (2004, 2007) calls the "analog aspects" of rhythm – that is, aspects such as sound choice, micro-timing, and techniques of articulation. Danielsen explains how the introduction of new interfaces – on both screens and hardware controllers – has, together with the increase in computational power, been "a critical factor in the development of opportunities to control these [analog] aspects of groove in desktop production" (Danielsen, 2020, p. 267). At the center of this development are the techniques for time tinkering that involve manipulating and sequencing waveforms.

First of all, digital audio sequencing allowed producers to create compelling grooves through precisely ordering sound at the micro level. While it is often used to simply correct mistakes or poor timing, the zooming-in capability of waveform editing can also generate new rhythmic feel through the alteration of the exact onset timing of sounds or other cutting and reordering operations at the micro level (Danielsen, 2010). For this kind of work, the synoptical and simultaneous presentation of sounds in the arrange view enables the careful positioning of them against one another and in accordance with the grid. In the context of sample- and mix-based music, sound events often have their own original rhythmic structure – one that is recontextualized and superimposed on the timeline of the new composition. Actually seeing the content of the waveforms down to the individual transients is key here because it allows one to efficiently cut up, trim, or nudge sounds ahead of or behind the beat in accordance with their content to achieve the desired timing.

Even in musical genres that adhere to a strict grid-based aesthetic, such as techno and electronic dance music (EDM), there is a lot of micro-editing going on. Producers report that they rely on the visual feedback of waveform manipulation and arrangement for many of their approaches to timing, all employed in order to combine on- and off-the-grid sounds and create rhythmic friction between these "loose" and "tight" sounds in a particular way (Brøvig-Hanssen et al., 2021). Moreover, some currently popular production techniques could not have arisen at all without waveform sequencing's capacities for micro-time manipulation. The layering of drum samples to create a new compound sound is one such technique, and another is vocal "comping" – the careful selection of words and phrases from a series of almost identical vocal takes to produce a "composite" audio recording.

In terms of sonic articulation, digital signal processing and automation afford endless opportunities to shape and manipulate sounds. Sound and timing interact in fundamental ways so that the alteration of the timbre or amplitude envelopes of sounds in the arrange view or editing mode impacts the sounds' timing as well. This relationship becomes apparent when one is drawing in automation curves – that is, curves that dictate how processing effects will be applied over the course of a track. The graphical spatialization of the time domain of arrange views in DAWs enables detailed programming related to how and when different signal processors operate at the micro level.

More specialized tools based on this principle have become popular as well. Dynamic range processors such as filters and compressors (including sidechain compression or compression triggered by a separate signal) have been particularly responsible for the new rhythmic feels in hip-hop and EDM music (Brøvig-Hanssen, Sandvik and Aareskjold-Drecker, 2020). Sidechaining's familiar "pumping effect" – wherein the sound rhythmically ducks and swells in the mix – is not visible in the arrangement itself, so one tinkers with it by adjusting the settings on the compressor. Via audio plugins that emulate and refashion this effect, however, one can manually draw in the curve or "shape" of the amplitude envelope visually. For example, in the popular plugin VolumeShaper from Cableguys – promoted with the tagline "a visual approach to volume" – one is invited to prototype and tinker with shaping amplitude envelopes to directly impact rhythm. By drawing in envelope curves or "shapes" on top of waveform representations, effects such as sidechain pumping and stuttering (the rhythmic cut-up of a signal) become customizable and flexible to produce (Figure 14.2).

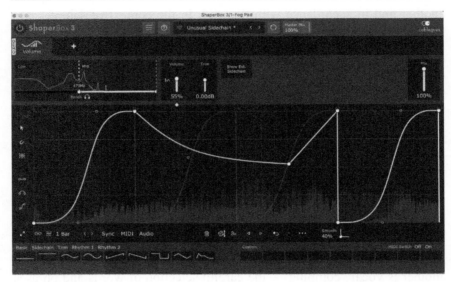

Figure 14.2 CableGuys' VolumeShaper 6 (screenshot by author).

Source: VolumeShaper 6 (n.d.)

Lastly, a whole repertoire of microtiming manipulation accompanies the concept of "time stretching" and other radical audio-warping procedures (see, for example, Danielsen, 2020, pp. 272–273; more on the idea of time stretching in the next section). Together, these examples clearly show how the spatial operations of waveform editing and arranging encourage experimentation with the timing and detailed shaping of sound's temporal envelopes at a micro level.

6 SLICING AND STRETCHING WAVEFORMS

In 1994, Propellerheads released their software ReCycle! in collaboration with Steinberg, intended as an add-on for their DAW Cubase that allowed users to alter a loop's tempo without affecting its pitch. Influenced by loop-slicing techniques popularized by drum machine producers, ReCycle! chopped the constituent parts of a drum loop into "slices," or smaller parts of the actual sample in its entirety. The software then instantly mapped each slice onto a keyboard or pad controller for performance and play-ful recombination; alternatively, the user could audit the different slices with a simple click of the mouse. As Charnas explains, programs such as ReCycle! represented a paradigmatic shift from older machines whose limitations "provoked the innovations of the producers who used them, and cultivated character too – patience, perseverance, focus, risk-taking . . . Tasks that used to take drum machine producers like Q-Tip, Pete Rock, and J Dilla hours now took computer producers seconds" (Charnas, 2022, p. 242). For example, J Dilla famously used an Akai MPC 3000 to chop his samples without any visual-spatial feedback whatsoever, using only the time codes on the small hexadecimal display to designate the various regions of longer samples to different pads on the interface. With the waveform view of ReCycle!, users were invited to create and move slice markers to prototype and experiment with the slice functionality in real-time. This use of the two-dimensional waveform representation to afford interaction with the functionality of loop slicing became instrumental to how the technique would develop in digital music-making later on.

Since the following installment of Akai's MPC series, the MPC 2000 (1998), most hardware samplers have had displays with waveform editing views and slicing modes with auto-chopping functions. The art of DJing today is associated as much with some kind of screen interface – replete with waveforms and slicing functionality – as with traditional turntablism (e.g., Serato's DJ Pro or Native Instruments' Traktor Pro).

The principle behind the technique for time compression and expansion that is based on spatial segmentation used in ReCycle! has its historical roots in wartime tape recorders, since popularized by Anton Springer's 1960s tape-based Tempophon. Voigtschild, Sterne, and Mills describe how it worked: "To change the playback speed, segments had to be discarded or repeated in such a way as to maintain consistency of sound" (n.d., para. 8; see also Sterne and Mills, 2020). While the algorithm's workings as it maintained consistency by expanding and compressing the sound between slices remained hidden beneath the interface like the Tempophon's tape heads before it, ReCycle! now allowed users to play around with slice points and other relevant parameters in the interface in real-time.

The introduction of Sonic Foundry's ACID Pro (1998) and Ableton's Live (2001) DAWs demonstrates how the possibilities of time stretching have long been framed in terms of agency and automation. ACID Pro was a loop-based sequencer that shipped with a library of prefabricated loops in different genres that were already tempo sliced and could, therefore, be dragged and dropped into the timeline arrange view, where they automatically adjusted and snapped to the tempo and key of a song. In introducing their own proprietary file format – soon nicknamed "acidized" loop files – Sonic Foundry effectively launched a new segment in the sample and loop market by commodifying time-sliced audio loops and linking them to a piece of software (a business model that remains viable today).

When importing audio from other sources, however, one had to rely on a hidden menu called "Beatmapper Wizard" – a classic Windows Wizard pop-up dialogue that took one through the steps of automatically beat-mapping audio. A video ad for ACID Pro opens with the question, "How does ACID work?" After a quick semi-ironic and overly technical description of the process of pitch and time manipulation, the question is asked once more: "But: how does ACID work?" The whispered answer: "It's magic" (DJ Puzzle, 2010). This exemplifies ACID Pro's emphasis on the allure of automaticity (and "wizardly magic") over user control. This kind of "black boxing" of the new abilities of computers as "magical" and automatic captures a widespread ethos of North American tech discourse surrounding ubiquitous computing and "organic" (i.e., invisible) interaction (Stahl, 1995; see also Emerson, 2014, ch. 1). Soon, other software like GarageBand and FruityLoops targeted this user group of amateurs and hobbyists as well, "wherein preset rhythms and chunky graphics gave music-making a feel of playing a video game" (Charnas, 2022, p. 241).

Ableton Live, on the other hand, was designed to provide unprecedented user control over the time domain. As its name suggested, it offered direct real-time control over time and pitch shift settings rather than hiding the relevant mechanisms and selling premade loops. It automatically conformed and "warped" disparate audio clips to the tempo of the Live project, and users could change the overall tempo of the project regardless of the sound sources. As in ReCycle!, Live invited direct user control over and experimentation with the slicing of waveforms. More importantly, however, it also enabled the actual stretching of waveforms right there in the main view, meaning that one could effectively time-shift parts of a sample by dragging its transients around in space. By the year 2008 or so, most other major DAWs followed Live and had their own pitch-and-time algorithms and waveform-stretching functions in place, from Pro Tool's "Elastic Audio" and Logic's "Flex Time" to Cubase's "Time Warp," all with variations upon the same standardized two-dimensional waveform view with its movable slice markers, automatic transient detection, and beat-matching functions. It all anticipated how people would soon expect audio to behave on a screen: as highly mutable mobiles. Whereas waveform representations have conventionally been considered indexical to time itself (functioning as a true inscription of real-life events), they have now, at least in the context of the DAW's "elasticity of audio," become indexical exclusively to the left-to-right spatial timeline grid on our screens.

7 TOUCHING WAVEFORMS

Although the concept of touching sound has a long history (see, for example, Parisi, 2018; Simon, 2018; Strauven, 2021), it was not until the success of the iPhone and iPad in the early 2010s that multitouch capabilities were added to waveform displays on a widespread basis.

In 2015, Akai released the first in a new line of MPC sampler workstations with large touchscreens, the MPC Touch. Whereas earlier MPCs had only a smaller LCD display, the new model replaced most of the control knobs and faders of past MPCs with a large multitouch display as the primary interface element besides the traditional grid of rubber pads. Here, Akai looked to combine its iconic MPC design and its tactile controls and rubber pads with the flexibility of a colorful screen with multitouch interaction. Ironically, despite the ongoing ideal of moving away from the computer screen altogether, many of the most successful controllers provide high-resolution screens with editing, slicing, and sequencing capabilities. It appears that the so-called return to standalone is contingent on striking a delicate balance between hardware tactility and software functionality. As D'Errico puts it, "the relationship between old and new interfaces [is] based not simply on remediation, in which the new refashions the old, but also on accumulation, as tools and techniques continue to converge" (D'Errico, 2022, p. 3).

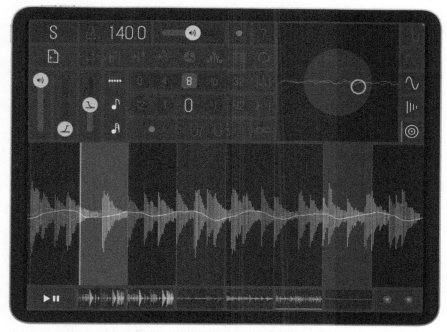

Figure 14.3 The SamplR iPad app (screenshot by author).

Source: See Alonso (n.d.).

A mobile app that showcases how multitouch screens can introduce new sensibilities regarding waveform representations is SamplR, developed and released by Marcos Alonso in 2012 (Figure 14.3).

In an early review, Kirn describes how the app exemplified a paradigmatic shift from "looking at" to "touching" sound:

> On computers and most hardware, waveforms have been a 'look, but don't touch' affair. Now, that view is coupled with multi-touch capabilities . . . With rhythmic slicing modes and multi-touch manipulation of samples, it's a lovely-looking way to surf sounds from your fingertips.
>
> (Kirn, 2012, para. 1)

As this chapter has shown, there had already been much more to waveform representations on screens than merely "looking" at them even before touchscreens arrived. Still, apps like SamplR built on the now-familiar concept of flattened waveforms and loop slicing while refashioning our interaction with them. For example, one can touch any part of a sound's envelope and drag one's finger across the sound in a manner reminiscent of turntable scratching or the manual operation of tape playback, though in this case, the waveform renders data about the content of the recording both visible and navigable. It operationalizes space and invites a kind of multitouch, granular exploration of sounds. By using more than one finger, one can trigger, loop, or sequence multiple parts of a sample of a loop simultaneously in real-time as a polyphonic expressive instrument.

Despite the many layers of mediation and chains of indices, then, the ability to produce sounds we are already accustomed to looking at on a screen by "touching" them feels strangely intuitive and immediate. SamplR anticipated a new range of interfaces that employed that same familiar waveform representation in their design but engendered new possibilities for controlling and experimenting with the temporal and sonic features of the sound in a way that the more metaphorical and skeuomorphic designs of the past did not.

8 CONCLUSIONS

This chapter has highlighted some important ways in which the visual representation of sound as waveforms represents and constitutes how recorded sound is often interacted with in the context of digital music production. Specifically, it has examined how such visual-spatial representations of sounds frozen in space afford a range of operations of temporal reorganization and manipulation. As waveforms have become ubiquitous in the current screen-saturated culture, they have also become a transparent and self-evident medium (Gitelman, 2006). But, as Chun reminds us, our media matter most when they seem not to matter at all – that is when they move from self-aware to embedded and habitual (Chun, 2017). The fact that organizing, stretching, and even touching two-dimensional waveforms are now considered to be among the most immediate and intuitive ways of interacting with recorded sound, despite the many layers of mediation and abstraction separating them from the original sound event, exemplifies how the capacities of visual-spatial representation have crystallized into self-evident mechanisms. Over time, we may have become so accustomed to interacting with sound as waveforms on screens that we take little notice of how those waveforms influence us, but it remains the case that working with sound that is flattened and spatialized on a two-dimensional surface has an enormous impact upon how we think about and interact with recorded sound. Through foregrounding how two-dimensional waveforms have become key for both structural thinking and various forms of expressive time tinkering, this chapter has added to existing research on the role of visualization of music in digital audio production.

To recall Scott de Martinville's vision of "reading" waveforms once more: we do not only read and interpret them any longer, we think with them; they not only represent present sound but also provide the means to produce it. By substituting the temporal domain with the visual-spatial domain, they (re)structure our relationship to time and invite fresh approaches to time tinkering and experimentation. Digital waveform representations entail an informatic relationship with the world by presupposing abstraction and reframing the event that they present to us. Galloway suggests that "in order to be in a relation with the world informatically, one must erase the world, subjecting it to various forms of manipulation, preemption, modeling, and synthetic transformation" (Galloway, 2012, p. 13). Waveform interfaces abstract sound to its essentials (amplitude against time) and, when successful, minimize visual and auditory clutter in favor of a structural understanding and time axis intervention. As this chapter has shown, an interaction with a visual representation of sound that defies the linear logic of musical experience not only constitutes how we conceive of music and its content across time but also actively changes how we interact with and produce musical rhythms. Despite the fact that software developers continue to try to emulate human activity, innovative tinkering with timing and groove is something that cannot easily be automated. This is why waveform interfaces for multimodal experimentation with timing are so central to the new rhythmic fabric of digital music. As Danielsen puts it, "A crucial aspect of this development [of new rhythmic feels] is the manner in which the new technologies allow for combining agency and automation, understood as creative strategies, in new compelling ways" (Danielsen, 2019, p. 595).

On a more general closing note, the design and use of the waveform interfaces discussed in this paper reflect and constitute broader cultural trends surrounding the fractal and modular organization of audiovisual "content" on screens and interfaces across media realms. The many screens on computers and mobile devices in the digital era do more than just provide information – they structure our relationship to data through graphical formats. According to Drucker, learning to interpret how visual forms not only present but also produce knowledge – what she calls "graphesis" – has become an essential contemporary skill (Drucker, 2014). Examining a seemingly quotidian graphical format such as waveforms that occupies a space between presentation and production, recording and composing, the immutable and the mutable, and the indexical and the symbolic tells us something bigger about the dynamics at play between digital media and music-making today.

REFERENCES

Alonso, M. (n.d.). *SamplR*. Available at: http://samplr.net/ [Accessed: 1 August 2022].

Artsy Voiceprint. (n.d.). Available at: https://artsyvoiceprint.com/ [Accessed: 1 August 2022].

Bell, A., Hein, E. and Ratcliffe, J. (2015). 'Beyond Skeuomorphism: The Evolution of Music Production Software User Interface Metaphors', *Art of Record Production Journal*, 9. Available at: www.arpjournal.com/asarpwp/beyond-skeuomorphism-the-evolution-of-music-production-software-user-interface-metaphors-2/ [Accessed: 30 August 2022].

Brett, T. (2019). 'Popular Music Production in Laptop Studios', in Hepworth-Sawyer, R., Hodgson, J. and Marrington, M., eds. *Producing Music*, 1st ed. New York: Routledge. https://doi.org/10.4324/9781315212241-11.

Brøvig-Hanssen, R. and Danielsen, A. (2016). *Digital Signatures: The Impact of Digitization on Popular Music Sound*. Cambridge, MA: The MIT Press.

Brøvig-Hanssen, R., Sandvik, B. and Aareskjold-Drecker, J. M. (2020). 'Dynamic Range Processing and Its Influence on Perceived Timing in Electronic Dance Music', *Music Theory Online*, 26(2). https://doi.org/10.30535/mto.26.2.3.

Brøvig-Hanssen, R., et al. (2021). 'A Grid in Flux: Sound and Timing in Electronic Dance Music', *Music Theory Spectrum*, 44(1). https://doi.org/10.1093/mts/mtab013.

Bruyninckx, J. (2018). *Listening in the Field: Recording and the Science of Birdsong*. Cambridge, MA: The MIT Press.

Charnas, D. (2022). *Dilla Time: The Life and Afterlife of J Dilla, the Hip-Hop Producer Who Reinvented Rhythm*. New York: MCD/Farrar, Straus and Giroux.

Chun, W. H. K. (2017). *Updating to Remain the Same: Habitual New Media*. Cambridge, MA and London: The MIT Press.

Danielsen, A. (2006). *Presence and Pleasure: The Funk Grooves of James Brown and Parliament*. Middletown, CT: Wesleyan University Press.

Danielsen, A., ed. (2010). *Musical Rhythm in the Age of Digital Reproduction*. Farnham, Surrey, England and Burlington, VT: Ashgate.

Danielsen, A. (2019). 'Glitched and Warped: Transformations of Rhythm in the Age of the Digital Audio Workstation', in Grimshaw-Aagaard, M., Walther-Hansen, M. and Knakkergaard, M., eds. *The Oxford Handbook of Sound and Imagination*, Volume 2. Oxford: Oxford University Press, pp. 593–609. https://doi.org/10.1093/oxfordhb/9780190460242.013.27 .

Danielsen, A. (2020). 'Desktop Production and Groove', in Bourbon, A. and Zagorski-Thomas, S., eds. *The Bloomsbury Handbook of Music Production*. New York: Bloomsbury Academic.

D'Errico, M. (2022). *Push: Software Design and the Cultural Politics of Music Production*. New York: Oxford University Press.

DJ Puzzle. (2010). *Acid – The Sonic Foundry Story 1998 – YouTube*. Available at: www.youtube.com/watch?v=3QmcV-E1xJY [Accessed: 11 August 2022].

Drucker, J. (2014). *Graphesis: Visual Forms of Knowledge Production*. Cambridge, MA: Harvard University Press.

Emerson, L. (2014). *Reading Writing Interfaces: From the Digital to the Bookbound*. Minneapolis: University of Minnesota Press.

Feaster, P. (2014). *A Brief History of the Waveform* (Stylus Radio). Available at: https://soundcloud.com/stylusradio/a-brief-history-of-the-1 [Accessed: 1 August 2022].

Galloway, A. R. (2012). *The Interface Effect*. Cambridge and Malden, MA: Polity.

Gitelman, L. (2006). *Always Already New: Media, History and the Data of Culture*. Cambridge, MA: MIT Press.

Harkins, P. (2020). *Digital Sampling: The Design and Use of Music Technologies*. New York: Routledge.

Joho345. (2011). 'Fairlight II Page R', *Wikimedia Commons*, licenced under CC BY-SA 3.0. Available at: https://commons.wikimedia.org/wiki/File:Fairlight_II_Page_R.png [Accessed: 31 August 2022].

Keil, C. (1987). 'Participatory Discrepancies and the Power of Music', *Cultural Anthropology*, 2(3), pp. 275–283. https://doi.org/10.1525/can.1987.2.3.02a00010.

Kirn, P. (2012). 'Samplr Is an OP-1-Inspired iPad App Focused on Touching, Slicing Waveforms', *CDM Create Digital Music*. Available at: https://cdm.

link/2012/11/samplr-is-an-op-1-inspired-ipad-app-focused-on-touching-slic-ing-waveform-samples/ [Accessed: 17 August 2022].

Kittler, F. (2017). 'Real Time Analysis, Time Axis Manipulation', *Cultural Politics*. Translated by G. Winthrop-Young, 13(1), pp. 1–18. https://doi.org/10.1215/17432197-3755144.

Krämer, S. (2006). 'The Cultural Techniques of Time Axis Manipulation: On Friedrich Kittler's Conception of Media', *Theory, Culture & Society*, 23(7–8), pp. 93–109. https://doi.org/10.1177/0263276406069885.

Krämer, S. (2017). 'Why Notational Iconicity Is a Form of Operational Iconicity', in Zirker, A., et al., eds. *Dimensions of Iconicity. Symposium on Iconicity in Language and Literature*. Amsterdam and Philadelphia: John Benjamins Publishing Company (Iconicity in language and literature, volume 15), pp. 303–320.

Kramer, S. and McChesney, A. (2003). 'Writing, Notational Iconicity, Calculus: On Writing as a Cultural Technique', *MLN*, 118(3), pp. 518–537. https://doi.org/10.1353/mln.2003.0059.

Kvifte, T. (2004). 'Description of Grooves and Syntax/Process Dialectics', *Studia Musicologica Norvegica*, 30(1), pp. 54–74. https://doi.org/10.18261/ISSN1504-2960-2004-01-04.

Kvifte, T. (2007). 'Digital Sampling and Analogue Aesthetics', in Melberg, A., ed. *Aesthetics at Work*. Oslo: Oslo Academic Press, pp. 105–128.

Lehrman, P. D. (1989, August). 'Digidesign Sound Tools', *Sound on Sound*, pp. 60–63. Available at: www.muzines.co.uk/articles/digidesign-sound-tools/5626.

Nash, J. (2021). 'Motormouth: An Essay in Sonic Recontextualization', in Hepworth-Sawyer, R., Paterson, J. and Toulson, R., eds. *Innovation in Music: Future Opportunities*. New York: Routledge, pp. 56–69.

Parisi, D. (2018). *Archaeologies of Touch: Interfacing with Haptics from Electricity to Computing*. Minneapolis: University of Minnesota Press.

Reuter, A. (2020). *The Digitalization of Musical Time and Space*. Doctoral dissertation. Copehagen: University of Copenhagen.

Siegert, B. (2015). *Cultural Techniques: Grids, Filters, Doors, and other Articulations of the Real*. Fordham University Press (Grids, Filters, Doors, and Other Articulations of the Real). https://doi.org/10.5422/fordham/9780823263752.001.0001.

Simon, V. (2018). *From Difficulty to Delight. The History and Politics of Touch-screens for Music Production*. Doctoral dissertation. Montreal: McGill University.

Sound Wave Picture. (n.d.). Available at: soundwavepic.com [Accessed: 1 August 2022].

Stahl, W. A. (1995). 'Venerating the Black Box: Magic in Media Discourse on Technology', *Science, Technology, & Human Values*, 20(2), pp. 234–258. https://doi.org/10.1177/016224399502000205.

Sterne, J. (2003). *The Audible Past: Cultural Origins of Sound Reproduction*. Durham: Duke University Press.

Sterne, J. (2006). 'What's Digital in Digital Music?', in Messaris, P. and Humphreys, L., eds. *Digital Media: Transformations in Human Communication*. New York: Peter Lang, pp. 95–109.

Sterne, J. and Mills, M. (2020). 'Second Rate: Tempo Regulation, Helium Speech, and "Information Overload"', *Triple Canopy*, 26. www.canopycanopycanopy.com/issues/26/contents/second-rate [Accessed: 11 July 2022].

Strauven, W. (2021). *Touchscreen Archaeology: Tracing Histories of Hands-on Media Practices*. Lüneburg: Meson Press.

Voigtschild, F., Sterne, J. and Mills, M. (no date). 'Anton Springer and the Time and Pitch Regulator', *Sound & Science: Digital Histories*. https://soundandscience.de/contributor-essays/anton-springer-and-time-and-pitch-regulator [Accessed: 15 June 2022].

VolumeShaper 6. (n.d.). *Cableguys* (website). Available at: www.cableguys.com/volumeshaper.html [Accessed: 31 August 2022].

Wiffen, P. (1985, December). 'Screen Test', *Electronics & Music Maker*, pp. 44–50.

Wiffen, P. (1988, August). 'Alchemy', *Sound on Sound*, pp. 48–51.

15

Levelling up chiptune

Nostalgic retro games console sounds for the ROLI Seaboard

Kirsten Hermes

1 INTRODUCTION

In the 70s and 80s, special chips were built that could transform electrical impulses from a computer into analogue sound waves. They allowed musicians and programmers to transform early games consoles, arcade machines and personal computers into musical instruments through computer code. From the technological restriction of these old devices, "chiptune" emerged, a lo-fi style of electronic music. The genre's unique sound, along with traditional pixel art, continues to inspire modern musicians, filmmakers and game designers.

This chapter explores chiptune as a lasting cultural symbol and discusses its continuing relevance in the modern day despite the fact that its roots lie in obsolete and restrictive technologies. The argument is made that nostalgia can be a springboard for innovation and new creative expression. To demonstrate this, a literature review is combined with a practice-led case study, where the author attempts to translate the nostalgia of chiptune to the domain of MIDI polyphonic expression. MIDI polyphonic expression (MPE) expands the expressive power of traditional MIDI controllers by allowing individual modulation data to be sent for each musical note in a chord (Official Midi Specifications, 2022) – a newer technology that is juxtaposed to the creative restriction of traditional chiptune. The author reflects on her preset pack "Chiptune Bubblegum" for the "Equator 2" MPE software synthesizer, which was published by ROLI in 2021 (ROLI and Hermes, 2021) to assess the questions: can a genre that thrives on technological and creative restriction be performed on complex and multidimensional electronic music instruments? Is MPE chiptune still "authentic" chiptune?

Section 2 provides an overview of the chiptune genre, from its beginnings to its current state of the art. Section 3 uses nostalgia and authenticity frameworks to investigate the purpose of chiptune in the modern day, exploring ways in which the perusal of obsolete technology can allow for new creative expression. Section 4 describes the practice-led research underlying the paper. Section 5 is a reflection on this work, also presenting feedback from ROLI and the public, leading into an overall discussion of the research questions. Section 6 concludes.

DOI: 10.4324/9781003118817-17

2 CHIPTUNE AS AN OLD AND NEW PHENOMENON

Chiptune is a Lo-fi electronic music style that emerged in the early 70s and 80s (McAlpine, 2018). For interactive applications such as video games and arcade machines, audio playback had to respond on the fly to user input, which was difficult to achieve with older audio storage devices such as tape cassettes or vinyl. Newly created sound-producing chips, however, allowed for real-time audio playback. In order to compose chiptune music, it was necessary to employ trackers, systems whereby parameters like the channel, sample or instrument number, effects, pitch and length of each note had to be coded separately. One peculiarity of traditional chips is their limited polyphony, resulting from the small number of available channels, and their restricted timbre palette, resulting from the limited number of available waveforms. Since it was impossible to create complex arrangements with many notes playing simultaneously, new compositional techniques were invented to overcome this challenge. For instance, arpeggios were used in order to convey harmony and simple noises were repurposed as drums. The unique sonic characteristics of older chips, as well as their unusual operation, set the scene for the chiptune sound as an artistic identity (Tomczak, 2008) and even a sonic brand (Hermes, 2022).

Chiptune continues to inspire musicians in the present day (McAlpine, 2018). According to Paul (2014), purists enjoy the arcane nature and difficulty of producing chiptunes on original or personally customized hardware. Chiptunes, in their strictest definition, are songs produced on the original audio hardware microchips found in older computers and games consoles (such as the Commodore 64 MOS 6581 SID chip or the Nintendo Entertainment System Ricoh 2A03 sound chip, Paul, 2014). Many chiptune purists can distinguish the sound of different systems, and some can even tell apart different trackers used to produce the songs (Paul, 2014). These musicians share a strong DIY ethic, feel connected through mutual curiosity and enjoy the intellectual challenge of making older technology work for them. In order to stay true to the genre's roots, many stick with trackers specifically made for each system (Farrell, 2020), such as SID Duzz'It for the Commodore 64. Some use newly created trackers, such as GoatTracker, which runs on a modern PC (Paul, 2014). Little Sound DJ (LSDJ), a music sequencer for Game Boys first created in the early 00s, is still popular among musicians. Hardware hacking is a common practice among chiptune enthusiasts, whereby musicians alter and recombine old electronics, sometimes as a part of more modern music setups. For example, customized Arduino computers (like the ArduinoBoy by Cat Skull Electronics) can be used to control old Game Boys with a modern MIDI keyboard. In the live performance, many artists (such as Cyanide Dansen) use DJ setups where two Game Boys and a mixer replace DJ decks. Purists limit modifications to the hardware level to maintain the limitations and errors in the original chip design (Paul, 2014).

Non-purists expand the aesthetics of classic sound chips into other music genres, such as pop, EDM or rock, incorporating the sound of typical chiptune waveforms. These include pulse, triangle, sawtooth and pseudo-random noise, along with compositional artifacts such as rapid arpeggiation (Paul,

2014). Some artists use VST software emulations (for example, Plogue Chip-sounds) in order to replicate the iconic chiptune sound. This broader definition allows for chiptune aesthetics to be embedded in a modern production workflow, where processing such as reverb, compression or delays can be added, along with non-chiptune instruments (Paul, 2014). For example, the band Anamanaguchi releases EDM music with chiptune elements on the Monstercat label and use the NES (the 1983 Nintendo entertainment system) as another band member in a "chip-punk" band ensemble (Paul, 2014).

The modern reincarnation of the 8-bit era is not just a musical phenomenon but includes visual, social, political and performative aspects (Márquez, 2014). Márquez (ibid) describes this as a movement that is socially constructed through artists' playful congregation around retro-gaming symbols. Modern games such as the Pokémon series, Stardew Valley (2016) and Terraria (2011) utilize various audiovisual elements reminiscent of the 8-bit era, such as pixel art, bright colors, chiptune sounds and orthographic projection. Chiptune and pixel art are common symbols for gaming in general: films such as Disney's "Wreck It Ralph" (2012) reference retro gaming in an entertaining way. Pixel art and chiptune are also referenced in Japanese pop culture-inspired art-making and represent cuteness in the "kawaii" movement: on Instagram, pastel-clad adults pose with plushies, Gameboys, Pokémon or Tamagotchi toys and adorn their images with pixeled stickers to evoke childhood memories. Retro game artifacts can also symbolize 90s rave culture, Europop and bubblegum pop aesthetics, which emerged at a similar time as later Game Boys and Tamagotchis.

3 BLENDING THE OLD AND NEW: NOSTALGIA AS A SPRINGBOARD FOR NEW CREATIVE EXPRESSION

The question arises as to why chiptune is still popular in the present day. An important reason is nostalgia, which, according to Wulf et al. (2018), is a key factor in explaining the recent success of retro gaming. The authors explain that engagement with past video games can significantly contribute to wellbeing and a sense of social identity. Obsolescence as artistic practice is not limited to chiptune – according to Bittanti (2009), it is a multifaceted cultural phenomenon at the intersection of technology, music, art and politics. The perusal of outdated technology and bygone sociocultural themes has not always been met with positivity, however. Philosopher Alain Badiou (2012, p. 62) stated that a significant political event will always require "the dictatorial power of a creation ex nihilo". In his seminal work "Retromania", Reynolds (2012) accuses current-day popular culture of lacking the artistic imperative to be original. Digital technology allows us to lose ourselves in vast amounts of cultural data, which, as Reynolds observes, has facilitated widespread remixing, covering and sampling of older music since the mid-90s. Reissues, revivals, band reunions and nostalgic TV shows are now a structural feature of pop, which Reynolds (2012) describes as a malaise that militates against distinctive work or originality. He concludes that forgetting is as essential in culture as it is existentially and emotionally necessary for individuals (ibid, 2012).

On the other hand, Samuel (2012) takes issue with the claim that our obsession with heritage is a symptom of national decay. Reynolds (2012) does admit that nostalgia can have a dissident potential. Márquez (2014) stresses that obsolete gaming devices can be sources of innovation and creativity. Nostalgia can have several advantages, one being the archival of a bygone cultural language. As Paul (2014) puts it, the sound of chiptune lets us have a conversation with the machines that construct our surroundings through the lens of a time when they had their own unique voices. But beyond archival, nostalgia allows us to see the past through the lens of the present. Boym (2001, p. 7) defines nostalgia (from νόστος, "return home", and ἄλγος, "longing") as a longing for a home that no longer exists or has never existed. Instead of remembering the past as it really was, we distort it in the context of what has happened since. Boym compares nostalgia to "a double exposure", where two images are superimposed: home and abroad, past and present, dream and everyday life (Boym, 2001, p. 296). This thinking can be traced back to Romantic theory: Abrams (1953) used "the Mirror and the Lamp" as metaphors of the mind, which can reflect external objects as they really are or recreate them in a different way, like a radiant projector. In other words, chiptune, seen through a modern lens, is different from what it originally was.

One of the attractive elements of chiptune music is that, from a modern perspective, it is a minimalist framework (Paul, 2014). From Igor Stravinsky (1970) and David Hockney (Gayford, 2016) to the Oulipo group, artists have recognized the advantages of working with a restricted palette. By limiting polyphony and timbre, practitioners can engage with interesting arrangement challenges and find their unique voices within a creatively restrained environment. Chiptune can be used as a symbol of rebellion against the latest technological developments (Márquez, 2014), implicitly critiquing the status quo of modern music production. The absence of DSP effects can spark innovative ways to mimic a modern DAW without the overwhelm of numerous commercial software options. For instance, delays can be created by duplicating the notes of a particular channel at a quieter volume, delayed in time. Traditionally, more nuanced chiptunes were remarkable, as they were more difficult to create. In 1988, Martin Galway spent 20 days coding a "guitar" solo for the "Times of Lore" title song, the kind of challenge that many modern practitioners still enjoy.

As was seen in section 2, pixel art and chiptune have become modern cultural symbols for childhood and teen memories, kawaii culture and gaming in general. Humans are dependent upon signs and systems of signs, and the human mind is inseparable from the functioning of these signs (Morris, 1971). Through these shared symbols, retro gaming can connect people. Paul (2014) describes chiptunes as a type of folk art that anyone can enjoy by downloading free software or buying a cheap second-hand game console (Paul, 2014). Chiptune enthusiasts can make friends within a knowledge community and exchange information about music, videos and games online and face-to-face. (Levy, 1997).

Overall, nostalgia seems to be a useful springboard for new creative expression, where artists build upon obsolete technology and existing compositional means to create new voices within a well-established framework of cultural symbols. But at what point is chiptune no longer chiptune? Is there such a thing as authentic chiptune? As a thing that is subjective and difficult to measure, authenticity has led to heated debates among scholars for decades. Negus and Astor (2021, p. 3) observe that authenticity has been "dismissed, deconstructed, left for dead, or simply discarded". Richard Middleton (1990, p. 139) wrote of the "debris of 'authenticity'" in his book "Studying Popular Music", and Georgina Born and David Hesmondhalgh (2000, pp. 1–58) declared that the subject has been "consigned to the intellectual dust-heap". Richard Peterson (1997) described authenticity as fabricated. Overall, according to Negus and Astor (2021), understanding of authenticity depends on our individual experiences, perceptions, circumstances and vocabularies. The authors stress that "what matters is not what authenticity is, but what it does, which is to express ourselves in specific ways, connect with people in particular places, and explain our understanding of other people" (2021, p. 25). Retro-leaning games and modern chiptune allow us to connect with an imagined past, our own version of the 80s. As Frith (1981, pp. 159–168) put it, "what matters is not whether the magic is real or not, but that people experience it". If it sounds like chiptune, it has the potential to evoke nostalgia – even if we were not really there at the time. According to Reid (2018), the affective relationality of chiptune creativity means that the chiptune fan identity is never obsolete, no matter whether original hardware chips or VST emulations are used – and this leaves much room for new creative expression.

4 MPE CHIPTUNE – A CASE STUDY

Under the moniker Nyokee, the author creates audiovisual art, combining retro games console sounds with analogue synthesizers, DAW production and 3D graphics visuals. In this section, the author reflects on her preset pack "Chiptune Bubblegum" for the "Equator 2" MPE software synthesizer, which was published by ROLI in 2021 (Figures 15.1 and 15.2). In addition to the preset pack itself, the author also produced a demo track and a performance video for potential customers, which was published on the ROLI YouTube channel and social media pages (Figure 15.3). The video demonstrates how some of the sounds can be used with the ROLI Seaboard, the ROLI LUMI keys, and a non-MPE Midi controller.

In juxtaposition to the technological restriction of old sound chips, modern electronic music instruments are becoming ever more complex, offering fine control over sonic parameters, both live and in the studio. In conventional MIDI devices, continuous controller messages are sent channel-wide. Moving a pitch bend control changes the pitch of all notes simultaneously. MIDI polyphonic expression (MPE) expands the expressive power of traditional MIDI controllers: modulation data can be sent for each musical note in a chord (Official Midi Specifications, 2022). This includes musical

Figure 15.1 Artwork for the "Chiptune Bubblegum" sound pack.

Figure 15.2 This QR code can be scanned to view the preset pack on the ROLI website.

Figure 15.3 This QR code can be scanned to watch the preset performance video.

performance parameters such as note-on velocity, pitch bend, channel pressure (aftertouch) and note-off velocity. Each note is assigned to a different MIDI channel and can be modulated individually. MPE controllers such as the ROLI Seaboard, the Haken Continuum Fingerboard or the TouchKeys are built to resemble real, acoustic instruments, which tend to be highly responsive to small movements (Hermes, 2022).

Through methods such as sampling, granular synthesis, pitch modulation (e.g., arpeggios with shifting speeds) and distortion, the author strived to replicate the sound of old games consoles within the Equator 2 MPE synthesizer while implementing expressive performance control. Sliding, gliding and pressing motions on the ROLI Seaboard controller were mapped to sonic changes in the synthesizer's intricate modulation matrix. Nostalgic timbres were placed in a new context, morphing and shifting into one another and moving around on a virtual stage, all depending on performance parameters. Section 4.1 provides an overview of the synthesizer and Seaboard and the following sections explain the technical approaches to making the sound pack.

4.1 Equator 2 and the ROLI Seaboard MPE controller

MPE requires specialized hardware and software. DAWs must be able to send and receive multiple channels, and synthesizers need to be able to decode the individual information for each note in a chord. In this example, the ROLI Equator 2 MPE soft synth was controlled with a Seaboard MIDI controller within Logic Pro X. ROLI Seaboard controllers have soft "piano" keys that the performer can press into and slide on, for example, to create vibrato, pitch bend and timbre variations, alongside sliders and an X-Y pad (Figure 15.4).

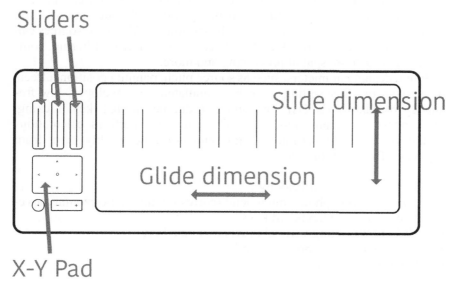

Figure 15.4 A schematic of the ROLI Seaboard Rise 25.

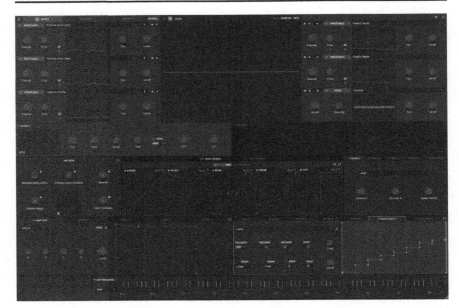

Figure 15.5 A screenshot of the Equator 2 interface.

Source: Copyright Luminary ROLI Ltd., showing the "Coinz" preset. The "routing" and "effects" tabs at the top lead to additional editing pages, as does the "mod matrix" tab (see also Figure 15.7).

Equator 2 (Figure 15.5) is a software synthesizer with six sound sources, each of which can be an oscillator (wavetable or virtual analog), a sampler, granular or a noise sound source. For each sound source, the user can control coarse and fine-tuning, panning and level, mute and solo and additional parameters specific to the chosen source. All sound sources can be fed through a filter block and an effects block offering filtering, compression, distortion, spatial processing and more.

Sound design parameters, such as source pitch, panning position, effects parameters or filter settings, can be modulated via envelopes, low-frequency oscillators (LFOs), multi-mods (editable graphs), key tracking, randomness and maths modifiers. The latter can perform calculations on the former. The most interesting modulation functionality stems from Equator's five MPE dimensions:

- *Strike*, i.e., note-on velocity,
- *Glide*, i.e., polyphonic pitch bend (corresponding to horizontal movement across the keyboard keys),
- *Slide*, representing vertical movement on a key,
- *Press*, polyphonic pressure, and
- *Lift*, note-off velocity.

Where no MPE controller is available, Equator 2 can be switched over to a standard MIDI mode whereby the listed items become:

- Note-on velocity,
- Pitch bend,
- Mod wheel,
- Pressure, and
- Note-off velocity.

Performers can additionally use macros for modulation, which correspond to an X-Y pad and three sliders on the Seaboard. All of these modulation sources can be combined creatively for complex and expressive sound design patches. The sound pack "Chiptune Bubblegum" contains 20 preset sets, including leads, basses, arpeggiated sounds, pads, percussive sounds and effects, whereby each preset was shipped as an MPE and standard MIDI version. Some of the preset sets were designed to mimic pure chiptune timbres, while others more broadly represent kawaii retro gaming culture and the 90s rave scene. In the following sub-sections, key sound design approaches are summarized.

4.2 Mimicking chiptune timbres

Typical chiptune timbres are noisy, pure waves. Within Equator's oscillator sound sources, suitable timbres were sought, and basic oscillator waveforms proved particularly useful (usually square, saw, pulse and triangle, and combinations thereof). The noise source could be used to enhance the lo-fi sound quality. The sound design process was supported by listening to chiptune references and by auditioning sounds created on a 90s Game Boy Color. In Equator's wavetable oscillator option, the wavetable position (i.e., the playback position in a wavetable) was occasionally modulated, creating the subtle timbral shifts that electrical currents can produce in hardware sound chips. The sampler was useful for storing real hardware chiptune sounds in the form of long notes recorded from the Game Boy Color. These recorded samples were blended with other sound sources. Filtering was used to further enhance the chiptune sound quality. For instance, a resonant bandpass filter, with the cut-off set to 1kHz, and a comb filter were applied to all sound sources for the sound "Chiptune Lead", giving it the typical nasal quality of an old computer speaker. Sound chips often produce an overdriven click sound at note onsets, which can be approximated by a fast drop in pitch. By drawing the corresponding shape into an envelope modifier and by mapping this to the source pitch, a fast octave drop could be created for the same lead sound.

For less chiptune-like and more "retro-rave" inspired sounds, the sound sources were used differently. For example, in "Candyfloss Sky", three detuned sawtooth oscillators create a timbre reminiscent of early 90s trance. "Villain Dub Bass" is a distorted dubstep bass consisting of wavetable and noise input sources that are fed through a low-pass filter. The filter cut-off, drive and resonance are controlled with a sinewave LFO, whose speed can be controlled further with the *Slide* MPE dimension. Presets such as "kawaii cat choir", or "anime angel choir" use recorded vocal samples that cannot be found in hardware chiptune but reference kawaii connotations of the chiptune movement in general.

4.3 MPE parameters and macros

The most common way in which MPE was used was to allow the performer to morph between chiptune timbres. *Press* and *Slide* were occasionally mapped to the volume levels of individual sound sources, subtly altering the blended, overall timbre. In "Coinz", pressing into a note increases the volume of a crackling noise sound source. Other times, MPE parameters were mapped to the cut-off of an overarching low-pass filter or to control vibrato. For vibrato, the pitches of the sound sources were modulated via a sinewave-shaped LFO, whose amplitude was mapped to an MPE parameter such as *Slide* (Figure 15.6).

In many presets, the performer can utilize macros to increase attack and release times, morphing plucked sounds into more ambient pads. Alternatively, she can alter the level of effects such as reverbs, delays, distortion, or modulation effects, or entirely "mangle" sounds to be less "musical", but more experimental. For instance, the "grain delay" effect, with its many pitch-shifted copies, can be brought in for an almost ghost-like, atonal soundscape.

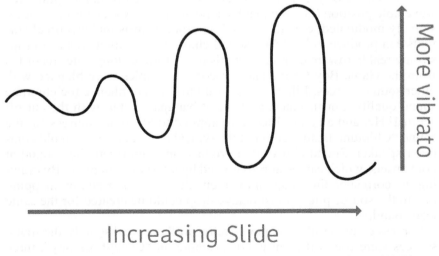

Figure 15.6 As the performer slides up on a Seaboard key (see also Figure 15.4), the LFO amplitude increases, and so do the pitch fluctuations that the LFO controls.

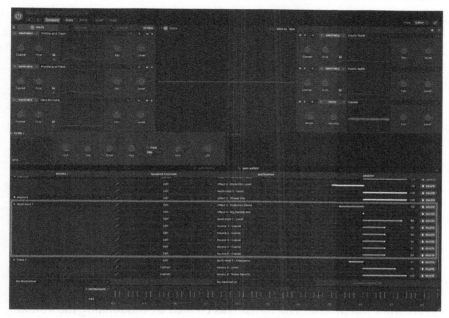

Figure 15.7 Multi-mod 1 is mapped to the coarse tuning of the first five sound sources.

Source: Copyright Luminary ROLI Ltd.

4.4 Arpeggios

Arpeggios are a typical feature of chiptune music and traditionally the only way to create harmony within the framework of limited polyphony. For many "Chiptune Bubblegum" presets, a multi-mod shape was programmed to resemble a staircase, with each step height representing pitch and each step depth representing the length of a note in an arpeggio (the multi-mod shape can be seen in the bottom right corner of Figure 15.5, and Figure 15.7 shows the mapping in the Mod Matrix). This overall shape is looped and mapped to the pitch of different sound sources. For added performance control, arpeggios (i.e., the multi-mod frequency) can be sped up or slowed down via the MPE dimensions (for example, *Slide* for the preset "Blippy Bloop" and *Press* for the preset "Coinz").

4.5 Rhythms

By mapping modifiers to the volumes of sound sources, interesting rhythms can be created, even while a note is held. For some sounds, macros were set up so that a performer could alternate between held notes and choppy rhythms. For example, in "arcade bass", a macro labelled "chopper" controls the blend between the amp envelope and a rhythmical multi-mod as input sources for the overall volume. The multi-mod is shaped like a pulse

Figure 15.8 Multi-mod controlling the volume level in the sound "Candyfloss Sky".

Source: Copyright Luminary ROLI Ltd.

wave that turns the sound on and off, resulting in stabbing, syncopated notes. A similar effect is employed in the polyphonic lead preset "Candyfloss Sky", except here, the user can alternate between long-held notes and stabbed rhythms via *Press* (Figure 15.8 shows the multi-mod shape, whose effect on the volume is mapped to *Press*).

"Trash Drums" is a preset that plays a complete drum arrangement while a note is held. The kick plays a four-to-the-floor rhythm while a snare plays on beats two and four. A 16th-note hi-hat completes the arrangement. Timbrally, the preset resembles noisy chiptune drums played in a reverberant warehouse. The hi-hat was created by modulating the volume of a white noise sound source via a sawtooth LFO. The snare is a pink noise sound source whose volume is controlled via a square wave LFO (effectively turning the sound on and off). The kick was created by modulating the pitch of a wavetable source, creating repeating, fast downwards sliding movements (via another sawtooth LFO). The speed of all LFOs can be controlled with the X-Y pad macro, therefore controlling the speed of the drum pattern overall. The addition of distortion, bit-crusher and compression effects gives the sound texture and grit. To add performability, the *Press* MPE dimension was mapped to alter the relative loudness of the three drum sounds, leading to interesting timbral shifts through the interaction with the distortion effects.

4.6 A higher level of abstraction

Not all presets directly represent individual chiptune sound sources. Some are more abstract representations of being surrounded by old sound chips, electronic toys or arcade machines that create a nuanced and morphing soundscape around the listener. "AI chatter" is such a preset: several wavetable sound sources, producing edgy and metallic timbres, stutter in and out of existence. This was achieved by mapping their volume levels and spatial positions to out-of-sync LFOs. Facilitated by multi-mod and pitch mapping, the sound sources also perform large pitch jumps. Several filtered white noise sources create subtle stabs and swishes, somewhat like whirring computer fans in an office.

The preset "Chibi Foley" references chibis, cute anime characters with oversized heads and childlike qualities. Samplers and granular sources were used to turn real-life recordings of bells and squeaky toys into a sustained, "cute" soundscape (a technique often used in Kawaii Bass music).

Via *Press*, a performer can change the timbre of a pad sound accompanying the bells and squeaks to resemble either a voice or a sustained bell. The sound also contains inharmonic Foley components (stemming from recordings of shakers and rattles), which can be played in isolation by turning up one of the macros.

In the preset "I think it's broken", a multi-mod controls the pitch of various sampler and wavetable sources via *Slide*, in a way that purposely sounds out of tune. A noise sample recorded from the Game Boy is mangled inside of a granular source in order to mimic the sound of speakers popping randomly. One of the macros, called "anger", can be used to overdrive the sound and make it extremely distorted. In all these cases, the sound design transcends the creation of virtual hardware chiptune instruments but places several imagined chiptune sound sources in a space with morphing spatial qualities. This is similar to the way in which some chiptune artists combine retro gaming timbres with more modern sounds, as discussed in section 2.

5 FEEDBACK AND DISCUSSION

This section presents feedback from ROLI, as well as the public, leading into a discussion that answers the overall research questions: can a genre that thrives on technological and creative restriction be performed on complex and multidimensional electronic music instruments? Is MPE chiptune still perceived to be "authentic" chiptune?

Overall, ROLI employees liked the concept of the preset pack from the outset ("so much fun!"). In an email exchange, one ROLI employee summarized the creative direction as "retro-gaming, chip-tune, old-school synths sounds morphing into bigger and more complex sounds via MPE/MW/Aftertouch/Macro modulation – giving a set of familiar, somewhat innocent sounds a new dimension with gestures that can take the sounds elsewhere". On YouTube, the ROLI account commented: "Great work! We hope this inspires everyone to be even more imaginative!" ROLI employees particularly appreciated the "off-the-wall" sounds in the pack. Creativity, expressivity and remarkability were seen as important features, while showcasing the technical capabilities of Equator 2 and the Seaboard. The presets needed to be "playable" and all MPE dimensions and macros needed to have a noticeable effect. The sounds also needed to sound pleasant across all musical octaves to make sure they were translatable to a wide range of use cases. In collaboration with ROLI, it was ensured that the preset pack fulfilled these requirements.

The public reactions to the demo video on YouTube and on social media were mixed. Positive comments included "legal", "AMAZING!!!" "great for kids", "ouhhhhh yeah" and various flame and clapping emojis. People wrote, "These sound rather awesome!", "cool track, nice job" and "omg I think it's broken is amazing!!". On the other hand, not everyone felt that the preset pack represented authentic chiptune. One commentator wrote: "chiptune or 8bit music are not related to [a] clamped and noisy sound", proceeding to point out other chiptunes on YouTube that are "on way another level". Another stated "These . . . didn't sound like chiptune (at all)". One angry comment read: "What a Trash Sound", to which another person replied, "who hurt you?".

Some people were unsure as to whether the preset pack would fit in with their creative process: "The demo is useful, but I prefer to see how the sound creator intended the sound to be used. I get it is creative, so anything goes. But I wasn't too inspired here . . . I like chiptune and fail to see how I can use these patches to make any of those songs." Another wrote: "OK but not something I would ever use. It is interesting to hear some of the 'chiptune' stuff from the past." Overall, the criticism related to both chiptune authenticity and the useability of the sounds within a creative context.

In general, it was challenging to create experimental and multidimensional sounds that were still simple and playable enough to fit into a standard DAW workflow. The Seaboard is a complex musical instrument that requires practice to be used effectively, and some of the presets have intense CPU demands. In addition, the demands of chiptune purists were difficult to satisfy while also staying true to the ROLI brand. The former is about raw, unmodulated timbres that only old sound chips can perfectly reproduce, while the latter is all about lifelike and expressive sounds played on complex and multidimensional electronic music instruments. Since Equator 2 is not primarily built with retro gaming sounds in mind, it was difficult to create believable chiptune within this framework. At first sight, complex modulation and the expressivity of real, acoustic instruments are at odds with the well-loved minimalism of music made on 80s sound chips. But this apparent dichotomy is at the core of what makes nostalgia a springboard for innovation. Rather than recreating the past as it was, it is recreated through the lens of the present. Is MPE chiptune still "authentic" chiptune? Probably not to some chiptune purists; but the creative expression was authentic nonetheless. Ableton founder Robert Henke stated in an interview in the author's recent monogram that "the core of artistic expression is finding your own voice within the tools you have available" (Hermes, 2022). A genre that thrives on technological and creative restriction needs to lose parts of its original identity in order to be performed on complex and multidimensional electronic music instruments – but old sound chips and modern MPE synths are more similar than they may first appear to be. Both satisfy a fascination with musical creativity expressed through engineering.

Overall, the preset sounds reference the feel of retro gaming through certain recognizable timbral qualities while also transcending them. As Márquez (2014, p. 78) puts it, "old, obsolete and 'dead' gaming devices can be sources of innovation and creativity in contemporary digital society". To work on the Seaboard, chiptune had to shift and morph away from its original sonic identity to an abstraction that can only be understood through the lens of a modern sociocultural movement. "MPE chiptune" replaces technological minimalism and hardware purism with increased expressive control. In a sense, just like the "objet sonore" in musique concrete (Schaeffer, 1966), timbres no longer have to be bound to their original sound sources, in this case, specific chips. One preset sound can represent several different instruments and timbres, representing a socio-cultural movement rather than accurately recreating distinct real-life sound sources. At the time of writing, the demo video had reached over 6,000 views on YouTube, and ROLI has invited the author to work on new freelance projects, including a spoken video about the role of the Seaboard in Nyokee's chiptune-infused creativity. As such, the project can be seen as a success.

6 CONCLUSION

From its roots in obsolete technology, decades after the first sound chips were built, chiptune has evolved into an interdisciplinary sociocultural phenomenon. Through its instantly recognizable sonic traits, chiptune can evoke nostalgia, connect people and support wellbeing. Nostalgia is not about representing the past as it was but about recreating it through the lens of the present. By using retro gaming as a springboard for innovation, the individual artistic expression becomes more important than strict genre traditions.

Purist hardware hackers rebel against the status quo in music production through a minimalist approach, while pop, rock and EDM artists broaden the genre definition into modern genres. With the inclusion of pixel art, retro gaming becomes an audiovisual symbol for sociocultural movements that include gamers, Japanese pop culture enthusiasts and anime fans. Building on the cultural capital of retro game symbolism, MPE chiptune transcends the hardware restrictions of obsolete games consoles and computers and instead gives the sounds of a bygone era advanced and expressive performance capabilities. Chiptune authenticity has many subjective definitions, allowing for a multitude of forms of artistic expression, and the "Chiptune Bubblegum" sound pack is one such expression.

REFERENCES

Abrams, M. (1953). *The Mirror and the Lamp: Romantic theory and the Critical Tradition*. Oxford: Oxford University Press.

Badiou, A. (2012). *The Rebirth of History*. London and New York: Verso.

Bittanti, M. (2009). 'So, When Did Planned Obsolescence Become an Artistic Practice?', in Quaranta, D., ed. *Playlist*. Gijón, Spain: LABoral, pp. 32–36.

Born, G. and Hesmondhalgh, D. (2000). 'Introduction: On Difference, Representation, and Appropriation in Music', in Born, G. and Hesmondhalgh, D., eds. *Western Music and Its Others: Difference, Representation, and Appropriation in Music*. Berkeley, CA: University of California Press, pp. 1–58.

Boym, S. (2001). *The Future of Nostalgia*. New York: Basic Books.

Farrell, G. (2020). *Game Boy Modding. A Beginner's Guide to Game Boy Mods, Collecting, History, and More!* San Francisco: No Starch Press.

Frith, S. (1981). 'The Magic That Can Set You Free: The Ideology of Folk and the Myth of the Rock Community', *Popular Music*, 1, pp. 159–168.

Gayford, M. (2016). *A Bigger Message: Conversations with David Hockney*, Revised ed. London: Thames and Hudson.

Hermes, K. (2022). *Performing Electronic Music Live*. Oxfordshire: Routledge.

Levy, S. (1997). *Hackers. Heroes of the Computer Revolution*. Harmondsworth: Penguin Books.

Márquez, I. (2014). 'Playing New Music with Old Games: The Chiptune Subculture', *Game*, 3, pp. 68–79.

McAlpine, K. B (2018). *Bits and Pieces: A History of Chiptunes*. Oxford: Oxford University Press.

Middleton, R. (1990). *Studying Popular Music*. Berkshire: Open University Press.

MIDI Association. (2022). *Official Midi Specifications* (website). Available at: www.midi.org/specifications.

Morris, M. N. (1971). *Writings on the General Theory of Signs*. Den Haag: Mouton.

Negus, K. and Astor, P. (2021). 'Authenticity, Empathy, and the Creative Imagination', *Rock Music Studies*, Advanced online publication.

Paul, J. (2014). 'For the Love of Chiptune', in Collins, K., Kapralos, B. and Tessler, H., eds. *The Oxford Handbook of Interactive Audio*. Oxford: Oxford University Press.

Peterson, R. (1997). *Creating Country Music, Fabricating Authenticity*. Chicago: University of Chicago Press.

Reid, G. (2018). 'Chiptune: The Ludomusical Shaping of Identity', *The Computer Games Journal*, 7, pp. 279–290.

Reynolds, S. (2012). *Retromania: Pop Culture's Addiction to Its Own Past*. London: Faber and Faber.

Samuel, R. (2012). *Theatres of Memory: Past and Present in Contemporary Culture*. New York: Verso Books.

Schaeffer, P. (1966). *Traité Des Objets Musicaux: Essai Interdisciplines*. Paris: Éditions du Seuil.

Stravinsky, I. (1970). *Poetics of Music in the Form of Six Lessons*. Translated by Arthur Knodel and Ingolf Dahl. London: Harvard University Press.

Tomczak, S. (2008). 'Authenticity and Emulation: Chiptune in the Early Twenty-First Century', in *International Computer Music Conference*, 24–29 August, Belfast, Northern Ireland.

Wulf, T., Bowman, N. D., Rieger, D., Velez, J. A. and Breuer, J. (2018). 'Video Games as Time Machines: Video Game Nostalgia and the Success of Retro Gaming', *Media and Communication*, 6(2), pp. 60–68.

MEDIA ARTEFACTS

Barone, E. (2016). *Stardew Valley*. Available at: Steam [Accessed: 19 August 2022].

Re-Logic. (2011). *Terraria*. Available at: Steam [Accessed: 19 August 2022].

Roli and Hermes. (2021). *Chiptune Bubblegum*. Available at: ROLI website [Accessed: 19 August 2022].

Spencer, C. (2012). *Wreck It Ralph*. Available at: Disney Plus [Accessed: 19 August 2022].

16

Forceful action and interaction in non-haptic music interfaces

Mads Walther-Hansen and Anders Eskildsen

1 INTRODUCTION

Music production, playing an instrument, or singing are musical activities that involve different forms of bodily gestures to generate and shape sound. New advances in motion-tracking technologies have fostered a renewed interest in understanding these gestures to better map them to relevant auditory parameters (Eskildsen and Walther-Hansen, 2020). Still, a key challenge for designing meaningful and intuitive user interfaces without haptic or visual feedback is to provide users with a clear sense of agency similar to that which characterizes everyday motor cognition.

To address this challenge, this study differentiates gestures that take the form of simulated *action* (e.g., when bodily movement in a sensory field activates an auditory object) from gestures that take the form of simulated *interaction* with a virtual environment (e.g., interaction with a virtual auditory object). But how do the terms *action* and *interaction* make sense when used in the design of new musical interfaces? Much of the psychological literature holds that any action is context-dependent and, therefore, always involves an element of interaction. You cannot step out of a situation to perform *pure actions*, and you cannot interact with your environment or anything in it without actions. For instance, picking a guitar string is an action, but the action is – as a minimum – based on the nature of the instrument and the sound it produces. You cannot *not* interact with the instrument.

Yet, while action and interaction are intimately intertwined in experience, one may experience a stronger or weaker form of agency in any specific situation (Gallagher, 2020). For example, in some situations, one may experience a strong causal relationship between intentional actions and the activation of an event in the external world. In other situations, one may feel that it is merely possible to respond to and modify sensory events already present in the environment. According to psychologists Daniel Wegner and Betsy Sparrow, "the human being has evolved a set of systems for the purpose of establishing knowledge of authorship of own action" (Wegner and Sparrow, 2007, p. 19). As a part of "the mind's effort to understand its own authorship" (Borgo, 2016, p. 117), actions that

DOI: 10.4324/9781003118817-18

occur in my immediate environment are processed in cognition, resulting in attributions of agency and causality to myself or other agents/factors in my environment.

If we accept that it is possible to differentiate action-like experiences from interaction-like experiences, then how can designers of new musical interfaces account for these differences, and why is this distinction important?

This chapter builds on the hypothesis that people with dissimilar musical training make sense of new non-haptic user interfaces for musical activity in different ways, and it explores variations in how users make sense of their bodily gestures when they activate or interact with sound. Some people may be predisposed to understand sound as something caused by their bodily actions; for instance, singers and instrumentalists who generate sound through and with their body and, accordingly, think of sound (in the act of singing and playing) as something that originates from their forceful *actions*. Others may instead conceive of sound as something that already flows outside the boundaries of their body; for instance, music producers who process sound with effects and dynamic adjustments in the act of mixing. In this case, body movements change the sound or make it audible as an effect of *interaction* with sound.

The chapter discusses how these two paradigms are usable as design principles for non-haptic music interfaces intended for users predisposed to either action-like musical practice or interaction-like musical practice. It is argued that designers should involve intended users early in the design process to understand their requirements and responses (see Zhang and Dong, 2016).

For this study, a pilot experiment with participants from the two user groups was conducted to qualify our thinking and to provide a foundation for further research. In the experiment, the optical hand-tracking controller, Leap Motion, was used as an interface, and a set of basic action- and interaction patterns based on force schemas were explored (Johnson, 1987). The aim is to outline two broad design paradigms that interface designers can use to make non-haptic music interfaces that appear intuitive for users.

2 ERGOMIMESIS

To explain the theoretical foundation for our design paradigms, it is necessary first to discuss the role of music technology in forming individual and culturally embedded habits in music-making and performance.

Thor Magnusson (2021, p. 178) has argued that new musical instruments are both confined to and delineated by specific cultural practices: "each technology or instrument presents a worldview, a field of exploration that is equally psychological, cultural and historical".

Magnusson proposes the notion of *ergomimesis* to explain how new instruments mimic or simulate older instruments; ergomimesis is the process of imitating or mimicking actions and physical features from one domain in another domain. It is, according to Magnusson (2018, p. 85), the "processual potential of an instrument" based on the traces of previous musical contexts. New music instruments may imitate material parts of older instruments and/or mimic immaterial motor actions derived from earlier instruments.

Since musical practitioners have different histories of using musical technologies and instruments, we can assume that individual bases for ergomimetic alignment between previous experience and new interfaces differ significantly. Thus, two aspects of discussion related to the notion of ergomimesis are of interest to our considerations about interface design. First, is it possible to meaningfully categorize users with comparable musical training into groups that will experience similar forms of resistance and possibilities in a specific new instrument? Second, based on the shared motor memory capacities of one group of users, is it possible to design interfaces that intuitively make more sense for this group than for users with dissimilar musical training?

3 UNIVERSAL AND LEARNED EMBODIED STRUCTURES

In this chapter, our embodied cognitive system is viewed as the locus of sense-making. The cognitive system guides thought and behavior in specific situations. It allows us to determine what is appropriate or desirable under different circumstances.

Embodied cognition refers to the hypothesis that both action and perception are the foundation for cognitive processing (Shapiro, 2011). Building on Kant's idea that understanding is founded on the forming of transcendental schemas in imagination (Kant, 1781/2003), George Lakoff (1987) and Mark Johnson (1987) proposed the term *image schemas* to refer to these foundational cognitive structures that govern both thought and action. Image schemas are structured representations of sense-information and thought embodied primarily through previous sensory-motor experiences, for example, through basic bodily actions and interactions with the world.

At a fundamental level, these schemas are intersubjective (by and large) because they are connected to basic forms of sensorimotor experiences that are common to most humans, such as the experience of being warm/cold, falling down/standing up, being inside/outside a containing building and so on. Basic embodied image schemas are thus sometimes considered universal, and several studies demonstrate that many such schemas are common across cultures. Likewise, studies in music cognition point to the prevalence of basic image-schematic structures in cognitive activities related to music (see Zbikowski (2008) for an overview), such as the verticality schema, which allows us to understand pitch on an up/down continuum. People form similar image schemas through childhood. These are later activated and often extended metaphorically in complex and varied ways (Lakoff, 2008) to make sense of more abstract experiences and actions such as listening to or performing music.

While basic, embodied sensory-motor experiences form the experiential basis for image schemas that are largely universal, our cognitive capacities are also influenced by situated learning processes (Beilock, 2009; Slepian and Ambady, 2014) that may be specific to communities or individuals. They are shaped and reshaped as we learn to reflect about and interact with the world in new ways throughout our lives, for instance, when learning a new instrument, reading a book about music production, or learning to use new technology. The relative importance and function of specific image schemas in individual cognitive operations thus change over time, which suggests that two people with dissimilar musical training may make sense of new music interfaces in fundamentally different ways. For example, studies of language use in musical communities suggest that concepts learned from verbal or written language profoundly affect preference judgments and conceptualizations of music and sound (Porcello, 2004). Also, as Paul Théberge (1997) has shown, the experienced sound of the very same technology changes over time; the sound of analog synthesizers that was experienced as cold and artificial in the early 1980s was described as warm and authentic during the 1990s. Thus, identical sound signals may activate different (and sometimes incongruent) cognitive metaphors in different communities, in different situations, and at different points in history (Walther-Hansen, 2020).

Kai Tuuri, Parviainen and Pirhonen (2017) have argued that meaningful human-technology action is based on historical, cultural, and individual user capacities. Accordingly, each new technology added to our daily routines affects the experience of the whole technological infrastructure in which we participate in everyday life: "Infrastructures always transform our perceptual capacities" (Tuuri, Parviainen and Pirhonen, 2017, p. 500).

Related to this, the authors state that "gesture recognition" is a misleading term because human-technology systems cannot fully grasp the complex web of meaning entangled in the specific mind-body producing the gesture. Gestures are thus more than "chunks of movement" to be picked up by sensors; gestures are inscribed with meaning (Tuuri, Parviainen and Pirhonen, 2017, p. 496). To understand how this meaning emerges in situated moments, bodily engagement in sound interaction should be understood on a more fundamental level. Ideally, the design of gesture-based interfaces should consider the meanings inscribed in the broader web of bodily actions the intended user performs on a daily basis. However, pursuing this ideal would entail a more comprehensive exposition into more existential questions of sounds' role in presence and sense-making in a technologically engineered environment – as previously discussed in Walther-Hansen and Grimshaw (2016). Here, the focus is on how users make sense of new interfaces for music based on their musical backgrounds.

4 SOUND, MOVEMENT, ENVIRONMENT, AND OUR COGNITIVE SYSTEM

There is a strong connection between sound and movement – in both listening and performance situations. Haueisen and Knösche (2001) have demonstrated how the sensory-motor system pianists use when they play the piano is also activated when they only listen to piano music. Likewise, seeing someone performing a piece of music on a traditional instrument without hearing the actual sound can evoke auditory images of that sound (Haslinger et al., 2005). Godøy and Leman (2010) go even further to argue that associative connections between body movement and music are, by and large, universal. Godøy (2010) points to air instrument performances where people easily mimic sound-producing gestures like strumming a guitar, even if they have no previous musical training. Yet this argument is only relevant if the instrumental sounds that form the basis of the gestural response are produced by known/traditional instruments, for example, when playing the air guitar. Non-haptic instruments that do not rely on past sound-gesture links still pose new research questions. How does one respond bodily to a sound or combination of sounds not causally related to known instruments? And how does one seek to activate sound when faced with silence and a non-haptic musical interface?

It is suggested here that previous musical experience may still play a role in the sound-gesture link when users make or perform music with new and unfamiliar interfaces. However, it is argued that these differences are related to broader taxonomies of musical practice (action-like vs. interaction-like music activities) rather than specific instrumental practices.

The argument involves two themes. First, variations in our cognitive capacities are related to differences in the conceptualization of sound. While fundamental embodied cognitive structures are largely shared, it is proposed that differences in music training intrude on the activation of specific schemas in music listening (as suggested by Godøy and Leman, 2010). Second, previous music training influences the ability to distribute cognitive tasks onto the world to reduce computational load (Magnusson, 2009). Music producers, for instance, usually use tangible technology to interface with the digital audio workstation, whether this technology is simply a mouse or mixer controller. However, these interfaces do not only work as transmitters of information from the user to the workstation. Interfaces provide haptic and visual feedback, allowing users to offload mental operations onto the environment. For instance, a mixing interface provides visual cues about pan position and level of sounds in the mix, and it offers limited – but visually present – options for sound editing. Musicians who use less or no technology to produce sound when performing music (such as singers) offload less information onto the environment. The singer's body is a music-making 'system' itself. For the digital music producer, that system requires, at a minimum, a computer and loudspeakers to function – besides the music producer's own body.

Every system provides constraints and opportunities for thought and action. Notably, a cognitive system is only a 'system' if it is possible to meaningfully determine its boundaries by individuating and distinguishing it from everything that does not belong to it. While most conceptions of embodied cognition imply that the body defines the limit of the cognitive system, the idea of extended cognition holds that the present environment forms a constituent part of an extended cognitive system (see Clark and Chalmers, 2010). For instance, when using a notebook to aid memory, when consulting a smartphone before making decisions, or when – in other ways – using the environment and technologies in it to perform specific tasks, the environment becomes essential.

Similarly, instrumentalists use auditory, visual, and haptic feedback from the environment in the act of playing. Removing these inputs would alter the performance. For instance, an instrumentalist does not have to remember all notes (abstract music symbols). Instead, he/she can simply react to the previously heard note to aid memory. In this way, instrumentalists use sensory objects in the environment to offload information and computational load (Magnusson, 2009).

Following the extended cognition paradigm, this also implies that music producers may feel more uncomfortable than singers and instrumentalists when faced with non-visual or non-haptic interfaces, as the visual and tangible feedback from technology usually has a decisive function in the music production task.

Based on these characteristics, how should we expect, on the one hand, singers and instrumentalists and, on the other hand, music producers to adapt to non-haptic interfaces designed on the basis of force schemas? Do they hold distinctive embodied capacities based on their previous musical training? And are these capacities constitutive of their ability to make sense of new music interfaces in an experimental setting?

5 FORCE SCHEMAS

To approach these questions from a practical design perspective, it is relevant to introduce a particular kind of image schema, namely that pertaining to the experience of *force dynamics*. Humans act upon objects in the world, and objects act upon them in various ways. However, forceful actions and interactions are not arbitrary; they have and generate structure (Talmy, 1985; Johnson, 1987). As we experience forceful encounters in the world, such as pressure, attraction, collision, containment, and so forth, these structures emerge and are activated, like other image schemas. In a previous paper, Anders Eskildsen and Mads Walther-Hansen (2020) explored how force dynamics – as a specific category of image schemas – could serve as the basis for designing more intuitive interfaces for musical expression. Here, it is discussed how users may have different conceptions of *force* in music making.

To examine these different conceptions, the pilot experiment distinguishes between two overall forms of force schemas: *action schemas* and *interaction schemas*. Action schemas are defined as clusters of gestalts that give structure to situations where the world is acted upon to activate sensory objects. Interaction schemas, on the other hand, provide structure to experience where we interact with objects in the world that are already there – objects that already possess inherent force structures. Obviously, all encounters with the world simultaneously contain elements of both action and interaction. However, the point here is that some experiences amplify action structures while other experiences amplify interaction structures. Likewise, some forms of music-making amplify one of the fundamental structures more than the other, and it is hypothesized that singers and instrumentalists are more accustomed to action patterns, while music producers are more accustomed to interaction patterns.

Six test examples were designed to further qualify the discussion of the two design paradigms – action and interaction. Three interfaces were designed on interaction patterns, and three were designed on action patterns. Each example combines several force schemas. The schemas are briefly introduced below.

5.1 Path schema

The path schema is the most basic design principle. A path contains a starting point, an endpoint, and an infinite number of intermediate points.

To meaningfully link physical movement with sound activation, the user should experience that the sound follows the trajectory of the hand movement metaphorically, for instance, by linking left-right movement to panning or linking vertical movement to pitch height. If the interface is designed from the interaction perspective, bodily motion activates metaphorical motion in a pre-existent sound. The user's motion alters the position of the sound. The action view, on the other hand, holds that there is no difference between sound and metaphorical movement. The sound movement is the sound. There is no non-moving sound.

5.2 Compulsion schema

The compulsion schema structures experience where an external force moves a physical or metaphorical object. If a sound is already present (the interaction perspective), a user may pull or push the sound along a specific trajectory. The sound has a force tendency towards rest (or another random movement), while the user has a force tendency towards movement, and that is what activates the interaction schema. If a sound is not already present in the field, forceful (rapid) user movements (action) can trigger the sound and movement along a specific trajectory.

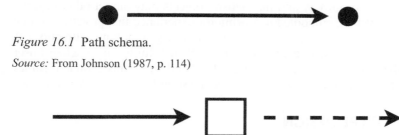

Figure 16.1 Path schema.

Source: From Johnson (1987, p. 114)

Figure 16.2 Compulsion schema.

Source: From Johnson (1987, p. 45)

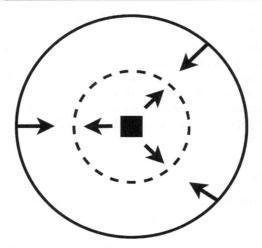

Figure 16.3 Containment restraint schema.

Source: From Johnson (1987, p. 21)

Figure 16.4 Attraction schema.

Source: From Johnson (1987, p. 47)

5.3 Containment restraint schema

When catching a fly with our hand, the closed hand constrains the movement of the fly. The hand provides containment control, while the fly has a tendency towards movement. It is possible to implement the containment restraint schema in the design of sensor-based interfaces, for example, by linking a closed palm to a restrained sound movement or compression (see Walther-Hansen, 2014).

5.4 Attraction schema

As in the case of gravity and magnetism, objects may attract other objects. This is a universal, embodied sensorimotor experience that governs a range of other, more abstract experiences of attraction (e.g., emotional attraction). A music interface may activate the attraction schema, for instance, when a user attracts the sound to the hand's position. The hand represents a force of attraction that pulls the sound towards it, while the sound itself tends toward rest.

6 PROTOTYPE DESIGN

To test the distinction between the action and interaction paradigm as a guiding principle in force dynamics-based interface design, three prototype interfaces were developed using the Leap Motion sensor (all software developed for this

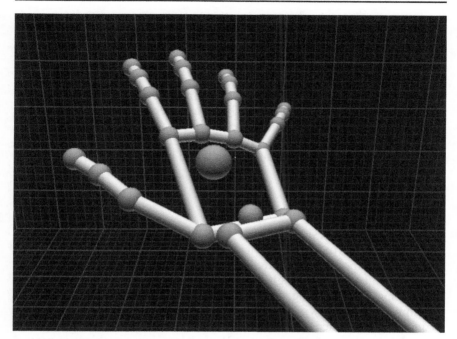

Figure 16.5 Skeletal hand tracking with the Leap Motion sensor.

project is open source and available online via the following URL: https://github.com/sparkletop/forceful-InMusic2022. Initially built for virtual reality applications, the Leap Motion sensor allows for fast and, under optimal conditions, precise skeletal tracking of hand and finger movement in 3D space.

The tracking data is pulled into SuperCollider using a small JavaScript bridge program that accesses the Leap Motion API. For simplicity, the interface prototypes draw upon a limited set of parameters:

- Horizontal and vertical hand position in the interaction zone
- Direction and velocity of hand movement
- Clench strength, i.e., the degree to which the hand is open/closed

These parameters are mapped to various synthetic sound designs, realized in SuperCollider. Crucially, for each of these three prototypes (1–3), two distinct sets of mappings were developed based on the action (A) and interaction (B) paradigms, respectively. This resulted in six interfaces (1A, 1B, 2A, 2B, 3A, and 3B).

6.1 Prototype interfaces 1A and 1B

The first sound design is based on tones generated with a low-pass-filtered square wave and a percussive envelope. The tones are similar to sounds that could be played with a keyboard or programmed with a MIDI sequencer/arpeggiator. Here, the main difference between the action and interaction mapping implementation lies in how new tones are triggered; in the action paradigm (1A), new tones are triggered whenever the hand crosses one of several vertical thresholds, whereas in the interaction paradigm (1B), tones are triggered automatically by a generative algorithm. 1A is thus strongly ergomimetic, resembling gestures associated with string instruments like harps, guitars, or tubular bells, where the instrumentalist strikes the strings or bells directly, in a sweeping motion, to produce sound. 1B is based on the containment restraint force schema (see section 5.3). The space of pitches and rhythmic structures available to the generative algorithm is confined and compressed by the vertical position and clench strength.

6.2 Prototype interfaces 2A and 2B

The second sound design is based on a type of sound synthesis akin to what is often referred to as physical modeling synthesis. Even though no mathematical model of a particular object is employed, noise bursts are produced and passed through a bank of ringing filters, a common strategy in physical modeling. This simulates an object brought into vibration through contact with another object and produces a set of resonant frequencies reminiscent of a ceramic or metallic surface. 2A employs the compulsion schema (see section 5.2), that is, when an object is moved by force or when objects collide or scrape against each other, thus only sounding when the user's hand is in motion. 2B allows the user to affect a generative algorithm already running, where the temporal density of noise bursts is constrained by how closed the user's hand is, which follows the containment restraint schema (see section 5.3). Both interfaces draw upon containment restraint to simulate control of dampening via ring times.

Table 16.1 Action and Interaction mappings for prototype interfaces 1A and 1B.

1A – Action	1B – Interaction
• Crossing vertical thresholds triggers new tones on a musical scale; upward motion triggers higher notes on a harmonic minor scale, and vice versa for downward motion • Horizontal motion controls stereo panning • Clench strength controls envelope release time; a closed palm leads to shorter release times	• Vertical position controls pitch and rhythm/articulation ('space'); upwards motion leads to longer attack and release times and higher pitches for generated tones as well as longer durations and 'space' • Horizontal motion controls stereo panning • Clench strength controls the number of scale degrees available to the generative algorithm; a closed palm leads to only one pitch step being available for random selection, while an open hand leads to a wider pitch set from which the algorithm can choose

Table 16.2 Action and Interaction mappings for prototype interfaces 2A and 2B.

2A – Action	2B – Interaction
• Vertical motion bends resonant frequencies; upward motion bends resonant frequencies slightly up • Horizontal motion controls stereo panning • Clench strength controls filter ring times; a closed palm leads to short ring times, like an object where vibration is partially dampened • Movement velocity controls the amplitude and density of noise bursts over time; no movement leads to silence, while faster movement leads to a denser, more constant production of sound	• Vertical motion controls resonant frequencies; upward motion moves frequencies up to an octave up • Horizontal motion controls stereo panning • Clench strength controls ring times and density of noise bursts over time; a closed hand leads to short ring times but a denser series of sounds

Table 16.3 Action and Interaction mappings for prototype interfaces 3A and 3B

3A – Action	3B – Interaction
• A two-dimensional vector for movement is measured whenever velocity crosses a predetermined threshold, simulating the 'striking' of an object; the direction of strike determines the trajectory of the tone in pitch (sliding up/down) and stereo space (moving left/right) • Strike power (velocity at time of 'impact') determines the length of the object's movement in pitch and stereo space	• Vertical motion controls pitch, intentionally filtered to produce glissandi; upward motion moves pitch up • Horizontal motion controls stereo panning, intentionally lagged to produce smooth motion in stereo space • Clench strength controls tremolo depth to allow for internal movement in the object

6.3 Prototype interfaces 3A and 3B

The third sound design is a drone based on a bank of detuned sawtooth wave oscillators processed with a low-pass filter and a tremolo effect. This sound is monophonic, rich in timbre, and suitable for lead synthesizers or bass lines. 3A and 3B are designed with different force schemas; 3A is based on the path and compulsion schemas (see sections 5.1 and 5.2), that is, sound emerges when a user strikes an invisible force with sufficient power (measured in velocity), causing the object to produce sound and move along the trajectory of the strike. 3B is based on the attraction schema (see section 5.4), in that the user's hand gradually attracts an invisible, sounding object that lingers when the hand is not present and continues to produce sound in the space.

7 CODA

The prototypes presented previously are examples of two design paradigms: action and interaction. The argument was based on image schema theory, which accounts for the effect of learned embodied structures on our individual cognitive capacities, and on Thor Magnusson's (2021) notion of ergomimesis, which concerns the design of musical interfaces by means of translating gestures from the context of one musical instrument to another. Also, the paper suggests, with reference to Kai Tuuri, Parviainen and Pirhonen (2017), that technological infrastructures – including infrastructures of music technology – influence gestural habits.

As previously argued, force dynamics may function as a useful design principle for non-haptic music interfaces (Eskildsen and Walther-Hansen, 2020). This paper argues that the suitability of specific force schemas is related to users' previous musical training and experience, and it explores in theory and practice how these force schemas can serve as design principles within the two paradigms to accommodate differences in user background.

Future research has yet to put the proposed design paradigms to the test. To initiate the discussion, six potential users – three singers and instrumentalists (user group 1) and three music producers (user group 2) – were asked to test the interface prototypes. From subsequent semi-structured interviews, it became clear that the design principles made sense to the participants. Still, it was not possible to determine if either user group preferred the action paradigm over the interaction paradigm or vice versa. The potential users found the most basic mappings intuitive, such as vertical hand movement mapped onto pitch, closed or open palm mapped onto release time (open and closed sound), and horizontal movement mapped onto panning. Participants found it more challenging to make sense of prototype interfaces based on the attraction and compulsion schemas.

It should be recognized that it may prove difficult to validate the proposed framework in laboratory settings. Many musical practitioners do not fit neatly into binary categorizations, such as *singers/instrumentalists* and *music producers*. While the focus of this chapter was to explore whether participants would find the six prototype interfaces intuitive and potentially useful, it appears from the answers in the interviews that the potential users saw the prototype test as a problem-solving task. This indicates that participants activated higher-level cognitive processes (conscious use of memory and imagination) when experimenting with the prototypes instead of lower-level cognitive processes that govern more automated tasks. For this reason, future research should explore the use of interfaces based on the proposed design framework in more natural settings such as rehearsal, performance, or music production situations.

REFERENCES

Beilock, S. L. (2009). 'Grounding Cognition in Action: Expertise, Comprehension, and Judgment', *Progress in Brain Research*, 714.

Borgo, D. (2016). 'Openness From Closure: The Puzzle of Interagency in Improvised Music and a Neocybernetic Solution', in Waterman, E. and Siddall, G.,
eds. *Negotiated Moments: Improvisation, Sound, and Subjectivity*. Durham
and London: Duke University Press, pp. 113–130.

Clark, A. and Chalmers, D. J. (2010). 'The Extended Mind', in Menary, R., ed.
The Extended Mind. Cambridge, MA: MIT Press, pp. 27–42.

Eskildsen, A. and Walther-Hansen, M. (2020). 'Force Dynamics as a Design
Framework for Mid-Air Musical Instruments', in *Proceedings of New Inter-
faces for Musical Expression (NIME)*, July 21–25. Birmingham, UK: Royal
Birmingham Conservatoire.

Gallagher, S. (2020). *Action and Interaction*. Oxford: Oxford University Press.

Godøy, R. I. (2010). 'Images of Sonic Objects', *Organised Sound*, 5(1), pp. 54–62.

Godøy, R. I. and Leman, M. (2010). *Musical Gestures. Sound, Movement, and
Meaning*. New York: Routledge.

Haslinger, B., Erhard, P., Altenmüller, E., Schroeder, U., Boecker, H. and Cebal-
los-Baumann, A. O. (2005). 'Transmodal Sensorimotor Networks During
Action Observation in Professional Pianists', *Journal of Cognitive Neuroscience*, 17, pp. 282–293.

Haueisen, J. and Knösche, T. R. (2001). 'Involuntary Motor Activity in Pianists
Evoked by Music Perception', *Journal of Cognitive Neuroscience*, 13(6),
pp. 786–792.

Johnson, M. (1987). *The Body in the Mind: The Bodily Basis of Meaning, Imagination, and Reason*. Chicago and London: The University of Chicago Press.

Kant, I. (1781/2003). *Critique of Pure Reason*. Translated by Marcus Weigelt.
London: Penguin Classics.

Lakoff, G. (1987). *Women, Fire and Dangerous Things: What Categories Reveal
about the Mind*. Chicago and London: The University of Chicago Press.

Lakoff, G. (2008). 'The Neural Theory of Metaphor', in Gibbs, R., ed. *Cambridge
Handbook of Metaphor and Thought*. Cambridge: Cambridge University
Press, pp. 17–38.

Magnusson, T. (2009). 'Of Epistemic Tools: Musical Instruments as Cognitive
Extensions', *Organised Sound*, 14(2), pp. 168–176.

Magnusson, T. (2018). *Ergomimesis: Towards a Language Describing Instrumental Transductions*. Porto: ICLI.

Magnusson, T. (2021). 'The Migration of Musical Instruments: On the Sociotech-
nological Conditions of Musical Evolution', *Journal of New Music Research*,
50(2), pp. 175–183. https://doi.org/10.1080/09298215.2021.1907420.

Porcello, T. (2004). 'Speaking of Sound: Language and the Professionalization of
Sound-Recording Engineers', *Social Studies of Science*, 34(5), pp. 733–758.

Shapiro, L. A. (2011). 'Embodied Cognition: Lessons from Linguistic Determin-
ism', *Philosophical Topics*, 39(1), pp. 121–140.

Slepian, M. L. and Ambady, N. (2014). 'Simulating Sensorimotor Metaphors: Novel Metaphors Influence Sensory Judgments', *Cognition*, 130,
pp. 309–314.

Talmy, L. (1985). *Force Dynamics in Language and Thought, The Parasession
on Causatives and Agentivity at the Twenty-First Regional Meeting*. Chicago,
IL: Chicago Linguistic Society.

Théberge, P. (1997). *Any Sound You Can Imagine: Making Music, Consuming Technology*. Hanover: Wesleyan University Press.

Tuuri, K., Parviainen, J. and Pirhonen, A. (2017). 'Who Controls Who? Embodied Control Within Human-Technology Choreographies', *Interacting with Computers*, 29(4), pp. 494–511.

Walther-Hansen, M. (2014). 'The Force Dynamic Structure of the Phonographic Container: How Sound Engineers Conceptualise the "Inside" of the Mix', *Journal of Music and Meaning*, 12.

Walther-Hansen, M. (2020). *Making Sense of Recordings – How Cognitive Processing of Recorded Sound Works*. New York: Oxford University Press.

Walther-Hansen, M. and Grimshaw, M. (2016). 'Being in a Virtual World: Presence, Environment, Salience, Sound', in *Proceedings of the 11th Audio Mostly Conference*. New York: ACM Digital Library, pp. 77–84.

Wegner, D. M. and Sparrow, B. (2007). 'The Puzzle of Coaction', in Ross, D., Spurrett, D., Kincaid, H. and Stephens, G. L., eds. *Distributed Cognition and the Will: Individual Volition and Social Context*. Cambridge, MA: MIT Press, pp. 17–38.

Zbikowski, L. M. (2008). 'Metaphor and Music', in Gibbs, R., ed. *The Cambridge Handbook of Metaphor and Thought*. Cambridge: Cambridge University, pp. 502–520.

Zhang, B. and Dong, H. (2016). 'User Involvement in Design – The Four Models', in Zhou, J. and Salvendy, G., eds. *Human Aspects of IT for the Aged Population – Designing for Aging*. Cham, Switzerland: Springer, pp. 141–154.

17

Artificial creativity and tools for understanding

Music, creative labour and AI

Matthew Lovett

1 INTRODUCTION

This chapter focuses on the relationship between artificial intelligence and human intelligence, and how we might think about that relationship in the context of music. The term 'Artificial Creativity' is used as a means to focus on whether – in the context of creativity – we should see AI as simply modelling human intelligence or if AI is asking us more searching questions about the nature of intelligence itself and thereby offering valuable perspectives on musical creativity.

To begin, it is worth reflecting briefly on the inception of artificial intelligence at the Dartmouth Summer Research Project on Artificial Intelligence in 1956. Central to the project was the contention that,

> Every aspect of learning or any other feature of intelligence can in principle be so precisely described that a machine can be made to simulate it. An attempt will be made to find how to make machines use language, form abstractions and concepts, solve kinds of problems now reserved for humans, and improve themselves.
>
> (McCarthy et al., 1955)

Two fundamental ideas emerge in this passage. Firstly, the idea that human intelligence can be mapped and simulated with machine technology. Secondly, the defining characteristic of human intelligence – which here is taken to be synonymous with intelligence per se – is that it is capable of modifying (improving) itself. More recently, IBM has developed this position, describing AI as 'the broadest term used to classify machines that mimic human intelligence', listing speech and facial recognition, decision making and translation as examples of the human tasks that AI has been used to predict, automate and optimise (Kavlakoglu, 2020).

An important distinction, however, appears in the Oxford English Dictionary. Here, Artificial Intelligence is defined as 'the capacity of computers or other machines to exhibit or simulate intelligent behaviour' (OED, 2022). This subtle shift to engaging with intelligence as something that exists in its own right, separate from its instantiation as human intelligence,

DOI: 10.4324/9781003118817-19

is hugely important. It is a shift that enables us to examine the many different forms that intelligence might take – human, machine or otherwise – but also consider that human intelligence may not necessarily be the blueprint for intelligence, or at least the standard against which other forms of intelligence are measured. In this sense, it may be that human intelligence may be no less artificial than so-called artificial intelligence.

The following analysis explores the relationship between artificial intelligence and human intelligence, what this might tell us about the nature of creativity, and how that might play out in the context of music. While the chapter engages with a variety of AI-music use cases in order to explore and illustrate these themes, it is not designed to provide an exhaustive account of AI in music. Instead, it engages with narratives concerning the threat posed by machines to human workers, identifies key vectors in how AI is being implemented in the context of music and work, and offers emergent perspectives on music and creativity.

2 AI AND MUSIC

The history of AI in music is peppered with hyperbolic claims about its significance and its capacity to shape the future of music, where a growing awareness of AI's increased presence in music speaks of an appreciable rise in the number of companies developing AI projects for music-related activities. In 2017, Stuart Dredge's article for the Guardian posed the question, 'AI and music: will we be slaves to the algorithm', describing how a 'burgeoning sector', consisting of start-ups and subsidiaries of major firms such as Google (Alphabet) and Sony, were developing AI systems for music creation and transformation (Dredge, 2017). By 2019, Scott Cohen, who was about to be appointed as Chief Innovation Officer at Warner Music Group, likened AI's potential to transform the music industry to the consequential impacts of hip hop and MTV in the 1980s, highlighting the central role that AI was playing in terms of organization, recommendation and search on music streaming platforms (Dredge, 2019).

These kinds of claims about the increasingly central role that AI could – or would – take in the music industry have been fuelled by relentless innovation and increased usage of AI tools across a wide range of music ecosystems. Companies such as LANDR (2022) and iZotope (2022) have long been working with AI to innovate in production and mastering, and the likes of Amper (2020), Boomy (2020), Loudly (2021) and AIVA (2022) have been developing tools for music creation, particularly aligned to the needs of creators working across non-musical forms (for example, games, film and social media). Launched in 2014 to offer AI-powered mastering services for musicians, LANDR now encompasses music distribution services, music sample libraries, virtual instruments (VSTs) and plug-ins for music processing. Similarly, music creation services, including Boomy and AIVA, complement their creative toolkits with licensing packages that reflect the AI's creative contribution to a finished track, offering a variety of payment and royalties models. In March 2022, the audio streaming platform SoundCloud acquired Musiio, an AI start-up launched in

2018, that produces audio tools that are able to 'tag, search and playlist large catalogues' (Musiio, 2022) and which have been described as having the capacity to '"listen" to music faster than any human possibly could' (Silberling, 2022). Other companies working in music and sound include Never Before Heard Sounds, who, since 2020, have been making 'cutting-edge technology expressive and useful for musicians [and building] machine learning instruments and create powerful audio tools' (Never Before Heard Sounds, 2022). LALAL.AI (OmniSale GMBH, 2022) specialises in separating and extracting instrumental and vocal components from audio files, and MatchMySound (2022) is an education service that listens to learners as they practice playing music and compares the performance to a score of the original piece, providing tips on how to improve.

3 VECTORS IN ARTIFICIAL INTELLIGENCE

While these examples are not a definitive list of the state of play as regards AI-for-music in 2022, even this brief snapshot allows us to observe important differences in how it is being used and what the consequences may be. The work of the economist Daniel Susskind enables us to articulate these differences in terms of AI's impact on music in the context of creative production and distribution. Susskind draws on a history of technological disruption to labour markets and examines how today's industrial machines, in the form of AI systems, are threatening to replace human labour across a wide range of commercial and industrial sectors. By offering cheaper, more convenient and, controversially, more effective services than their human counterparts, he sees that intelligent machines look set to operate as an increasingly 'substituting force' (Susskind, 2020).

In this sense, we can see such a substituting tendency in the design and implementation of the likes of LANDR, Amper, MatchMySound and Musiio, as these companies offer to outsource a range of established and emergent services (the likes of mastering, music education and playlist curation) to AI-powered automation. At the same time, a company such as Never Before Heard Sounds, in seeking to deploy AI as a tool to enhance human creativity and productivity, offers what Susskind describes as a 'complementing force' (Susskind, 2020). Here, technological systems are designed to enhance, rather than replace, human performance at a given task, thereby offering new opportunities for innovation and employment to balance the substituting force of technology.

Susskind discusses the step-change brought about by AI systems over the past decade in problem-solving and decision-making processes. Rather than focusing on how a given task is performed, the neural networks and machine learning processes that operationalise AI are designed to operate pragmatically, and focus instead on how well that task is performed; in other words, it is the outcome that matters, rather than the route taken. This has led to a situation where AI systems are not being built to do things in the way that humans do but better; instead, they are built to complete a task in the most optimal way. By invoking the concepts of 'complementing' and 'substituting' forces, Susskind is referencing a history of the impact of technology on the workplace, which has been characterised by technology's capacity to create new roles for human workers at the same time as it has made workers redundant in established roles. Susskind's view is that artificial intelligence has destabilised this balance; that the proliferation of substituting technologies now threatens to permanently outstrip the capacity of complementing technologies to create new forms of employment.

Susskind goes on to suggest that in the context of contemporary labour markets, AI systems are increasingly replacing humans via a process he calls 'task encroachment' (Susskind, 2020). Susskind's analysis suggests that machines are not competing for humans' jobs in a straightforward manner or simply replacing their human counterparts. Instead, he suggests that the change is occurring at the level of the individual tasks that come together to constitute a job that a human would be employed to do. He maps task encroachment across three domains of work: manual (for example, operating machinery, driving vehicles, repairing appliances), cognitive (secretarial work, bookkeeping and accounting, bank and post office clerks) and affective (customer service roles in hospitality and call centres, but also, in the context of music, affective labour can be characterised as work that is intended to create an emotional response in others), suggesting that machine labour is now encroaching into each of these areas. Ultimately, Susskind's concern is that technological task encroachment could lead to 'structural technological unemployment', a phrase he uses to denote a future scenario where there are too few jobs available that require humans (Susskind, 2020).

4 HOLLY+ AND THE CENTAUR

As already mentioned, the AI start-up Never Before Heard Sounds (NBHS) has made use of machine learning to create audio tools for musicians. In 2021, they collaborated with the musician Holly Herndon and the technologist Mat Dryhurst to launch Holly+, a project that transformed participant-generated audio into a new piece of music that had been 'sung' in Herndon's voice (Herndon, 2021). NBHS describes how models can be trained on an instrument or an ensemble to capture particular sonic characteristics but can also be trained to 'capture playing styles and articulation which is unique to an individual, place, time or culture' (Never Before Heard Sounds, 2022). Trained on an extensive set of Herndon's vocal recordings, the Holly+ model combines the textural and timbral qualities of this training set with the pitches and rhythms of up to five minutes of user-generated audio content (uploaded to the Holly+ website) to create a new piece of audio which, in the words of NBHS themselves, 'is imperfect and idiosyncratic', and which can produce 'unexpected (and sometimes bizarre) combinations of the model's training dataset and the input performance' (Never Before Heard Sounds, 2022).

In its quest to harness human and machine creativity so as to create music that neither could have produced alone, the Holly+ project reflects the ambitions of Garry Kasparov in his vision for what he referred to as 'advanced chess' (Chessgames.com, 2021). Having been beaten in 1997 by the chess computer Deep Blue, the then-chess grandmaster developed advanced chess as an approach to playing the game that paired humans with computer programmes in order to achieve results that exceeded the capabilities of either humans or machines playing alone. Kasparov went on to compete alongside the chess programme Fritz 5 in the first Advanced Chess event in 1998 (Chessgames.com, 2021), and for a time, interest in this style of gameplay – also known as 'centaur chess' and 'freestyle chess' (Cassidy, 2014), (Nilsen, 2013) – grew.

As with advanced chess, so too with Holly+. Never Before Heard Sounds, by partnering AI technology with the genetic, cultural, social and creative contributions of human participants, is a musical centaur. While these innovations are compelling, and NBHS's ambition to harness technology within an ethically-informed production framework is laudable, Susskind's view is that it is only a matter of time before human-machine centaurs are outperformed by machines alone. Centaurs will only offer optimum possible performance across a range of domains – either in chess, the economy or, indeed, music – as long as the computer half of the centaur is not able to bring to the partnership what the human half can. As with his rationalisation for the relentless progression of task encroachment, where roles are incrementally eroded rather than being displaced wholesale, for Susskind, since computers are increasingly able to replicate human performance across a number of domains, the opportunity for human contribution diminishes. While we may be accustomed to thinking about different types of tasks across different domains – for example, manual, cognitive or interpersonal – these distinctions only hold insofar as they require 'manual, cognitive or personal capabilities when performed by human beings' (Susskind, 2020). Essentially, developments in artificial intelligence have made these distinctions redundant, and it is a serious underestimation of a machine's capacity to encroach into the domain of human labour to assume that the *human* approach to fulfilling a task is the *only* way to fulfil that task.

There are clearly differences between completing a work-related task and creating music, although the outcomes as far as a listener might be concerned – in other words, the production of something that is pleasing and/or interesting to listen to – may not be that different. While it remains to be seen whether Susskind's misgivings about the time-limited nature of human-machine performance will be borne out in the context of music creation, his articulation of the collapse of manual and cognitive domains nonetheless challenges us to reconsider what we think musical creativity might be, and how the processes of making music operate.

5 REPLACEMENT ANXIETY

Susskind's sense is that the complementing force of technology – the force that creates new roles for human employment in the wake of technological disruption – will, in the last instance, not withstand the relentless and all-encompassing power of its opposite, the substituting force.

In discussing their products, the likes of LANDR and iZotope, another sector-leading specialist in AI-driven audio production technology, communicate carefully constructed messages that both promote the virtues of intelligent production tools whilst at the same time celebrating and re-affirming the important roles that humans play in the audio production process.

LANDR's Product Director emphasises that the software does not think of 'AI-mastering as a question of OR, but rather as an AND that assists creators when needed' (Bourget, in Price, 2022) and positions the LANDR toolset as a tool for producing feedback during the production process, rather than producing a finished product to professional standards, ready for public consumption. iZotope offer a range of AI-driven 'Assisted Audio Technology' tools that use machine learning to offer a range of editing and production services. In a similar vein, Melissa Misicka, Director of Brand Marketing at iZotope, positions the Assisted Audio Technology tools as a studio assistant. Whilst Misicka draws the analogy of the assistive tools functioning as 'a studio assistant who can take that first pass at repairs or a mix for you while you go get a coffee' and who can enable a seasoned audio professional to '[get] to a starting point more quickly' (Misicka, in Price, 2022), it is clear that, whilst the mastering engineer's role may not be threatened, at least not yet, other roles are being replaced: in this case, the studio assistant.

iZotope's segmenting of the production workflow into creative activity and 'time-consuming' production tasks is precisely what task encroachment describes: the fragmentation of holistic processes into a set of sequential tasks that can be accomplished – often more efficiently – by automated systems. In this sense, iZotope, LANDR and their ilk are transforming the world of audio production, not by replacing human jobs wholesale, but by altering the nature of the work involved in the production workflow that takes music creation from inception to distribution and public consumption.

In 2016, *Sound On Sound* ran an article in which a number of prominent mastering engineers voiced their opinions on LANDR and similar automated services. The general response was that – for various reasons – human mastering engineers would continue to outperform their disruptive AI counterparts. As Justin Evans, one of LANDR's co-founders asked, 'In the '40s, mastering was part of the job of a transferring engineer. Then vinyl and radio changed that. Now we are living in a streaming world. What should mastering be now?' (Evans, in Inglis, 2016).

Such questions of what mastering 'should be' and the changing nature of the environment in which mastering exists and operates are very much giving shape to the question that AI is increasingly asking us about music and its associated practices.

6 UNDER CONSTRUCTION

The history of AI concerns the quest to understand intelligence, and whilst the Dartmouth Summer Research Project was originally focused on modelling and replicating human intelligence, models of intelligence have emerged that have enabled us to think more broadly about what intelligence is and how it works. Indeed, Susskind's work on outcome optimisation demonstrates that, in a practical sense, intelligence – human or otherwise – is not necessarily what we think it is. Just as we might want to consider the changing nature of music-related labour, we can also pause to consider the extent to which our understanding of intelligence itself is evolving.

The philosopher Reza Negarestani defines what is 'human' not as an evolutionary animal but as an idea that is historically constructed. He says, 'we can never elide the distinction between the totality of the human idea – that is the totality of its history – with what we appear to ourselves to be in any specific historical moment' (Negarestani, 2020, p. 127).

Negarestani's point is that what we might think of as some kind of perpetual human essence that exists for all time is, in fact, something that is entirely tethered to its historical moment. He goes further to say that whilst humans are rational lifeforms, rationality in itself is not something that is exclusive to humans, proposing that rationality can be associated with any lifeform 'that satisfies its criteria (the power of judgement, and theoretical and practical reason) or falls under its concept' (Negarestani, 2020, p. 132). Rather than being something that is a necessarily human faculty, rationality – in Negarestani's reading – instead becomes a means to take apart an anthropocentric view of intelligence and our conceptions of the world more widely. What is more, he proposes that the human is 'historically collective and is under construction' (Negarestani, 2020, pp. 127–128). 'Historically collective' means that although we might think about and experience intelligence at the level of the individual, it is, in fact, the expression of a collective history, and his assertion that the human is 'under construction' means just that: humans are not finished. We are merely a snapshot, at any given moment, of a process-in-motion through time, a snapshot that is entirely located within its temporal moment. Such snapshots do not present a view of the human as a completely finished and evolved entity, and neither are they an expression of the entire history of human-ness, resolved into one fragmented moment. What we take to be 'human' is simply a momentary expression of a set of histories that have led up to a moment of consideration; an appraisal of a process, rather than a distillation of an essence.

Taking the idea of the collective further, Negarestani suggests that the 'mind is ultimately understood as the dimension of structure, or a configuring factor; something which can only be approached via an essentially deprivatised account of discursive (linguistic) apperceptive intelligence' (Negarestani, 2018, p. 3). This is absolutely central for Negarestani; that the mind, which we think of as an individual, isolated thing, is, in fact, formed via its use of language, something that is shared. He conceptualises this as 'the intrinsic social frame' of intelligence, which refers to a wider arc in Negarestani's work; his view that – given that we are only able to think because our thoughts are mediated through language, and that language by its very nature is a shared, social construct – then intelligence must, by definition, operate as a shared, social phenomenon.

All of this adds up to suggest that, no matter what we might think it is that are modelling artificial intelligence on – leaving aside the question of whether it is actually possible to emulate that model or not – it is highly likely that we shall be mistaken in our understanding and apprehension of what human intelligence even is.

7 CONCLUSIONS . . . ARTIFICIAL CREATIVITY

Artificial musical creativity – a zenith of AI research and development – has continued to evolve, both in terms of the approach taken to facilitating AI-enhanced creativity as well as how the resultant pieces of music can be used. AIVA (2022) offers users the opportunity to compose using preset styles (including modern cinematic, tango, fantasy, sea-shanty and many more besides) or in the style of a pre-existing track. The latter reflects an approach often used by directors, where a temporary piece of already-existing music is placed alongside a film sequence to convey a sense of the desired mood or atmosphere that they are trying to achieve or even the genre of music they would like a composer to create. Shortcutting this process, AIVA's 'compose with influences' function enables visual creators to upload a template track from which the AI can generate an original piece of music that can be used without the complications of either paying for permission to use an already-existing piece of music or having to negotiate with a composer to commission a score that meets a director's require-ments. To accompany its dynamic approach to music creation, AIVA also offers users a suite of rights packages that allow for a variety of access and ownership of its AI-generated music, enabling free but limited access through a monthly subscription that gives subscribers full ownership of any music they create using AIVA, and extensive (although still not com-plete) access to their content.

Boomy, whose landing page offers users the chance to 'create original songs in seconds, even if you've never made music before', is clearly more overtly focused on servicing a market concerned with creating content for social media platforms such as TikTok and YouTube (Boomy Corporation, 2020). The website also offers visitors a glossary of musical terms, pro-viding simple explainers for key terms such as composition, production, mixing and tempo, provides simple tutorials to enable creators to sing over the AI-generated tracks, and offers a pricing system that enables royalty payments to be shared between Boomy and content creators themselves.

While AIVA and Boomy are embracing the social media environment, it is worth reflecting on the musician Taryn Southern's comments from 2018 who – when asked whether she felt that using AI to create music was 'cheat-ing' – responded, 'if music is concretely defined as this one process that everyone must adhere to in order to get to some sort of end goal, then, yes, I'm cheating [however], the music creation process can't be so narrowly defined' (Southern, in Deahl, 2018). What is interesting about these three examples of AI-powered music creation is that they each speak to the way in which the roles traditionally played by composers and songwriters are indeed being eroded by AI. However, each of these scenarios also suggests that there is more happening here than simple task encroachment or worker displacement. Although – as may be expected – Amper co-founder Michael Hobe was keen to stress Amper's emphasis on empowering creatives rather than replacing musicians' jobs – saying that his interest lay in enabling 'more people to be creative and [allowing creatives to] further themselves' (Hobe, in Deahl, 2018), Southern's remark about how we might define creativity may be more to the point.

Dadabots, an AI-music project, described by its creators CJ Carr and Zack Zukowski as 'a cross between a band, a hackathon team, and an ephemeral research lab' is focused on creating music and collaborating with other musicians (Dadabots, 2022). Clearly framed as a set of experiments and explorations into the capabilities of AI to produce music – rather than a commercial offering in the vein of LANDR and iZotope – Dadabots has created a number of short-form musical artefacts along with a series of projects that span more extended timeframes. Human Extinction Party was a 100-day-long livestream of 'Neural Death Metal' in the style of the band Cannibal Corpse. Outerhelios was a 'Neural Free Jazz' livestream. For this project, the neural network was trained on the saxophonist John Coltrane's album Interstellar Space, which it listened to sixteen times, enabling it to continuously produce music in the style of the saxophone-drums partnership of Coltrane alongside Rashid Ali. Excerpts from the Human Extinction Party and Outerhelios livestreams are now archived as ten-hour videos on YouTube (Dadabots, 2022). Also from 2019, the Relentless Doppelgänger project, described as 'Neural Technical Death Metal', is an infinitely evolving and continuous livestream of music inspired by the Canadian death metal band Archspire.

Of all the Dadabots projects, the extended play livestreams and the indefinitely enduring Relentless Doppelgänger most concretely reflect the questions raised by LANDR and iZotope. We cannot ignore Susskind's challenge to think about how such systems are fracturing and fragmenting once-familiar and trusted job roles and creative labour activities. However, just as Dadabots' are creating more music and Musiio are listening to and categorising music faster than any human can comprehend, what we think music is, and what we think it is for is also changing. The question may not be so much will this or that music production tool put humans out of work, but instead, will music survive AI in any way that we will still recognise it?

To conclude. Reflecting on Susskind's theory of task encroachment, while it is compelling, these music-based developments in AI suggest that maybe his ideas could be taken further. AI does not simply atomise jobs into tasks, replace the task, then incrementally replace the job. Instead, AI is impacting the entire creative process. AI does the making so that humans don't have to; it identifies the audience, it does the listening and, because of this, AI sets the framework for what is made in the first place. At the same time, however, it is becoming increasingly clear that we must recognise that human intelligence, which is often the recipient of the music produced by the machines carrying out these various tasks may not be fixed either; in other words, the human creativity that AI is seemingly technologically displacing may be no less 'artificial' itself. If humans and machines are equally artificial – which is to say that both are intelligences under construction and that neither can lay claim to having an originary provenance over the nature of intelligence – this would suggest that music itself is no more fixed than its human or machine makers or listeners. Music has always moved and evolved in relation to the way that makers (musicians), tools (for example, instruments, studios) and institutions (for example, states, corporations, legal governance frameworks, rights agencies) have changed. AI may be accelerating change at the moment, but in many ways, its lasting legacy may be that it has helped us to see more clearly the artificial creative processes that fundamentally underpin music. Creativity under construction. Humans as activators of intelligence, rather than the sole source of intelligence. The human is a construction and a coming-together of a set of vectors, suggesting that we humans are also artificial, the product of a non-human set of processes. In this sense, the history of music is the history of artificial intelligences artificially creating music, no more or less artificially than any number of manufactured intelligent machines.

REFERENCES

AIVA. (2022). *The Artificial Intelligence Composing Emotional Soundtrack Music*. Available at: www.aiva.ai [Accessed: May 2022].

Amper Music. (2020). *Music for Your Defining Moment*. Available at: www.ampermusic.com [Accessed: April 2022].

Boomy Corporation. (2020). *Make Instant Music. Share It with the World*. Available at: https://boomy.com [Accessed: May 2022].

Cassidy, M. (2014). *Centaur Chess Shows Power of Teaming Human and Machine*. Available at: www.huffpost.com/entry/centaur-chess-shows-power_b_6383606 [Accessed: April 2022].

Chessgames.com. (2021). *Advanced Chess Matches*. Available at: www.chessgames.com/perl/chesscollection?cid=1017919 [Accessed: April 2022].

Dadabots. (2022). *FAQ*. Available at: https://dadabots.com/music.php [Accessed: May 2022].

Deahl, D. (2018). *How AI-generated Music Is Changing the Way Hits Are Made*. Available at: www.theverge.com/2018/8/31/17777008/artificial-intelligence-taryn-southern-amper-music [Accessed: May 2022].

Dredge, S. (2017). *AI and Music: Will We Be Slaves to the Algorithm?* Available at: www.theguardian.com/technology/2017/aug/06/artificial-intelligence-and-will-we-be-slaves-to-the-algorithm [Accessed: April 2022].

Dredge, S. (2019). *Scott Cohen: 'Every 10 Years Something Kills the Music Industry'*. Available at: https://musically.com/2019/01/29/scott-cohen-every-10-years-something-kills-the-music-industry/ [Accessed: April 2022].

Herndon, H. (2021). *Holly+*. Available at: https://holly.mirror.xyz/54ds2IiOnvthjGFkokFCoaI4EabytH9xjAYy1irHy94 [Accessed: May 2022].

Inglis, S. (2016). *LANDR, CloudBounce & The Future of Mastering*. Available at: www.soundonsound.com/techniques/landr-cloudbounce-future-mastering [Accessed: May 2022].

iZotope. (2022). *iZotope Products*. Available at: www.izotope.com/en/products. html [Accessed: April 2022].

Kavlakoglu, E. (2020). *AI vs. Machine Learning vs. Deep Learning vs. Neural Networks: What's the Difference?* Available at: www.ibm.com/cloud/blog/ ai-vs-machine-learning-vs-deep-learning-vs-neural-networks [Accessed: April 2022].

LANDR. (2022). *Instant Mastering. Professional Results*. Available at: www. landr.com/en/online-audio-mastering/ [Accessed: May 2022].

Loudly. (2021). *Create Awesome Music in Seconds: Studio-quality Music, the Easy Way*. Available at: www.loudly.com/aimusicstudio [Accessed: May 2022].

MatchMySound. (2022). *Welcome to MatchMySound*. Available at: https://match-mysound.com [Accessed: April 2022].

McCarthy, J., Minsky, M., Rochester, N. and Shannon, C. (1955). *A Proposal for the Dartmouth Summer Research Project on Artificial Intelligence*. Available at: http://jmc.stanford.edu/articles/dartmouth/dartmouth.pdf [Accessed: April 2022].

Musiio. 2022. *Use Artificial Intelligence to Help Automate Your Workflows*. Available at: www.musiio.com [Accessed: April 2022].

Negarestani, R. (2018). *Intelligence and Spirit*. Falmouth: Urbanomic Media.

Negarestani, R. (2020). 'On an Impending Eternal Turmoil in Human Thought', in Garayeva-Maleki, S. and Munder, H., eds. *Potential Worlds: Planetary Memories & Eco-Fictions*. Zurich: Migros Museum für Gegenwartskunst, YARAT Contemporary Art Space and Scheidegger & Speiss.

Never Before Heard Sounds. (2022). *Never Before Heard Sounds*. Available at: https://heardsounds.com [Accessed: April 2022].

Nilsen, M. (2013). *Humans Are on the Verge of Losing One of Their Last Big Advantages Over Computers*. Available at: www.businessinsider.com/com-puters-beating-humans-at-advanced-chess-2013-11?r=US&IR=T [Accessed: April 2022].

OED | Oxford English Dictionary. (2022). *Artificial Intelligence*. Available at: www.oed.com/viewdictionaryentry/Entry/271625 [Accessed: April 2022].

OmniSale GMBH. (2022). *About Us: LALAL.AI*. Available at: www.lalal.ai/ about/ [Accessed: April 2022].

Price, A. (2022). *Artificial Intelligence in Music Production – Friend or Foe?* Available at: https://audiomediainternational.com/artificial-intelligence-in-music/ [Accessed: May 2022].

Silberling, A. (2022). *SoundCloud Acquires Musiio, an AI Music Curator, to Improve Discovery*. Available at: https://techcrunch.com/2022/05/03/sound-cloud-acquires-musiio-ai-music-discovery/ [Accessed: May 2022].

Susskind, D. (2020). *A World Without Work: Technology, Automation and How We Should Respond*. London: Allen Lane.

18

From digital assistant to digital collaborator

M. Nyssim Lefford, David Moffat, and Gary Bromham

1 INTRODUCTION

Sanders and Simons (2009) describe co-creation as "any act of collective creativity that is experienced jointly by two or more people. How is co-creation different from collaboration? It is a special case of collaboration where the intent is to create something that is not known in advance" (n.p.). Co-creators do not necessarily bring the same skills, nor are they necessarily equal partners in authorship. Nevertheless, combining the expertise and situational awareness of multiple and varied creative agents can unearth new creative potential – even if not all the participating creative agents are "people". Intelligent Digital Mixing Assistants (IMAs) such as those found in products by Izotope, Synchro Arts and Sound Radix are becoming increasingly popular in music mixing, the stage of music production in which recorded elements are balanced and processed for the distribution format. Utilising various signal analysis techniques and artificial intelligence (AI), assistants can detect, manage or help resolve a variety of sound engineering related issues such as equalisation, dynamic range compression or loudness. Amershi et al. (2019) refer to such systems as "AI-infused" or "systems that have features harnessing AI capabilities that are directly exposed to the end user" (Amershi et al., 2019). IMAs rarely have direct control and autonomy over the problem area. The mixer chooses when and how to apply the tool. System designers generally offer and sell IMAs as mixing tools that "take care of the technical aspects and physical constraints of music production" (De Man, Stables and Reiss, 2019). The label *assistant*, like "wizard" or "tool", has instilled "asymmetry" (Reeves and Nass, 1996, p. 160) into mixer-tool interaction design, perhaps limiting what these tools might contribute to mixing practices. This study explores how mixer-IMA interactions might be further developed.

To investigate the possibilities, a survey was conducted of the system design literature in domains that have more extensive experience with human-AI interaction (HAI) and automation than audio. IMA interaction design sits at the intersection of automation design and use, human-automation interaction (HAI) and human-AI interaction, as well as cognitive

DOI: 10.4324/9781003118817-20

systems engineering. This study draws insight from all these areas to identify mixing-relevant interaction design recommendations. Tsiros and Palladini (2020) used a similar approach, adapting HAI and Human-AI interaction research in other fields to design an AI-infused channel for a live mixing console. The findings of our study suggest that what is currently possible in mixing may be expanded by communicating particular kinds of content in interactions between the mixer and IMA. These insights are offered not as a "position" for how HAI in IMAs should develop but rather as interaction design approaches. It is hoped that these findings will inspire more complex and facilitative mixer-IMA interactions.

IMAs – assistants – are but one class among the many intelligent audio or production tools that have been developed to date. There are fully automatic mixing systems such as the web-based Faders DAW built by Stables et al. from the DMT lab at Birmingham City University (https://faders.io/) and RoEx, a team of researchers in intelligent music production from C4DM at Queen Mary University and led by David Ronan, which embraces a similar web-based philosophy (www.roexaudio.com/). There are tools that fully automate some mixing tasks, such as the recently launched Izotope Neutron 4, as discussed in what follows (www.izotope.com/en/products/neutron.html), and there are also many generative music systems that compose, synthesise and, in some cases, render mixed music (www.ampermusic.com/). Some systems are fully autonomous. However, the scope of this study is constrained to IMA *user-tool* interactions. Unlike their fully autonomous cousins, since IMAs are typically *tools* designed and sold to *mixers*, it is assumed that IMAs are not meant to supplant the mixer but to facilitate the mixing process and, importantly, to serve the creative process of the mixer. The latter goal may be accomplished by decreasing the cognitive load that technical concerns place on mixers. This study offers additional means of facilitation. Furthermore, it is assumed that the creative aspects of mixing form the core of authorship in mixing, and in keeping with the user-tool frame, this study considers mixing scenarios in which the mixer proceeds with the assumption that the IMA cannot impinge on the mixer's authorship. These assumptions limit the applicability of the findings. Not all mixers will adopt these perspectives. Creative, generative systems have been designed that are intended to overtly assert their own authorship. Perhaps one of the most famous examples of this is an AI-based painting system called AARON, developed by the artist Harold Cohen (1995). Cohen has described the complex, collaborative relationship he developed with AARON, one that is difficult to describe as a user-tool relationship since each learns from and adapts to the other in highly sophisticated ways. Another example is David Cope's Experiments in Musical Intelligence or EMMY (Cope, 2004) which, although designed by Cope, composed autonomously. Music production will no doubt see a wide variety of creator-tool relationships, but these are beyond the scope of the present study.

Much can be learned about mixer-IMA interactions from observing human-human interactions. In all areas of professional music production, including mixing, work is often delegated among individuals with roles that are associated with particular responsibilities. These include, for example, the creator or artist, facilitating or actuating producers and technicians or engineers. IMAs may be used (or are assumed) to fulfil (some of) an engineer's or producer's responsibilities, in particular those areas of technical expertise that can be robustly modelled and codified. Another thing (human) producers and engineers do is supply expertise about genre conventions, for example, associated instrument timbres. These kinds of normative patterns, as well as entire genres that value adherence to conventions or rule sets, have proven relatively easier to model robustly for IMAs than those that are more free aesthetically or creatively. Therefore, IMAs may hold particular appeal in genres that value strict adherence to genre conventions, for example, K-pop, J-pop and EDM.

However, conformity monitoring is hardly the only role an IMA might play in mixing. As users interact more with AI-infused tools and new interaction designs are introduced, new "behavioral opportunities" (Naikar, 2018) can emerge. Humans may seek out new potential actions for themselves or IMAs, or mixers may spontaneously adopt afforded capacities that are well adapted to a specific mixing situation. According to Naikar (2018), sociotechnical working environments (like mixing) are, to some extent, dynamically self-organising. Hence, "models of human-automation interaction that focus on 'who should do what' or on 'who should be responsible for what' fail to appreciate how complex cognitive work is carried out" (Naikar, 2018, p. 62). IMA capabilities, mixing practices and mixer-IMA working methods are all co-evolving, and new approaches to HAI can spur constructive developments.

2 INTELLIGENT SOCIOTECHNICAL SYSTEMS

After investigating the use and disuse of robotics and automation in automotive industry assembly lines, Shimada and MacDuffie (1986) concluded that "technology becomes a meaningful concept only after the role of human resources, interlocking and interacting with hardware, is included." Adding machine intelligence to automation adds many layers of complexity to the interlocked state. In mixing, both the human user and IMA have intelligence about mixing, though (for the time being) it is obvious how their areas of expertise differ. Regardless, when they share expertise to produce work, in essence, together, they form one cognitive system in which capacities are distributed. To utilise their capacities, both the mixer and IMA require information from the other in order. At the very least, the IMA needs to know which functions are desired, and in many cases, parameter settings for those functions must be chosen by the mixer. Alternatively, the mixer's own actions are influenced by IMA actions. The sharing of information and the coordination of expertise require effective communication.

Roughly speaking, at present, IMAs are experts in those aspects of mixing for which optimal values and rules can be established (Pestana and Reiss, 2014). They can measure the physical properties of signals and compare signals to models and ideals. They can enact mixing axioms that can be quantified. Alternatively, humans understand subjective experience, emotion, social interaction among humans, context, and aesthetics. They have a theory of mind that helps them to predict how listeners are likely to respond to particular sounds in a particular mix. Mixing requires finding a balance between technical and aesthetic perspectives. A mix with evocative sounds rendered with appalling audio quality is likely to be as unsuccessful as a mix of excellent audio quality devoid of emotion. An effective approach to HAI in mixing is one that promotes reaching a balance among concerns. Human-machine communications that encourage the user and tool to establish "interdependence" (Reeves and Nass, 1996), where users and tools rely on the capabilities of and information from the other, is one component of such interactions.

3 AUTONOMY AND AUTHORITY

In interdependent relationships, actors have autonomy and authority to act within the ambit of their expertise, capacities and responsibilities. If actors cannot perform and contribute their own work, there is no interdependence. In other domains, there are various modes of automation application that are employed in different circumstances. "Direct teleoperation and complete autonomy are often thought of as two extremes" (Johnson et al., 2011, pp. 172–173) in a range of possible interaction scenarios. Mixing does not require "teleoperation" but there are analogous modes in which an IMA is used much as any other signal processor, where all parameters are set by the mixer. In such scenarios. the IMA has no autonomy, does not participate in the mixer's decision-making and there is no interdependence. Interdependence happens when actors' actions are influenced by and simultaneously influence other actors' actions (Johnson et al., 2011). The degree of interdependence may vary from scenario to scenario as "any needed resource or power within the action-perception loop of an agent [human or machine] defines a possible dimension of dependence or autonomy" (Castelfranchi, 2000 via Johnson et al., 2011, p. 177). In mixing, an IMA may have capacities to detect physical characteristics in signals that the human user cannot perceive. In such a scenario, there would be a high degree of dependence and IMA autonomy, but there are also qualities humans, but not IMAs, can detect. "The ideal [dependence] is not a fixed location along this [teleoperation-autonomy] spectrum but may need to vary dynamically along the spectrum as context and resources change" (Johnson et al., 2011, p. 173). Johnson et al. (2011) argue that "an understanding of the potential interdependencies" should be a criterion for designs that ensure degrees of autonomy, capabilities and interactions [that] are "appropriate" (p. 173).

Without debating how exactly the information should be displayed to or collected from the user, useful content to communicate about interdependence, autonomy and authority may include the following:

- Giving the mixer granular control over IMA actions (i.e., teleoperation)
- The mixer's attention can be directed to parameters that can be set manually, suggesting ways to reduce the IMAs' autonomy

- Conversely, the IMA might confirm that it should optimise, or optimise given certain tolerances or boundary conditions, without mixer input to the process

4 SHARED CONTEXT

The autonomy granted to the IMA and the perceived appropriateness of whatever action it takes under the direction of the mixer is dependent on the context. "Context reputedly explains everything in the environment that influences our perceptions, cognitions and actions" (Sober, 2009 via Lawless, Mittu and Sofge, 2017, p. 309). Numerous contextualising factors impact mixing decisions and the balance struck between technical and aesthetic interests. The context is shaped by both physical and immaterial constraints that include the musical content, artist, aesthetic and commercial goals and the availability of financial resources and time, as well as genre conventions and norms. Much of this information is inaccessible to an IMA without mixer input.

The sharing of contextualising Information requires bidirectional communication. For example, IMAs could propose contextualising factors to the mixer. An example of this interaction strategy already exists in Izotope's Mix Assistant (Izotope Neutron 3, 2022), which can autonomously generate a rough mix at the start of the mixing process. The IMA asks the user to choose what instruments are to be "foregrounded" in this rough mix, in other words, to prioritise or add weights to instruments in a mix. The IMA can then use these weighting factors along with mixing axioms and/or other rules to generate a mix likely to seem appropriate, if not preferable, to the mixer. Izotope's own marketing suggests that the generated mix is only a rough balance or starting place for more creative, human decision-making.

Taking this further, richer bidirectional communication about the appropriateness of the rough mix rendered could produce a more nuanced shared context for future actions. To appreciate what actions are appropriate in a context, "communication must incorporate both a sensitivity to its circumstances, and built-in resources for the remedy of troubles in understanding that inevitably arise" (Suchman, 1987, p. 21). Conceivably, the mixer and IMA could, for example, negotiate what is to be foregrounded and prioritised based on the specifics of the material and genre. The IMA could offer prompts based on mixing axioms and genre conventions. "In the context of computers . . . A desirable feature of a shared context is that machines can use it to explain their decisions, situations, or perspectives to their human collaborators" (Wollowski et al., 2020, p. 416). Increasing the shared context would provide the IMA with information about the mixer's goals and expectations, and this can be used as a basis for suggesting to the mixer appropriate IMA functionality and for customising future IMA actions and user queries. Also, the IMA would have information to better predict and "update or convey how user actions will impact future behaviours of the AI system" (Amershi et al., 2019, p. 3). Amershi et al. (2019) advocate human-AI interaction designs that "encourage granular feedback. Enable the user to provide feedback indicating their preferences during regular interaction with the AI system" (p. 3).

Communications may:

- Propose contextualising factors to the mixer
- Prompt mixers to prioritise elements based on expressed genre conventions and mixing axioms
- Query mixers about goals and expectations
- Convey how mixer actions will impact future IMA behaviours
- Offer granular feedback

Lawless, Mittu and Sofge (2017) argue that context may actually be illusory (Lawless, Mittu and Sofge, 2017), but "whether an AI program automatically 'knows' the context and yet still improves performance, it may not matter whether context is real, uncertain or illusory" (Lawless, Mittu and Sofge, 2017, p. 310). On the one hand, interactions to share context could seem quite laborious to mixers. On the other hand, such interactions would foster interdependence and encourage mixers to reflect more deeply on their choices – which can facilitate creativity. Whether or not mixers will utilise this kind of creative scaffolding is a matter of trusting the IMA and the benefits of communicating with it. Trustworthiness is one of the cornerstones of automation and, therefore, of IMA design.

5 TRUST AND TRANSPARENCY

"People respond to technology socially" (Lee and See, 2004, p. 50). Social expectations shape how users view and experience technology behaviour and interaction, but also, "trust helps . . . by acting as a social decision heuristic" (Kramer, 1999 via Lee and See, 2004, p. 52). In non-audio applications of automation, it has been observed that automated systems "earn the trust" of users through reliable performance (Parasuraman and Riley, 1997, p. 244). Trust is developed by the AI by performing actions that can be anticipated by a user (Jacovi et al., 2021). Communication can help IMAs to appear trustworthy. According to Klein et al. (2005), trust in interaction and in the coordination of any joint activity (with automation or humans) requires the "ability to predict the actions of other parties with a reasonable degree of accuracy. It follows that each party also has a responsibility to make his or her actions sufficiently predictable to enable effective coordination" (p. 148). This "interpredictability" (Klein et al., 2005) presupposes that the actions of the automation or AI are transparent to the mixer. Transparency in automation is "the quality of an interface pertaining to its ability to afford an operator's comprehension about an intelligent agent's intent, performance, future plans and reasoning process" (Mercado et al., 2016; via Yang et al., 2017, p. 409). It is important to "make clear why the system did what it did. Enable the user to access an explanation of why the AI system behaved as it did" (Amershi et al., 2019, p. 3).

In human-robot interactions, Lyons and Havig (2014) observe that "notions of shared intent and shared awareness are key objectives related to transparency" (Lyons and Havig, 2014, p. 184). Transparency can mitigate distrust. However, transparency can also lead to distrust and uncertainty if too much or irrelevant information is provided (Lyons and Havig, 2014). An effective way to communicate transparently is to communicate the limits of an assistants' functionality or capacities. This information might be conveyed alongside suggestions about the appropriateness of functionality.

To earn trust, communicate:

- About The IMA's "intent, performance, future plans and reasoning process" (Mercado et al., 2016; via Yang et al., 2017, p. 409)
- To explain the rationale behind IMA actions and why IMA actions occurred. Make explanations accessible after the fact
- About the limits of IMA capabilities
- About the potential appropriateness of specific IMA functionality
- But avoid too much or irrelevant information

"Trust influences reliance on automation" (Lee and See, 2004, p. 76). Lee and See (2004) describe trust "as the attitude that an agent will help achieve an individual's goals in a situation characterized by uncertainty and vulnerability" (p. 54). Professional music production is uncertain. Just as there is no way to guarantee the audience's reaction to a finished mix, there is no way to guarantee that the use of an IMA for any particular task will contribute to the improvement of a mix. Most likely, mixers will reconsider their reliance many times over during the mixing process. There are many factors that can contribute to decisions about reliance. Mistrust in automation has been known to occur when the user has misunderstandings about automation capabilities. "Disuse signifies failures that occur when people reject the capabilities of automation" (Lee and See, 2004, p. 50). People may also misjudge automation performance or ascribe inaccurate or unreasonable expectations. In industrial applications, it has been observed that "initial expectations of perfect automation performance can lead to disuse when people find the automation to be imperfect" (Dzindolet et al., 2002 via Lee and See, 2004, p. 69). Disuse due to failures of trust also occurs when insufficient communication makes it difficult for the user to monitor the system or if there is the wrong kind of communication between the user and automation, for example, if the system often "cries wolf" due to unnecessarily low thresholds for triggering alarms/alerts (Parasuraman and Riley, 1997).

Users of (non-mixing) automation systems have also exhibited tendencies to trust when they should not. "Overtrust is poor calibration in which trust exceeds system capabilities" (Lee and See, 2004, p. 55). "Excessive trust can lead operators to rely uncritically on automation without recognizing its limitations" (Parasuraman and Riley, 1997, p. 237). Users can exude an "automation bias" and "inappropriate decision making linked to overreliance on automation" (Parasuraman and Riley, 1997, p. 240). "Complacency effects" occur when the user's task and cognitive loads are high, and they respond to these demands with "an active reallocation of attention" (Parasuraman and Manzey, 2010, p. 384) away from tasks and decisions the automation can presumably manage autonomously and without monitoring.

To avoid disuse and complacency, IMAs can:

- Communicate about capabilities and limitations and explain IMA performance
- Provide mixers with information about IMA self-monitoring
- Periodically direct the mixer's attention to monitoring IMA actions

6 SHARED AWARENESS

No matter how an intelligent system communicates about mixing and about its own capabilities, a mixer's understanding or belief in an IMA's abilities to make relevant contributions is shaped by their own experience and tacit and formal knowledge of mixing, automation and AI. Among mixers, understanding and knowledge can vary greatly. Mixers vary greatly in both technical and creative expertise. One thing that separates a less experienced mixer from an experienced one is their respective abilities to guide the song in a creative and stylistically appropriate direction. This requires making decisions about when it is appropriate to follow the norms of a given genre or break the musical rules. Knowledge and experience influence mixer awareness of potential and problems. Less experienced users may not share the same level of awareness or ability to assess what is relevant, probable or uncertain in a given situation. "Dynamically presenting uncertainty information leads operators to employ more appropriate attention allocation strategies" (Kunze et al., 2019, p. 356). A lack of awareness could lead a mixer to automation complacency, which, in music production, may almost be a form of deference (to an expert system). Less experienced users, especially those with limited critical listening skills, may trust the IMA to make good corrections or suggestions or at least ones that are better than those the mixer may make.

This might be somewhat alleviated with HAI designs that "help the user understand what the AI system is capable of doing" (Amershi et al., 2019, p. 3). An IMA might also make certain inferences about mixers' situational awareness based on the mixer's behaviour, patterns in queries and mixing axioms. That information can be used to generate prompts to attend to certain technical issues that are seemingly not being given attention and that have a high probability of being consequential for the mix. Disclosing information about probability also helps to establish a shared awareness, particularly of the IMA's limitations. A mixer may choose to ignore potential outcomes with low probability but there could be consequences for IMA's inferences that are inaccurate; for example, it could make the IMA appear less reliable.

To increase a mixer's situational awareness, an IMA can communicate:

- Regularly about its perspective of the situation. For example, as the mix changes, the IMA can collect new information from signal

analyses run in the background and then deliver regular technical observations about the state of the mix to the user
- By tracking mixer actions, queries and patterns in the functionality accessed, the mixer's awareness may be inferred, and from that, the IMA can identify and communicate about potentially problematic issues not receiving attention.

Bi-directional communication can establish not only a shared technical conceptual space but potentially a shared creative conceptual space as well.

7 CO-CREATION

Sharing awareness aligns the mixer's and the IMS's perspectives of a mix, at which point HAI could move beyond enabling the coordination of joint activity between technical and creative actors to enable sustained inter-subjective activity. Staying within the limits of user-tool relationships, an IMA could offer creative decision support and could do so without challenging the mixer's authorship by assuming a facilitative "producer" role in interactions. To maintain this stance, the IMA would have low autonomy and no authority to make any decisions about the creative direction of the mix. Nevertheless, by sharing awareness of the creative as well as the technical conceptual space, the IMA becomes, in essence, a creative agent or co-creator. "Co-creativity allows participants to improvise based on decisions of their peers" (Davis et al., 2015, p. 113). At least, the IMA could, if not improvise, adapt to the mixer's creative activities.

Presently, commercially available IMAs offer functionality that helps mixers match pre-defined genre conventions and norms (Pestana and Reiss, 2014; De Man, Stables and Reiss, 2019), and based on mixing axioms and genre conventions, an IMA could suggest creative decision heuristics. Relatedly, based on mixer actions, information provided by the mixer and/or potentially machine learning, the IMA may be able to predict what patterns appear to be emerging and suggest actions to render them more overtly. The same basic strategy of leveraging comparisons to idealised models and axioms can be used to offer other forms of decision support. Boden has previously proposed the development of creative "agents" that are capable of "helping us by suggesting, identifying and even evaluating differences between familiar ideas and novel ones" (Boden, 2010, p. 164). An IMA could evaluate the proximity of choices to genre conventions and inform the mixer without necessarily offering specific suggestions for modification. The same sort of benchmarking can provide the IMA with information that can help map out a shared creative conceptual space, for example, between genres. This can be used to direct the mixer's attention to potentially relevant aesthetic considerations, help the mixer ideate and also provide the IMA with means to recalibrate for subsequent comparisons.

Another indirect way to map out a conceptual space is for mixers to supply the IMA with reference mixes (similar to Singh et al., 2021). The IMA could use its signal analyse capabilities to generate comparisons between the provided and created mixes along pre-defined parameters and direct the mixer's attention towards similarities and differences. This kind of directing of attention would (in many cases) increase the mixer's awareness and thereby provide information for creative decision-making.

Assuming some kind of conceptual space can be mapped out, for example, relative to pre-existing models of genre, the IMA could facilitate the mixer's explorations of the creative conceptual space. Many models of creative ideation have been proposed, and some of those have been represented in logic or code. Notably, Boden (2004, 2010) has proposed several modes of creative activity: "combinational" where creative activity generates new combinations of existing form, "exploratory" where the creative activity involves novel ways to navigate a conceptual space of possibilities and "transformational" activities that lead to wholly new forms or possibilities in the conceptual space. All modes, in essence, require some form of exploration of a structured conceptual space (Boden, 1998). IMAs are already positioned to make suggestions in well-structured scenarios. Rather than making suggestions based on genre, IMAs could, for example, suggest approaches to combining genres. These suggestions would still need to be based on axioms or rules of some sort, but not necessarily genre-based rule sets.

If exploring the creative conceptual space remains too ill-structured, Boden's modes might be turned towards technological affordances. With at least a partial shared awareness of both creative possibilities as well as technical degrees of freedom, mixer and IMA could co-interrogate the functionality and affordances of available technology to find appropriate potential treatments. The IMA could predict probable outcomes of the application of proposed functions and alert the mixer to the likely effects. Co-interrogations might include not only the IMA's functionality but also the affordances of other (less intelligent) tools.

Ultimately, the more the IMA understands the mixer's intentions and creative goals, the more the decision support can be adapted to the creative work being undertaken. Since creative goals may be difficult to specify, particularly using semantics available to an IMA (for example, as in Stables et al., 2014), bi-directional communications might incorporate relative comparisons (e.g., multidimensional scaling) or by choosing positions on a 2-dimensional, x-y plane, as one would find in the graphical user interface of a physical modelling synthesiser. The mixer also needs to be able to access explanations of how the IMA is trying to enable creativity. The reasoning behind the IMA's creative decision support is, in itself, information that the mixer can use to make creative decisions. Without these explanations, prompts, information and suggestions may feel irrelevant to the mixer's creative ideation and decision-making.

An IMA can participate in co-creative activities by facilitating the mixer's creative decision-making. Facilitation may be delivered by communicating:

• Prompts to direct the mixer's attention
• About proximity of choices to genre conventions

- About rendering patterns more overtly
- About how the creative conceptual space may be explored
- To co-interrogate technological affordances
- About the IMAs facilitation strategy

At the time of writing, looking at the development of AI in other domains, it is fair to say that such functionality is not technically achieved yet; however, it is also not far out of reach. C-creative systems may not yet be real-time (commercial) systems or demonstrate the deep domain knowledge expected, particularly when compared with a human co-creator. Therefore, as IMAs grow increasingly more intelligent, it remains to be seen how human mixers will work out, work with, work around and, indeed, misappropriate intelligent creative collaborators.

In music production, the distribution of work to various experts and the social, technical and economic structures that bind collaborators have been and continue to be researched extensively. The study presented here focused specifically on the structuring of interactions between a mixer and an IMA, a very low-level and particular type of interaction. However, that interaction can be positioned within a broader context of the production environment. The "idea of configuring the environment so that it affords particular types of action also works on a more macro, temporal and structural level" (Zagorski-Thomas and Bourbon, 2020, p. 142). Latour's Actor-Network Theory (ANT) (Latour, 1996; Law, 1992) is one model that has been proposed for structuring collaborative relationships in music production, no doubt in part because Latour allows that technology, which is so integral to music production, can be a node in a network of actors. Hence, at a macro level, IMAs may be viewed as a new type of actor in the context of the ANT. Some researchers using ANT to analyse music productions choose to "let technological devices 'speak' for themselves by activating them within specific 'performance ecosystems' that include context-specific tools, techniques, studio personnel and audience feedback among other things" (Williams, 2012 cited in Zagorski-Thomas and Bourbon, 2020, p. 36). And if they are granted this autonomy, since it has been argued previously that sharing awareness can align the mixer's and the IMA's perspectives with regards to the implementation of mixing tasks and creative decision making, it is also worth considering whether mixer and IMA might be enabled to share awareness of the collaboration process. Shared perspectives on the social organisation of production and approaches to collaboration generally may present further opportunities for the IMA to collaborate with a mixer. This is yet another layer of intelligence that could be developed in emerging IMA technology.

8 CONCLUSIONS

Intelligent Digital Mixing Assistants (IMAs) are mixing tools that "take care of the technical aspects and physical constraints of music production" (De Man, Stables and Reiss, 2019). In practical terms, for mixers, in theory, this means less of their cognitive load is occupied by technical concerns, and therefore more attention may be dedicated to creative matters. However, music mixing involves not only integrating varied perspectives and varied types of technical and aesthetic knowledge but also prioritising technical versus aesthetic information as situations demand, balancing the personal styles of mixers and genre conventions and distributing the authority to take decisions as situations and tasks demand. Current IMAs provide little assistance, facilitation and scaffolding in this work.

Human-automation interaction (HAI) in music production is an emerging field, and some early assumptions, while understandable, do not necessarily best serve the creative process of mixing. Developments in HAIs in other domains have shown that user-tool communications can be rich and dynamic when the tool encourages the reciprocation of knowledge. With more and more complex bi-directional communication between the mixer and IMA, the IMA could more clearly communicate about its capacities, limitations and intelligence. Thereby, the mixer would be in a better position to determine how much autonomy and authority should be given to the IMA in particular tasks, and overall, the system would be more trustworthy and transparent. Bi-directional communication would also allow the mixer and IMA to share pertinent information about the mixing context and goals generally, as well as specific situations. Interactions can subsequently take on more of an intersubjective and co-creative dimension.

REFERENCES

Amershi, S., Weld, D., Vorvoreanu, M., Fourney, A., Nushi, B., Collisson, P., Suh, J., Iqbal, S., Bennett, P. N., Inkpen, K. and Teevan, J. (2019, May). 'Guidelines for human-AI interaction', in *Proceedings of the 2019 Chi Conference on Human Factors in Computing Systems*. NY, USA: ACM, pp. 1–13.

AmperMusic. (2022). *www.ampermusic.com*. Available at: www.ampermusic.com/ [Accessed: 9 June 2022].

Boden, M. A. (1998). 'Creativity and Artificial Intelligence', *Artificial intelligence*, 103(1–2), pp. 347–356.

Boden, M. A. (2004). *The Creative Mind: Myths and Mechanisms*. London and New York: Routledge Taylor and Francis Group.

Boden, M. A. (2010). *Creativity and Art: Three Roads To surprise*. Oxford: Oxford University Press.

Castelfranchi, C. (2000, August). Founding agent's' autonomy'on dependence theory. In Proceedings of the 14th European Conference on Artificial Intelligence (pp. 353–357). Amsterdam https://dl.acm.org/doi/proceedings/10.5555/3006433

Cohen, H. (1995). 'The Further Exploits of AARON, Painter', *Stanford Humanities Review*, 4(2), pp. 141–158.

Cope, D. (2004). *Virtual Music: Computer Synthesis of Musical Style*. Cambridge, MA: MIT Press.

Davis, N., Hsiao, C. P., Popova, Y. and Magerko, B. (2015). 'An Enactive Model of Creativity for Computational Collaboration and Co-creation', in *Creativity in the Digital Age*. London: Springer, pp. 109–133.

De Man, B., Stables, R. and Reiss, J. D. (2019). *Intelligent Music Production*. Routledge.

Dzindolet, M. T., Pierce, L. G., Beck, H. P. and Dawe, L. A. (2002). 'The Perceived Utility of Human and Automated Aids in a Visual Detection Task', *Human Factors*, 44, pp. 79–94.

Faders. (2022). *Faders.io*. Available at: https://faders.io/ [Accessed: 9 June 2022].

Izotope Neutron 3 (Computer Software). (2022). *Izotope Neutron 3*. Available at: www.izotope.com/en/products/neutron.html.

Jacovi, A., Marasović, A., Miller, T. and Goldberg, Y. (2021, March). 'Formalizing Trust in Artificial Intelligence: Prerequisites, Causes and Goals of Human Trust in AI', in *Proceedings of the 2021 ACM Conference on Fairness, Accountability, and Transparency*, pp. 624–635. Available at https://dl.acm.org/doi/pdf/10.1145/3442188.3445923.

Johnson, M., Bradshaw, J. M., Feltovich, P. J., Jonker, C. M., Van Riemsdijk, B. and Sierhuis, M. (2011). 'The Fundamental Principle of Coactive Design: Interdependence Must Shape Autonomy', in *Coordination, Organizations, Institutions, and Norms in Agent Systems VI: COIN 2010 International Workshops, COIN@ AAMAS 2010, Toronto, Canada, May 2010, COIN@ MALLOW 2010, Lyon, France, August 2010, Revised Selected Papers*. Berlin: Springer Berlin Heidelberg, pp. 172–191.

Klein, G., Feltovich, P. J., Bradshaw, J. M. and Woods, D. D. (2005). 'Common Ground and Coordination in Joint Activity', *Organizational Simulation*, 53, pp. 139–184.

Kramer, R. M. (1999). 'Trust and Distrust in Organizations: Emerging Perspectives, Enduring Questions', *Annual Review of Psychology*, 50, pp. 569–598.

Kunze, A., Summerskill, S. J., Marshall, R. and Filtness, A. J. (2019). 'Automation Transparency: Implications of Uncertainty Communication for Human-Automation Interaction and Interfaces', *Ergonomics*, 62(3), pp. 345–360.

Latour, B. (1996). 'On Actor-Network Theory: A Few Clarifications', *Soziale welt*, pp. 369–381.

Law, J. (1992). 'Notes on the Theory of the Actor-Network: Ordering, Strategy, and Heterogeneity', *Systems Practice*, 5(4), pp. 379–393.

Lawless, W. F., Mittu, R. and Sofge, D. (2017, March). '(Computational) Context. Why It's Important, What It Means, Can It Be Computed?', in *2017 AAAI Spring Symposium Series*.

Lee, J. D. and See, K. A. (2004). 'Trust in Automation: Designing for Appropriate Reliance', *Human Factors*, 46(1), pp. 50–80.

Lyons, J. B. and Havig, P. R. (2014, June). 'Transparency in a Human-Machine Context: Approaches for Fostering Shared Awareness/Intent', in *International Conference on Virtual, Augmented and Mixed Reality*. Cham: Springer, pp. 181–190.

Mercado, J. E., Rupp, M. A., Chen, J. Y. C., Barnes, M. J., Barber, D. and Procci, K. (2016). 'Intelligent Agent Transparency in Human–Agent Teaming for Multi-UxV Management', *Human Factors*, 58(3), pp. 401–415.

Naikar, N. (2018). 'Human – Automation Interaction in Self-Organizing Sociotechnical Systems', *Journal of Cognitive Engineering and Decision Making*, 12(1), pp. 62–66.

Parasuraman, R. and Manzey, D. H. (2010). 'Complacency and Bias in Human Use of Automation: An Attentional Integration', *Human Factors*, 52(3), pp. 381–410.

Parasuraman, R. and Riley, V. (1997). 'Humans and Automation: Use, Misuse, Disuse, Abuse', *Human Factors*, 39(2), pp. 230–253.

Pestana, P. D. and Reiss, J. D. (2014, January). 'Intelligent Audio Production Strategies Informed by Best Practices', in *Audio Engineering Society Conference: 53rd International Conference: Semantic Audio*. Audio Engineering Society. London. https://www.aes.org/conferences/53/

Reeves, B. and Nass, C. (1996). *The Media Equation: How People Treat Computers, Television, and New Media Like Real People*. Cambridge: Cambridge University Press.

RoEx. (2022). *www.roexaudio.com*. Available at: www.roexaudio.com/ [Accessed: 9 June 2022].

Sanders, L. and Simons, G. (2009, December). 'A Social Vision for Value Co-creation in Design', *Open Source Business Resource*, 27.

Shimada, H. and MacDuffie, J. P. (1986). *Industrial Relations and "Humanware" – Japanese Investments in Automobile Manufacturing in the United States*. Available at: https://dspace.mit.edu/bitstream/handle/1721.1/48159/industrialrelati00shim.pdf;sequence=1.

Singh, S., Bromham, G., Sheng, D. and Fazekas, G. (2021). 'Intelligent Control Method for the Dynamic Range Compressor: A User Study', *Journal of the Audio Engineering Society*, 69(7/8), pp. 576–585.

Sober, E. 2009. The Power of Context. Getting Beyond Labels and Limitations. The 99th Monkey (blog), Psychology Today, July 10, 2009. www.psychologytoday.com/blog/the-99th-monkey/200907/the-power-context

Stables, R., Enderby, S., De Man, B., Fazekas, G. and Reiss, J. D. (2014). *SAFE: A System for Extraction and Retrieval of Semantic Audio Descriptors*. Available at: https://qmro.qmul.ac.uk/xmlui/bitstream/handle/123456789/12589/De%20Man%20SAFE%20A%20SYSTEM%20FOR%202014%20Published.pdf?sequence=2&isAllowed=y.

Suchman, L. A. (1987). *Plans and Situated Actions: The Problem of Human-Machine Communication*. Cambridge: Cambridge University Press.

Tsiros, A. and Palladini, A. (2020, July). 'Towards a Human-Centric Design Framework for AI Assisted Music Production', in *Proceedings of the International Conference on New Interfaces for Musical Expression*, pp. 399–404.

Williams, S. (2012). 'Tubby's Dub Style: The Live Art of Record Production', in *The Art of Record Production: An Introductory Reader for a New Academic Field*. Ashgate Publishing, pp. 235–246.

Wollowski, M., Bath, T., Brusniak, S., Crowell, M., Dong, S., Knierman, J., Panfil, W., Park, S., Schmidt, M. and Suvarna, A. (2020). 'Constructing Mutual Context in Human-Robot Collaborative Problem Solving with Multimodal Input', in *Human-Machine Shared Contexts*. Academic Press, pp. 399–420.

Yang, X. J., Unhelkar, V. V., Li, K. and Shah, J. A. (2017, March). 'Evaluating Effects of User Experience and System Transparency on Trust in Automation', in *2017 12th ACM/IEEE International Conference on Human-Robot Interaction (HRI)*. IEEE, pp. 408–416.

Zagorski-Thomas, S. and Bourbon, A., eds. (2020). *The Bloomsbury Handbook of Music Production*. New York, NY: Bloomsbury Publishing.

19

Analyse! Development and integration of software-based tools for musicology and music theory

Martin Pfleiderer, Egor Polyakov, and Christon-Ragavan Nadar

1 INTRODUCTION

One central area of music research is musical analysis: the detailed examination of various aspects of musical composition (form, harmony, melody, rhythm, timbre and instrumentation, etc.), which are first considered analytically and then interpreted and contextualised with regard to overarching issues. Findings of musical analysis strongly contribute to music historiography as well as to music theory and aesthetics. In all musicological, music pedagogical and artistic study programs, methods of music analysis are, therefore, a core competence for which usually several courses or seminars are provided.

The overarching goal of music analysis is to describe individual pieces of music as precisely as possible through analytical examination in order to work out their special features in comparison to certain stylistic conventions and to present the music to various possibilities of interpretation. In doing so, entire personal or historical styles of music are often characterised in a generalised manner, which would, however, presuppose the analysis of hundreds or thousands of scores. At this point, new methods of statistical music analysis come in, using computer routines to facilitate the immense work of analysing larger corpora of music (Cook, 2004; Neuwirth and Rohrmeier, 2016). While many of these corpus studies use musical scores as data material, there are approaches, especially in the fields of ethnomusicology, jazz and popular music research, and electroacoustic music, that analyse digitised recordings by resorting to methods of digital signal processing and music information retrieval. In addition, there are computer-aided approaches to comparing interpretations, so-called performance research, which have also been carried out in the context of music psychology.

There are now numerous freely available software tools that can be used to analyse various aspects of sheet music or audio files and to graphically illustrate the findings. They are particularly well suited for handling large amounts of data for statistical corpus analyses as well as for search routines in entire music repertoires. Moreover, these computer-based tools enable

DOI: 10.4324/9781003118817-21

novel music-analytic approaches to both sheet music and audio files and can be seen as valuable complements to conventional approaches. However, these new possibilities have so far found only little echo in music analysis teaching, seminars and exercises practiced in universities.

Therefore, it was the aim of a one-year project situated at the University of Music Franz Liszt in Weimar, Germany, to design and test teaching modules that take up new digital approaches and methods and test them with students of musicology, music theory, and music pedagogy (see https://analyse.hfm-weimar.de). With the help of these approaches and software tools, students should learn to analyse pieces of music (sheet music or audio) and compare them with respect to certain musical characteristics and issues. For advanced courses, these approaches are extended to statistical corpus analysis and to the possibilities of a targeted search of musical elements and patterns within scores. Sheet music and audio data as well as suitable software, have been provided via an internet platform by linking them to freely accessible internet resources. On this basis, several teaching modules with introductions and practical analysis tasks for lecturers and students were developed, evaluated, optimised and finally made available to all interested parties free of charge via the project website.

The project offers opportunities to link research more closely to teaching in the sense of inquiry-based learning and to connect music research (musicology, music theory, music pedagogy) in general more closely to developments in the digital humanities. In addition to new analytical issues, further application perspectives of the teaching modules lie within the practice of teamwork within analysis courses, which is still rarely practiced in the humanities in comparison to the natural or computer sciences. This includes a possible transfer to school teaching as well as the involvement of laypersons interested in music.

Against the background of this project, perspectives for methods and software tools for computer-aided sheet music analysis are outlined. Since the field of computer-based music score analysis is rather young, the main focus of the paper lies in the comparison and evaluation of several computational approaches and software solutions. In the first sections, the advantages (and disadvantages) of various computational approaches to the analysis of music scores, different data formats for sheet music and recently developed Jupyter Notebooks are discussed in detail. Thereafter, section 3 introduces a newly designed analysis tool based on the parsing of MusicXML data into a pandas DataFrame (according to the Python library pandas) that enables new opportunities for the visualisation of scores, for their statistical investigation and for the search of various tonal and rhythmic patterns in one score or over several scores. Then, the online presentation of the tools and corresponding tutorials is sketched (section 4). While the paper is dedicated to sheet music, the project's approaches to online tutorials for audio analysis are only briefly mentioned. Finally, the merits and shortcomings of the new tools as well as future perspectives of computational sheet music analysis are discussed.

2 BACKGROUND

2.1 Overview: computational music analysis

Since the mention of the possibility of various music-related calculations with Babbage's Analytical Engine in the notes of Ada Lovelace (Roure and Willcox, 2017), there was always a link between advancements in computational technology and the adoption of new methods in music analysis, music representation and music composition. Although many practical and historical aspects of this development, especially in the 1970s–80s, are crucial for the understanding of the current state of computer-aided musicology (Hewlett and Selfridge-Field, 1991), only a few concepts and formats from that time are still relevant today. The limitations of computer systems of that era required strict customisation of databases used in research. In many cases, this imposed a heavy restriction on what parameters or values from sheet music could be processed and usually led to very specialised datasets that could barely be used outside of their original purpose.

The emergence of efficient and affordable personal computers since the mid-1980s combined with the expanding availability of the internet led to the development of new tools and formats that were much more general-purpose by design and were built around accessible online databases. Examples are ABC music and Humdrum, which were developed during the 1990s and are still in use today. The rise of new interdisciplinary scientific fields, such as music information retrieval, combined with a shift towards performance-based analysis within the field of computer-assisted musicology in the 1990s (Schüler, 2007), led to a noticeable push in the evolution of new audio-related analytic tools and environments. So, during the 2010s, the most prolific tools for audio-related research were released and are still available today, such as the Sonic Visualiser (Cannam, Landone and Sandler, 2010) and the FMP Notebooks (Müller and Zalkow, 2019). They combine state-of-the-art functionality for audio analysis with great accessibility, thus making them not only useful tools for music research but also for several educational purposes.

Music21 is a Python-based analysis toolkit for sheet music that combines great functionality with a simple programming interface (Cuthbert and Ariza, 2010). However, it still relies heavily on code interaction and requires at least some experience with command-line tools and informatics in general. With the development of Jupyter Notebooks in the late 2010s, a web-based interactive Python environment that provided an accessible GUI for code interaction, there was a new opportunity to re-evaluate the current state of sheet music analysis tools, bringing them on par with the aforementioned tools for audio analysis and including them into educational programs. In the following sections, several analysis tools and sheet music formats are evaluated in more detail with an explicit focus on educational contexts.

2.2 Approaches to the analysis of music scores

In general, there are a variety of tools available today that can be used for processing sheet music data. Apart from easily accessible piano roll visualisation tools for MIDI files (e.g., in various digital audio workstations), one is obliged to use specialised tools or environments to generate other visual representations or extract any kind of statistical data. While there are many of these tools available, our project focused mainly on evaluating two music-related visual programming languages, Max/MSP and OpenMusic, along with the music score analysis tools Humdrum and music21. This choice is mainly justified by the necessity for many music departments to use open source or already widely available commercial software (such as Max/MSP); for the same reason, the MIDI toolbox (Eerola and Toiviainen, 2004), which requires an expensive Matlab license, is not included.

User-friendly solutions for the analysis of sheet music files are well-known and well-documented visual programming languages such as Max/MSP or OpenMusic. Both do not require any profound programming knowledge and represent a good playground for testing certain analytic approaches (Manzo, 2011; Fang, 2012). Especially remarkable is the wide variety of available possibilities to process and visually represent sheet music data within both environments. This includes not only the common music notation representation as a score but also various types of piano rolls or even graphic functions. Altogether, all these elements can be combined into clearly structured algorithmic networks that can represent certain musical processes or analytic tasks. The outstanding visual accessibility of code and object interaction makes it possible to intuitively explore the exact effect of certain algorithmic manipulations on the pitch and/or duration structure of the imported music sheets. However, the lack of any scalable options for the processing of large amounts of sheet music data makes both environments not an optimal choice for any corpus-related tasks. Also, various extensions or workarounds may be needed for importing sheet music in data formats different from MIDI. Overall, both softwares are rather beginner-friendly, visually oriented and interactive solutions requiring that specific scientific or didactic goals are adjusted to their limitations and benefits. In particular, the real-time interaction as well as the sonification of analysed or generated sheet music, can be seamlessly implemented in both environments and successfully used in an educational context (Poliakov, 2020).

Humdrum, originally created by David Huron in the 1980s, is a general-purpose software system designed to assist music researchers (Huron, 1999). Although there exist a lot of Humdrum script implementations in different programming languages and environments, no dedicated GUI version was developed until the release of Verovio Humdrum in 2017. Verovio Humdrum is a web-based viewer and editor for sheet music in **kern data format, which is the primary music encoding method of

Humdrum. Beside various editing and format converting functions, Verovio Humdrum is also capable of several analyses or so called "filter" tasks, e.g., finding motif imitations or certain chords and intervals. While the overall functionality of Verovio Humdrum seems to be limited in its default form, it can still be highly customised to meet certain scientific goals, such as in the Josquin (Kolb, 2016) or Tasso (Ricciardi and Sapp, 2020) research projects. Sadly, the customisation of Verovio Humdrum requires a high level of programming skills and thus is hardly usable as an educational tool. Also, the **kern data format scheme can be very unintuitive to work with, especially if permanent control of analysed or processed data is required.

Music21 is a Python-based, modular and object-oriented toolkit for analysing, searching and transforming sheet music (Cuthbert and Ariza, 2010). It was developed in the late 2000s as a more accessible alternative to Humdrum. Especially useful are the sheet music rendering capabilities of music21, which allow seamless usage of visual notation at any point. In particular, the code interaction with music21 is very clear and intuitive and, therefore, suitable for educational purposes, even if a basic knowledge of Python may be beneficial. Many functions included in music21 are aimed toward several analytic approaches, such as statistics, chord analysis, motif search or various types of feature extraction (see Cuthbert and Ariza, 2010 for examples).

To sum up, while visual programming languages and their environments are very intuitive and user-friendly, they have restricted usability that does not align with the goals of this project. Music21 offers a lot of powerful and easily accessible analytic capabilities but still requires some programming competence. While Verovio Humdrum can offer similar functionality even in a web-based application without any code commands, it has to be customised for the use case of music analysis beforehand. Since the knowledge required for Verovio Humdrum customisation clearly exceeds the Python code competencies within educational contexts, the project team decided to use music21.

2.3 Data formats for sheet music

Most of the aforementioned tools are built around data formats such as MIDI, **kern, MusicXML or MEI. Despite various conversion methods, however, these formats are still not fully compatible with each other. Moreover, in some cases, part of the data is altered during conversion (López, Vigliensoni and Fujinaga, 2019). Therefore, using only natively supported formats for certain tools or environments is strongly advised. Furthermore, there is a significant difference between older and younger formats. Older formats such as ABC notation, **kern, or even MIDI, to some extent, reduce the information available in sheet music to basic properties such as pitch and duration added by several optional values (e.g., dynamics or lyrics). In contrast, younger formats such as MusicXML and MEI are designed to contain additional layers of information about the visual appearance of sheet music, such as margins, font types or note system brackets. MEI can even include several annotated digitalised versions of a certain sheet music manuscript (Seipelt, 2020) and is currently going to be widely used as a reference standard in various digital edition projects. Although MEI offers many more options for scientific use, it is still barely adopted by any commercial or open-source scorewriter software. However, there is a clear need for editing the sheet music files as a preparation for analysis. Thus, the project team decided to use MusicXML since it is supported by most commercial and open-source editors and all the analysis tools mentioned previously. Despite being highly standardised, MusicXML files lead both to several compatibility issues, in particular, while opening files encoded with older versions (especially 1.x), and to severe rendering issues while opening the same file in different editors (especially in Finale and MuseScore). While software licenses of commercial editors are rather expensive, there are free alternatives such as MuseScore. Since one of the principles of our project was to only use freely available open-source software solutions, the MuseScore editor was used and recommended within the project.

2.4 Jupyter Notebooks as an easy-to-handle tool

Since its introduction in 2013, Jupyter Notebooks has quickly been established as a valuable scientific and educational tool. Jupyter Notebooks are literate programming documents that can be edited within browser software. They combine code, text, and execution results with visualisations and all sorts of rich media (Pimentel et al., 2019). The FMP Notebooks (Notebooks for Fundamentals of Music Processing, see Müller and Zalkow, 2019) are Python-based Jupyter Notebooks. Right now, they can be considered a reference as a scientific and educational resource, especially for various audio-related tasks as well as music information retrieval in general. They are bundled into eight chapters that contain countless code examples for feature extraction and visual representation. In particular, the chapters and Notebooks about sheet music and symbolic music representation were inspiring for us as the starting point for the project. More or less, the project's Notebooks were built as a kind of extension of the FMP Notebooks into topics more specialised in sheet music analysis. Moreover, the environment management proposed by FMP Notebooks (installation of Anaconda or Miniconda with yml file for environment configuration) was applied to the project tools while providing much more detailed installation tutorials aimed especially at students and musicians without any computational background.

Another useful feature of Jupyter Notebooks, which is used in FMP Notebooks as well as in CAMAT is the export of html files. A Notebook, all media included, could be saved as an html file that can be easily put online as a dedicated web page. This can be especially useful for getting an idea of a certain script/code before running it in a Jupyter Notebook or in a Python environment. In an educational context, Jupyter Notebooks could easily be shared by students with tutors or within learning groups.

3 COMPUTER-ASSISTED MUSIC ANALYSIS TOOL (CAMAT)

At the beginning of the project, the overall goals and structure of the tutorials for sheet music analysis were defined: introduction (parsing of files and piano roll representation), statistical analysis, corpus analysis and pattern search. Since there was already familiarity with music21 and the FMP Notebooks, similar libraries and module structures were incorporated for the analysis tasks. Unfortunately, after several tests with the corpus data and with several music21 libraries, there was a requirement for certain optimisations which finally led to the development of CAMAT. The source code, including some provisional documentation, is currently available on GitHub (see https://github.com/Christon-Ragavan/ CAMAT). In the following section, CAMAT's structure and features are discussed in detail.

3.1 Xml parser, pandas DataFrames and issues with MusicXML

One of the first problems during project runtime was persistent error messages during processing MusicXML files with dense chord/polyphonic structures while using music21 as a parser. It mainly concerned some piano and organ sheet music that included a particularly high number of tied notes distributed over multiple voices. Despite trying various available methods, the project team was not able to pinpoint the issue using music21. Therefore, a new parser module was designed and implemented. Python's pandas library was integrated as a container for parsed information so the data could easily be accessed and modified according to the project's needs.

In detail, two particular problems needed attention and modification of the parsed MusicXML data. After checking the correct properties of every note in parsed chords, it turns out that the proper tie information for every single note within a chord was often scattered over multiple voices and was not always consistent with the according MusicXML tags (<chord> tag contain information about ties or other features of every note included). This also may be a reason for the problems we encountered while using music21 with MusicXML. Additionally, the detection of anacrusis or pickup measures was incorrect in most cases. Interestingly enough, while the problem with chords could be solved – only all the necessary information had to be found and matched within available MusicXML tags – the second problem led to the discovery of a deeper issue within the MusicXML syntax. In MusicXML, there is actually no specialised tag structure defined for any kind of measure duration description; thus, you are obliged to calculate it by yourself. As MusicXML is a format built for engraving sheet music, there is no need for tracking the exact durations of every measure anyway since you only care about the correct reproduction of a sheet. This is also not needed for any kind of playback within a score editor since you simply execute the note or rest

	Onset	Duration	Pitch	Octave	MIDI	Measure	LocalOnset	Voice	PartID	PartName	MeasureOnset	MeasureDuration	MeasureDurDiff	TimeSignature	TimeSignatureAdjusted	Upbeat	ChordTag	TieType	GraceTag
0	0.0	6.0	G	4	67.0	1	0.0	1	1	[Superius]	0.0	12.0	0.0	3/1	12/4	False	none	none	none
1	6.0	2.0	A	4	69.0	1	6.0	1	1	[Superius]	0.0	12.0	0.0	3/1	12/4	False	none	none	none
2	8.0	4.0	B	4	71.0	1	8.0	1	1	[Superius]	0.0	12.0	0.0	3/1	12/4	False	none	none	none
3	12.0	4.0	C	5	72.0	2	0.0	1	1	[Superius]	12.0	12.0	0.0	3/1	12/4	False	none	none	none
4	16.0	2.0	B	4	71.0	2	4.0	1	1	[Superius]	12.0	12.0	0.0	3/1	12/4	False	none	none	none
...	...	...	...	...	...	...	...	...	...	...	...	...	...	...	...	...	...	...	...
1048	1100.0	2.0	F	3	53.0	109	4.0	1	4	Contrabassus	1060.0	12.0	8.0	3/1	12/4	True	none	none	none
1049	1102.0	2.0	G	3	55.0	109	6.0	1	4	Contrabassus	1060.0	12.0	6.0	3/1	12/4	True	none	none	none
1050	1104.0	4.0	D	3	50.0	109	2.0	1	4	Contrabassus	1060.0	12.0	6.0	3/1	12/4	True	none	none	none
1051	1108.0	4.0	rest	rest	NaN	110	0.0	1	4	Contrabassus	1072.0	12.0	0.0	3/1	12/4	False	none	none	none
1052	1112.0	8.0	G	3	55.0	110	4.0	1	4	Contrabassus	1072.0	12.0	0.0	3/1	12/4	False	none	none	none

Figure 19.1 Excerpt of several metric features within pandas DataFrame in CAMAT.

events in order. Since the correct metric profiling had to be preserved, however, it was crucial to develop several scripts for validation of the total duration of given measures and to recognise the correct metrical position of all events within. This led to the integration of a simple time-line model. This model converts every available event within a voice into a set of onsets and offsets according to both the defined time signature and the chosen rhythmic resolution. While a quarter note duration was used as a baseline for the model, full fraction and float value support were also included, especially for cases with very short or unusual time signatures and note values. Moreover, a method to adjust all available time signatures to the smallest possible denominator ("TimeSignatureAdjusted") was developed and was used for metric profile calculation in scores with multiple time signatures. An example of a typical set of metric features can be found in Figure 19.1.

Overall, through the implementation of a customised MusicXML parser and various scripts for correct chord and metric profile recognition, a very reliable and robust approach to data extraction has been established that has built a solid basis for various statistical data calculations (see section 3.3) and motif searches (see section 3.4).

3.2 Piano roll visualisation

CAMAT saves the parsed score in a strict timeline structure that can easily be visualised as a piano roll. A piano roll is a simple descriptive notation with a two-dimensional arrangement of all played notes: the y-axis corresponds to the absolute pitch, the x-axis to the passage of time or the bars. It easily uncovers the fabric of the various voices and, therefore, the overall musical texture (Figure 19.2). In CAMAT, different instruments or voices are represented in different colours (see legend at top right). Additionally, a convenient filter function can be used to select and evaluate individual bars or sections as well as individual voices. For the implementation, matplotlib was used for rendering. However, there were problems with visualising large scores, which makes matplotlib very slow, even on powerful computer systems. To avoid these issues, a selection filter was added, which allows to manually select only certain parts of the score (certain voices or measures) and to adjust it to the setup.

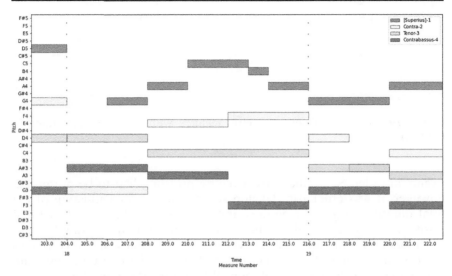

Figure 19.2 Example of a piano roll visualisation in CAMAT.

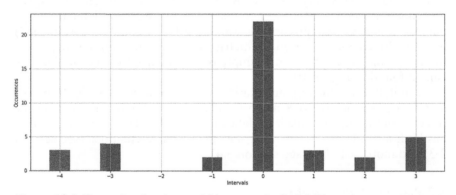

Figure 19.3 Example of an interval histogram in CAMAT.

3.3 Statistical features

With CAMAT, several statistical enquiries can easily be made. Within the current version, frequency distributions (tables, histograms and 3D plots) of the following basic musical features are available: frequencies of pitches and pitch classes, frequencies of interval steps or jumps within a voice (Figure 19.3) and frequencies of note duration values as well as a so-called metric profile that adds up all the notes that sound at particular metric positions. This allows for the fast exploration of basic tonal, melodic, rhythmic and metric characteristics of a composition. Additionally, pitch, pitch class and duration could be combined into two-dimensional frequency distributions and 3-D plots (Figure 19.4). These are just the most basic statistical features that could easily be extended by taking the data from the pandas DataFrame.

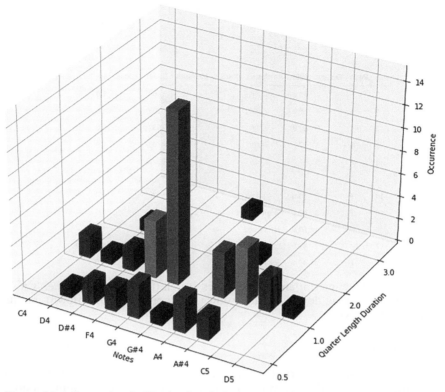

Figure 19.4 Example of a 3D plot for pitch classes vs. duration values in CAMAT.

It is possible to export the frequency distributions as CSV files that can be opened and read with spreadsheet software in order to further process the data. This may be necessary, especially in the context of corpus studies. As with the piano rolls, various filter functions can be used to select individual bars, sections or individual voices.

3.4 Pattern search

Part of CAMAT is a basic search for interval series that works on the full score or selected parts and sections. It could also be used for searching for a certain pitch pattern or motif, including its rhythmic variations and transpositions. The interval sequences to be searched for have to be entered as semitone steps, e.g., [2, 2, −4] (= two whole tones upwards followed by a major third downwards). The output is given as a list of the occurring instances with an indication of the starting note, the voice, the measure and the position in the measure ("LocalOnset") as well as the onset position within the overall score ("Onset") (Figure 19.5). In addition, the frequencies of the results for different starting tones (pitch classes) can be displayed.

```
In [10]:   results_02 = mp.core.search.simple_interval_search(xml_file,
                                          interval=[2, -2, -1, 1, -5],
                                          return_details=True)
           results_02
```

Out[10]:

	Pitch	Octave	MIDI	PartName	PartID	Measure	Onset	LocalOnset
0	F	4	65.0	Violin I	1	1	0.0	1.0
1	F	4	65.0	Violin I	1	9	24.0	1.0
2	B-1	5	82.0	Violin I	1	152	453.0	1.0
3	F	5	77.0	Violin I	1	159	474.0	1.0
4	F	5	77.0	Violin I	1	179	534.0	1.0
...	...	...	...	...	...	...	...	...
14	F	3	53.0	Viola	3	179	534.0	1.0
15	F	3	53.0	Violoncello	4	1	0.0	1.0
16	F	3	53.0	Violoncello	4	9	24.0	1.0
17	B-1	2	46.0	Violoncello	4	119	354.0	1.0
18	F	2	41.0	Violoncello	4	179	534.0	1.0

Figure 19.5 Example for an interval series search ([2, -2, -1, 1, -5], i.e., whole tone up, whole tone down, semitone down, semitone up, fourth down) and its results in CAMAT.

3.5 Corpus statistics

Basic corpus statistics are integrated into CAMAT. Various features from several scores could be compared with each other. In the current version, the comparative queries focus on the frequencies of the following characteristics of each voice or all voices of one or several sheet music files: the total amount of measures, time signatures used, ambitus including lowest and highest note, frequencies of the 12 pitch classes and frequencies of interval steps (up and down). One can choose between absolute frequencies and relative frequencies (percentages). The results of these queries are displayed in tables in the Jupyter Notebook (Figure 19.6) and can easily be exported as a CSV file.

4 ONLINE PRESENTATION OF TOOLS AND TUTORIALS

The project website (https://analyse.hfm-weimar.de) contains all freely accessible educational material (introductions, tutorials, Jupyter Notebooks, sheet music files) that was used and tested in several analysis courses at the Department of Musicology and the Centre of Music Theory, Music University Franz Liszt Weimar, during summer 2021 and winter 2021/22. During this time, the feedback from students and lecturers during the courses led to many optimisations of both the educational material and the software tools.

The website is divided into the following sections: Audio Analysis, Sheet Music Analysis, Sheet Music Database, Installation of the Software,

Out[5]:

	FileName	PartID	PartName	TotalPart	TotalMeasure	PitchMin	PitchMax	Ambitus	TimeSignature	C	C#	D	D#	E	F	F#	G	G#	A	A#	B	<5	-5	-4	-3	-2	-1	0	1	2	3	4	5	5<
0	MoWo_K171_COM_1-1_StringQuar_003_00867	1	Violino I	1	159	A3	A#6	30	[3/4, 4/4]	41	0	66	119	0	59	2	55	51	31	83	4	30	20	19	37	91	78	33	79	36	8	7	20	52
1	MoWo_K171_COM_1-1_StringQuar_003_00867	2	Violino II	1	159	G3	A#5	27	[3/4, 4/4]	60	0	62	110	1	76	2	56	49	29	102	5	19	13	10	27	137	87	36	70	56	23	15	20	38
2	MoWo_K171_COM_1-1_StringQuar_003_00867	3	Viola	1	159	C3	D#5	27	[3/4, 4/4]	23	0	32	57	0	45	0	40	31	18	60	5	18	18	19	15	55	43	14	39	22	12	11	21	24
3	MoWo_K171_COM_1-1_StringQuar_003_00867	4	Violoncello	1	159	D#2	G4	28	[3/4, 4/4]	26	2	22	49	0	33	0	21	19	8	57	4	40	7	9	1	20	22	16	24	53	3	1	30	14
4	MoWo_K171_COM_1-1_StringQuar_003_00867	AllParts	AllParts	4	159	D#2	D#6	48	[4/4, 3/4]	150	2	182	335	1	214	4	172	150	86	302	18	107	58	57	80	303	230	99	212	167	46	34	91	128
5	MoWo_K171_COM_2-1_StringQuar_003_00868	1	None	1	51	G3	G#5	25	[3/4]	8	7	5	40	1	19	2	21	24	4	35	3	3	2	10	10	25	22	48	16	3	11	3	8	8
6	MoWo_K171_COM_2-1_StringQuar_003_00868	2	None	1	51	G3	F5	22	[3/4]	21	21	5	17	0	8	0	6	6	4	16	0	2	2	5	7	16	13	29	11	6	2	2	3	6
7	MoWo_K171_COM_2-1_StringQuar_003_00868	3	None	1	51	D#3	C4	24	[3/4]	9	6	6	28	0	12	0	8	12	1	16	0	2	0	2	14	24	9	16	5	4	5	2	5	8
8	MoWo_K171_COM_2-1_StringQuar_003_00868	4	None	1	51	D#2	C4	21	[3/4]	9	6	5	17	0	6	0	17	21	1	29	0	8	2	7	1	6	7	40	7	15	1	0	11	3
9	MoWo_K171_COM_2-1_StringQuar_003_00868	AllParts	AllParts	4	51	D#2	G#5	41	[3/4]	47	40	20	102	1	45	2	52	63	10	96	3	13	6	24	32	71	53	133	39	28	19	7	27	25
10	MoWo_K171_COM_3-1_StringQuar_003_00869	1	None	1	29	G3	D#6	32	[4/4]	44	1	35	37	5	20	18	39	12	13	17	25	14	17	18	17	39	19	11	39	24	11	6	5	27
11	MoWo_K171_COM_3-1_StringQuar_003_00869	2	None	1	29	G3	G5	24	[4/4]	35	2	36	21	2	14	11	47	14	23	23	9	11	21	18	17	30	27	12	27	23	14	5	15	16
12	MoWo_K171_COM_3-1_StringQuar_003_00869	3	None	1	29	C3	A4	21	[4/4]	22	0	23	15	1	12	9	27	5	5	11	6	10	1	11	18	25	6	10	12	9	6	5	5	17
13	MoWo_K171_COM_3-1_StringQuar_003_00869	4	None	1	29	C2	D#4	27	[4/4]	23	1	24	23	1	12	3	48	8	7	12	4	26	2	8	9	7	14	32	12	13	11	4	13	14
14	MoWo_K171_COM_3-1_StringQuar_003_00869	AllParts	AllParts	4	29	C2	D#6	51	[4/4]	124	4	118	96	9	58	41	161	39	48	63	44	61	41	58	76	101	66	65	90	69	42	20	38	74
15	MoWo_K171_COM_4-1_StringQuar_003_00870	1	None	1	162	G3	G6	36	[3/8]	48	1	45	52	1	83	0	66	33	19	98	0	28	3	2	15	123	50	63	31	68	9	5	9	39
16	MoWo_K171_COM_4-1_StringQuar_003_00870	2	None	1	162	G3	D#6	32	[3/8]	30	0	46	73	0	65	0	45	23	18	72	1	21	6	15	20	71	40	44	40	51	2	16	11	35
17	MoWo_K171_COM_4-1_StringQuar_003_00870	3	None	1	162	C3	D#5	27	[3/8]	26	0	33	70	1	52	0	47	25	10	96	0	12	2	27	26	46	33	91	23	37	9	17	11	25
18	MoWo_K171_COM_4-1_StringQuar_003_00870	4	None	1	162	D2	A#3	20	[3/8]	7	0	23	89	0	26	0	18	33	7	116	0	33	7	5	4	13	10	153	28	20	0	9	25	12
19	MoWo_K171_COM_4-1_StringQuar_003_00870	AllParts	AllParts	4	162	D2	G6	53	[3/8]	111	1	147	284	3	226	0	176	54	114	382	1	94	18	49	65	253	133	351	122	176	20	47	56	111

Figure 19.6 Example for results of a corpus statistic inquiry with CAMAT.

Resources and Documentation (including links to other projects and to some publications), as well as a short project description. Versions in English, German and, for most of the resources, in Spanish are provided.

4.1 Sheet music analysis

With regard to sheet music analysis, three options are offered in parallel: music21 with Jupyter Notebooks, music21 with I-MaT and CAMAT with Jupyter Notebooks. All tutorials and all Jupyter Notebooks for music21 and CAMAT are available in German and English. The contents of all Jupyter Notebooks can be previewed independently of a Python installation as html previews. Finally, for the visualisation of scores as piano rolls, an additional display option with the Sonic Visualiser is offered.

From the music21 Python library for symbolic music representation and processing, several modules for visualisation, statistical investigation (frequency distribution of pitch, pitch classes, duration values, etc.) and motif search have been taken. On that basis, five tutorials have been prepared using several music examples. Based on CAMAT and the pandas DataFrames structure, there are four tutorials focussing on piano rolls, statistical investigations, pattern search and corpus statistics as described in sections 3.2–3.5. All these tutorials can be executed as Jupyter Notebooks. Therefore, a rudimentary knowledge of Python command syntax is required, which is provided in the tutorials. The scores are displayed within Jupyter Notebooks in the browser if a score editor (e.g., MuseScore) has been installed. Another prerequisite for running the Jupyter Notebooks is the installation of Anaconda or Miniconda, as well as the Python environment developed for the project.

However, the handling of the programming code was very unfamiliar to many of the students. To lower this access threshold, another tool was programmed by a student assistant that has the full analysis functions presented within the music21 tutorials but can be operated without any knowledge of Python. While the installation of this Interactive Music Analysis Tool (I-MaT) is relatively simple, the installation of the Python environment is still necessary for running the tool. The tool is executed in a command window. There, various options could be selected without using Python code by entering digits proposed by menu boxes. The results are displayed partly in the command window and partly in external programs for graphics or spreadsheets. Unfortunately, an implementation of CAMAT with I-MaT or with a GUI could not be realised during the project runtime.

As reported previously, Jupyter Notebooks are a very good flexible solution to handle programming code in a transparent and user-friendly manner. However, in the courses, the installation of the Python environment and the Jupyter Notebooks turned out to be a barrier to using the tools. There were several problems related to installation processes and code interaction. Since there are quite a few pitfalls here, detailed installation instructions are provided on the website and supplemented by video tutorials.

4.2 Sheet music database

The sheet music database provided by the project's website includes several thousand sheet music files listed by composer name, which can be used for students' analysis projects, especially for corpus analysis. The scores come from a number of online databases freely available on the internet as well as other research databases and can be used in compliance with Creative Commons licensing. All these score data are converted to MusicXML format using music21. The files can be easily loaded into a score editor, viewed there and listened to (with MIDI sound). Unfortunately, the individual MusicXML files could not have been checked for errors, and, therefore the quality of the data strongly varies depending on the selection. However, a cross-checked sub-corpus of the sheet music database was generated, corresponding to a short (and rather subjective) synopsis of European music history. This sub-corpus includes MusicXML files with scores of vocal music, piano solos, string quartet and symphony, which were checked for quality and with respect to possible errors. This selection also contains all the scores used within the tutorials for sheet music analysis.

4.3 Additional online tutorials and tools for audio analysis

As an additional offering, introductions and tutorials for the analysis of music recordings (Audio Analysis) are included within the educational project and on the website. For a long time now, methods for music analysis have not only referred to the music scores of European music history (historical musicology) but also encompass sound documents from other musical cultures (ethnomusicology) as well as recordings from the history of jazz and popular music (jazz and popular music research). Various computer-based methods for transcription, visualisation and analysis have been adapted, such as spectrograms or descriptive features developed in music information retrieval. The Audio Analysis sites encompass an introduction and two tutorials on spectral representation using the free software Sonic Visualiser (Audio Basics), as well as a short introduction to the field of music information retrieval and to a set of algorithms for sound, chroma and beat analysis freely available as Vamp plugins (Audio Advanced). In addition, there is a tutorial on corpus analysis using the Sonic Annotator and a tutorial on the Sonic Visualiser as a tool for transcription.

5 DISCUSSION

The project aims to contribute to the emerging field of computational music analysis by establishing free computer tools for educational contexts. Emphasis was put on sheet music since most courses in musicology and music theory focus on the analysis of scores. A web-based hub of various resources has been developed, including online introductions and tutorials to freely accessible software tools, as well as a database of free music scores in the MusicXML format. Following an evaluation of several existing tools, music21 libraries and Jupyter Notebooks have been used. However, two additional tools were implemented: The Interactive Music Analysis Tool (I-MaT) can be handled without knowledge of Python commands while providing the full functionality of the music21 Jupyter Notebooks. This is an advantage, especially for students with no programming experience. Moreover, a new tool library for music analysis called CAMAT has been designed that uses a simple timeline model implemented in pandas DataFrames. This solution is open for extensions, e.g., for additional search routines in regard to various tonal, rhythmic or harmonic patterns. With these tools, it is possible to visualise musical textures via piano rolls, to investigate the frequency distribution of pitches, pitch classes, intervals, duration values, notes on different metric positions, etc. – possibilities that are introduced and exemplified in the tutorials.

However, there are still desiderata. Most of all, there is a need for tools for reliable harmonic analysis according to various approaches of music theory. Moreover, during the oral evaluation in several analysis courses, a demand was articulated (by students as well as by the teaching staff) for a general reflection of the merits of computational tools and its mainly quantitative approaches within music analysis methodology. In particular, the goals and purposes of a statistical and comparative approach were questioned and extensively discussed. These discussions echoed Nicholas Cook's objection against computational approaches, according to that "the value of analysis consists primarily in the lengthy process of making it. . . At the end of it, you have a knowledge of the music – you might call it an intimacy – that you did not have at the outset, and there is a sense in which the final graph is significant mainly as a record of this learning process" (Cook, 2004, p. 107). Sometimes, these intimate processes and learning effects are missing within an unthinking usage of computer tools. However, Cook stresses that "[t]he value of objective representations of music, in short, lies principally in the possibility of comparing them and so identifying significant features, and of using computational techniques to carry out such comparisons speedily and accurately" (Cook, 2004, p. 109). Nonetheless, in educational contexts, there seems to be a kind of gap between understanding the functionality of a certain tool and its successful usage within a certain analytical issue or use case. While it is evident that computer tools can successfully and reliably substitute rather monotonous tasks such as counting pitches or finding interval patterns, there have to be more analytical examples that demonstrate that the distribution of pitches or interval patterns can actually contribute to a better understanding of the compositions or corpora and their distinct style. As a first step in this direction, appropriate examples of statistical queries and pattern searches are included within the tutorials that showcase analytical issues and findings within 'real scores', e.g., a Mozart string quartet, a mass by Josquin or a string quartet by Beethoven. These tutorials should encourage students to try the tools out with the music they like and/or are familiar with. Additionally, an online hub has been launched where everybody is welcome to upload their own analytical use cases as PDF files and find inspiration by examining analytical findings made by other students with the help of the tools.

6 OUTLOOK

Alongside the maintenance and optimisation of the already available resources, as well as further improvements in practical integration of our tools within running music analysis courses, the general functionality of CAMAT could be expanded into several directions.

First of all, the timeline data concept using pandas DataFrames for extracting sheet music information along with certain basic musical features presents the potential to be expanded towards a variety of analytical tasks. For example, CAMAT could easily be used for the synchronisation of note events with audio or sensor data as well as for more advanced search routines implementing various binary matrix solutions, e.g., searches for chord progression or fuzzy motif and pattern search – which was already requested by many students and colleagues. In this way, CAMAT could form a starting point for several scientific and educational extensions that will be approached in the near future. Besides, everybody is free to take the existing Python scripts from GitHub and contribute to their further development.

Additionally, we are working towards support of the MEI format in order to ensure full compatibility with current and prospective digital editions of sheet music – not least in order to improve the quality of the scores available for computational analysis. Moreover, we are looking forward to evaluating the Verovio interface as an alternative approach for the implementation of several CAMAT functions and testing its practical accessibility in comparison with Jupyter Notebooks. The unique combination of sheet music rendering, editing and analysis functions within a single browser-based interface that barely requires any code interaction could constitute an easy-to-handle extension of our current approach.

7 ACKNOWLEDGEMENTS

The project *Computergestützte Musikanalyse in der digitalen Hochschullehre* was funded by the Thuringian Ministry for Economy, Science and Digital Change and the Stifterverband, see www.stifterverband.org/digital-lehrfellows-thueringen/2020/pfleiderer (accessed 22 December 2022).

REFERENCES

Cannam, C., Landone, C. and Sandler, M. (2010). 'Sonic Visualiser: An Open Source Application for Viewing, Analysing, and Annotating Music Audio Files', in *MM '10: Proceedings of the 18th ACM International Conference on Multimedia*. New York: Association for Computing Machinery, pp. 1467–1468.

Cook, N. (2004). 'Computational and Comparative Musicology', in Clarke, E. and Cook, N., eds. *Empirical Musicology. Aims, Methods, Prospects*. Oxford and New York: Oxford University Press, pp. 103–126.

Cuthbert, M. S. and Ariza, C. (2010). 'Music21: A Toolkit for Computer-Aided Musicology and Symbolic Music Data', in Stephen Downie, J. and Veltkamp, R. C., eds. *11th International Society for Music Information Retrieval Conference (ISMIR 2010)*, August 9–13. Utrecht, Netherlands: International Society for Music Information Retrieval, pp. 637–642.

Eerola, T. and Toiviainen, P. (2004). *MIDI Toolbox. MATLAB Tools for Music Research*. Jyväskylä: University of Jyväskylä.

Fang, M. (2012). *Utilizing OpenMusic as a Tool for the Analysis of Lutoslawski's Chain2.* London: LAP LAMBERT Academic Publishing.

Hewlett, W. B. and Selfridge-Field, E. (1991). 'Computing in Musicology, 1966–91', *Computers in Human*, 25, pp. 381–392. https://doi.org/10.1007/BF00141188.

Huron, D. (1999). *Music Research Using Humdrum. A User's Guide*. Available at: http://ccarh.org/publications/manuals/humdrumuserguide/humdrum-usersguide-1998.pdf [Accessed: 22 December 2022].

Kolb, P. (2016). 'The Josquin Research Project. http://josquin.stanford.edu/', *Zeitschrift der Gesellschaft für Musiktheorie*, 13(2), pp. 351–354. https://doi.org/10.31751/920.

López, N. N., Vigliensoni, G. and Fujinaga, I. (2019). 'The Effects of Translation Between Symbolic Music Formats: A Case Study with Humdrum, Lilypond, MEI, and MusicXML', in *Music Encoding Conference 2019*. Available at: https://napulen.github.io/publication/effects_of_translation/ [Accessed: 22 December 2022].

Manzo, V. J. (2011). *Max/MSP/Jitter for Music: A Practical Guide to Developing Interactive Music Systems for Education and More*. New York: Oxford University Press.

Müller, M. and Zalkow, F. (2019). 'FMP Notebooks: Educational Material for Teaching and Learning Fundamentals of Music Processing', in *Proceedings of the International Conference on Music Information Retrieval (ISMIR)*. Delft, The Netherlands. Available at: www.audiolabs-erlangen.de/resources/MIR/FMP/data/C0/2019_MuellerZalkow_FMP_ISMIR.pdf [Accessed: 22 December 2022].

Neuwirth, M. and Rohrmeier, M. (2016). 'Wie wissenschaftlich muss Musiktheorie sein? Chancen und Herausforderungen musikalischer Korpusforschung', *Zeitschrift der Gesellschaft für Musiktheorie*, 13(2), pp. 171–193. https://doi.org/10.31751/915.

Pimentel, J. F., Murta, L., Braganholo, V. and Freire, J. (2019). 'A Large-Scale Study About Quality and Reproducibility of Jupyter Notebooks', in *2019 IEEE/ACM 16th International Conference on Mining Software Repositories (MSR)*, pp. 507–517. https://doi.org/10.1109/MSR.2019.00077.

Poliakov, E. (2020). 'Computerbasierte Analyse und visuelle Repräsentationsformen der Musik im Kontext der neuesten Entwicklungen im Bereich Computer/Multimedia und deren Integration in musikologische Forschung und Lehre', *Schriften Online: Musikwissenschaft*, 11, pp. 148–170. Available at: https://nbn-resolving.org/urn:nbn:de:bsz:14-qucosa2-723858 [Accessed: 22 December 2022].

Ricciardi, E. and Sapp, C. (2020). *Editing Italian Madrigals in the Digital World: The Tasso in Music Project*. http://doi.org/10.17613/17a5-2b65.

Roure, D. C. and Willcox, P. (2017). 'Numbers into Notes: Digital Prototyping as Close Reading of Ada Lovelace's "Note A"', in *Digital Humanities 2017*, Montreal, Canada. Available at: https://dh2017.adho.org/abstracts/540/540. pdf [Accessed: 22 December 2022].

Schüler, N. (2007). 'From Musical Grammars to Music Cognition in the 1980s and 1990s: Highlights of the History of Computer-Assisted Music Analysis', *Musicological Annual*, 43(2), pp. 371–396. https://doi.org/10.4312/mz.43.2.371-396.

Seipelt, A. (2020). Digitale Edition und Harmonische Analyse mit MEI von Anton Bruckners Studienbuch. Aktuelle Perspektiven. Bericht über die Jahrestagung der Gesellschaft für Musikforschung 2019 in Paderborn und Detmold, Bd. 3', in *Detmold: Musikwissenschaftliches Seminar der Universität Paderborn und der Hochschule für Musik Detmold*, pp. 105–113. Available at: https://nbn-resolving.org/urn:nbn:de:bsz:14-qucosa2-727492 [Accessed: 22 December 2022].

20

A new morphology

Strategies for innovation in live electronics performance

Mattias Petersson

1 INTRODUCTION

The general starting point for this study is an investigation into how different agents in musicking systems involving live electronics can work and co-evolve together. One of the main aims is to gain knowledge about how live electronics ensembles, understood as scalable systems of interconnected human and non-human agents, can aid in revealing the adaptation process required by a participating musician. Patched-up systems of agents can be studied on macro-, meso- and micro-levels. Thus, by zooming in or out, the possibilities of studying such systems span from individual (functions of) agents to complex networks of ensembles. A second aim of this study is to better understand how to create models for musical interaction that enable an awareness of all constituent agents as necessary for a certain kind of musicking. Building on such a mindset, another overarching aim is to begin uncovering the idiomaticity of the live electronic instrument, to better understand it as an epistemic tool (Magnusson, 2009) and to reach for its ontological foundations. In this chapter, I propose an understanding of the live electronic instrument as a modular system of human and non-human agents – a cybernetic system in which the distribution of agencies becomes a defining part of the instrumentality. With this understanding, the use cases presented in this study may contribute to establishing a basis for a new musical morphology for live electronics.

1.1 Background

The Royal Live Electronics ensemble (RLE) was founded by the author in 2006 at the Royal College of Music in Stockholm (KMH). It is included in the curriculum for the first two years of the bachelor program in electro-acoustic composition and is also available as an elective course for other students. In practice, the arrangement means that the ensemble usually consists of between 10–16 musicians and can vary quite a lot between the years, both in terms of instrumentation and the students' previous experience of live electronics performance. Because of the general lack of standards within the field of live electronics, a fundamental concept of RLE has been to keep

DOI: 10.4324/9781003118817-22

individual instrumental setups open in terms of aesthetics and technology. The ambition has instead been to build further upon any prior knowledge and instruments that the students bring. In acknowledging that an adaptation process on the meso-level (i.e., instrument setups) is necessary for all players in such an ensemble combined with a macro-level perspective on the ensemble as a whole, a formation of a shared ensemble voice is enabled.

Hence, RLE is not a laptop orchestra (LOrk). However, a simplified version of PLOrk's (see plork.princeton.edu) meta-instrument concept, as described by Smallwood et al. (2008), has been used. For RLE, this consists of one mono speaker per player and a small mixer shared with one other player. This otherwise open arrangement can seem blurry compared to more conceptually driven ensembles. A foundational question that emanates from the work with RLE is how we deal with this blur in practice and how this feature instead can be turned into a catalyst for reaching the aims of this study. Other, more concrete questions that follow include how we revise our setups to fit the ensemble situation, what it is that causes the need for adaptation and how it is carried out, and also in what way this process can facilitate and stimulate the formation of the musicians' individual voices. However, to limit the scope, this study focuses on our understanding of the instruments themselves and how they are situated in a musicking context.

1.2 Research questions

The following research questions will be addressed in this study:

- How are live electronic instruments understood by musicians and composers in the context of live electronics ensembles?
- How do the pieces, strategies and systems presented in this study relate to the situated understanding of the instrument?

To answer these questions, the study combines an empirical data set comprised of strategies, pieces and systems used both during the course and in collaborative projects. Further, a survey aimed towards students participating in RLE was carried out, and the results were then subject to a thematic analysis. The complete design of the study is further described in what follows.

2 FOUNDATIONS

This section outlines the theoretical, aesthetic, and practical foundations for this study and the basis for the Royal Live Electronics Ensemble's course curriculum. To understand the nature of live electronics and how it might differ from other musical instruments, a critical reflection on this issue is used as a point of departure. This leads to a more sociological perspective based on the concept of musicking systems design combined with posthuman views of agency and shared experiences. Finally, some examples of how the work within KMH's ensemble has been shaped according to these ideas are presented.

2.1 Musical instruments

Understood as a material object, a musical instrument carries "sonic and musical possibilities and limitations, with its own history of development" (Alperson, 2008, p. 37). This shapes our awareness and understanding of different types of music. Striving for a "more robust philosophical view of musical instruments" (ibid. p. 38), Alperson argues for an inclusion of immaterial aspects in its ontology, stating that "[t]he moment they are musical instruments they are musically, culturally, and conceptually situated objects" (ibid. p. 42). He explains how electronic instruments, in general, and software-based ones in particular, shine light on the fact that it is the intention behind the instruments, along with their usage, that defines them rather than their material properties.

Akin to Alperson, Thor Magnusson states that an "instrument is concretised music theory" (Magnusson, 2019, p. 5) and an epistemic tool (Magnusson, 2009). This embedded theory and knowledge implies that the instrument maker, the musician or the composer – who, of course, can be one and the same person – has had an intention with their approach to the constituent components of what is to be used as a musical instrument. A conscious aesthetic ambition is included from the beginning. A possibly significant difference between traditional acoustic and electronic musical instruments seems to be hinted at in these ambitions. In the first case, one departs from *a single existing tradition* of practice with sonorous ideals and idioms that a musician adheres to, together with others within the same guild. This involves accepting the sum of aesthetic choices made within a tradition of luthiers, a well-defined instrumental idiomaticity and the context from which it springs. When it comes to the field of live electronics, one is confronted with the initial task of assembling an instrument. This task is often a continuous process of trial and error, using different combinations of tools, that usually results in an eclectic, unique collection of sound-generating and sound-manipulating entities with disparate genre belongings and aesthetic roots. Here, the instrument becomes *a manifestation of several combined paradigms and traditions* composed by one musician. Further, the instrument is not something you have to accept as a fixed object. It can be changed dynamically as new musical ideas and needs arise. Of course, all musical instruments develop as new performers discover and explore new affordances, but in the case of live electronics, even the physical core of a setup can change radically, not only the relational dynamics between musician and instrument.

Electronic instruments often show this ability to mutate. Per-Anders Nilsson (2011) uses two parallel timelines to describe the phenomenon: The first is *Design Time,* where the actual instrument building and the creation of conditions for a certain kind of musicking happen. The second is *Play Time,* which describes the actual music making where a musician makes use of a design's affordances (Gibson, 1977). In some contexts, however, these processes merge. For example, in a modular synthesiser, the instrumentality is not defined by the modules themselves but by how they are interconnected. With the help of patch cables, control signals can be applied to different musical parameters, and by re-patching a few cords, radically different results can be achieved. The unpatched modular synth is thus nothing more than a possible future actualisation, as different patches are perceived as different instruments. In the same way, a live electronics ensemble can be understood as a modular system in which each specific setup actualises a certain instrumentality. To achieve a robust conceptualisation of such systems, a cybernetic perspective is useful.

Technically, most musical instruments consist of one or more sound-generating or sound-processing functions. These functions can be enclosed in one or more physical or virtual bodies, which in turn can be affected by manual as well as automatic and algorithmic processes. However, as pointed out by Alperson (2008), a musicking intent is necessary for these functional bodies to come into existence as musical instruments. Informed by cybernetics, Herbert Heyde (1975) made an attempt to describe musical instruments as systems of human and non-human agents connected in a feedback network. According to this view, different agencies in a system evolve together (Latour, 1991, p. 117) and merge into a cyborg. Applying a view on musical instruments as cybernetic entities thus reveals that a player is required for its actual becoming. Similarly, Alperson argues that "our understanding of the musical art" (Alperson, 2008, p. 37) is defined by "the musician playing the musical instrument" (ibid.). He concludes that "[w]hat counts is that an object takes its place in the world of musical practice as something that can be used as a musical instrument" (Alperson, 2008, p. 38).

In the case of live electronic instruments, the non-human agencies can actively affect one another, and a cybernetic perspective emphasises how such instruments can be reconfigured to also change their "dimensionality of control" (Pressing, 1990, p. 14). An addition of a new device to an existing instrument setup, changes not only the local possibilities for expressiveness inherent in this specific tool but also the affordances of the system on a global level. The agents themselves and how they are patched together can change – even during a performance. Is an ontology for such instruments even possible to consider? What can we know about an instrument with such radically transforming affordances?

The unstable, fluctuating state significant for live electronic instruments is perhaps one of their most defining characteristics and is possibly most clearly manifested in the live coding community. A typical performance in this scene involves a few lines of code projected behind the performer, allowing the audience to follow the process of real-time modifications and edits that move the music in different directions. There are of course several aesthetic currents within this scene, but the basic, and still very influential, ideas were formulated as a manifesto (Ward et al., 2004) by a loose association of live coders called *TopLap* already in the early 00s.

Live coding further blurs the boundaries between Design Time and Play Time (Nilsson, 2011). It is not obvious where a composition begins and the instruments it is performed on end. A change in the code can simultaneously build a new instrument and change the structure of the composition. The musician thus has the power to dissolve the traditional division of roles. In performing her piece *Wezen–Gewording*, Marije Baalman confirms that "[i]t is hard to distinguish if a particular segment of code is part of the instrument, of the composition, or even the performance, or perhaps all of these at the same time" (Baalman, 2016, p. 229). Such a system of interconnected agencies is permeated with flux and blurriness but also enables embodied and artistic understanding of the current state of the patch.

2.2 Interactive music(king) systems

A frequently used strategy for live electronics performances is to create an interactive music system (IMS) for musicians to play with. For example, feedback systems such as no-input mixers and self-resonating vibrotactile instruments (SRI), as found in the work of Alice Eldridge and Chris Kiefer (see, e.g., Eldridge et al., 2021) and in my own piece *Sinew0od* (see Petersson and Ek, 2022), involves musicians engaging in constant negotiation with IMS, with varying degrees of stability. The creative use of artificial intelligence and machine learning (see, e.g., Visi and Tanaka, 2021), accessible tools like the *Fluid Corpus Manipulation* library (2022) and where the AI becomes an active co-player with an aesthetic agenda of its own (see, e.g., Gioti, 2021) are other examples pointing in this direction.

Acknowledging the social, cultural and immaterial aspects of such systems (see, e.g., Small, 1998; Latour, 2007), but also the cybernetic perspectives on musical instruments discussed previously, an expanded understanding of the concept as interactive *musicking* systems is used in this chapter. Similar systems are described by De Souza (2018) as *Orchestra Machines*, which conceptually includes traditional symphony orchestras as well as laptop ensembles such as PLOrk (Smallwood et al., 2008), but also The Machine Orchestra (Kapur et al., 2011) in which the players collectively control robotic instruments. The latter ensembles explore ideas of shared control of sonic structures by means of networked computers in various ways.

In a book chapter, pianist Deniz Peters draws from experiences working with a particular IMS and suggests that "instrumentality can be distributed in the sense that it can be established across various instruments and various players" (Peters, 2016, p. 69). By means of microphones and transducer speakers, he describes how a violin and various flutes could be given bi-directional agency to both influence and be influenced by the piano. Peters explains the phenomenon of their "trio [having] become a quartet. The fourth, semi-autonomous voice suggests that, next to the separate instruments, the interconnectedness of the instruments creates a new instrument" (ibid, p. 74).

An example of how these systems can be expanded with network technologies is the recent *Global Hyperorgan* project (Harlow et al., 2021), in which the *TCP/Indeterminate Place Quartet* (see Ek et al., 2021) created a scenario for telematic musicking with hyperorgans, connecting instruments in Piteå and Amsterdam. Utilising a live coding interface together with an electric MIDI guitar, a clarinet and various gestural controllers, a modular IMS with shared agencies distributed among the two geographically dispersed organs, was established.

To develop ideas and strategies for performance, RLE has for several years collaborated with the UK-based ensemble *Dirty Electronics* (2022) led by John Richards at De Montfort University in Leicester (see Kungl.

Musikhögskolan, 2014; sonodrome, 2014). Their work of composition and performance begins on the workbench with instrument design and conceptualisation. This method, where the making and the shared experience of the building process are foundational, arguably leads to a significantly deeper understanding of the instrument than if someone else had built it for you. It also raises questions regarding to what extent the instrument and the piece are inseparable and where the work identity lies. As another example of when the boundary between Design Time and Play Time (Nilsson, 2011) gets blurry, Richards (2011) discusses whether the schematics of an instrument or even the instrument itself can be considered a score and where we should draw the line between making and playing. The process is also characterised by testing different solutions to problems together, and often participants are encouraged to explore a shared instrumentality during the design process. During RLE's visit to Leicester in 2014, the group set out to build a simple instrument called *The Bed of Nails* as an introductory workshop (see Figure 20.1). It consists of a simple, open

Figure 20.1 The Bed of Nails by John Richards and Dirty Electronics, built by Mattias Petersson.

circuit that can be closed by touching nails connected to a small amplifier. The body's ability to conduct current and its resistance are utilised and have a direct effect on the sonic affordances. This was then expanded into a shared instrument requiring two bodies to close the circuit by placing a Bed of Nails between them at the feet. When the bare feet are in contact with the instrument, the musicians can influence the sound by touching each other. It became an improvisational piece for five instruments and ten musicians conducted by Richards (sonodrome, 2014 at 6:53).

3 DESIGN OF THE STUDY

The study takes off from the theoretical and conceptual foundations presented previously. An analysis of the aesthetic and pedagogic foundations of the RLE course, paired with a critical reflection on how the live electronic instrument can be understood, have led me to adopt a sociologically driven perspective based on the concept of musicking systems design, combined with a posthuman view on agency and shared experiences. Examples of strategies, composed pieces and systems shaped according to these ideas are presented in what follows. Thus, the pieces presented are part of the empirical data set.

A survey was also conducted for this study. The questions were aimed primarily at the students who participated in the course during the autumn semester of 2019 but also some students who took the course earlier responded. Several of the respondents have been involved in RLE for many years and can therefore be considered to have extensive experience of this particular ensemble. The answers were collected anonymously, and the students received information about the purpose of the study and that the results would be used as a basis for future research. Ten students responded to the questionnaire. A thematic analysis of the survey results has been made.

The presented strategies, pieces and systems have been analysed and correlated with both the intentions behind them and the results of the survey. As a teacher, I have, besides composing pieces and designing IMS for the course, also participated as a musician in the ensemble. Therefore, an empirical approach where the survey results and the experiences of collaboration with the Dirty Electronics ensemble are compared with my own development in terms of instrument design and playing with and composing for live electronics. The notion of the ensemble as a scalable musicking system and shared instrumentality lays a foundation for the methodology.

3.1 Ethical considerations

The comparison of the different subjective viewpoints presented in the study, both by students and other professionals in the field, constitutes a fundamental analytical perspective. Hence, while the methods used in the study and the results they generate cannot be considered completely free from bias, the advantages of a pre-understanding are essential for the analysis. The respondents to the survey have been anonymised but were aware that they responded directly to their teacher, which can influence their responses. The author of the study is also the originator of both course content and analysed course material to a large extent. While this provides an inside perspective crucial to the study, it inevitably makes the analysis less objective. Informed consent has been obtained from all named students.

4 STRATEGIES, PIECES, SYSTEMS

To enable a modular approach for live electronic musicking, taking into account not only instrument setups but also the various aesthetic traditions and preferences human and non-human agents carry, the notions of 'piece' and 'authorship' need consideration. Within RLE, an outspoken ambition has been that improvisation concepts and compositions should preferably facilitate negotiation of both roles and structure as well as open up for the individual player's formation of voice by means of instrument design. Hence, a collective approach towards musical results is often necessary. Many of the strategies that have been proven useful for such musicking situations include rule-based improvisation structures. Such pieces often start off as very open but are collectively steered and re-composed by the ensemble during the rehearsal process. When successful, these musicking systems can evoke a collective musical consciousness and a distributed instrumentality, as described by Deniz Peters (2016). In the following, a series of examples of such interactions through strategies, pieces and systems used in the context of RLE are presented.

4.1 Variations II

One recurring example of a piece with these qualities is Johns Cage's *Variations II* (1961), where the realisation of the score itself requires an elaborate procedure (see, e.g., Pritchett, 2000). Five students from RLE collaborated to make their version of the score (see Figure 20.2) for a concert at the Museum of Modern Art in Stockholm (Moderna Museet, 2012), and this score has since been reused several times in both rehearsal and concert contexts.

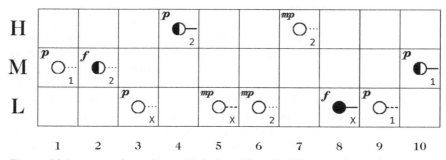

Figure 20.2 A page from Cages Variations II realised by members of The Royal Live Electronics Ensemble in Stockholm, 2012.

In the score, L, M and H indicate registers (Low, Mid, High). Each box denotes a pre-agreed time period (e.g., one minute) to perform the assigned audio event(s) within. The numbers 1 and 2 in each box indicate how many times the specified audio event should occur. X means that the player can choose any number of events. The character of the sound is specified with circles. A white circle indicates a tonal sound, a black one denotes a complex, noisy sound and a black and white circle means something in between. The lines that follow the circles indicate the profile and length of the sound. A dotted line refers to a short event, a dashed one to a medium and a solid line to a long sound. The practical implications of long and short are up to the musician and the ensemble to negotiate within the given time period. Traditional dynamic designations are also found in the score.

4.2 Find & replace

Although not specific to live electronics ensembles, an effective method to strengthen the notion of a shared musicking system is to work with distributed rhythmic patterns in the ensemble. In such exercises, it is obvious that everyone is equally important for some kind of groove to occur and that everyone has agency within the group. An observation made over the years is that these exercises often lead to individual musicians becoming more inclined to take initiatives in other types of exercises as well. Besides simple rehearsal concepts, more formalised pieces based on these ideas have been performed by RLE. One example is the piece *Find & Replace* (Petersson, 2019a), which revolves around an animated score (see Figure 20.3) where the musicians alternate between three different roles:

- Beat – play a repeated rhythmic pattern with the indicated length in beats.
- Find – find and play the first resulting pattern that comes to mind as you listen to the current, collectively produced, beat.
- Replace – contrast the ensemble beat with longer, non-percussive sounds.

While performing the piece, the players follow a blinking metronome with the option of an added tempo-synced delay line that bounces each player's sounds around the room, enhancing the collectively produced groove.

In the animated score pictured in Figure 20.3, every numbered ray in the star polygon is a musician in the ensemble. While the star itself remains fixed during a performance, the outer circles, denoting musical functions, change dynamically. The circled numbers assign a Beat pattern function to the respective player, and the digit indicates the length of the pattern to be played. In the pictured version of the score, there are patterns of 5, 7 and 9 beats. Those patterns are always negotiated within the ensemble during rehearsals but usually settle on fairly simple ones (e.g., playing a sound on every first and last beat) and should be repeated as long as the respective ray points to it. Players with the same pattern number have been visualised

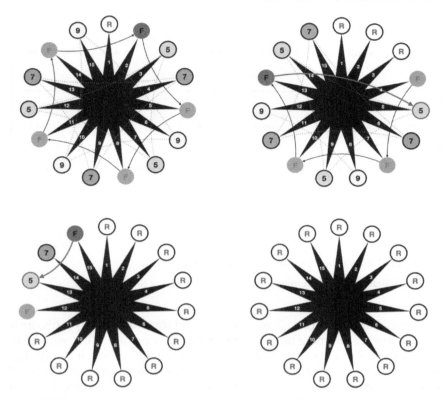

Figure 20.3 From the animated score for *Find & Replace*.

*Source:*Petersson (2019a)

with dashed lines and the numbers are also colour-coded to strengthen the awareness of other members within these subgroups. The Find function, indicated by an F and coloured red, is assigned to one player at a time and arrows show how this soloist function will move between players for the coming periods. As the piece progresses, the pattern functions are gradually replaced by extended, non-percussive sounds. This is indicated by an R in the score. The image at the bottom right is the penultimate in the score. There, all rhythmic patterns have been replaced by continuous sounds.

4.3 Oblique strategies

When Brian Eno and Peter Schmidt created their famous deck of cards called *Oblique Strategies* in 1975, the premise was that it would aid decision-making when you got stuck in the studio. Each card has more or less clear suggestions for how to move forward in the creative process. Based on a selection of these cards, excluding the most studio-specific, I composed a generative, animated score that serves as a basis for improvisation (Petersson, 2010).

The score is projected on the wall so that the audience can follow along, and each musician is presented with their own deck of cards. Sometimes,

Listen to the quiet voice	Repetition is a form of change	Use an unacceptable color
Don't be afraid of things because they're easy to do	Humanize something free of error	You can only make one dot at a time
Towards the insignificant	Remember those quiet evenings	Only one element of each kind

Figure 20.4 From the dynamic score of *Oblique Strategies*.

Source: Adapted for live electronics ensemble by Petersson (2010)

cards are changed for one player at a time, and sometimes everyone's cards are changed at the same time. In this piece, the structure is determined to some extent. For example, once a time unit is decided upon, it always has the same total duration, and the timing between different types of card changes is predictable. However, chance controls the order of the different players' changes and which cards show up. Further, the same player cannot get the same card multiple times. The piece begins with the projection fading in, and the musicians are instructed to select a starting sound and fade it in along with the score. Then, they follow the instructions of the cards (see Figure 20.4) throughout the piece.

This piece has been played quite a few times with varying types of ensembles, and even if the same ensemble plays it twice, it can have very different results. Since you never get the same series of cards, the musicians must enter a state where they are prepared for everything and, at the same time, balance what they do with the instructions on the card with the currently prevailing structure in the ensemble as a whole. The piece has also proved useful for an ensemble such as RLE, where prior knowledge in improvisation can vary greatly. Here, everyone can participate in any capacity, and it quickly becomes clear that practice makes the piece better. The suggestions on the cards also immediately force the player to explore instrumental affordances, which in turn reveal any unintentional limitations in individual setups, thus enabling useful adaptations to be made.

4.4 Focus and Oblique Focus

After working with my adaptation of *Oblique Strategies* since 2010, I made a variant of it called *Focus* (Petersson, 2019b). Here, Eno's and Schmidt's, often quite esoteric, suggestions are replaced by more direct,

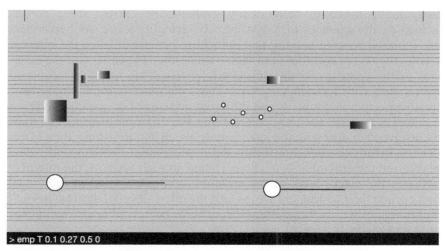

> emp T 0.1 0.27 0.5 0

Figure 20.5 A prototype card from an early version of *Oblique Focus*.

*Source:*Petersson (2022)

musically applicable keywords during the performance. The cards now suggest what the player should focus on at the moment. Some examples of used keywords are *Initiative, Affect, Unison, Repetition, Opposites, Simplicity, Mimicry* and *Memory*. These words were inspired by Cornelius Cardew's list of "Virtues that a musician can develop" in the essay *Towards an ethics of improvisation* (Cardew, 1971). Instead of projecting the score in its entirety, in this version, the cards were distributed to the players over a local network so that everyone could follow along via their smartphone or laptop.

As part of this study, *Focus* has also been tested as an IMS for one musician by the author. Using the same instrument normally used as a performer in the RLE ensemble (a self-made SuperCollider-based system controlled by a Snyderphonics Manta (Snyder, 2011)), with the addition of a modular synthesiser, the score was played several times. A shorter time unit was used for these performances, allowing for intuitive, memory-based, in-the-moment comparisons between different run-throughs.

In a recent development of this system called *Oblique Focus* (Petersson, 2022) the players can 'live-code' new cards for other players using a symbolic language based on a combination of Pierre Schaeffer's taxonomy of sounds and recent sound notation research (e.g., Sköld, 2018, 2019, 2020) (see Figure 20.5). Here, the machine itself can also be allowed to interfere to various degrees, e.g., by handing out new cards for everyone after a period of low activity.

4.5 Summary

The strategies, pieces and systems presented in this section can all be understood as interactive musicking systems in which the players are individually asked to aesthetically evaluate the current sonic corpus guided by the agencies of a dynamically changing score. As performers are required to take actions that somehow benefit or alter the musical whole, they must consider both their own aesthetic agendas and the agencies of the context and the musicking system. This leads to a constant negotiation with instrument setups. Thus, the other ensemble members, their respective instruments and the dynamic scores become co-players in a complex system, not only patched into the different instrument setups themselves but also with the agency to re-patch and transform their affordances. In turn, this also transforms the artistic voice of both the individual player and the ensemble as a whole. Hence, in such systems, the interplay between the macro-level of the ensemble, the meso-level of individual players and their instrument setups, and the micro-level of discrete devices and functions within these setups can often be perceived as an intelligence with an agenda of its own.

5 RESULTS OF THE SURVEY

Since the survey was aimed towards Swedish-speaking students only, all the responses are in Swedish. In the section below, the student from whom the quote originates is indicated as (S#) following their words, translated by the author. The edits, shown in brackets, are made for grammatical reasons only. To interpret the survey results, five different labels were used as a basis for a thematic analysis:

1   The instrument as a dynamic process
2   Adaptation as practice
3   Aesthetic vs. technical needs
4   Ensemble roles
5   Ensemble size

The first theme involves respondents describing how their instruments were continuously developed and refined during the course and how all "rehearsals made [them] realise something that need[ed] to be changed" (S7). The answers here suggest that a dynamic change of instruments is part of the practice of a live electronics musician and how this includes the "build[ing of] an instrument that [one] needs for a given situatio[n]" (S8). In this category, software environments like Max or SuperCollider are mentioned as more suitable than hardware because they provide the necessary flexibility.

A second, clearly discernible theme (related to the first) is the notion of *adaptation as practice*. Respondents in this category describe how using "an instrument [he/she already] knew to focus on the interplay rather than on learning [a new] instrument" (S1) enables a new understanding of instrumental affordances. The adaptation of the instrument emanates from the ensemble situation, and the process seems very similar to practising a traditional instrument.

The third theme concerns responses discussing *aesthetic vs. technical needs*. This involves expanding sonic possibilities in order to deviate from the music theory and aesthetics embodied within an existing setup. One respondent describes how they transformed from using "mostly noise" to also being able to "play notes and rhythm because the pieces that were played required these musical qualities" (S6). These respondents depart from a need for aesthetic rather than technical adaptation but can also be interpreted as if the act of expanding one's sonic possibilities (e.g., through technical adaptation) is not a big deal but a part of the duties of a live electronics musician.

Several respondents directly or indirectly mention how certain instruments and ways of playing work less well in the ensemble. This fourth theme, labelled *ensemble roles*, includes one respondent describing how they intended to use processed singing but refrained from doing so due to the fear of being ascribed a soloist function. Obviously, the acoustic voice will stand out in the room if all other sounds stem from speakers. Another respondent explains how they have "reduced [their] instrument to one voice" (S2), unlike the usual starting point where they, as a solo artist, "[rather is] a conductor of the machine as an electronic/digital orchestra" (S2). In other words, DAW-based setups (e.g., Ableton Live, Bitwig, etc.) are often considered to be full digital orchestras intended to be handled by one person.

The last theme derived from the survey analysis is the matter of *ensemble size*. Several respondents express that the size of the ensemble is what forced the need for adaptations, and they also emphasise the importance of being able to be silent. Some expressed a frustration over the great colossus that a 15-musician large live electronics ensemble constitutes. Many of the instruments used can easily outpower all others sonically. Especially at the beginning of the course, each student's table with instruments tends to comprise a full live electronics orchestra in itself. One respondent says that there can be a desire to show off your self-made instrument and to try it for real when you get a chance, which can easily conflict with the necessary ensemble discipline. When there is no conductor, a lot of responsibility is placed on the individual players to keep this discipline. At the same time, the sessions need a recurring element of instrument demonstrations with the ambition to share new ideas and build an understanding of the limitations and possibilities that exist in the ensemble.

6 DISCUSSION

Acknowledging a live electronics ensemble as a modular system of human and non-human agents implies that what was usually considered a 'small' ensemble in a traditional musicking context should often be understood as a complex and very large orchestra machine (De Souza, 2018) when live electronics are involved. While a string quartet will remain a string quartet, four live electronic players could indeed be a quartet of full orchestras.

Thus, in developing interactive musicking systems for live electronics ensembles, one needs to take this hidden ensemble size into account.

In contrast to the open IMS described in this chapter, there are pieces where a custom-made instrument is provided by the composer. According to both the survey results and the experiences from collaborating with the Dirty Electronics ensemble, this seems to strengthen the notion of the musical work as something static. Such pieces often leave little room for interpretation and tend to reduce the performer's musicianship to an administrator on a technical level. Both the interpretation and the piece identity are, to a large extent, built into the instruments in these cases. To unlock a more active musicianship, the shared experience of building such instruments, as practised by Dirty Electronics, seems beneficial.

Regarding the first research question, the discussed strategies and pieces, together with the survey data, expose a clear notion of the live electronic instrument as something being subject to more or less radical changes. The development of a functional instrument setup is described as a dynamic process. This process is a consequence of both technical and aesthetic needs, exposed by factors such as pieces, ensemble size, being able to play in sync, being able to react, making it possible to shift focus quickly and so on. Besides developing musicianship skills, practising live electronics also includes thinking of and understanding how to effectively adapt and transform an instrumental setup to solve these issues. This demands knowledge both within digital and analogue lutherie as well as composition and performance.

The second research question can be answered in different ways according to the results of this study. On an overarching level, all types of musicking force the player to explore instrumental affordances, which in turn reveals any unintentional limitations, thus enabling useful adaptations to be made. However, open, modular interactive musicking systems like *Oblique Strategies* or the Bed of Nails collaborative piece, show fluctuating properties that are similar to the instruments themselves. This appears to be a useful pedagogic strategy as it encourages the musician towards an explorative approach to both instrumental and sonic affordances in each specific musicking situation. Returning to Alperson (2008), our understanding of music is shaped by our instruments, but the ability to understand and shape an instrument according to the musical need seems crucial for a skilled live electronic musician.

While performing *Focus* as a solo piece, I often felt the need to re-patch the modular system as new cards came up. The aleatoric agencies of the dynamic score became intertwined with the instrument and me as a performer. For example, if the card asks me to focus on *mimicry*, the question is what to mimic. With a notion that I oversee all ongoing processes, the only thing I can mimic is my own playing, which in practice simply implies continuing with what I am doing at the moment. Instead, allowing for a mindset where different modules and sub-patches are autonomous agents or co-players enables a much more radical interpretation. This can, for example, include embodying and articulating auditory or visual phenomena caused by the system itself, e.g., by enhancing oscillator beatings with other sounds or translating the LED intensity of a random generator into gestures.

Acknowledging the fluctuating nature of live electronic systems as one of their most defining instrumental features seems necessary to unleash their full potential. The cybernetic perspectives of musical instruments, as discussed earlier in this chapter, are crucial for understanding this flux. A safe space for musicking, where performers can share experiences, co-evolve with human and non-human agencies and make creative use of the blurry lines between pieces, instruments and players, seems to be a way forward.

Traditional musical instruments that have survived for centuries have probably done so because of a particularly favourable balance between cause and effect, evaluated in front of audiences and refined together with other musicians. The live electronic instrument, understood as a dynamic process of change in which a musical voice is formed, could be developed in a similar way. Seemingly, the framework of a live electronics ensemble that includes several human agents can unlock awareness of the agencies our instruments exert on us and how we, as musicians, form our voices in negotiation with them. A main aim of any live electronics ensemble should therefore be to create a beneficial environment for causal relationships. In such an environment, we can develop the necessary strategies and understanding required for a new morphology of live electronic musicking. Basic reflections on the ontology of the musical instrument, like Alperson's (2008) and Peters' (2016), can support this quest. But thoughts about the fusion of instrument, system, composition and performance that Richards (2011) and Baalman (2016) discuss, as well as ideas from the live coding and modular synthesiser communities, can also further contribute to a developed theoretical basis.

REFERENCES

Alperson, P. (2008, Winter). 'The Instrumentality of Music', *Source: The Journal of Aesthetics and Art Criticism*, 66.

Baalman, M. A. J. (2016). 'Interplay Between Composition, Instrument Design and Performance', In *Musical Instruments in the 21st Century: Identities, Configurations, Practices*. Singapore: Springer, pp. 225–241. https://doi.org/10.1007/978-981-10-2951-6_15.

Cardew, C. (1971). 'Towards an Ethics of Improvisation', in *Treatise Handbook*. Online resource. Available at: www.ubu.com/papers/cardew_ethics.html [Accessed: 15 August 2020].

De Souza, J. (2018). 'Orchestra Machines, Old and New', *Organised Sound*, 23(2), pp. 156–166. https://doi.org/10.1017/S1355771818000031.

Dirty Electronics. (2022). *Dirty Electronics*. Available at: www.dirtyelectronics.org/ [Accessed: 23 August 2022].

Ek, R., Östersjö, S., Visi, F. and Petersson, M. (2021). 'The TCP/Indeterminate Place Quartet: A Global Hyperorgan Scenario', *NIME*. https://doi.org/10.21428/92fbeb44.7714e834.

Eldridge, A., Kiefer, C., Overholt, D. and Ulfarsson, H. (2021, June 1). 'Self-resonating Vibrotactile Feedback Instruments||: Making, Playing, Conceptualising :||', in *NIME 2021*. NIME 2021, Shanghai, China. https://doi.org/10.21428/92fbeb44.1f29a09e.

Fluid Corpus Manipulation. (2022). *Fluid Corpus Manipulation*. Available at: www.flucoma.org/ [Accessed: 23 August 2022].

Gibson, J. J. (1977). 'The Theory of Affordances', in *Perceiving, Acting, and Knowing: Toward an Ecological Psychology*. Hillsdale, NJ: Erlbaum, pp. 67–82.

Gioti, A.-M. (2021). 'A Compositional Exploration of Computational Aesthetic Evaluation and AI Bias', in *NIME 2021*. NIME 2021, Shanghai, China. https://doi.org/10.21428/92fbeb44.de74b046

Harlow, R., Petersson, M., Ek, R., Visi, F. and Östersjö, S. (2021, June 1). 'Global Hyperorgan: A Platform for Telematic Musicking and Research', in *NIME 2021*. NIME 2021, Shanghai, China. https://doi.org/10.21428/92fbeb44.d4146b2d.

Heyde, H. (1975). *Grundlagen des natürlichen Systems der Musikinstrumente*. Leipzig: Deutscher Vlg für Musik.

Kapur, A., Darling, M., Diakopoulos, D., Murphy, J. W., Hochenbaum, J., Vallis, O. and Bahn, C. (2011). 'The Machine Orchestra: An Ensemble of Human Laptop Performers and Robotic Musical Instruments', *Computer Music Journal*, 35(4), pp. 49–63. www.jstor.org/stable/41412946.

Kungl. Musikhögskolan. (2014). *Dirty Electronics & Royal Live Electronics 10/10 2014* [Video]. YouTube. Available at: www.youtube.com/watch?v=SEPVvPU5R6o.

Latour, B. (1991). 'Technology Is Society Made Durable', in Law, J., ed. *A Sociology of Monsters: Essays on Power, Technology, and Domination*. London and New York: Routledge, pp. 103–131.

Latour, B. (2007[2005]). *Reassembling the Social: An Introduction to Actor-Network-Theory*. Oxford: Oxford University Press.

Magnusson, T. (2009). 'Of Epistemic Tools: Musical Instruments as Cognitive Extensions', *Organised Sound*, 14, pp. 168–176. https://doi.org/10.1017/S1355771809000272.

Magnusson, T. (2019). *Sonic Writing. Technologies of Material, Symbolic & Signal Inscriptions*. New York: Bloomsbury Academic.

Moderna Museet. (2012). *John Cage special! Moderna Museet i Stockholm*. Available at: www.modernamuseet.se/stockholm/sv/aktiviteter/john-cage-special/ [Accessed: 23 August 2022].

Nilsson, P. A. (2011). *A Field of Possibilities Designing and Playing Digital Musical Instruments*. Diss. Göteborg: Göteborgs universitet.

Peters, D. (2016). 'Instrumentality as Distributed, Interpersonal, and Self-Agential: Aesthetic Implications of an Instrumental Assemblage and Its Fortuitous Voice', in *Musical Instruments in the 21st Century: Identities, Configurations, Practices*. Singapore: Springer, pp. 225–241. https://doi.org/10.1007/978-981-10-2951-6_15.

Petersson, M. (2010). *Oblique Strategies for Live Electronics Ensemble* (musical score). Stockholm: STIM.

Petersson, M. (2019a). *Find & Replace for Live Electronics Ensemble* (musical score). Stockholm: STIM.

Petersson, M. (2019b). *Focus for Live Electronics Ensemble* (musical score). Stockholm: STIM.

Petersson, M. (2022). *Oblique Focus for Live Electronics Ensemble* (musical score). Unpublished work in progress.

Petersson, M. and Ek, R. (2022). 'Exploring Sinew0od', *ECHO, A Journal of Music Thought and Technology*, 3. https://doi.org/10.47041/QPSR1612.

Pressing, J. (1990, Spring). 'Cybernetic Issues in Interactive Performance Systems', *Computer Music Journal*, 14(1), New Performance Interfaces 1, pp. 12–25.

Pritchett, J. (2000), *David Tudor's realization of John Cage's Variations II*. Available at: www.rosewhitemusic.com/cage/texts/Var2.html [Accessed: 22 August 2022].

Richards, J. (2011). *Lead and Schemas. Institute of Contemporary Arts: Roland Magazine, 9*. Available at: www.dirtyelectronics.org/docs/ICA_Roland_09.pdf [Accessed: 22 August 2022].

Sköld, M. (2018). 'Combining Sound-and Pitch-Based Notation for Teaching and Composition', in *TENOR'18 – Fourth International Conference on Technologies for Music Notation and Representation*. Montreal, Canada: TENOR, pp. 1–6.

Sköld, M. (2019). 'The Visual Representation of Spatialisation for Composition and Analysis', in *Nordic Sound and Music Computing Conference*. Stockholm, Sweden: The Royal Institute of Technology, pp. 70–77. https://doi.org/10.5281/zenodo.3755978.

Sköld, M. (2020). 'The Notation of Sound for Composition and transcription: An adaptation of Lasse Thoresen's Spectromorphological Analysis', in Gottfried, R., Hajdu, G., Sello, J., Anatrini, A. and MacCallum, J., eds. *Proceedings of the International Conference on Technologies for Music Notation and Representation – TENOR'20/21*. Hamburg, Germany: Hamburg University for Music and Theater, pp. 106–113.

Small, C. (1998). *Musicking: The Meanings of Performing and Listening*. Hanover, NH: University Press of New England.

Smallwood, S., Trueman, D., Cook, P. R. and Wan, G. (2008, Spring). 'Composing for Laptop Orchestra', *Computer Music Journal*, 32(1), pp. 9–25.

Snyder, J. (2011). 'Snyderphonics Manta Controller, a Novel USB Touch-Controller', in Jensenius, A. R. ed. *Proceedings of the International Conference on New Interfaces for Musical Expression—30 May—1 June 2011*. Oslo, Norway: NIME, pp. 413–416.

sonodrome. (2014). *Dirty Electronics and KMH Live Electronics Ensemble* [Video]. YouTube. Available at: www.youtube.com/watch?v=nwW0P2GGQWQ.

Visi, F. G. and Tanaka, A. (2021). 'Interactive Machine Learning of Musical Gesture', in *Handbook of Artificial Intelligence for Music*. Cham: Springer International Publishing, pp. 771–798.

Ward, A., Rohrhuber, J., Olofsson, F., Mclean, A., Griffiths, D., Collins, N. and Alexander, A. (2004). 'Live Algorithm Programming and a Temporary Organisation for its Promotion', in *Proceedings of the README Software Art Conference, vol 289*. Aarhus: README_2004, pp. 243–261.

Index

Note: Numbers in **bold** indicate a table. Numbers in *italics* indicate a figure on the corresponding page.

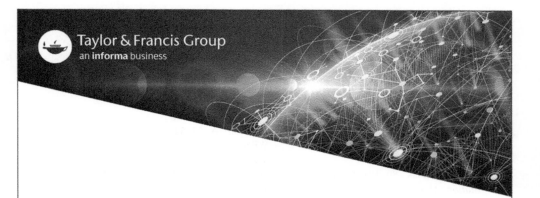

For Product Safety Concerns and Information please contact our EU representative GPSR@taylorandfrancis.com Taylor & Francis Verlag GmbH, Kaufingerstraße 24, 80331 München, Germany

Printed and bound by CPI Group (UK) Ltd, Croydon, CR0 4YY
08/06/2025
01897009-0015